# ♥1 Alice IN THE COUNTRY OF Hearts

Volume 2

Created by
QuinRose X Soumei Hoshino

HAMBURG // LONDON // LOS ANGELES // TOKYO

## *Alice in the Country of Hearts Volume 2*
## Created by QuinRose X Soumei Hoshino

Translation - Beni Axia Conrad
English Adaptation - Magda Erik-Soussi
Copy Editor - Jill Bentley
Retouch and Lettering - Star Print Brokers
Production Artist - Michael Paolilli
Graphic Designer - Al-Insan Lashley

Editor - Cindy Suzuki
Print Production Manager - Lucas Rivera
Managing Editor - Vy Nguyen
Senior Designer - Louis Csontos
Art Director - Al-Insan Lashley
Director of Sales and Manufacturing - Allyson De Simone
Associate Publisher - Marco F. Pavia
President and C.O.O. - John Parker
C.E.O. and Chief Creative Officer - Stu Levy

A  Manga

TOKYOPOP and 🐢 are trademarks or registered trademarks of TOKYOPOP Inc.

TOKYOPOP Inc.
5900 Wilshire Blvd. Suite 2000
Los Angeles, CA 90036

E-mail: info@TOKYOPOP.com
Come visit us online at www.TOKYOPOP.com

ISBN: 978-1-4278-1770-9

First TOKYOPOP printing: March 2010
10  9  8  7  6  5  4
Printed in the USA

# Alice in the Country of Hearts

# ハートの国のアリス

## ~ Wonderful Wonder World ~

2

QuinRose × Soumei Hoshino

ハートの国のアリス
～ Wonderful Wonder World ～
2nd

# CONTENTS

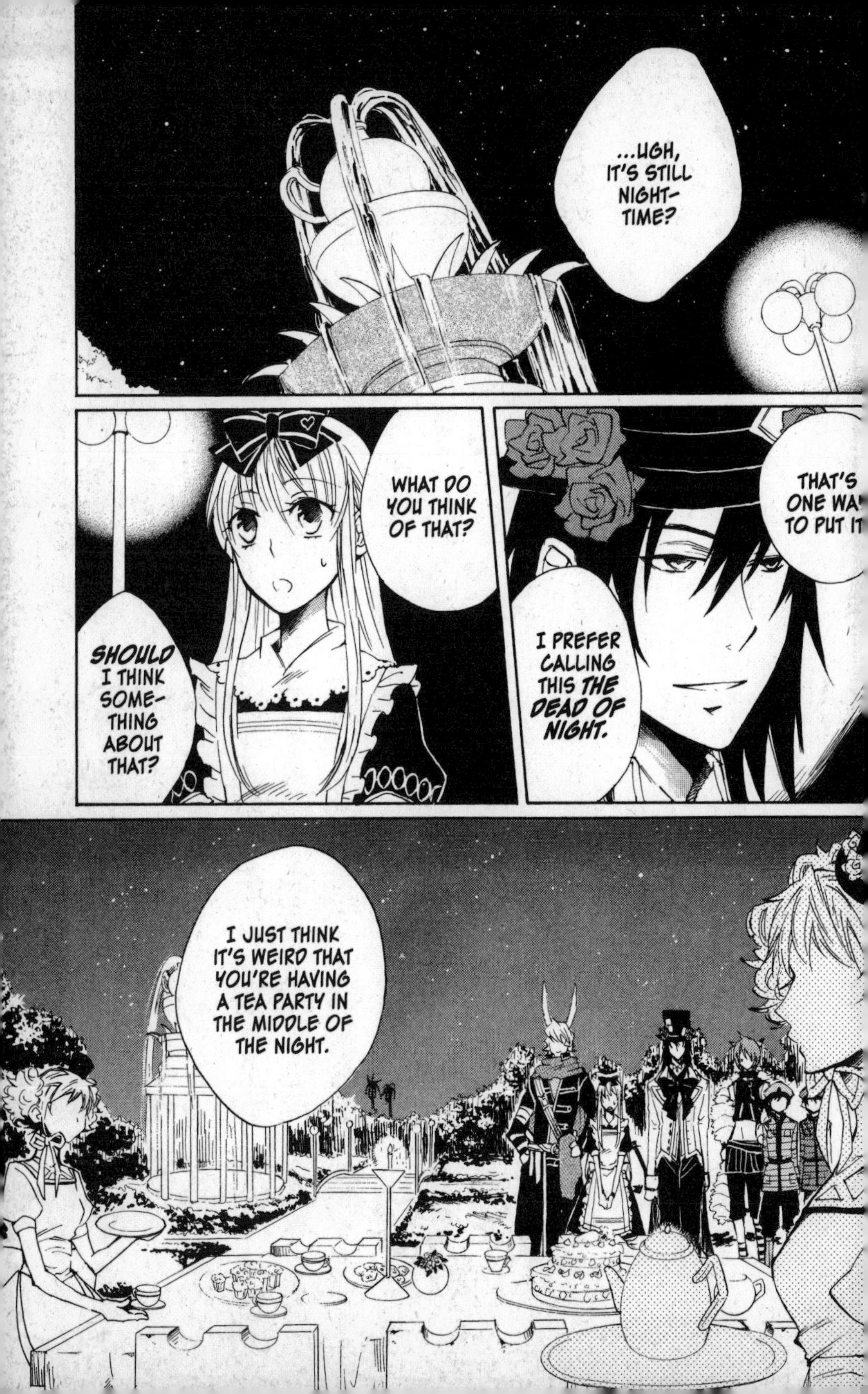
...UGH, IT'S STILL NIGHT-TIME?
THAT'S ONE WA TO PUT IT
I PREFER CALLING THIS *THE DEAD OF NIGHT.*
WHAT DO YOU THINK OF THAT?
*SHOULD* I THINK SOME-THING ABOUT THAT?
I JUST THINK IT'S WEIRD THAT YOU'RE HAVING A TEA PARTY IN THE MIDDLE OF THE NIGHT.

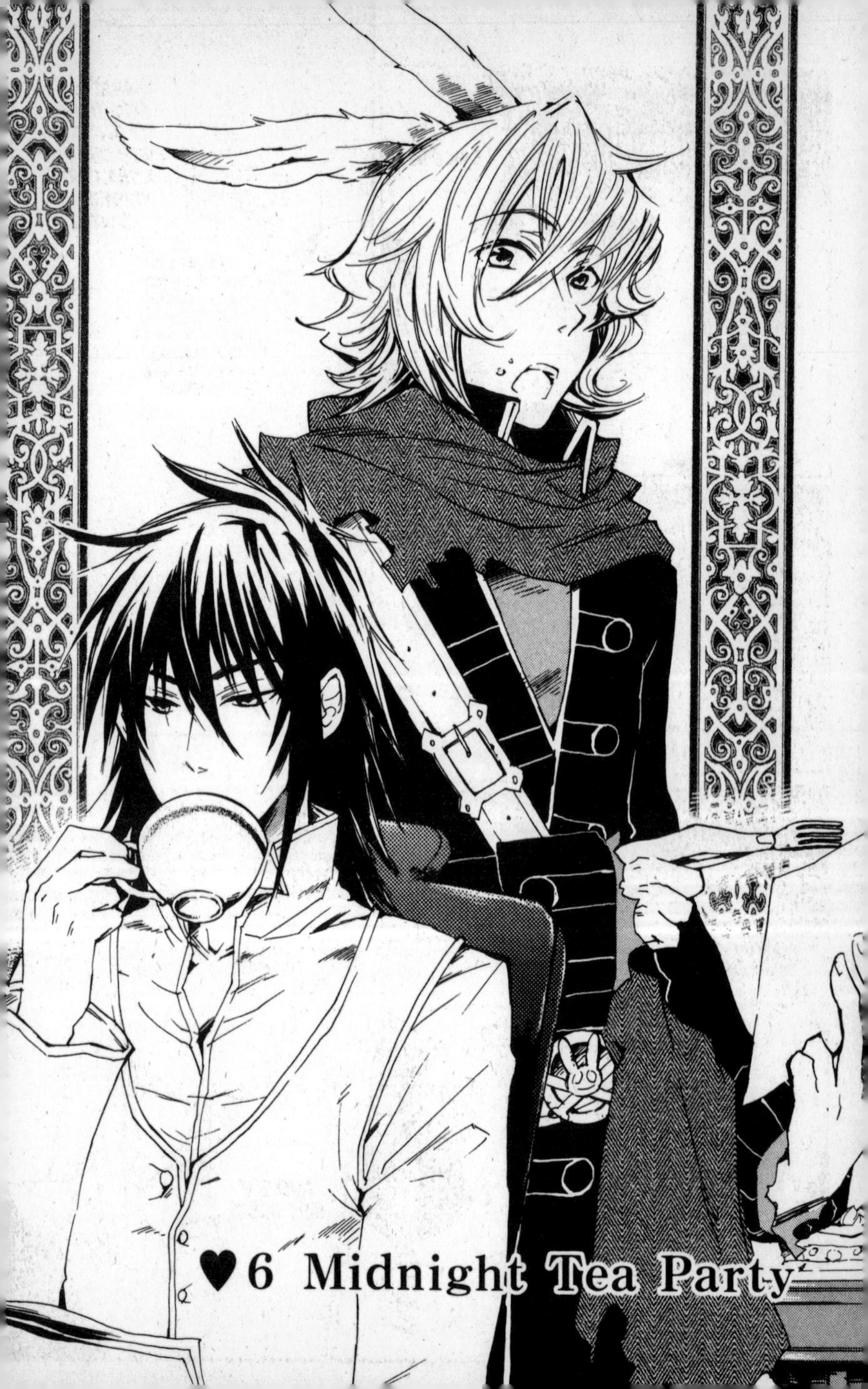
♥6 Midnight Tea Party

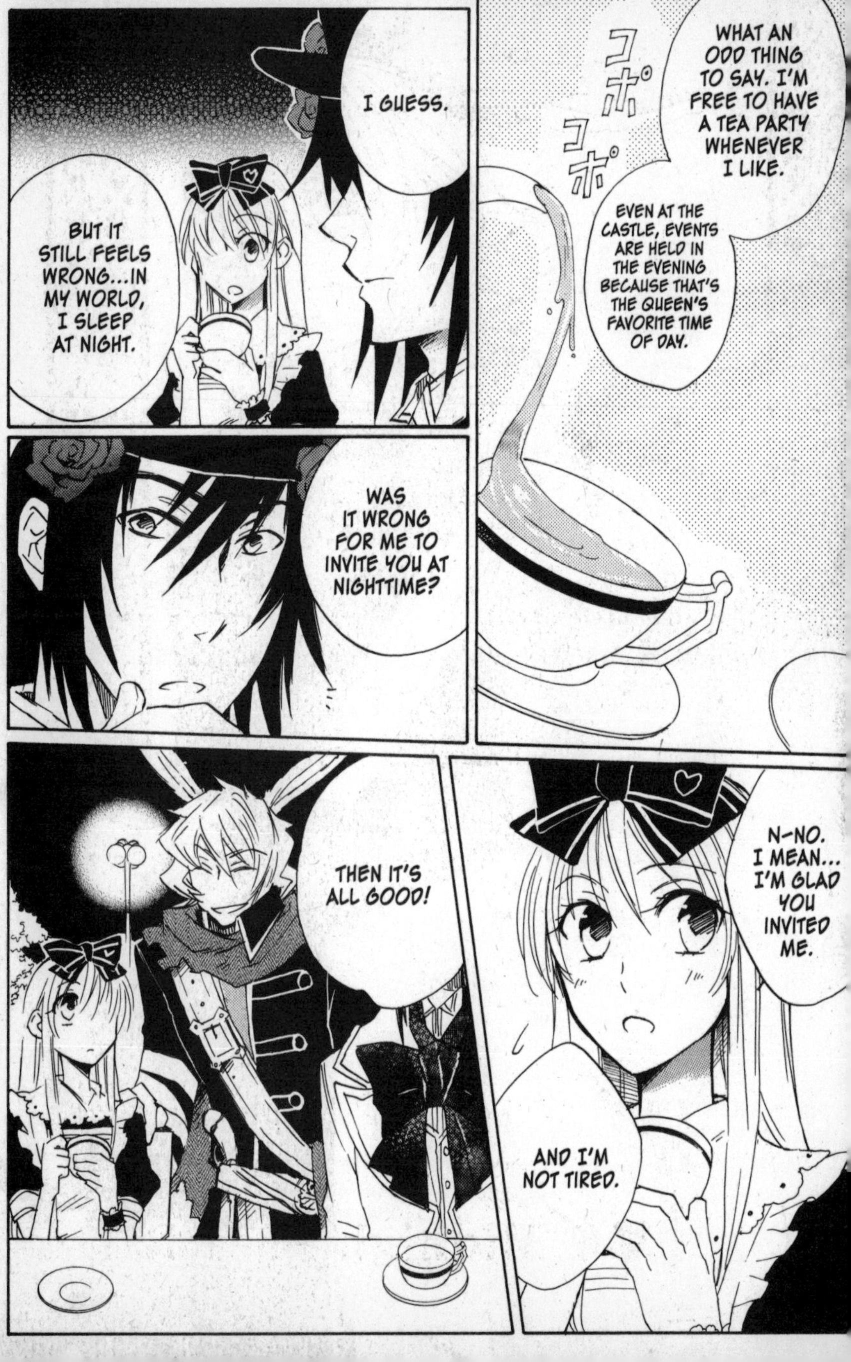
WHAT AN ODD THING TO SAY. I'M FREE TO HAVE A TEA PARTY WHENEVER I LIKE.
コポコポ
EVEN AT THE CASTLE, EVENTS ARE HELD IN THE EVENING BECAUSE THAT'S THE QUEEN'S FAVORITE TIME OF DAY.
I GUESS.
BUT IT STILL FEELS WRONG...IN MY WORLD, I SLEEP AT NIGHT.
WAS IT WRONG FOR ME TO INVITE YOU AT NIGHTTIME?
N-NO. I MEAN... I'M GLAD YOU INVITED ME.
AND I'M NOT TIRED.
THEN IT'S ALL GOOD!

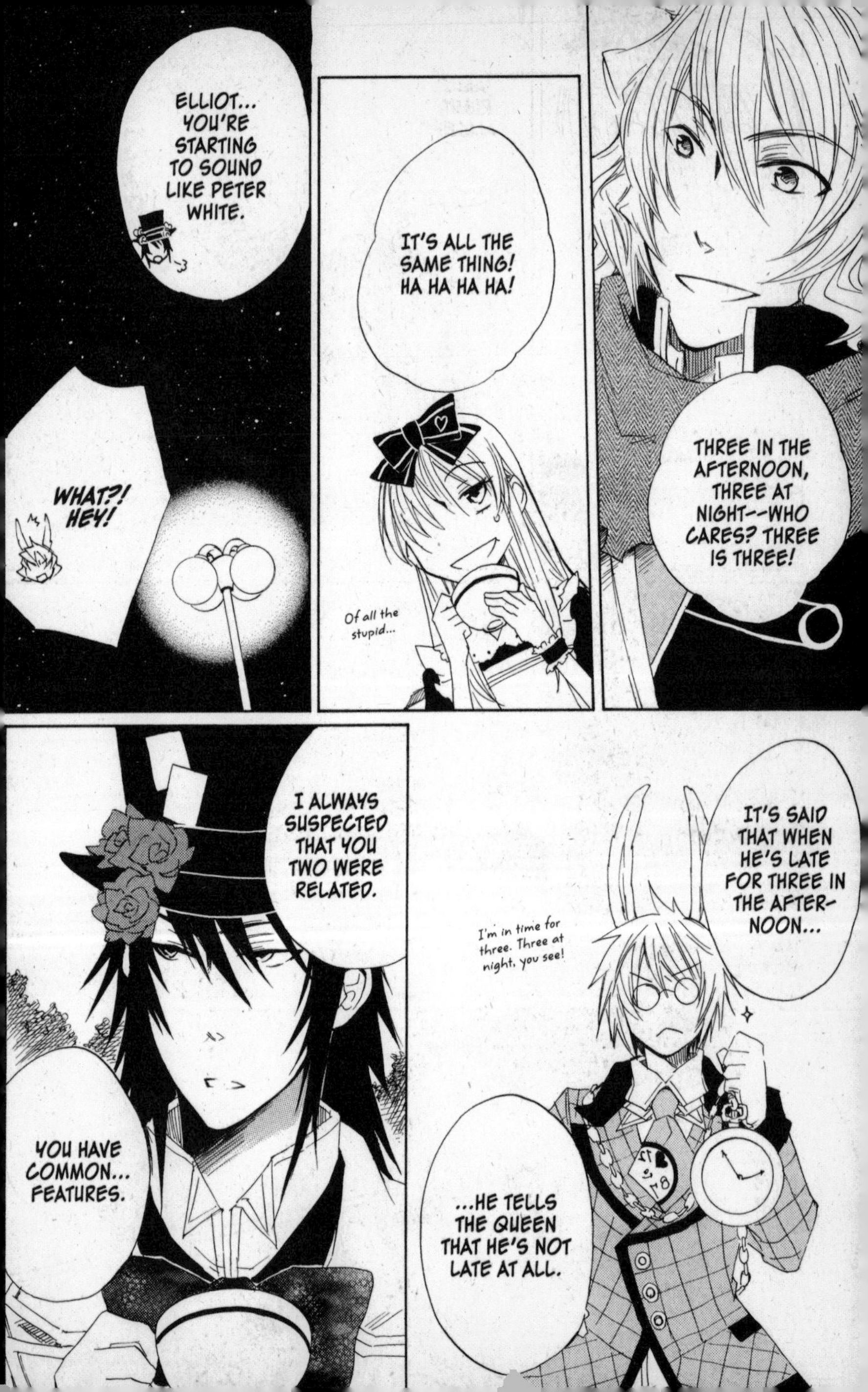
THREE IN THE AFTERNOON, THREE AT NIGHT--WHO CARES? THREE IS THREE!
IT'S ALL THE SAME THING! HA HA HA HA!
Of all the stupid...
ELLIOT... YOU'RE STARTING TO SOUND LIKE PETER WHITE.
WHAT?! HEY!
IT'S SAID THAT WHEN HE'S LATE FOR THREE IN THE AFTER-NOON...
I'm in time for three. Three at night, you see!
...HE TELLS THE QUEEN THAT HE'S NOT LATE AT ALL.
I ALWAYS SUSPECTED THAT YOU TWO WERE RELATED.
YOU HAVE COMMON... FEATURES.

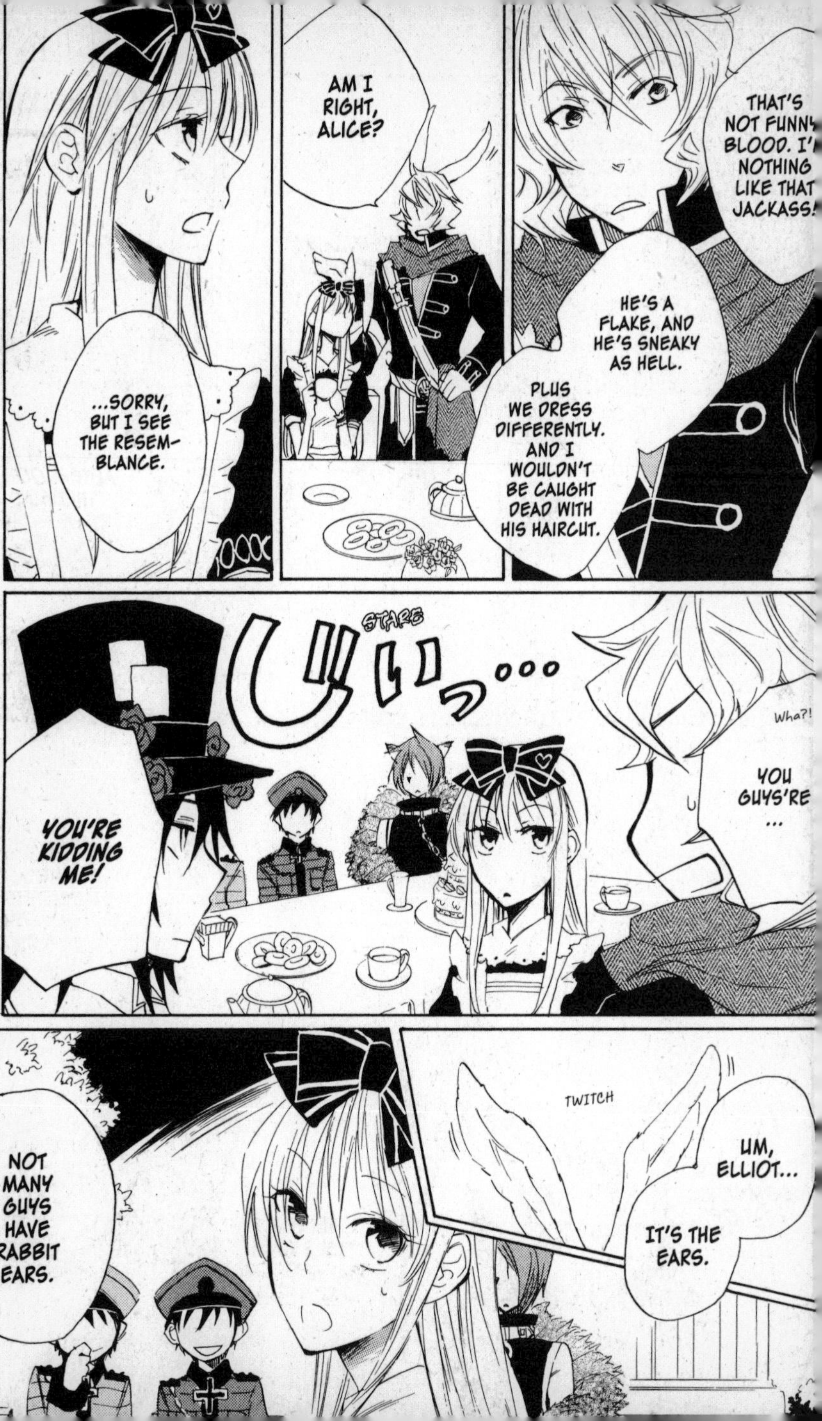
THAT'S NOT FUNNY BLOOD. I' NOTHING LIKE THAT JACKASS!
HE'S A FLAKE, AND HE'S SNEAKY AS HELL.
PLUS WE DRESS DIFFERENTLY. AND I WOULDN'T BE CAUGHT DEAD WITH HIS HAIRCUT.
AM I RIGHT, ALICE?
...SORRY, BUT I SEE THE RESEM- BLANCE.
Wha?!
YOU GUYS'RE ...
STARE
YOU'RE KIDDING ME!
TWITCH
UM, ELLIOT...
IT'S THE EARS.
NOT MANY GUYS HAVE RABBIT EARS.

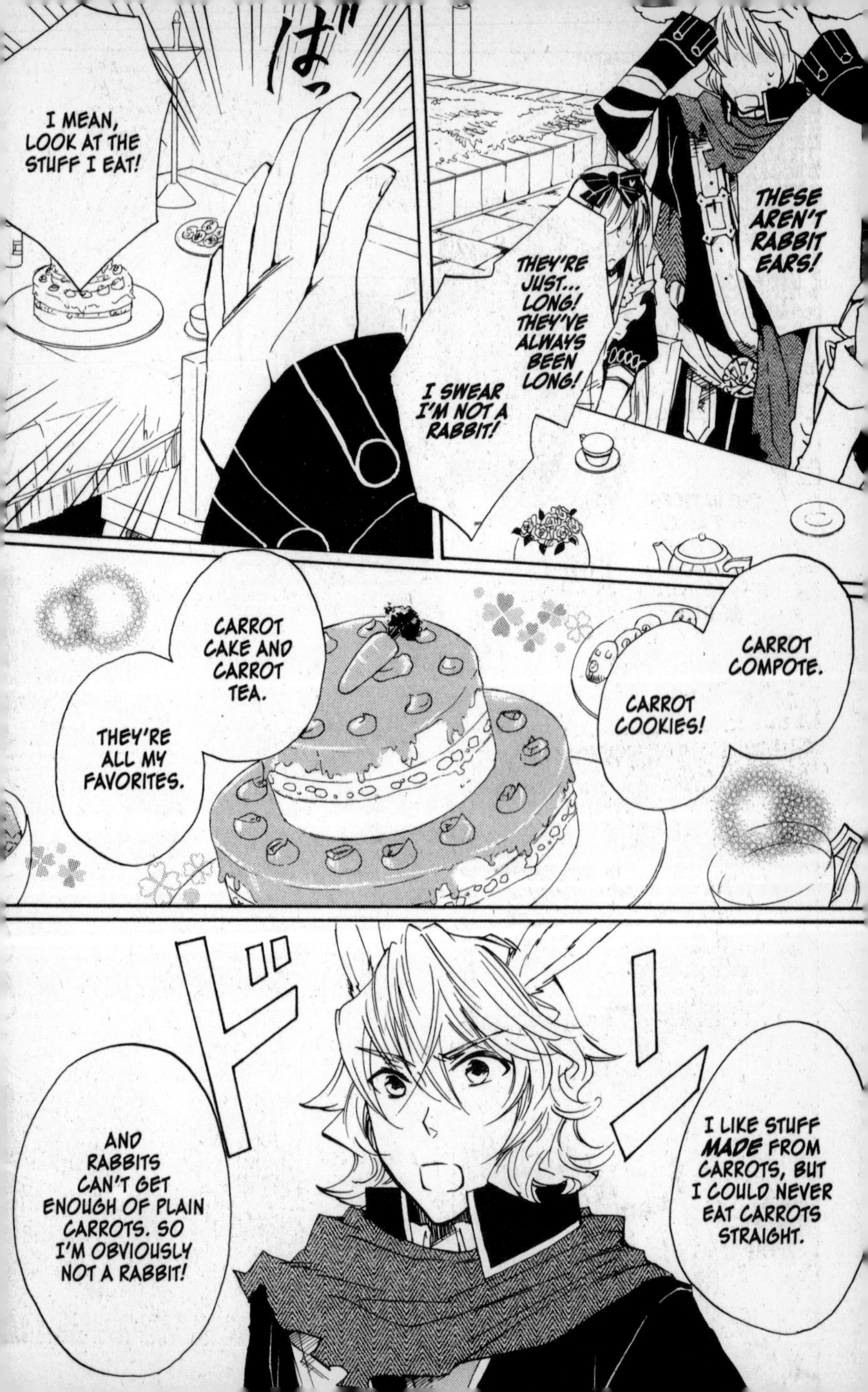
THESE AREN'T RABBIT EARS!
THEY'RE JUST... LONG! THEY'VE ALWAYS BEEN LONG!
I SWEAR I'M NOT A RABBIT!
ばっ
I MEAN, LOOK AT THE STUFF I EAT!
CARROT COMPOTE.
CARROT COOKIES!
CARROT CAKE AND CARROT TEA.
THEY'RE ALL MY FAVORITES.
I LIKE STUFF *MADE* FROM CARROTS, BUT I COULD NEVER EAT CARROTS STRAIGHT.
ドーン
AND RABBITS CAN'T GET ENOUGH OF PLAIN CARROTS. SO I'M OBVIOUSLY NOT A RABBIT!

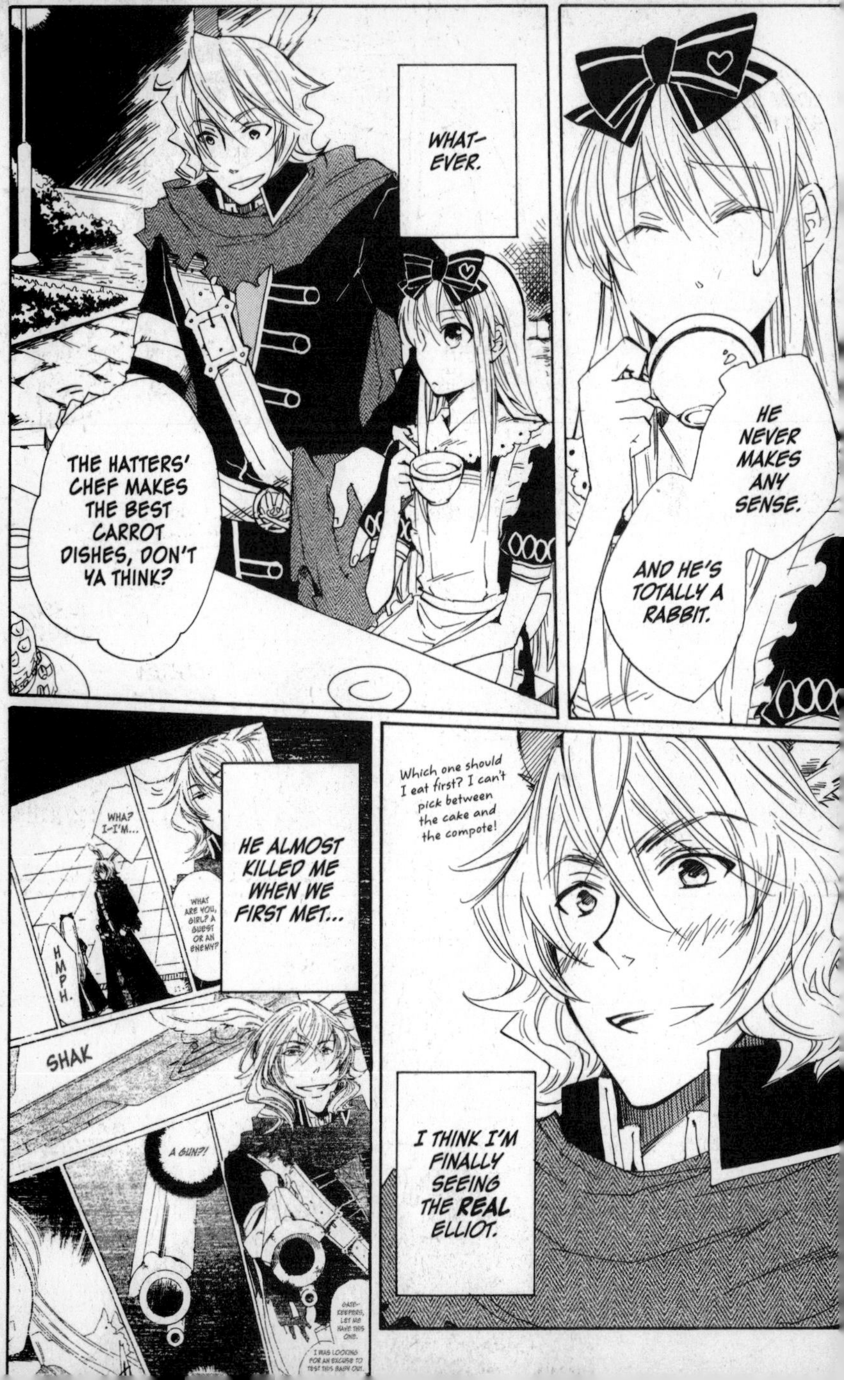
HE NEVER MAKES ANY SENSE.
AND HE'S TOTALLY A RABBIT.
WHAT-EVER.
THE HATTERS' CHEF MAKES THE BEST CARROT DISHES, DON'T YA THINK?
Which one should I eat first? I can't pick between the cake and the compote!
I THINK I'M FINALLY SEEING THE REAL ELLIOT.
HE ALMOST KILLED ME WHEN WE FIRST MET...
WHAT ARE YOU, GIRL? A GUEST OR AN ENEMY?
WHA? I-I'M...
HMPH.
SHAK
A GUN?!
GATE-KEEPERS, LET ME HAVE THIS ONE.
I WAS LOOKING FOR AN EXCUSE TO TEST THIS BABY OUT.

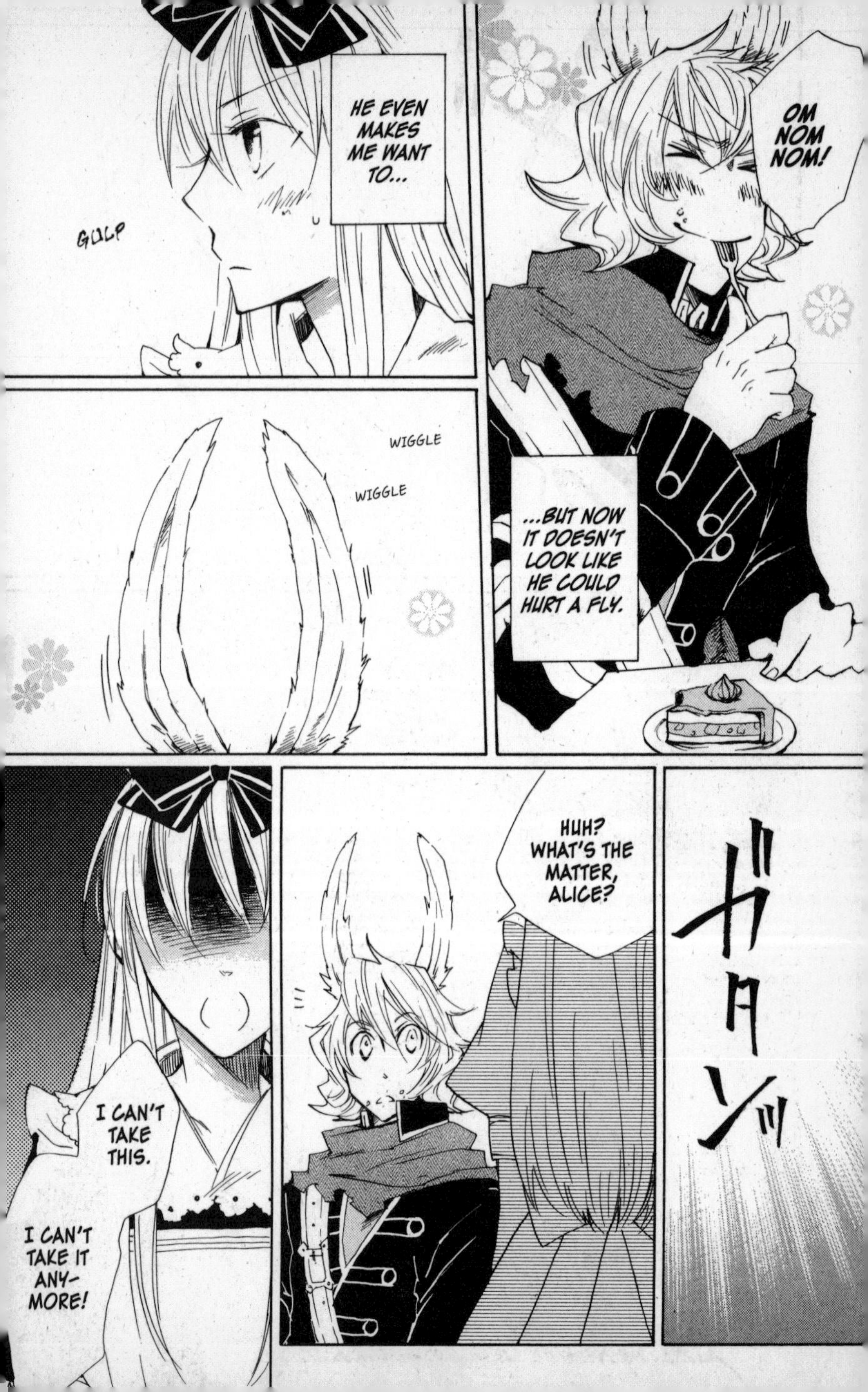
OM NOM NOM!
...BUT NOW IT DOESN'T LOOK LIKE HE COULD HURT A FLY.
HE EVEN MAKES ME WANT TO...
GULP
WIGGLE
WIGGLE
ガタンッ
HUH? WHAT'S THE MATTER, ALICE?
I CAN'T TAKE THIS.
I CAN'T TAKE IT ANY-MORE!

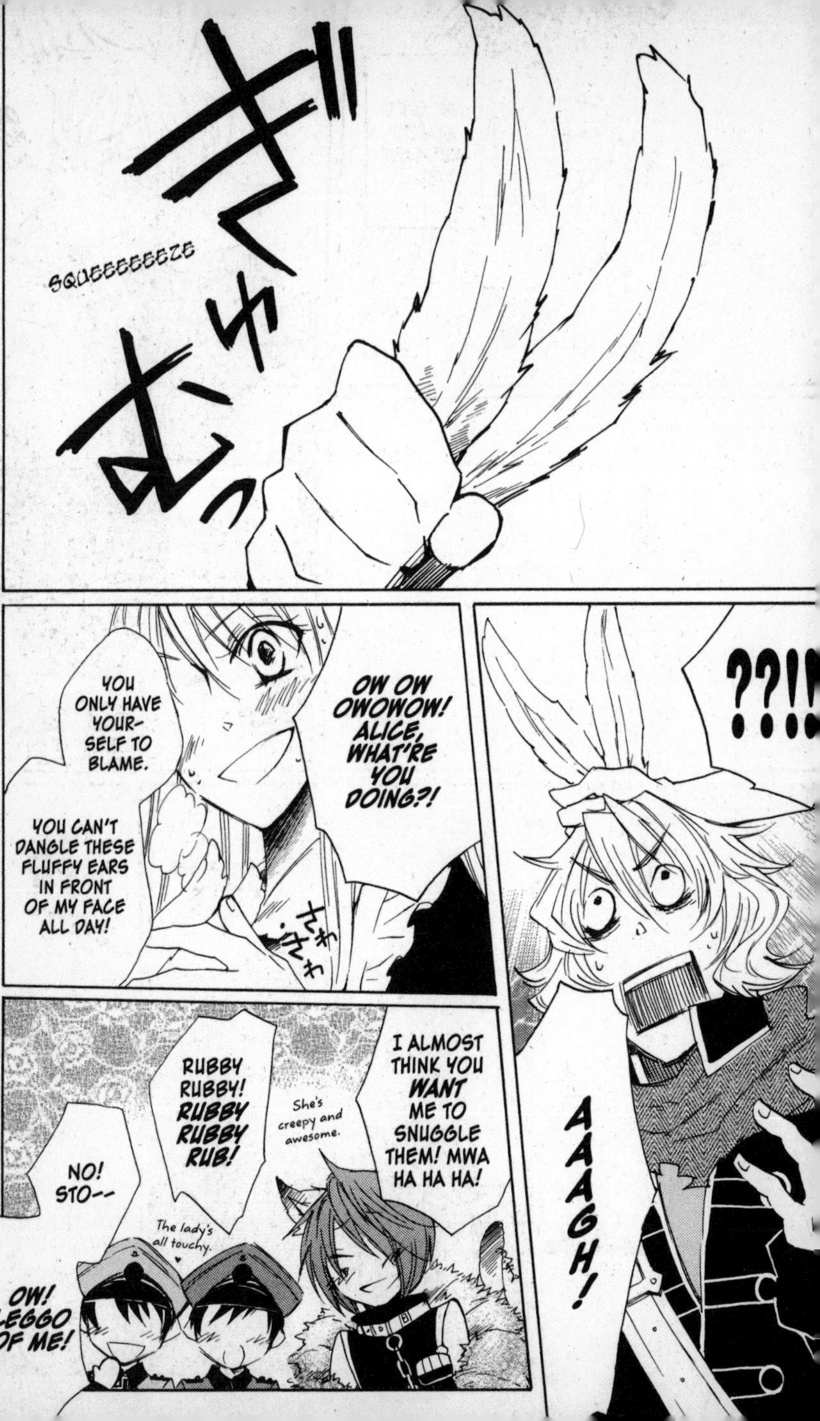
ぎゅむっ
SQUEEEEEEZE
??!!
AAAAGH!
OW OW OWOWOW! ALICE, WHAT'RE YOU DOING?!
YOU ONLY HAVE YOUR-SELF TO BLAME.
YOU CAN'T DANGLE THESE FLUFFY EARS IN FRONT OF MY FACE ALL DAY!
さわさわ
I ALMOST THINK YOU WANT ME TO SNUGGLE THEM! MWA HA HA HA!
She's creepy and awesome.
RUBBY RUBBY! RUBBY RUBBY RUB!
NO! STO--
The lady's all touchy.
OW! LEGGO OF ME!

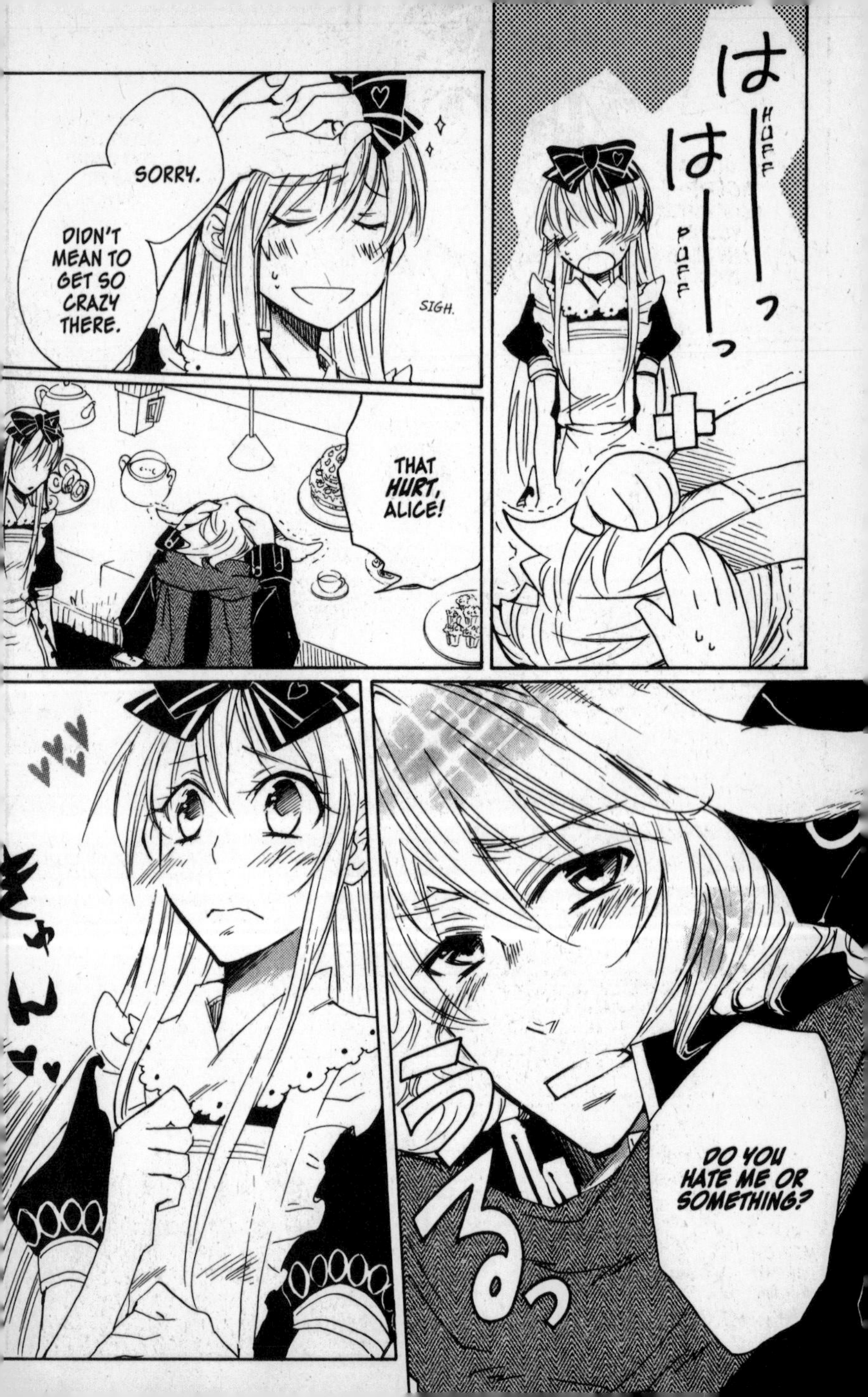
はーっ
HUFF
はーっ
PUFF
SORRY.
DIDN'T MEAN TO GET SO CRAZY THERE.
SIGH.
THAT HURT, ALICE!
DO YOU HATE ME OR SOMETHING?
うるっ
きゅん

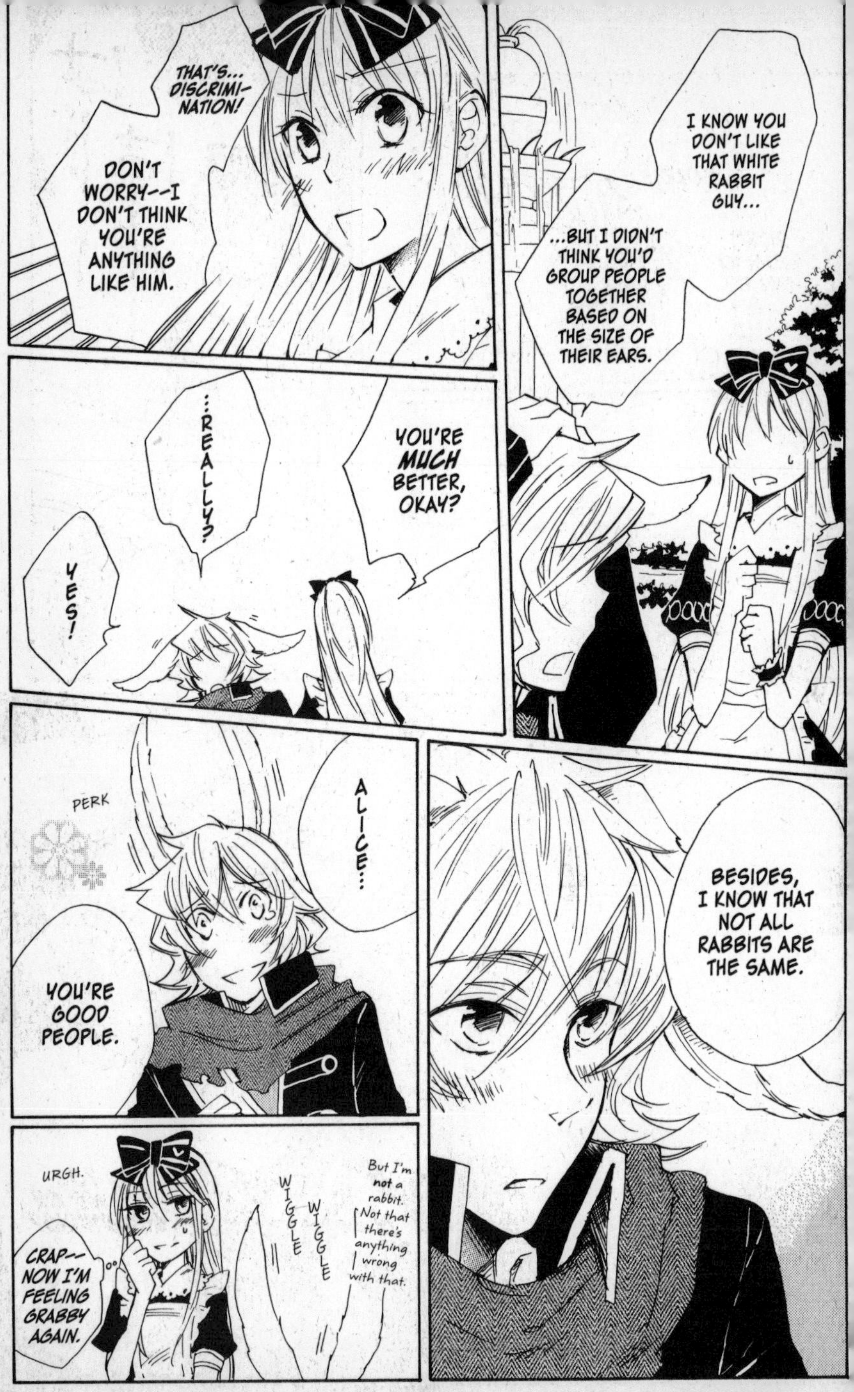
I KNOW YOU DON'T LIKE THAT WHITE RABBIT GUY...
...BUT I DIDN'T THINK YOU'D GROUP PEOPLE TOGETHER BASED ON THE SIZE OF THEIR EARS.
THAT'S... DISCRIMINATION!
DON'T WORRY--I DON'T THINK YOU'RE ANYTHING LIKE HIM.
YOU'RE *MUCH* BETTER, OKAY?
...REALLY?
YES!
BESIDES, I KNOW THAT NOT ALL RABBITS ARE THE SAME.
ALICE...
PERK
YOU'RE GOOD PEOPLE.
But I'm **not** a rabbit. Not that there's anything wrong with that.
WIGGLE WIGGLE
URGH.
CRAP--NOW I'M FEELING GRABBY AGAIN.

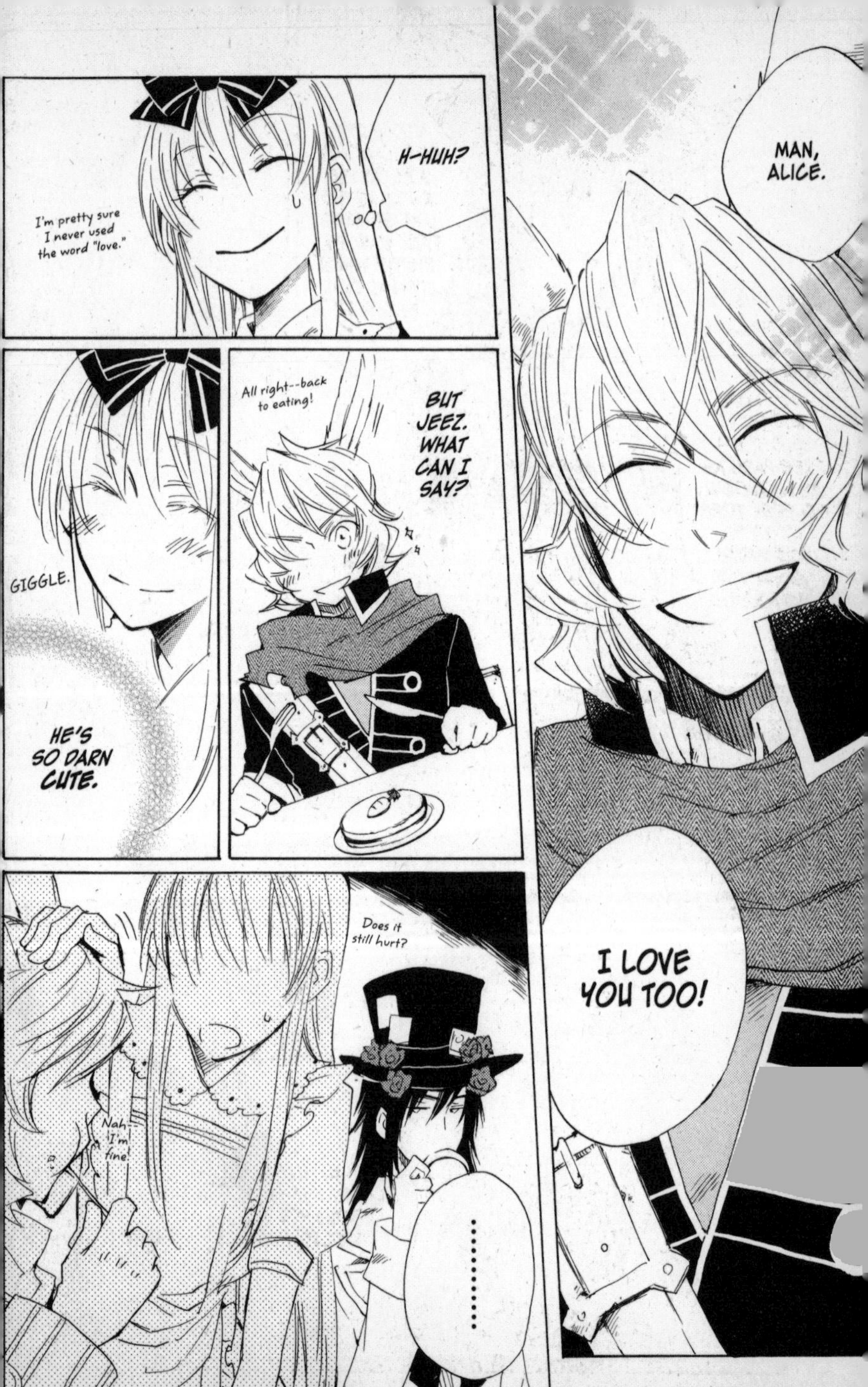
MAN, ALICE.
I LOVE YOU TOO!
H-HUH?
I'm pretty sure I never used the word "love."
BUT JEEZ. WHAT CAN I SAY?
All right--back to eating!
GIGGLE.
HE'S SO DARN CUTE.
Does it still hurt?
Nah--I'm fine.
.........

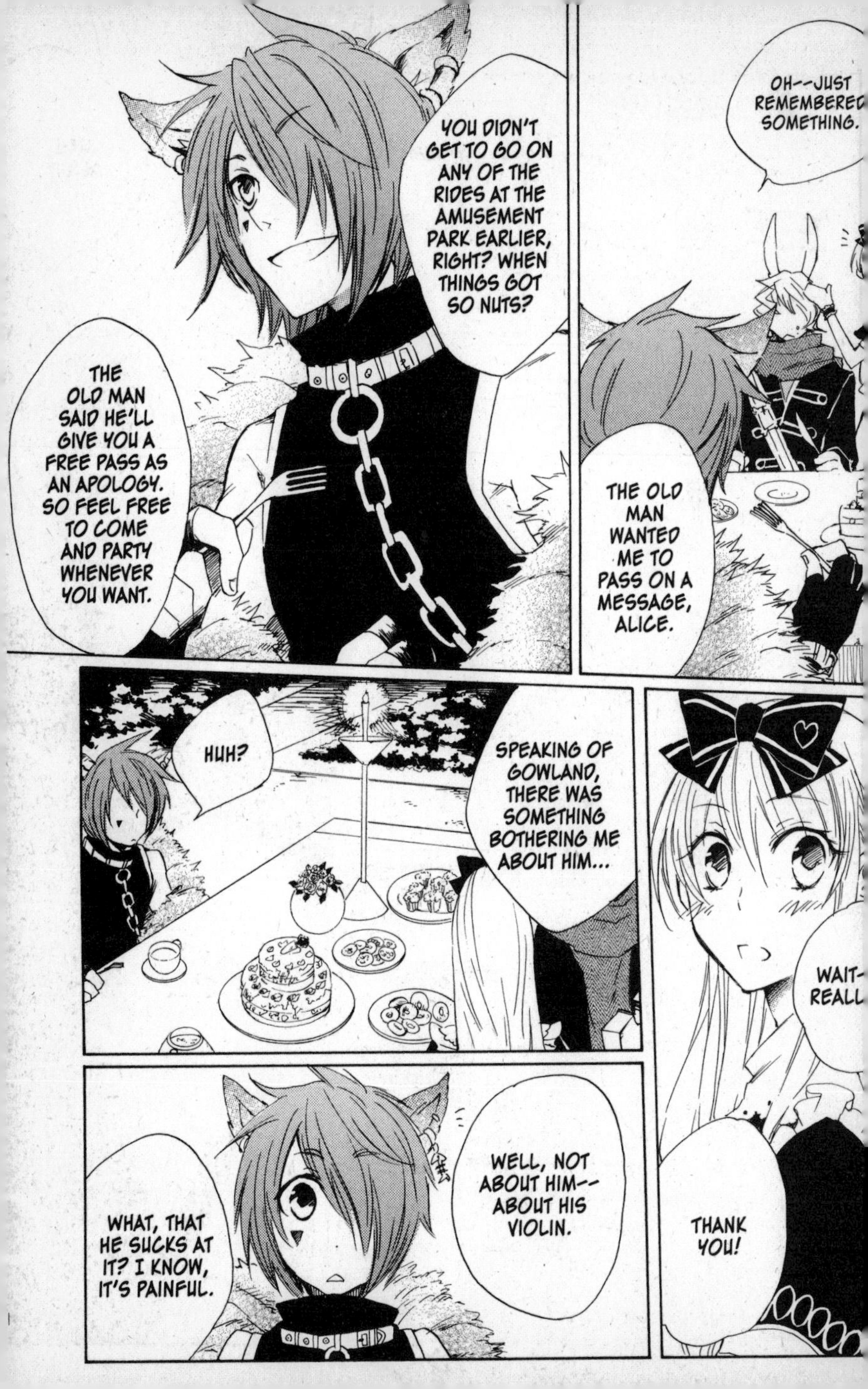
OH--JUST REMEMBERED SOMETHING.
THE OLD MAN WANTED ME TO PASS ON A MESSAGE, ALICE.
YOU DIDN'T GET TO GO ON ANY OF THE RIDES AT THE AMUSEMENT PARK EARLIER, RIGHT? WHEN THINGS GOT SO NUTS?
THE OLD MAN SAID HE'LL GIVE YOU A FREE PASS AS AN APOLOGY. SO FEEL FREE TO COME AND PARTY WHENEVER YOU WANT.
WAIT- REALL
THANK YOU!
SPEAKING OF GOWLAND, THERE WAS SOMETHING BOTHERING ME ABOUT HIM...
HUH?
WELL, NOT ABOUT HIM-- ABOUT HIS VIOLIN.
WHAT, THAT HE SUCKS AT IT? I KNOW, IT'S PAINFUL.

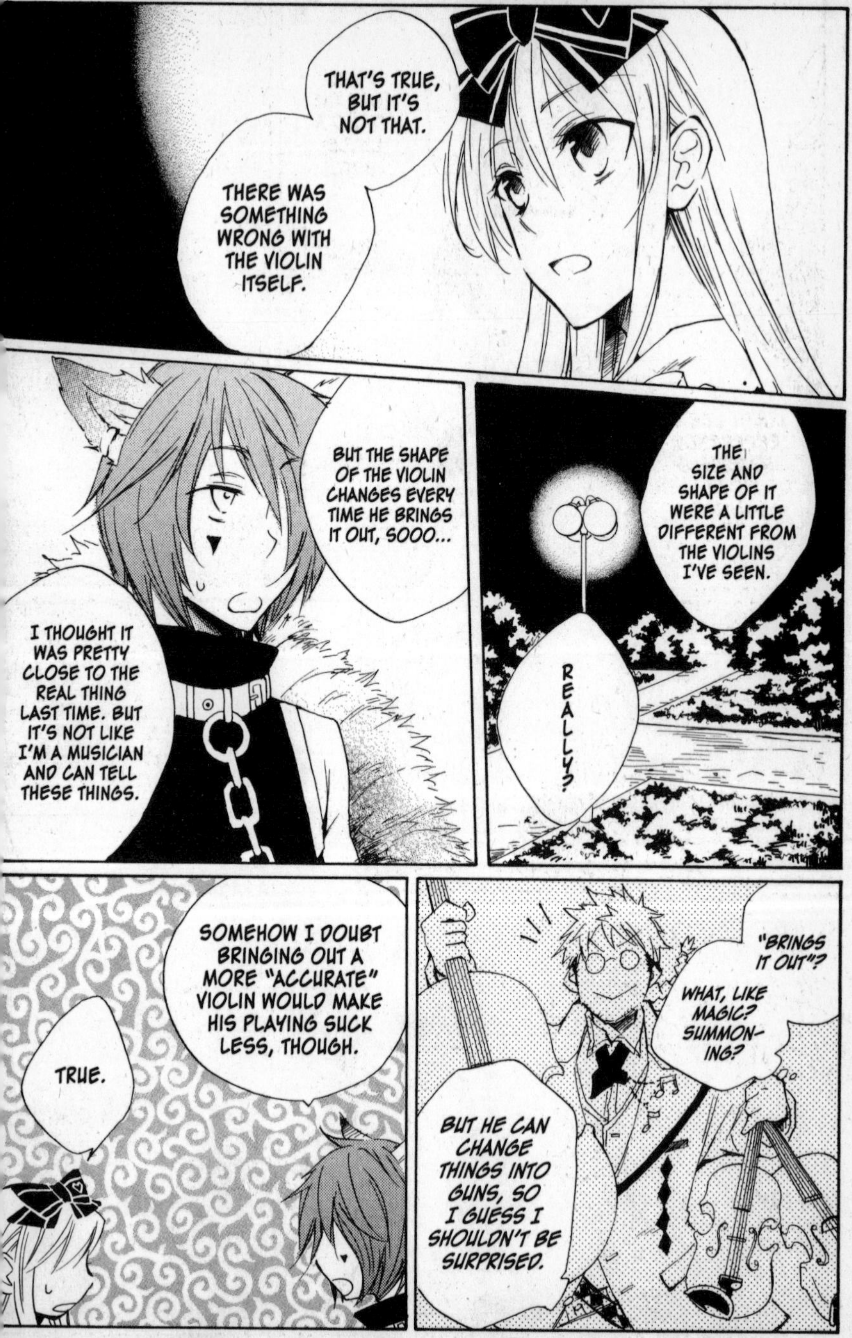
THAT'S TRUE, BUT IT'S NOT THAT.
THERE WAS SOMETHING WRONG WITH THE VIOLIN ITSELF.
THE SIZE AND SHAPE OF IT WERE A LITTLE DIFFERENT FROM THE VIOLINS I'VE SEEN.
REALLY?
BUT THE SHAPE OF THE VIOLIN CHANGES EVERY TIME HE BRINGS IT OUT, SOOO...
I THOUGHT IT WAS PRETTY CLOSE TO THE REAL THING LAST TIME. BUT IT'S NOT LIKE I'M A MUSICIAN AND CAN TELL THESE THINGS.
"BRINGS IT OUT"?
WHAT, LIKE MAGIC? SUMMON-ING?
BUT HE CAN CHANGE THINGS INTO GUNS, SO I GUESS I SHOULDN'T BE SURPRISED.
SOMEHOW I DOUBT BRINGING OUT A MORE "ACCURATE" VIOLIN WOULD MAKE HIS PLAYING SUCK LESS, THOUGH.
TRUE.

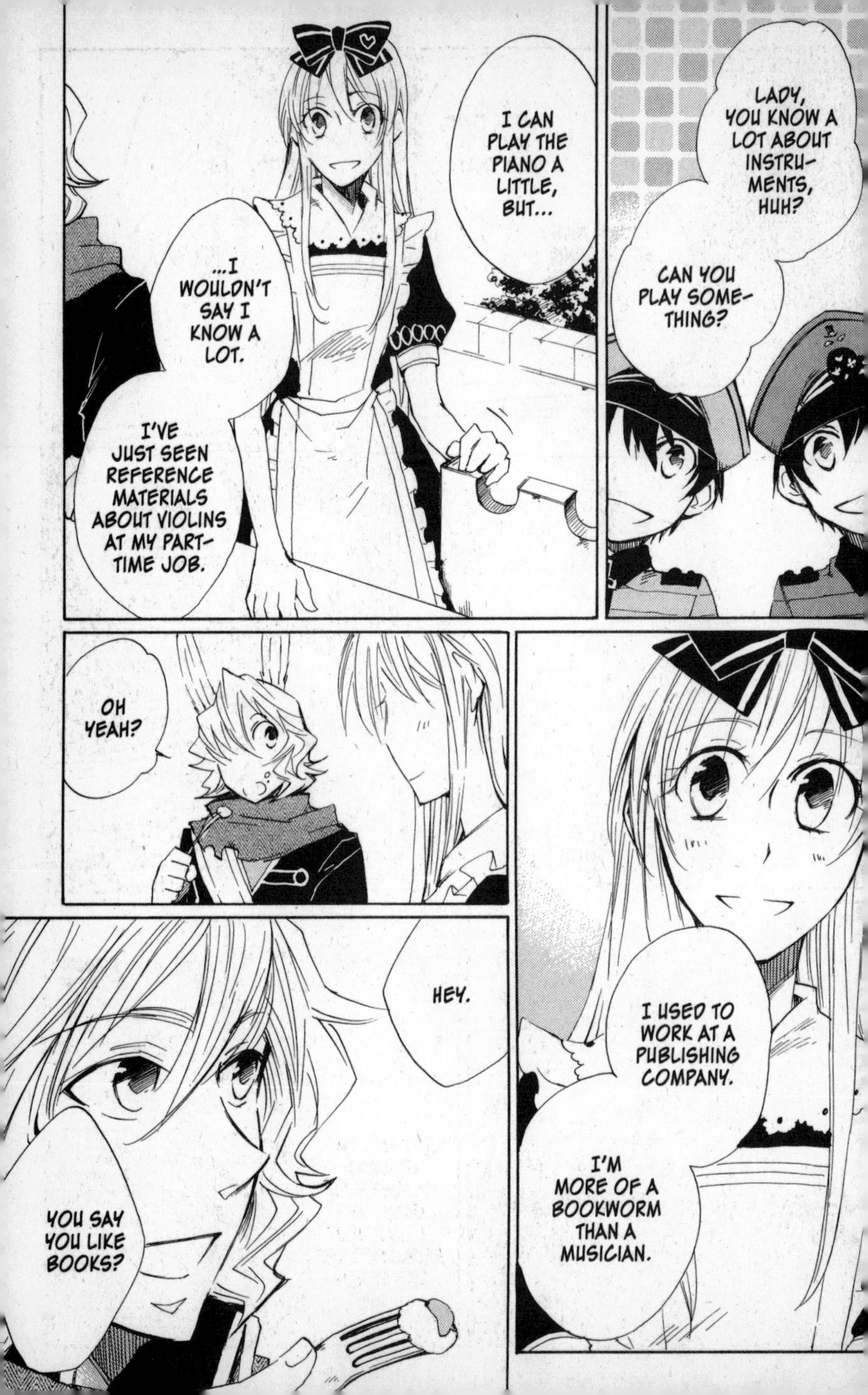
LADY, YOU KNOW A LOT ABOUT INSTRU-MENTS, HUH?
CAN YOU PLAY SOME-THING?
I CAN PLAY THE PIANO A LITTLE, BUT...
...I WOULDN'T SAY I KNOW A LOT.
I'VE JUST SEEN REFERENCE MATERIALS ABOUT VIOLINS AT MY PART-TIME JOB.
I USED TO WORK AT A PUBLISHING COMPANY.
I'M MORE OF A BOOKWORM THAN A MUSICIAN.
OH YEAH?
HEY.
YOU SAY YOU LIKE BOOKS?

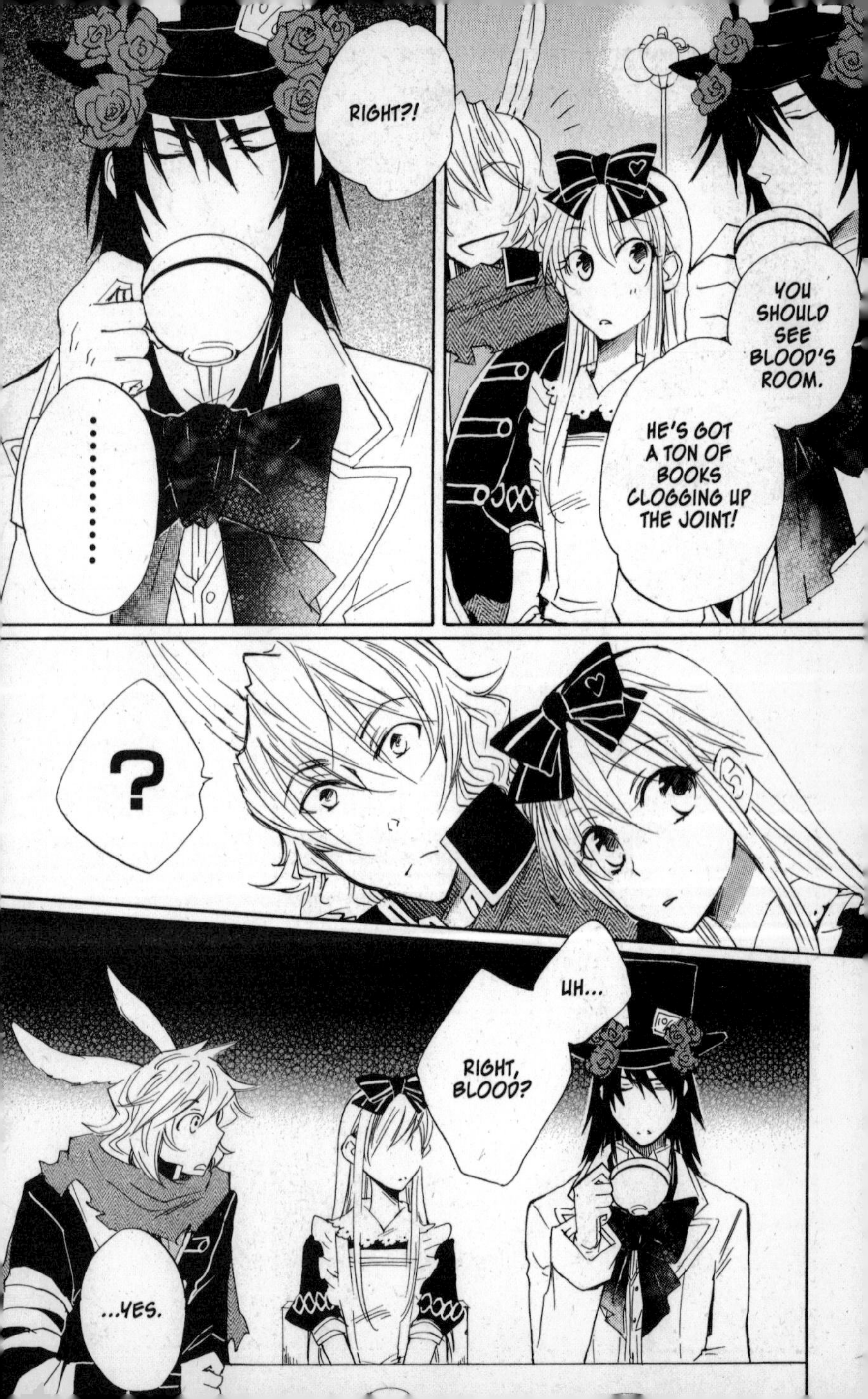
YOU SHOULD SEE BLOOD'S ROOM.
HE'S GOT A TON OF BOOKS CLOGGING UP THE JOINT!
RIGHT?!
......
?
UH...
RIGHT, BLOOD?
...YES.

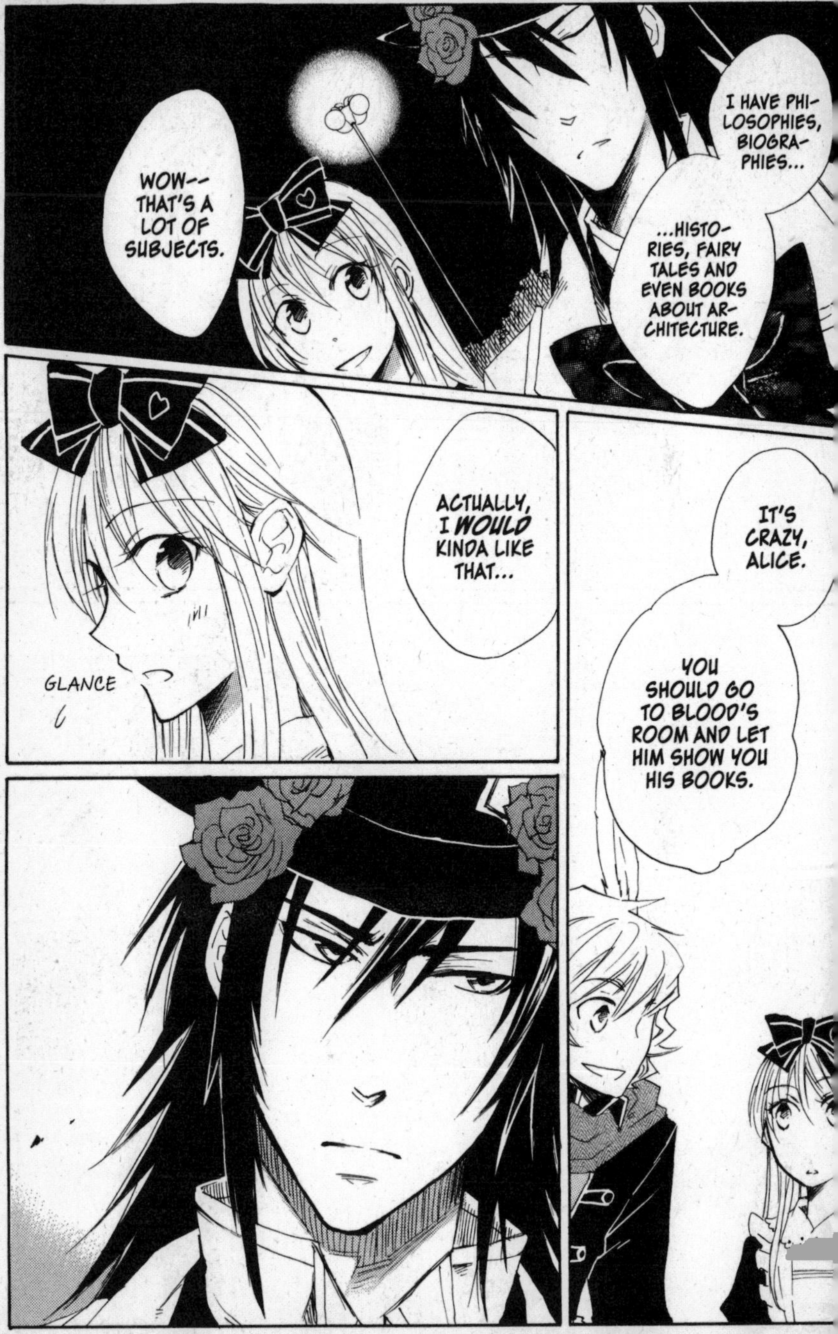
I HAVE PHILOSOPHIES, BIOGRAPHIES...
...HISTORIES, FAIRY TALES AND EVEN BOOKS ABOUT ARCHITECTURE.
WOW--THAT'S A LOT OF SUBJECTS.
IT'S CRAZY, ALICE.
YOU SHOULD GO TO BLOOD'S ROOM AND LET HIM SHOW YOU HIS BOOKS.
ACTUALLY, I *WOULD* KINDA LIKE THAT...
GLANCE

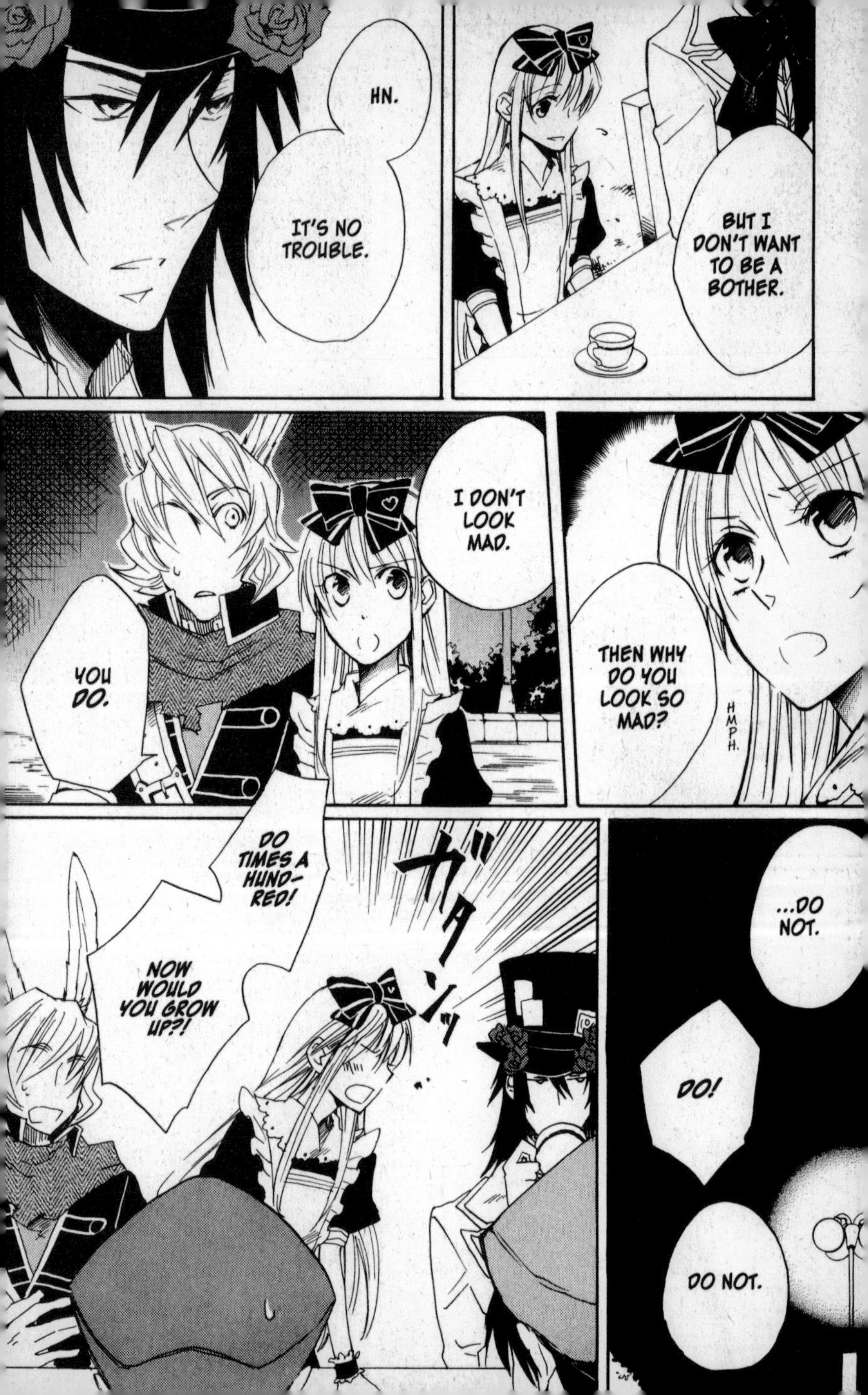
BUT I DON'T WANT TO BE A BOTHER.
HN.
IT'S NO TROUBLE.
THEN WHY DO YOU LOOK SO MAD?
HMPH.
I DON'T LOOK MAD.
YOU DO.
...DO NOT.
DO!
DO NOT.
DO TIMES A HUNDRED!
ガタンッ
NOW WOULD YOU GROW UP?!

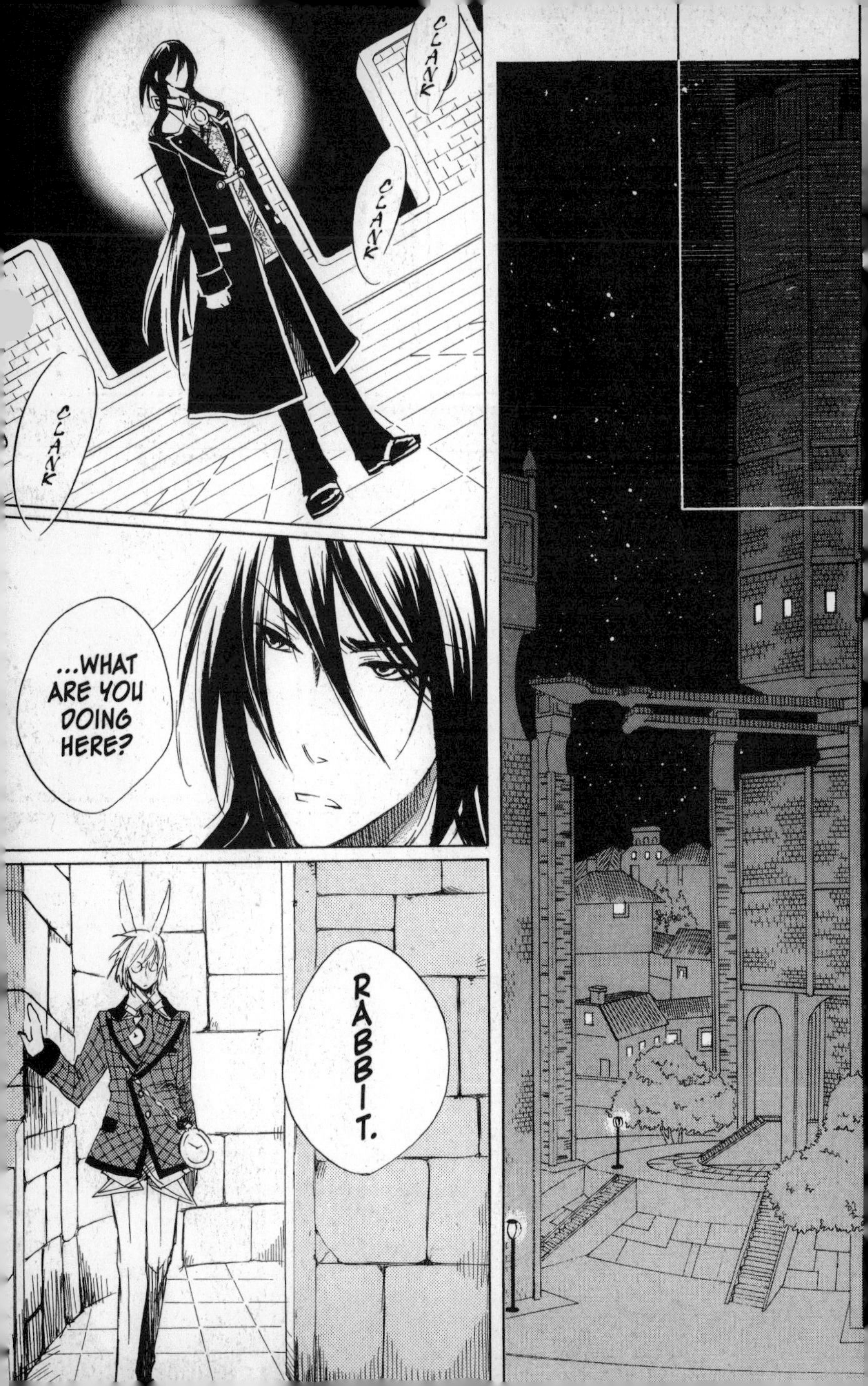
CLANK
CLANK
CLANK
...WHAT ARE YOU DOING HERE?
RABBIT.

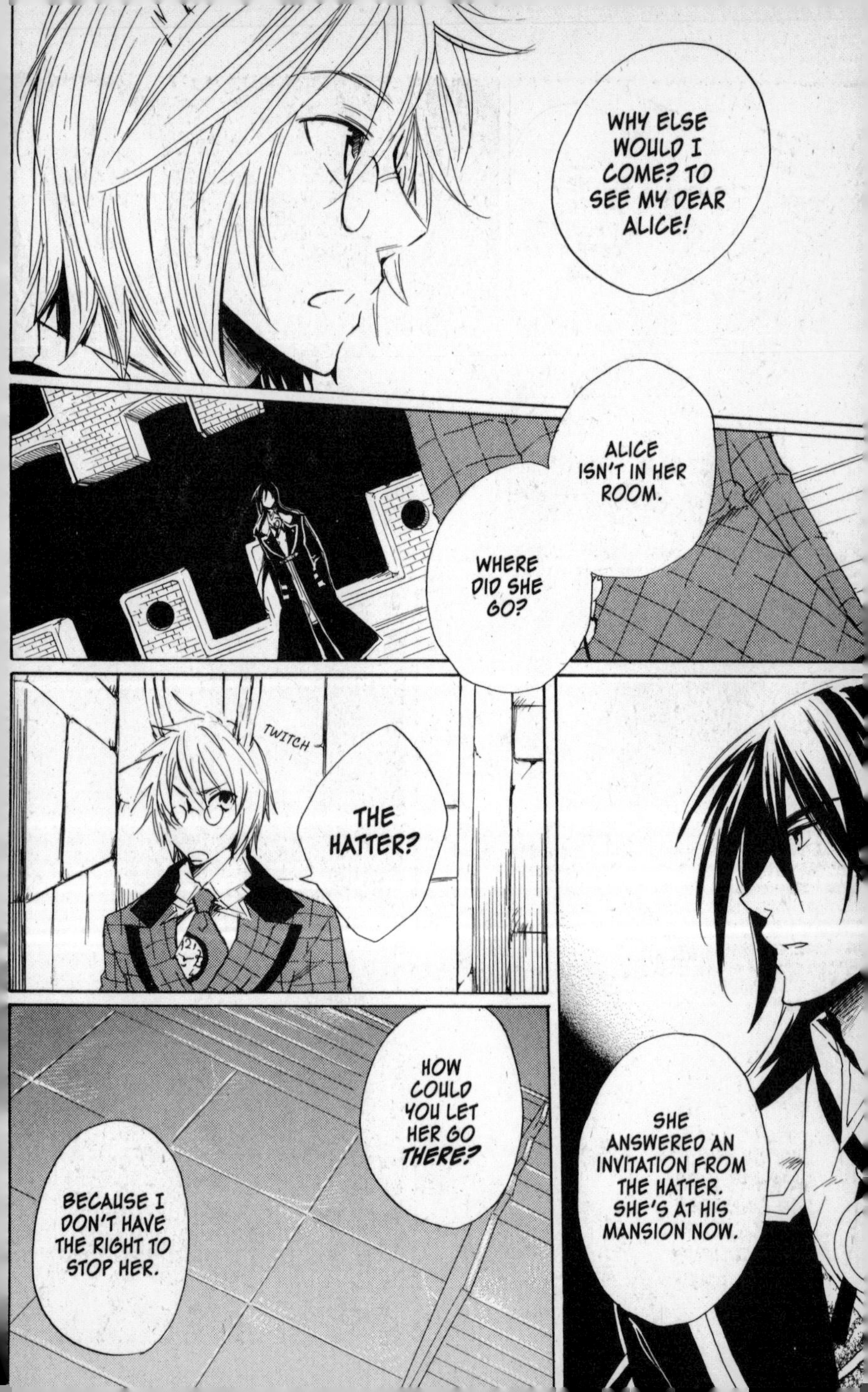
WHY ELSE WOULD I COME? TO SEE MY DEAR ALICE!
ALICE ISN'T IN HER ROOM.
WHERE DID SHE GO?
SHE ANSWERED AN INVITATION FROM THE HATTER. SHE'S AT HIS MANSION NOW.
TWITCH
THE HATTER?
HOW COULD YOU LET HER GO *THERE?*
BECAUSE I DON'T HAVE THE RIGHT TO STOP HER.

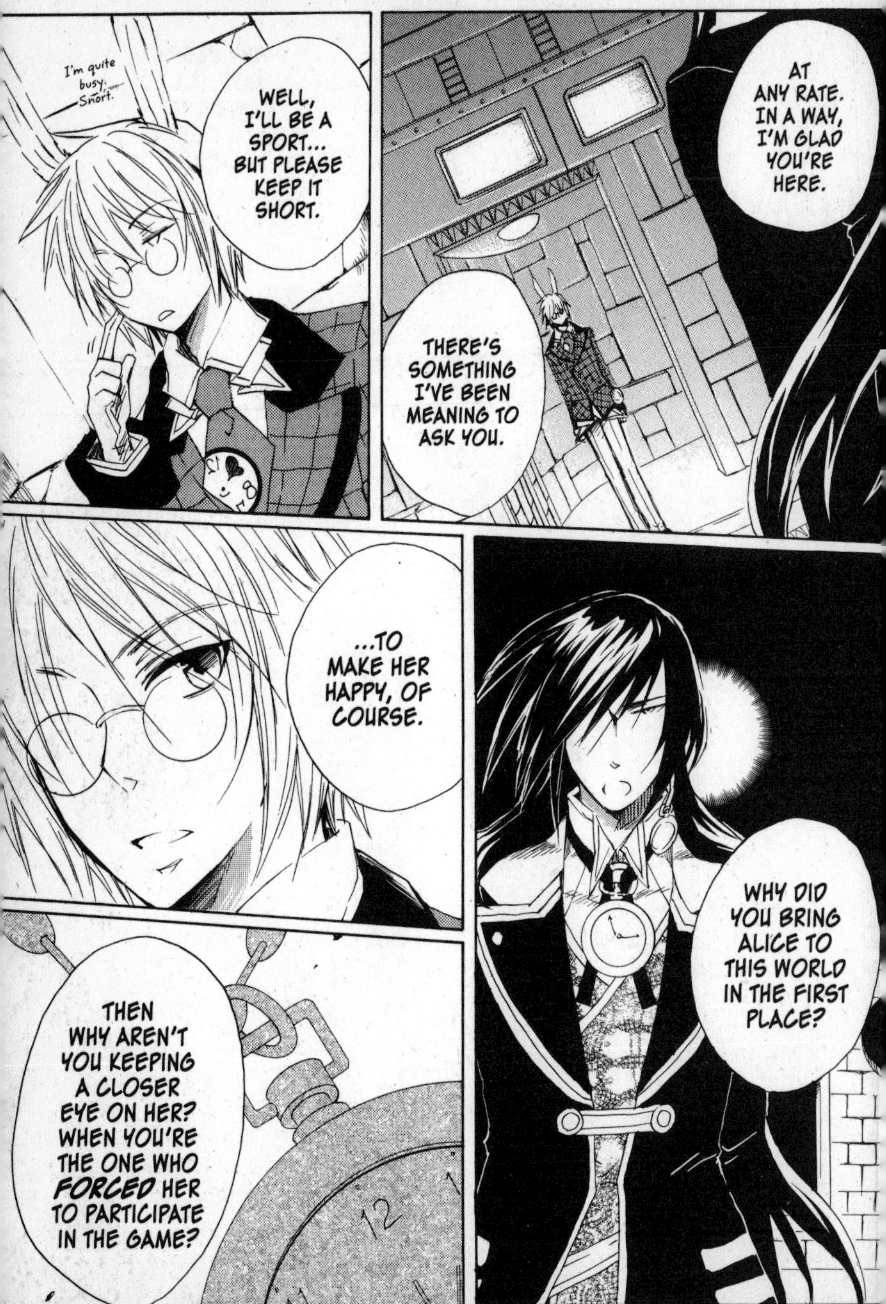
AT ANY RATE. IN A WAY, I'M GLAD YOU'RE HERE.
THERE'S SOMETHING I'VE BEEN MEANING TO ASK YOU.
WELL, I'LL BE A SPORT... BUT PLEASE KEEP IT SHORT.
I'm quite busy. Snort.
WHY DID YOU BRING ALICE TO THIS WORLD IN THE FIRST PLACE?
...TO MAKE HER HAPPY, OF COURSE.
THEN WHY AREN'T YOU KEEPING A CLOSER EYE ON HER? WHEN YOU'RE THE ONE WHO *FORCED* HER TO PARTICIPATE IN THE GAME?

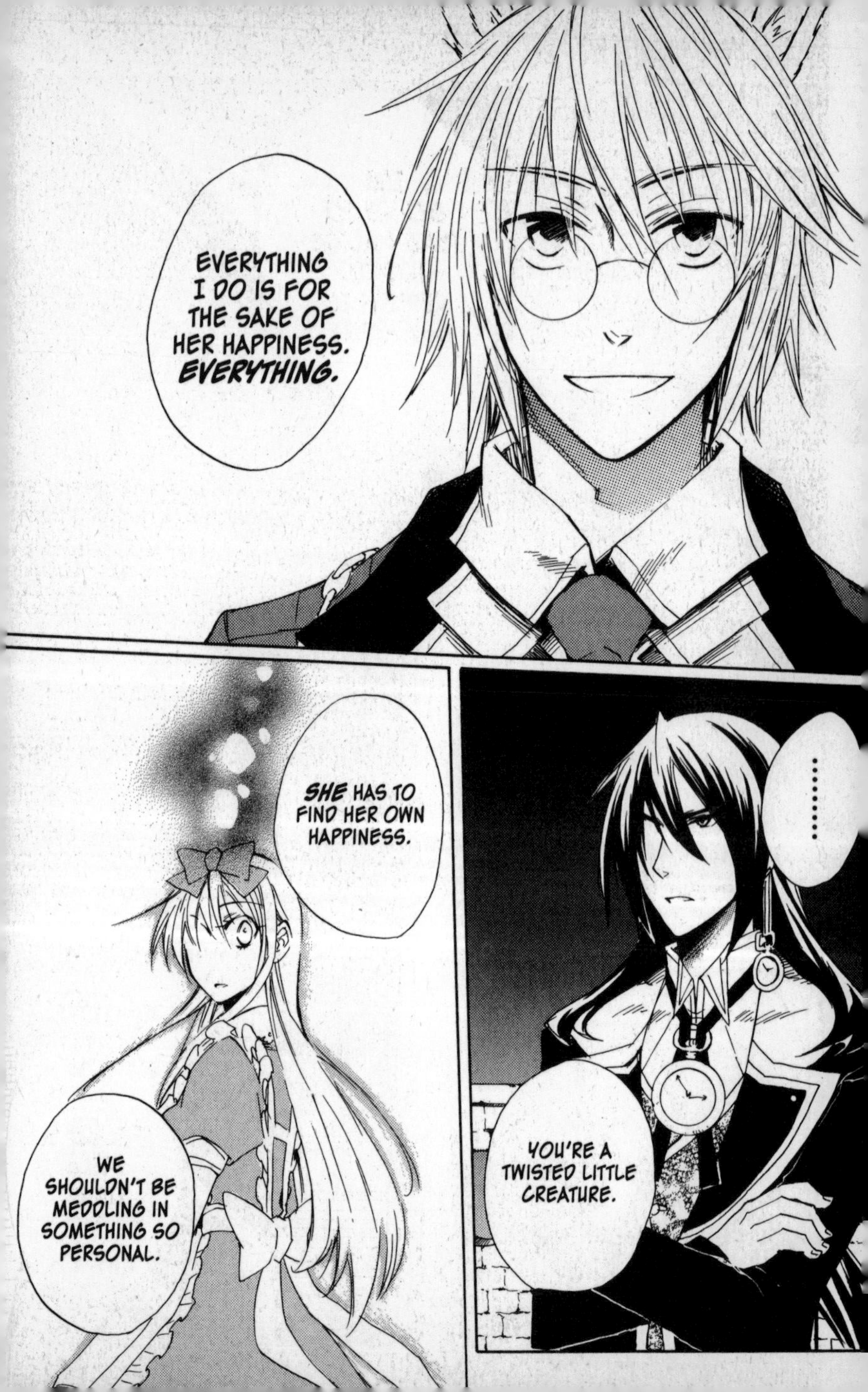
EVERYTHING I DO IS FOR THE SAKE OF HER HAPPINESS. *EVERYTHING.*
......
YOU'RE A TWISTED LITTLE CREATURE.
*SHE* HAS TO FIND HER OWN HAPPINESS.
WE SHOULDN'T BE MEDDLING IN SOMETHING SO PERSONAL.

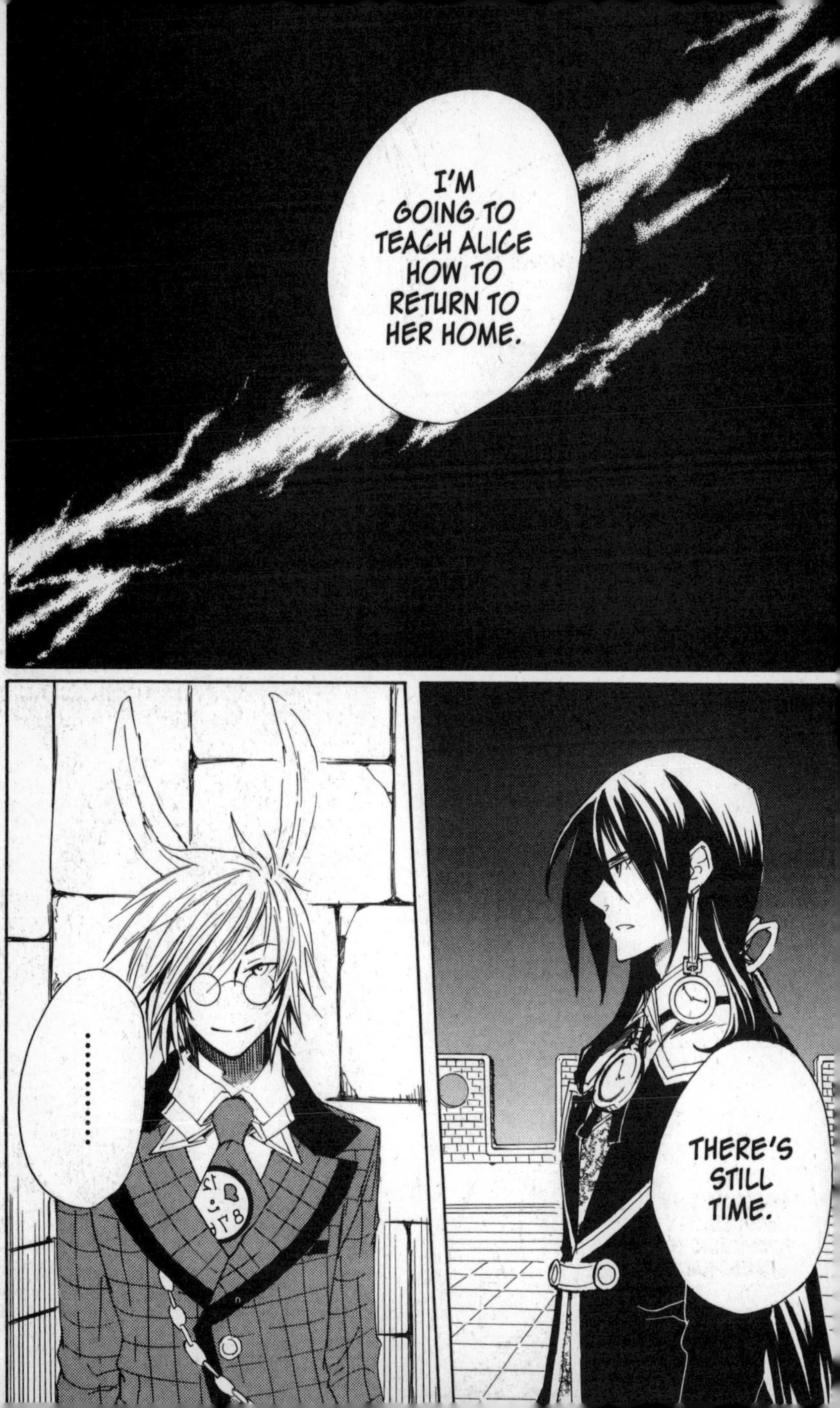
I'M GOING TO TEACH ALICE HOW TO RETURN TO HER HOME.
THERE'S STILL TIME.
......

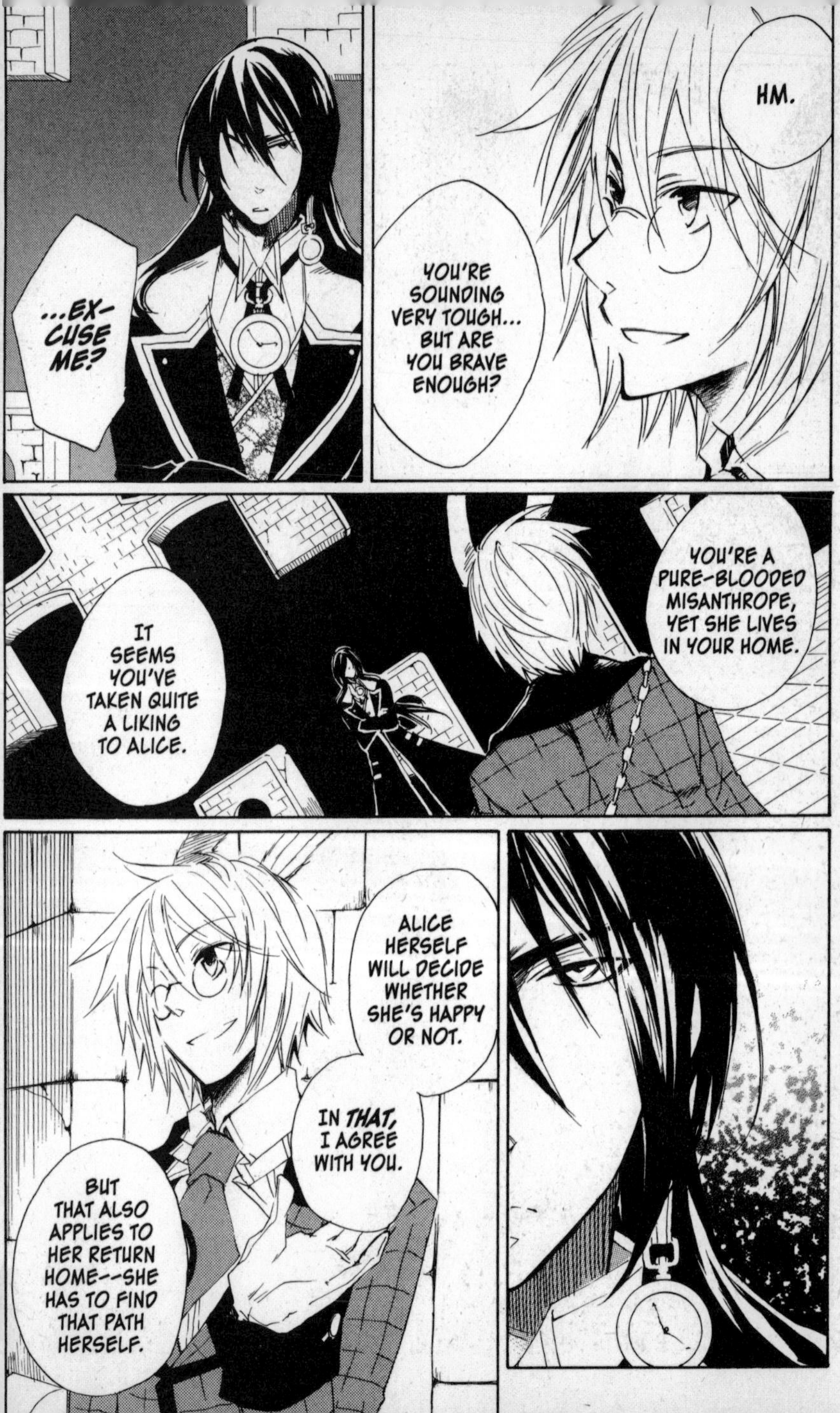
HM.
YOU'RE SOUNDING VERY TOUGH... BUT ARE YOU BRAVE ENOUGH?
...EX-CUSE ME?
YOU'RE A PURE-BLOODED MISANTHROPE, YET SHE LIVES IN YOUR HOME.
IT SEEMS YOU'VE TAKEN QUITE A LIKING TO ALICE.
ALICE HERSELF WILL DECIDE WHETHER SHE'S HAPPY OR NOT.
IN *THAT*, I AGREE WITH YOU.
BUT THAT ALSO APPLIES TO HER RETURN HOME--SHE HAS TO FIND THAT PATH HERSELF.

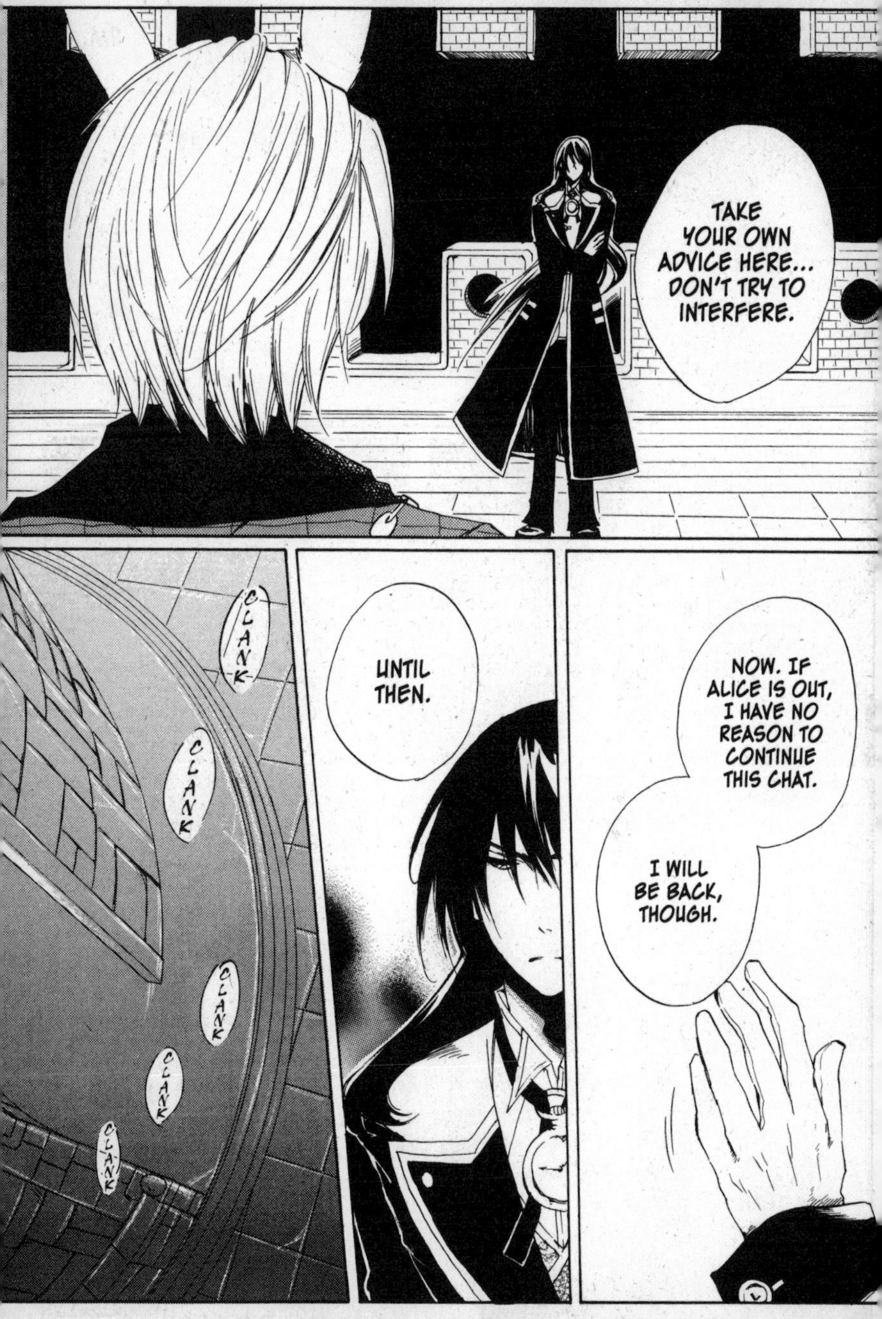
TAKE YOUR OWN ADVICE HERE... DON'T TRY TO INTERFERE.
NOW. IF ALICE IS OUT, I HAVE NO REASON TO CONTINUE THIS CHAT.
I WILL BE BACK, THOUGH.
UNTIL THEN.
CLANK
CLANK
CLANK
CLANK
CLANK

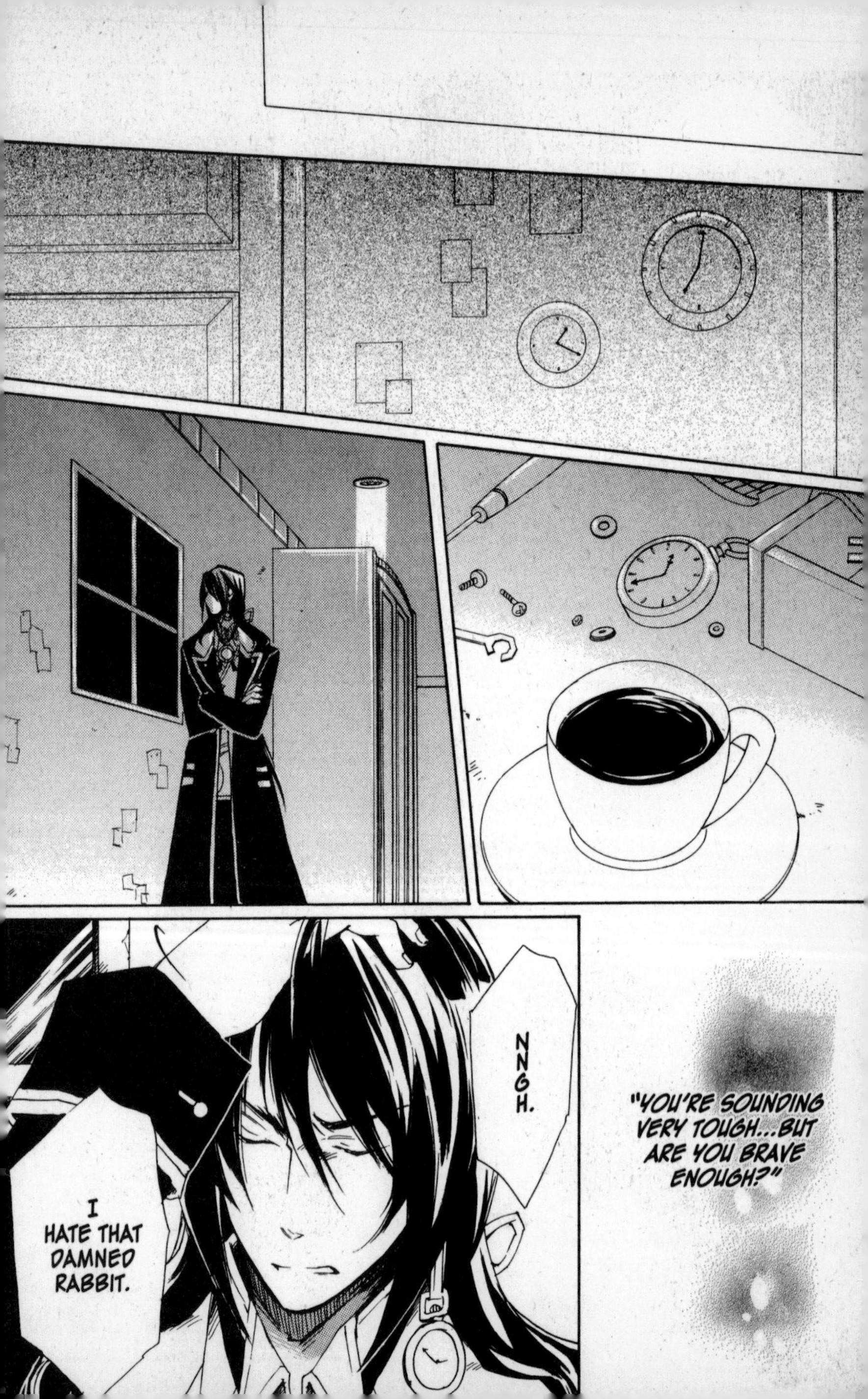
"YOU'RE SOUNDING VERY TOUGH...BUT ARE YOU BRAVE ENOUGH?"
NNGH.
I HATE THAT DAMNED RABBIT.

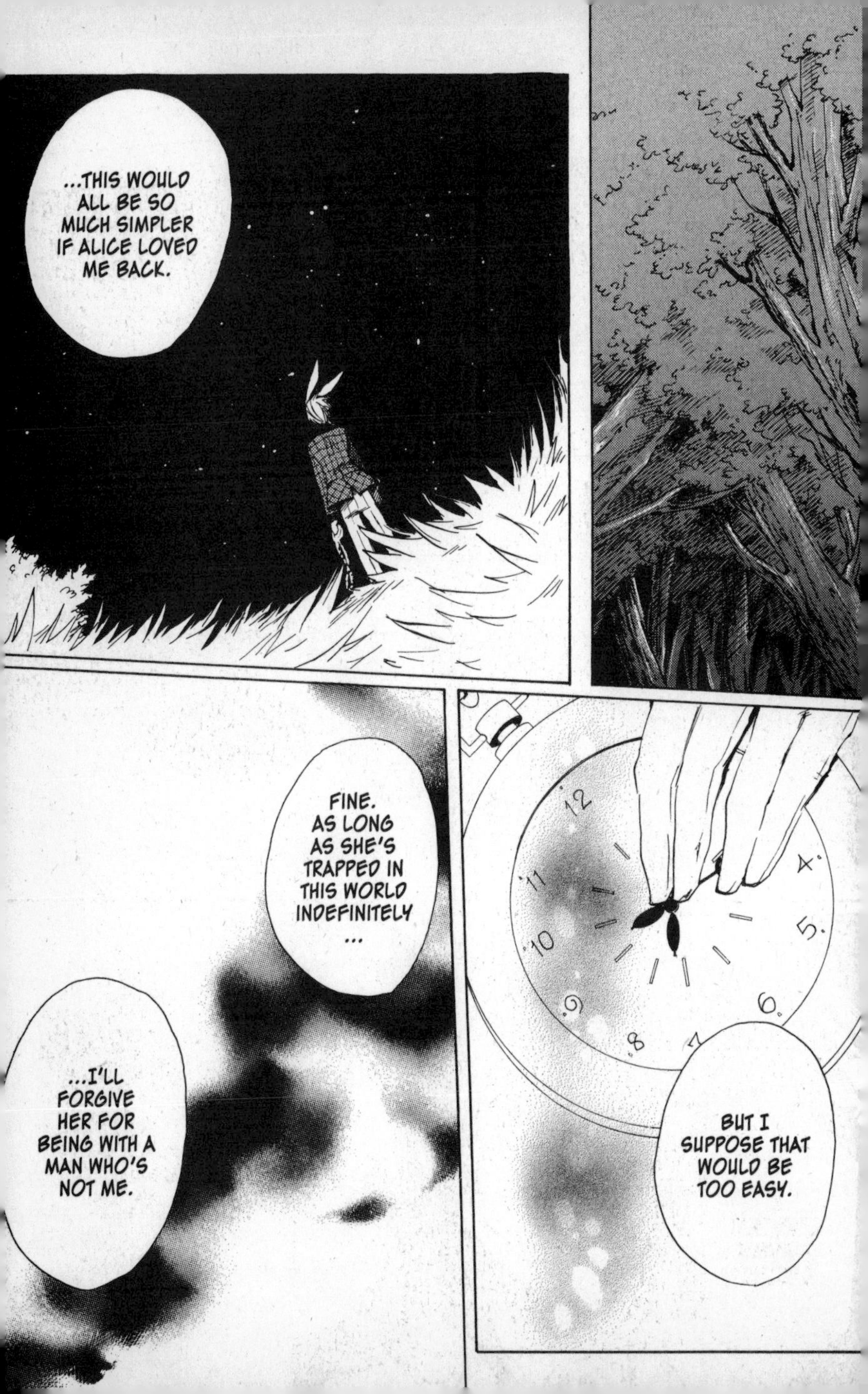
...THIS WOULD ALL BE SO MUCH SIMPLER IF ALICE LOVED ME BACK.
BUT I SUPPOSE THAT WOULD BE TOO EASY.
FINE. AS LONG AS SHE'S TRAPPED IN THIS WORLD INDEFINITELY...
...I'LL FORGIVE HER FOR BEING WITH A MAN WHO'S NOT ME.

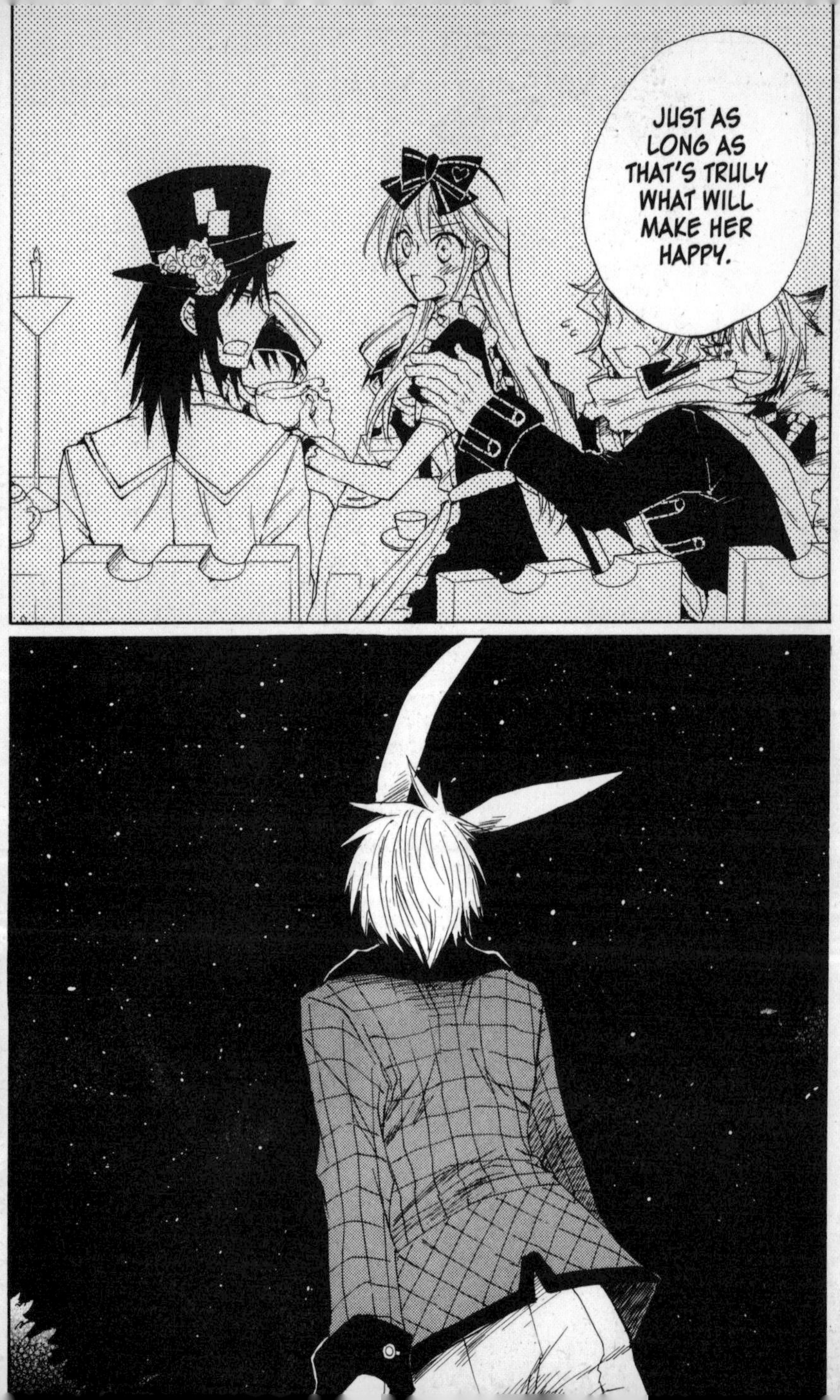
JUST AS LONG AS THAT'S TRULY WHAT WILL MAKE HER HAPPY.

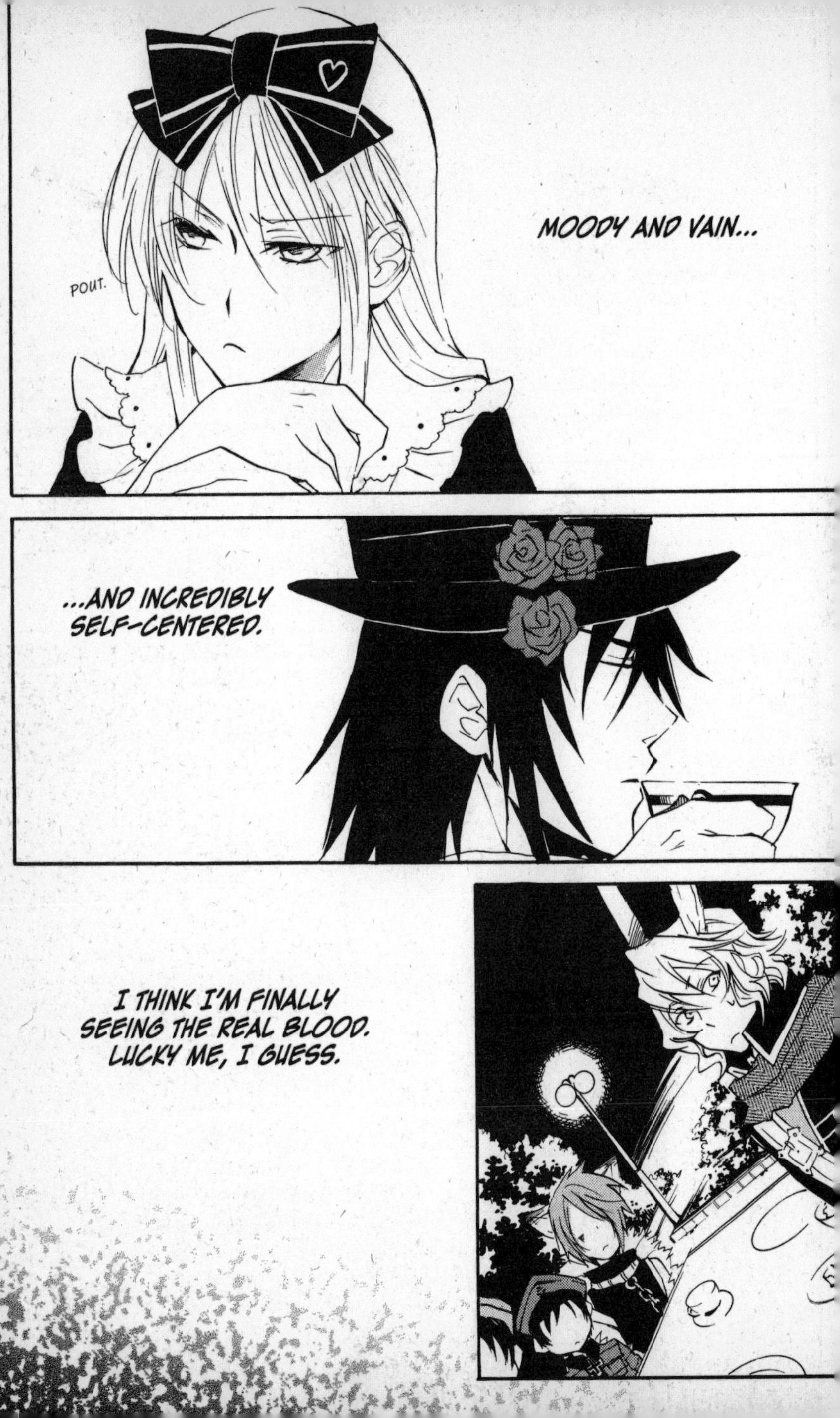
MOODY AND VAIN...
POUT.
...AND INCREDIBLY SELF-CENTERED.
I THINK I'M FINALLY SEEING THE REAL BLOOD. LUCKY ME, I GUESS.

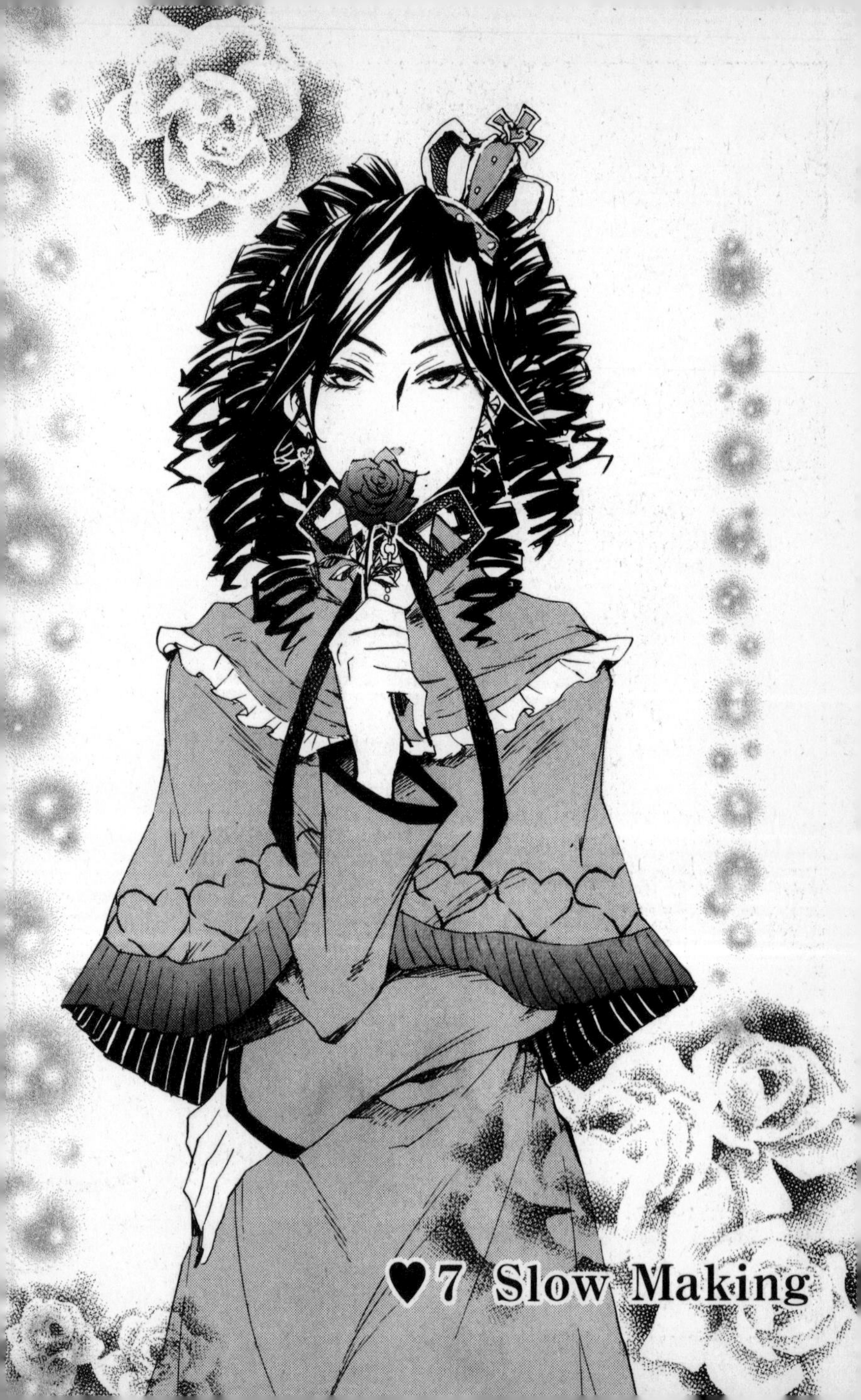
♥7 Slow Making

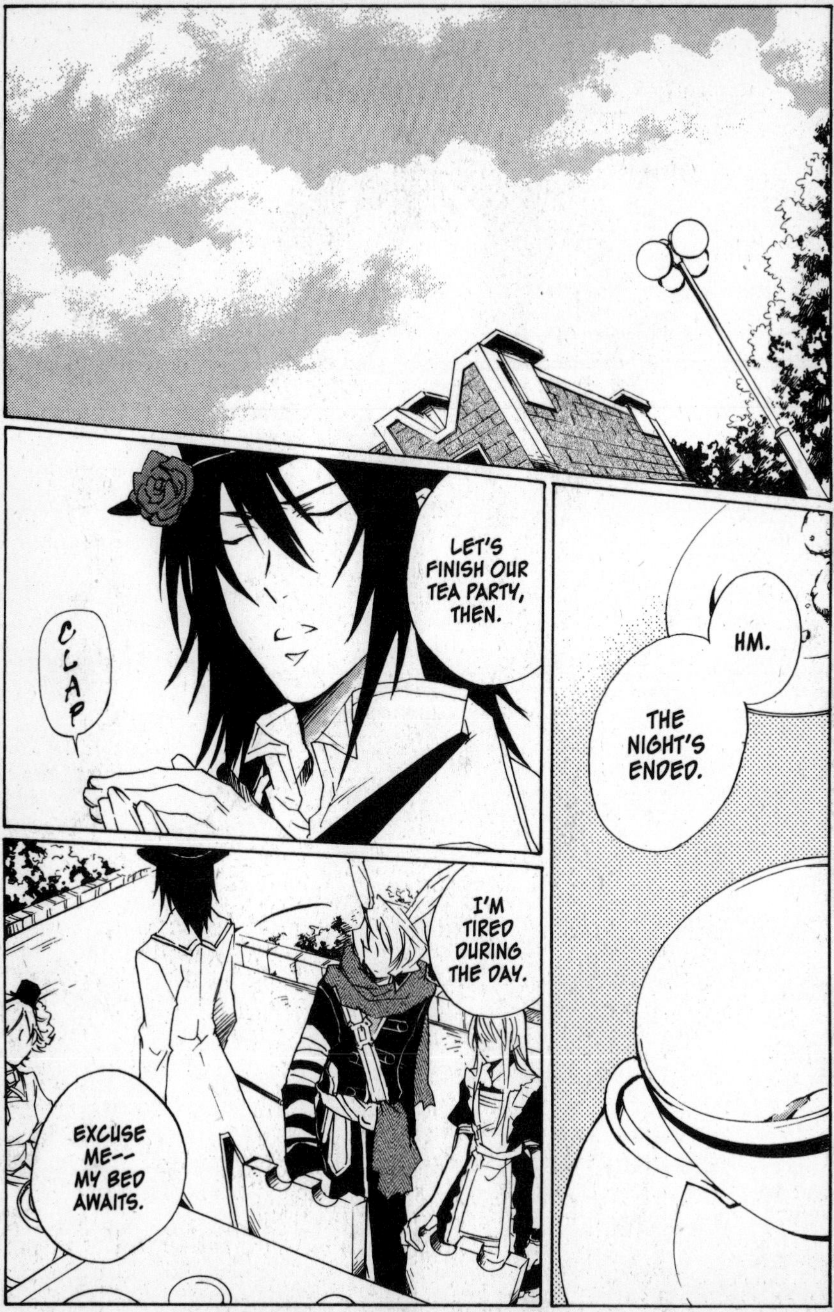
HM.
THE NIGHT'S ENDED.
LET'S FINISH OUR TEA PARTY, THEN.
CLAP
I'M TIRED DURING THE DAY.
EXCUSE ME-- MY BED AWAITS.

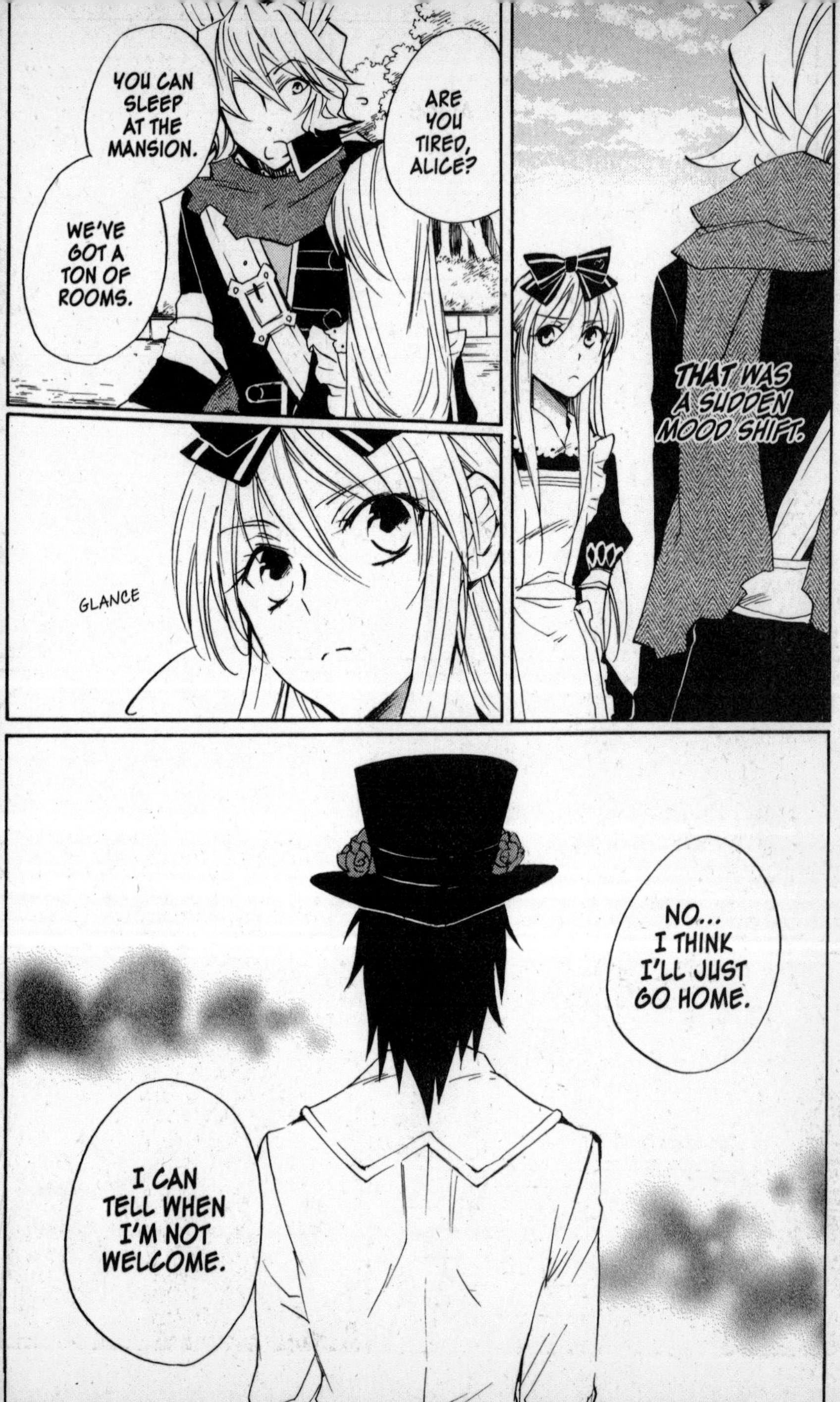
THAT WAS A SUDDEN MOOD SHIFT.
ARE YOU TIRED, ALICE?
YOU CAN SLEEP AT THE MANSION.
WE'VE GOT A TON OF ROOMS.
GLANCE
NO... I THINK I'LL JUST GO HOME.
I CAN TELL WHEN I'M NOT WELCOME.

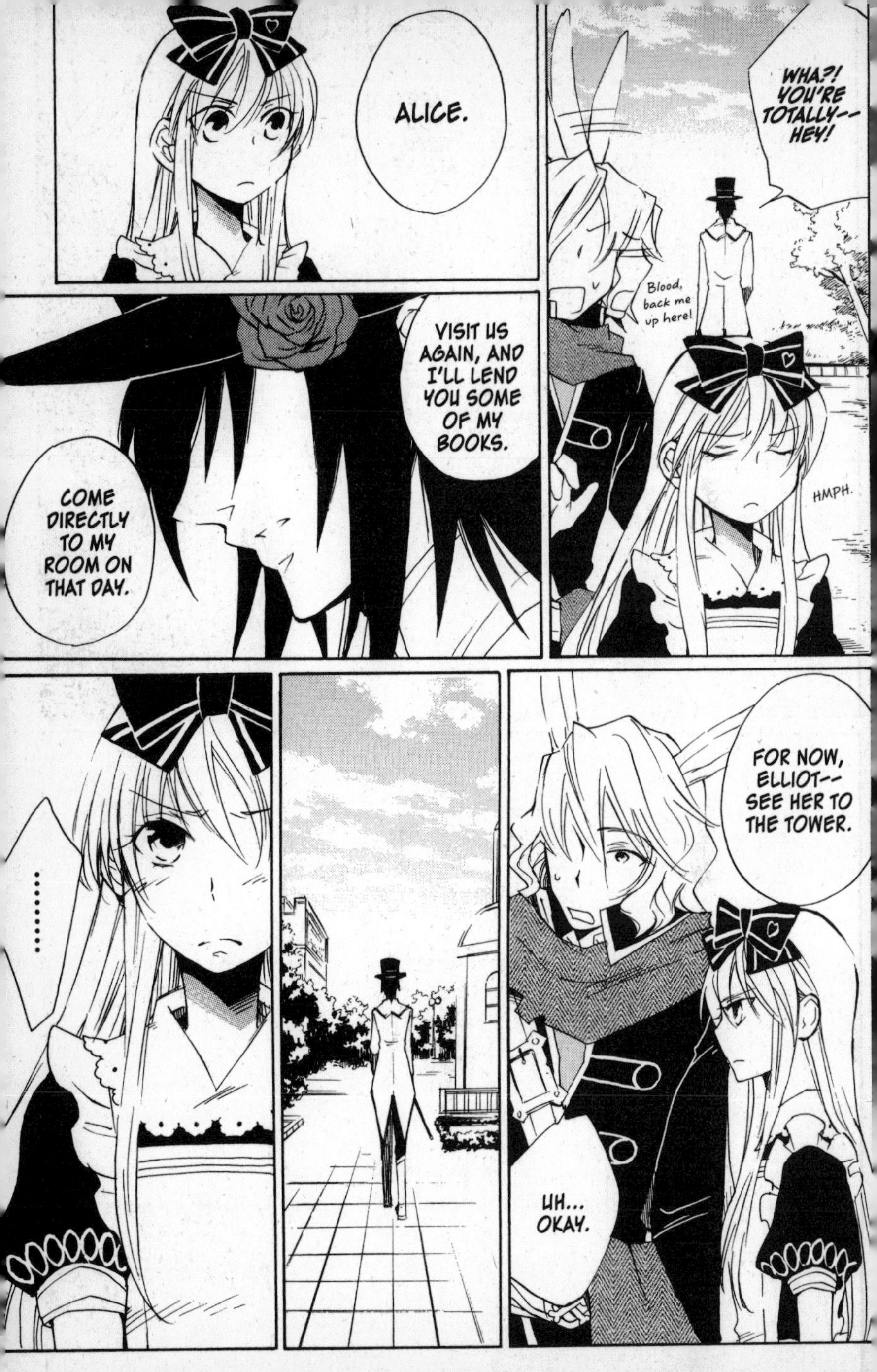
WHA?! YOU'RE TOTALLY-- HEY!
Blood, back me up here!
HMPH.
ALICE.
VISIT US AGAIN, AND I'LL LEND YOU SOME OF MY BOOKS.
COME DIRECTLY TO MY ROOM ON THAT DAY.
FOR NOW, ELLIOT-- SEE HER TO THE TOWER.
UH... OKAY.
.......

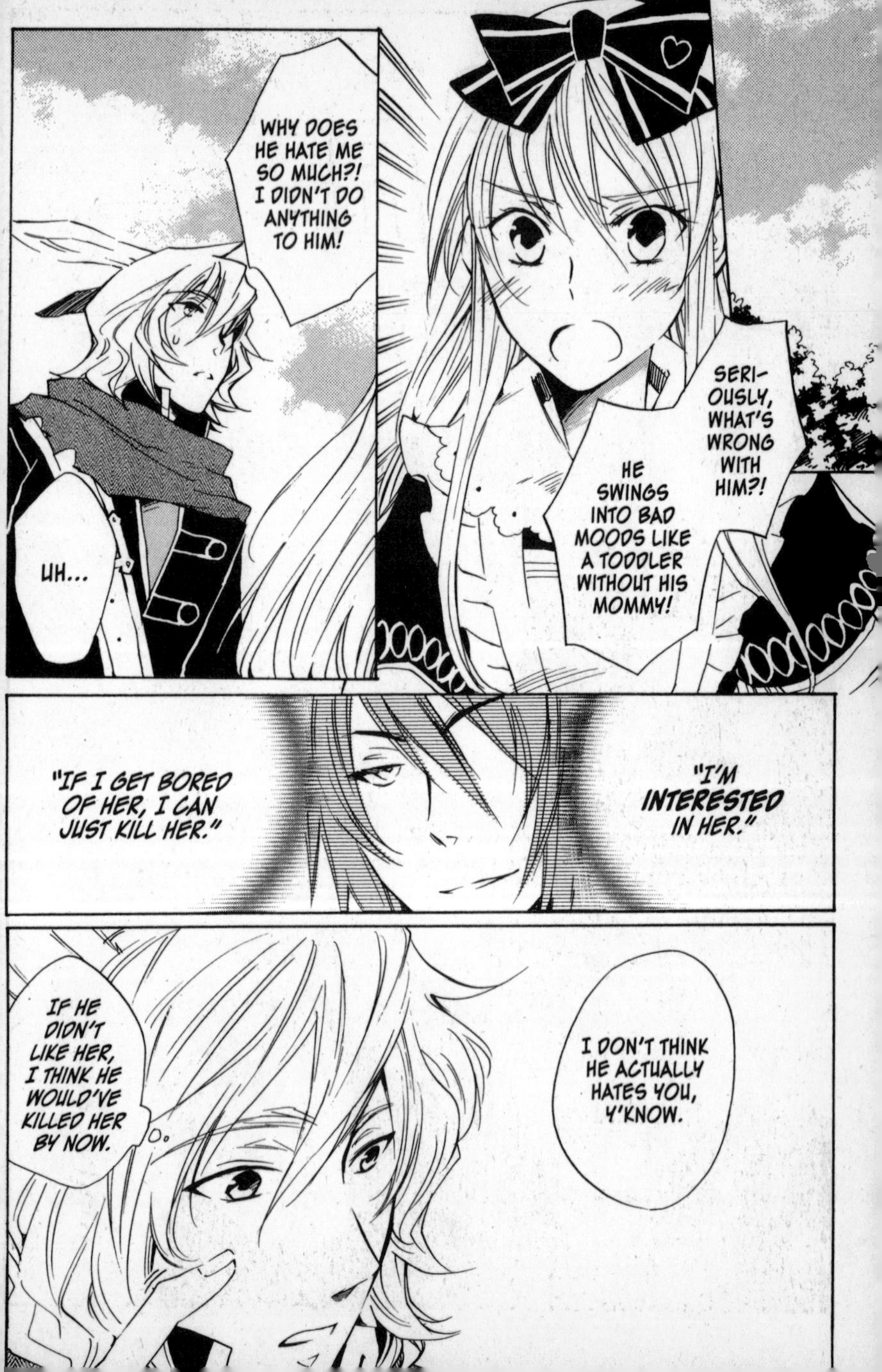
SERI-OUSLY, WHAT'S WRONG WITH HIM?!
HE SWINGS INTO BAD MOODS LIKE A TODDLER WITHOUT HIS MOMMY!
WHY DOES HE HATE ME SO MUCH?! I DIDN'T DO ANYTHING TO HIM!
UH...
"I'M *INTERESTED* IN HER."
"IF I GET BORED OF HER, I CAN JUST KILL HER."
I DON'T THINK HE ACTUALLY HATES YOU, Y'KNOW.
IF HE DIDN'T LIKE HER, I THINK HE WOULD'VE KILLED HER BY NOW.

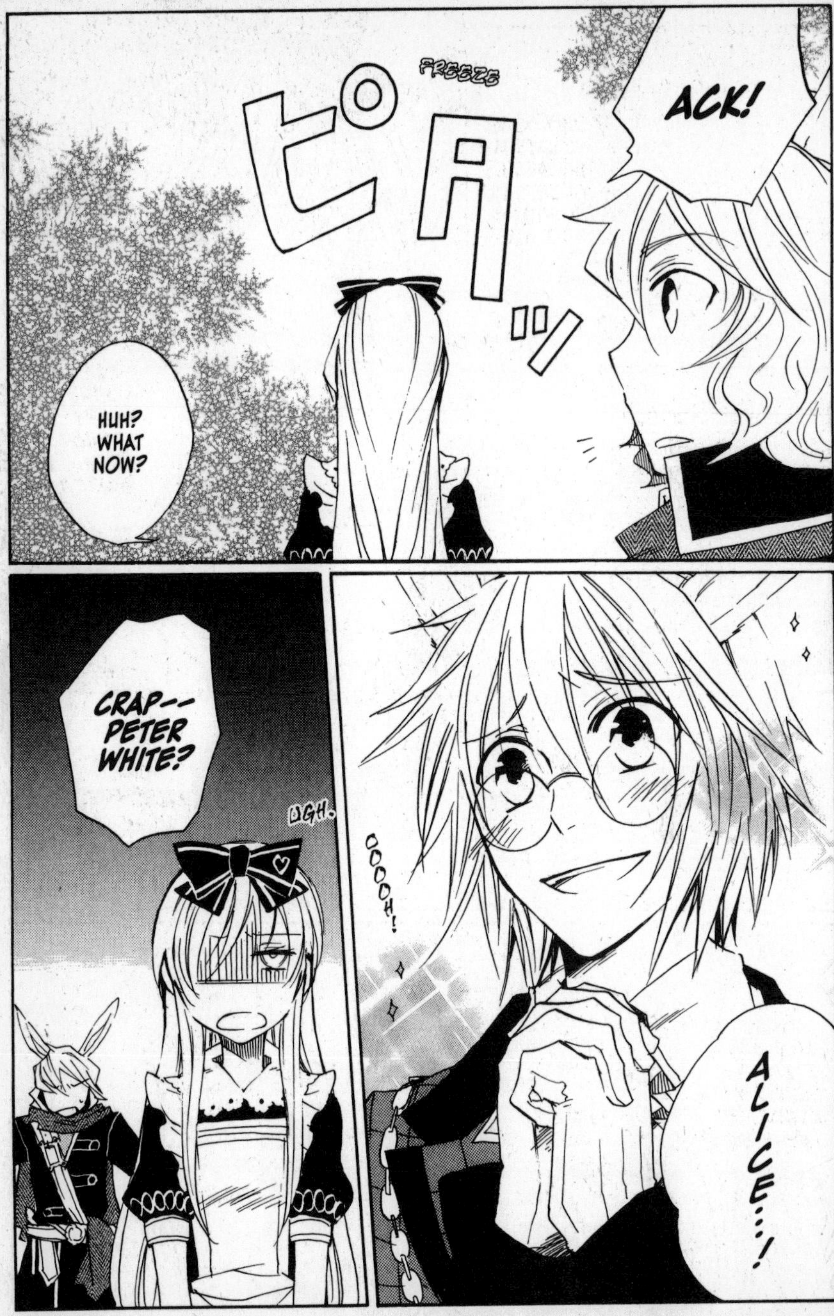
ACK!
ピタッ
FREEZE
HUH? WHAT NOW?
OOOOOH!
ALICE...!
CRAP-- PETER WHITE?
UGH.

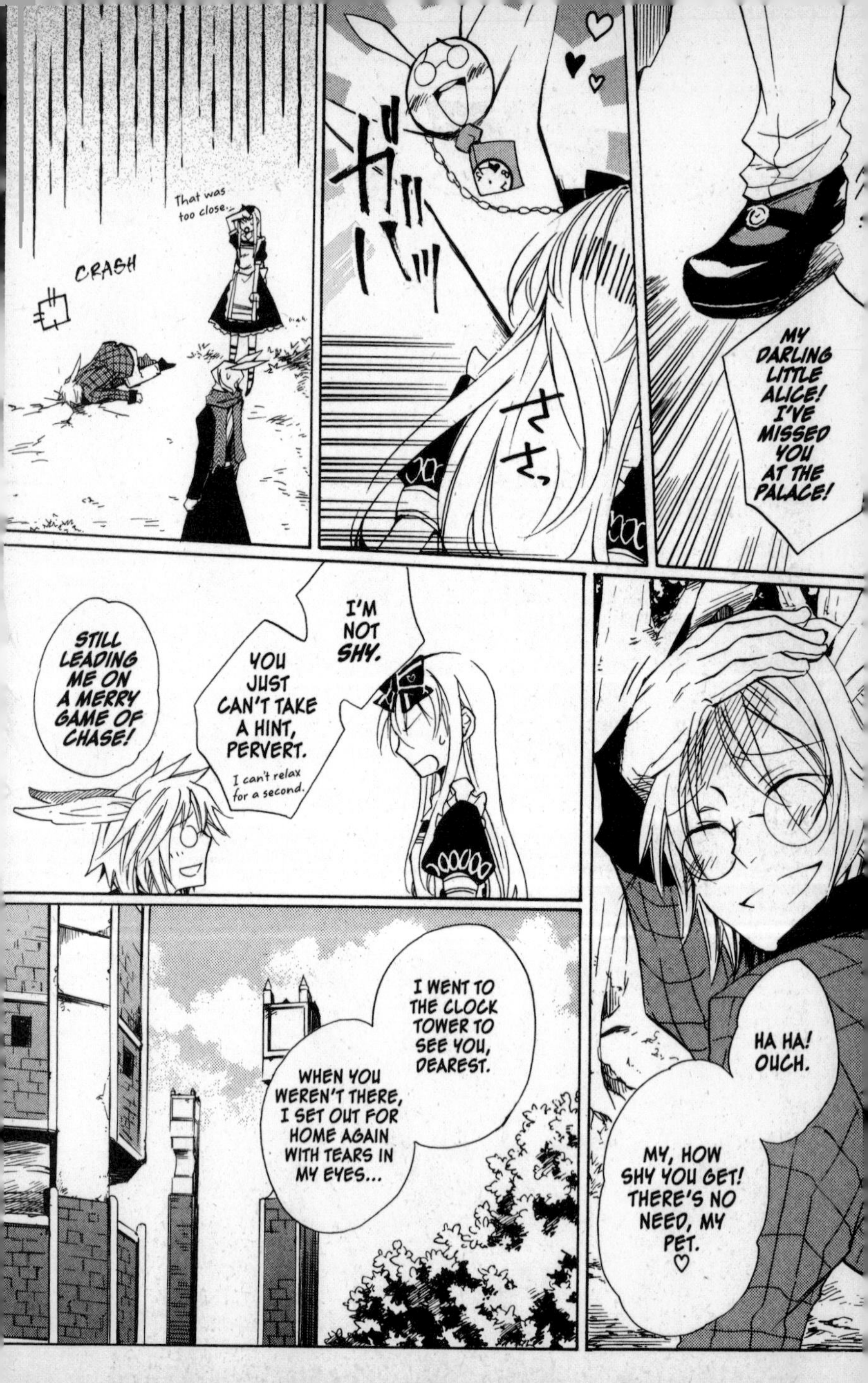

MY DARLING LITTLE ALICE! I'VE MISSED YOU AT THE PALACE!
ガバッ
さっ
That was too close.
CRASH
HA HA! OUCH.
MY, HOW SHY YOU GET! THERE'S NO NEED, MY PET. ♡
I'M NOT SHY.
YOU JUST CAN'T TAKE A HINT, PERVERT.
I can't relax for a second.
STILL LEADING ME ON A MERRY GAME OF CHASE!
I WENT TO THE CLOCK TOWER TO SEE YOU, DEAREST.
WHEN YOU WEREN'T THERE, I SET OUT FOR HOME AGAIN WITH TEARS IN MY EYES...

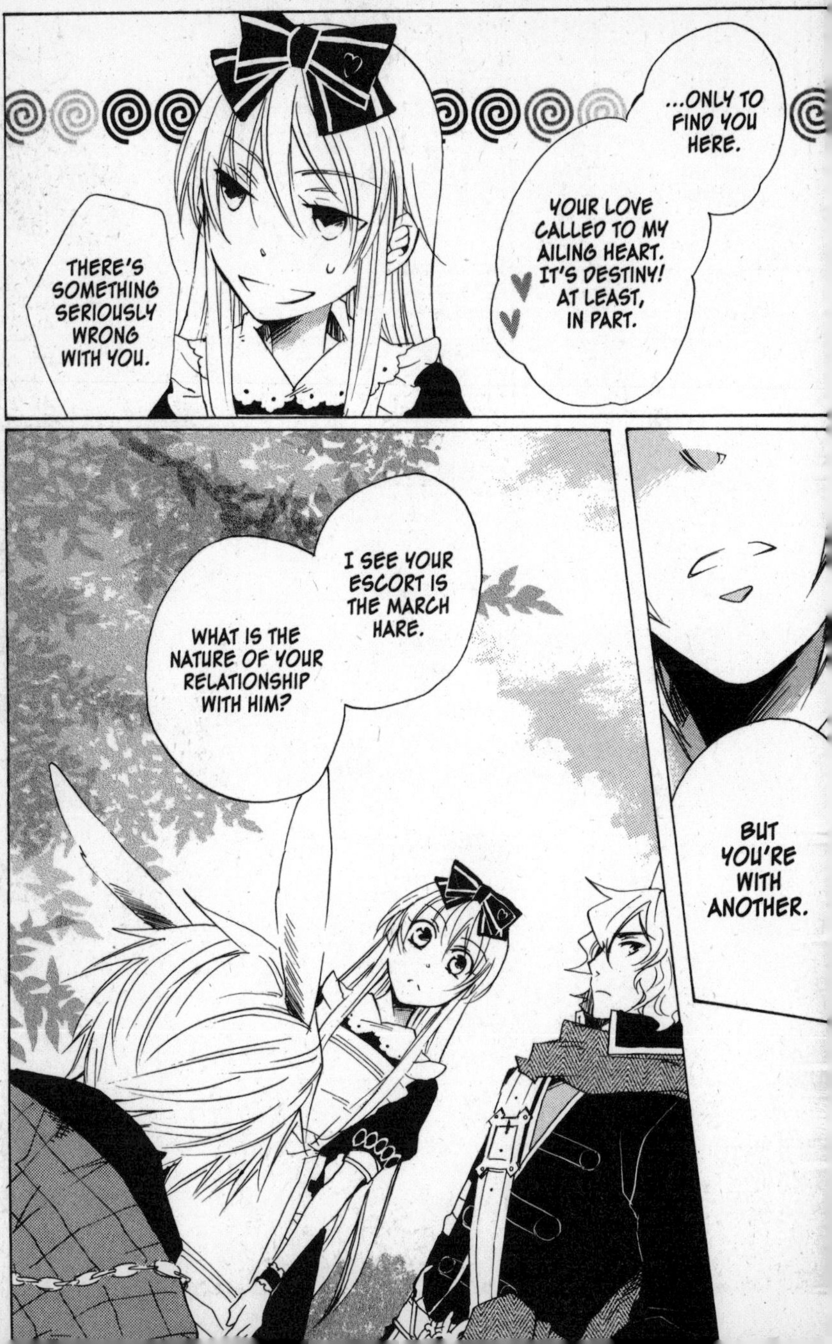
...ONLY TO FIND YOU HERE.
YOUR LOVE CALLED TO MY AILING HEART. IT'S DESTINY! AT LEAST, IN PART.
THERE'S SOMETHING SERIOUSLY WRONG WITH YOU.
BUT YOU'RE WITH ANOTHER.
I SEE YOUR ESCORT IS THE MARCH HARE.
WHAT IS THE NATURE OF YOUR RELATIONSHIP WITH HIM?

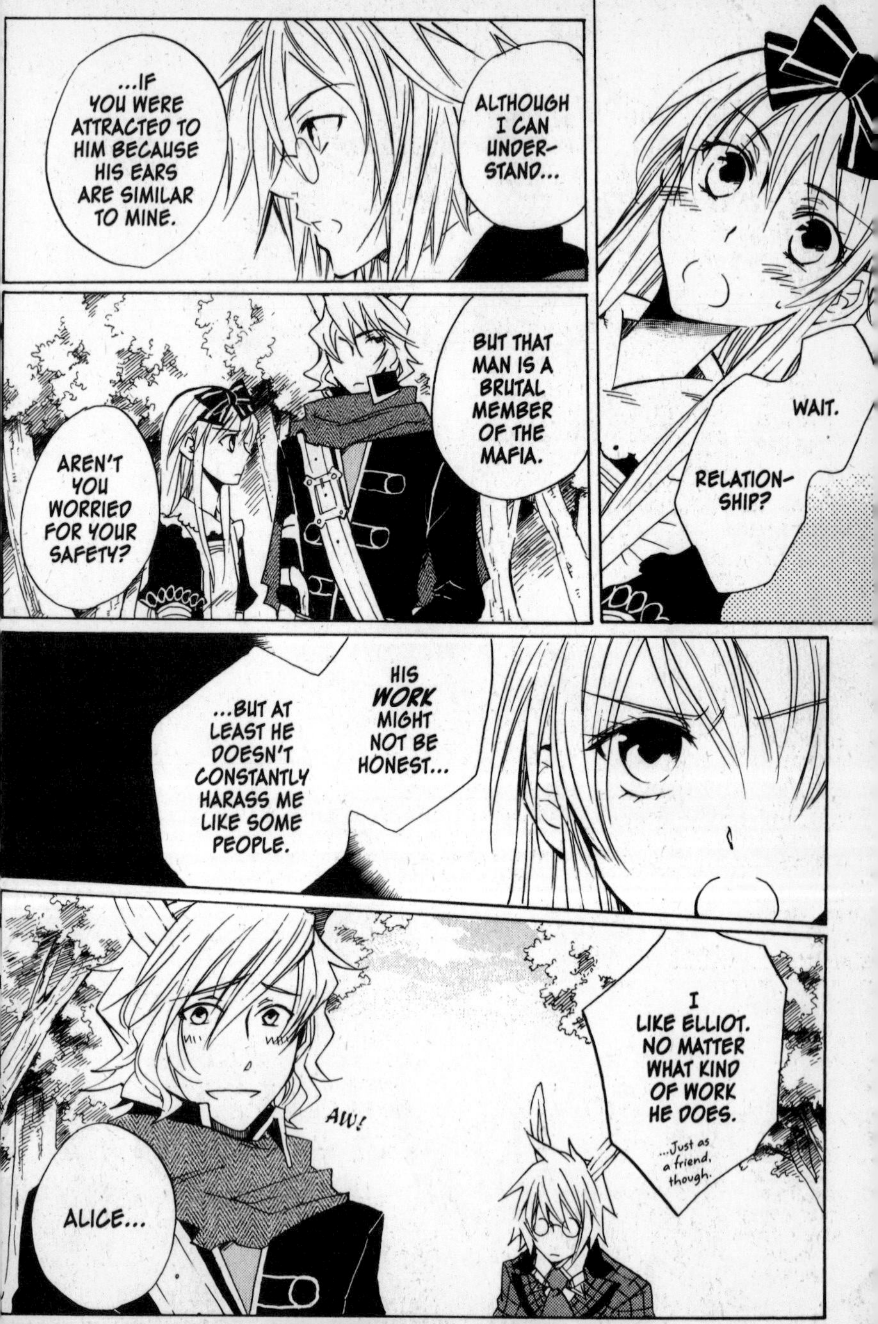
WAIT.
RELATIONSHIP?
ALTHOUGH I CAN UNDERSTAND...
...IF YOU WERE ATTRACTED TO HIM BECAUSE HIS EARS ARE SIMILAR TO MINE.
BUT THAT MAN IS A BRUTAL MEMBER OF THE MAFIA.
AREN'T YOU WORRIED FOR YOUR SAFETY?
HIS *WORK* MIGHT NOT BE HONEST...
...BUT AT LEAST HE DOESN'T CONSTANTLY HARASS ME LIKE SOME PEOPLE.
I LIKE ELLIOT. NO MATTER WHAT KIND OF WORK HE DOES.
...Just as a friend, though.
AW!
ALICE...

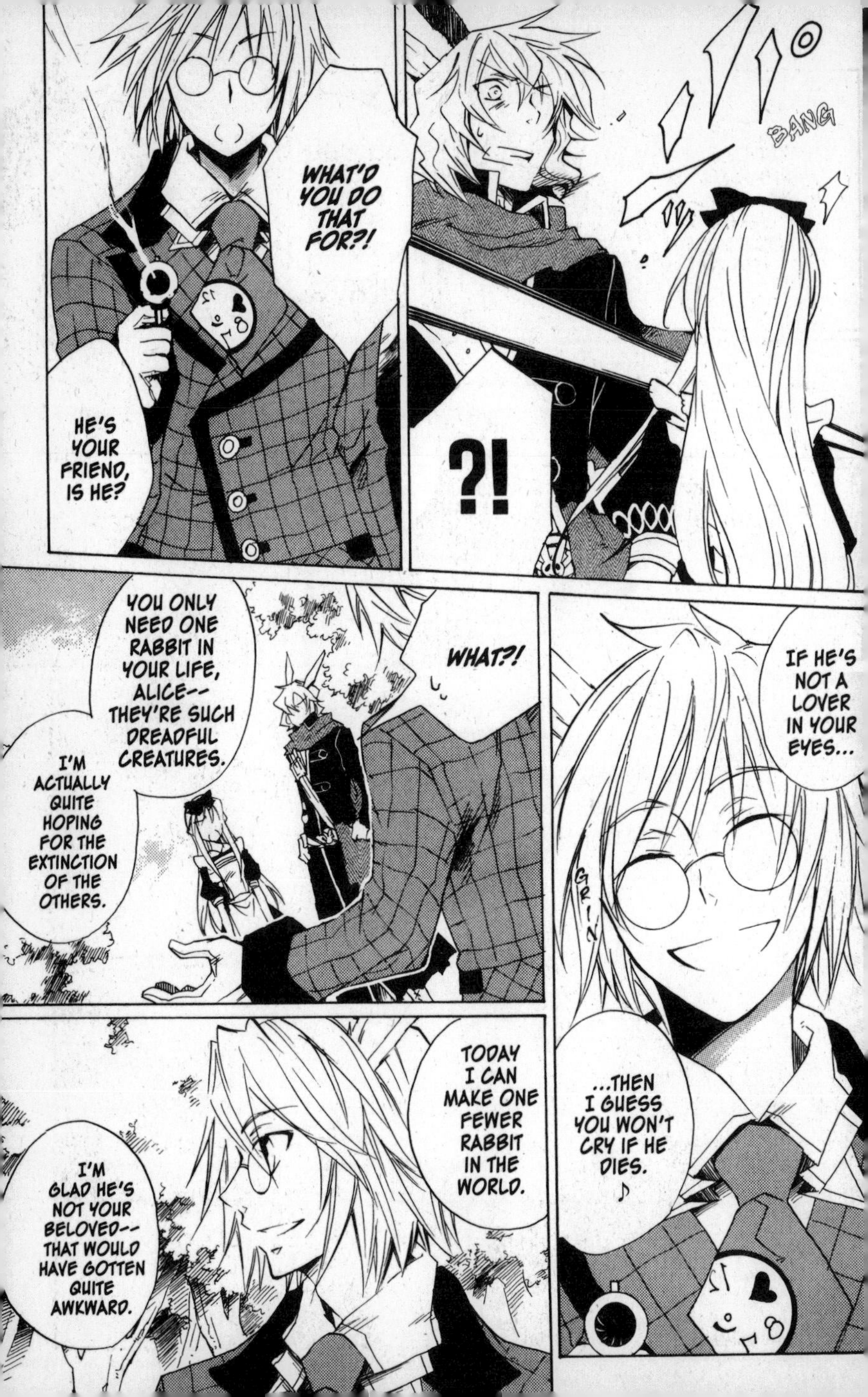
BANG
?!
WHAT'D YOU DO THAT FOR?!
HE'S YOUR FRIEND, IS HE?
IF HE'S NOT A LOVER IN YOUR EYES...
GRIN
...THEN I GUESS YOU WON'T CRY IF HE DIES. ♪
WHAT?!
YOU ONLY NEED ONE RABBIT IN YOUR LIFE, ALICE-- THEY'RE SUCH DREADFUL CREATURES.
I'M ACTUALLY QUITE HOPING FOR THE EXTINCTION OF THE OTHERS.
TODAY I CAN MAKE ONE FEWER RABBIT IN THE WORLD.
I'M GLAD HE'S NOT YOUR BELOVED-- THAT WOULD HAVE GOTTEN QUITE AWKWARD.

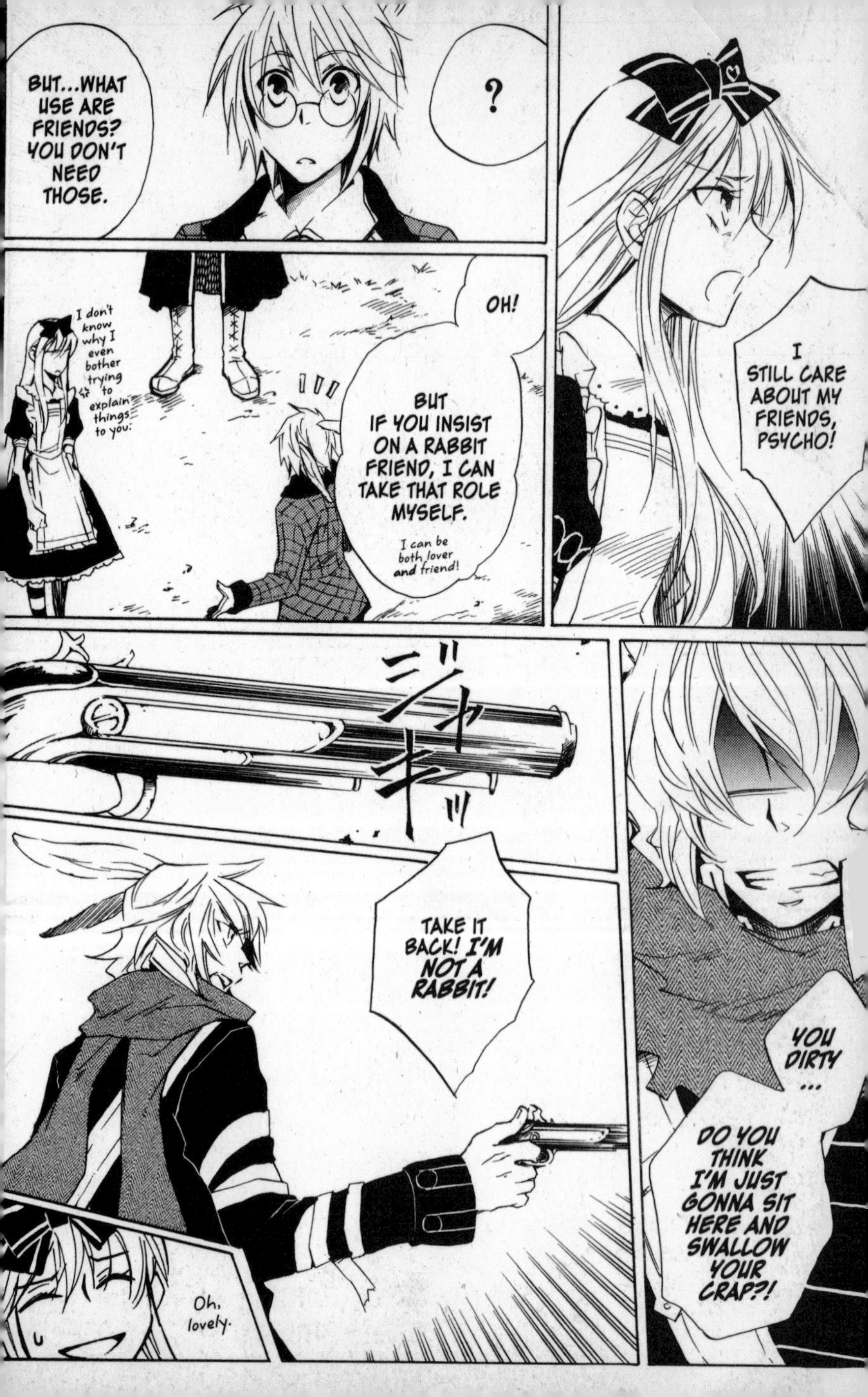

I STILL CARE ABOUT MY FRIENDS, PSYCHO!
?
BUT...WHAT USE ARE FRIENDS? YOU DON'T NEED THOSE.
OH!
BUT IF YOU INSIST ON A RABBIT FRIEND, I CAN TAKE THAT ROLE MYSELF.
I can be both lover and friend!
I don't know why I even bother trying to explain things to you.
YOU DIRTY...
DO YOU THINK I'M JUST GONNA SIT HERE AND SWALLOW YOUR CRAP?!
ジャキッ
TAKE IT BACK! I'M NOT A RABBIT!
Oh, lovely.

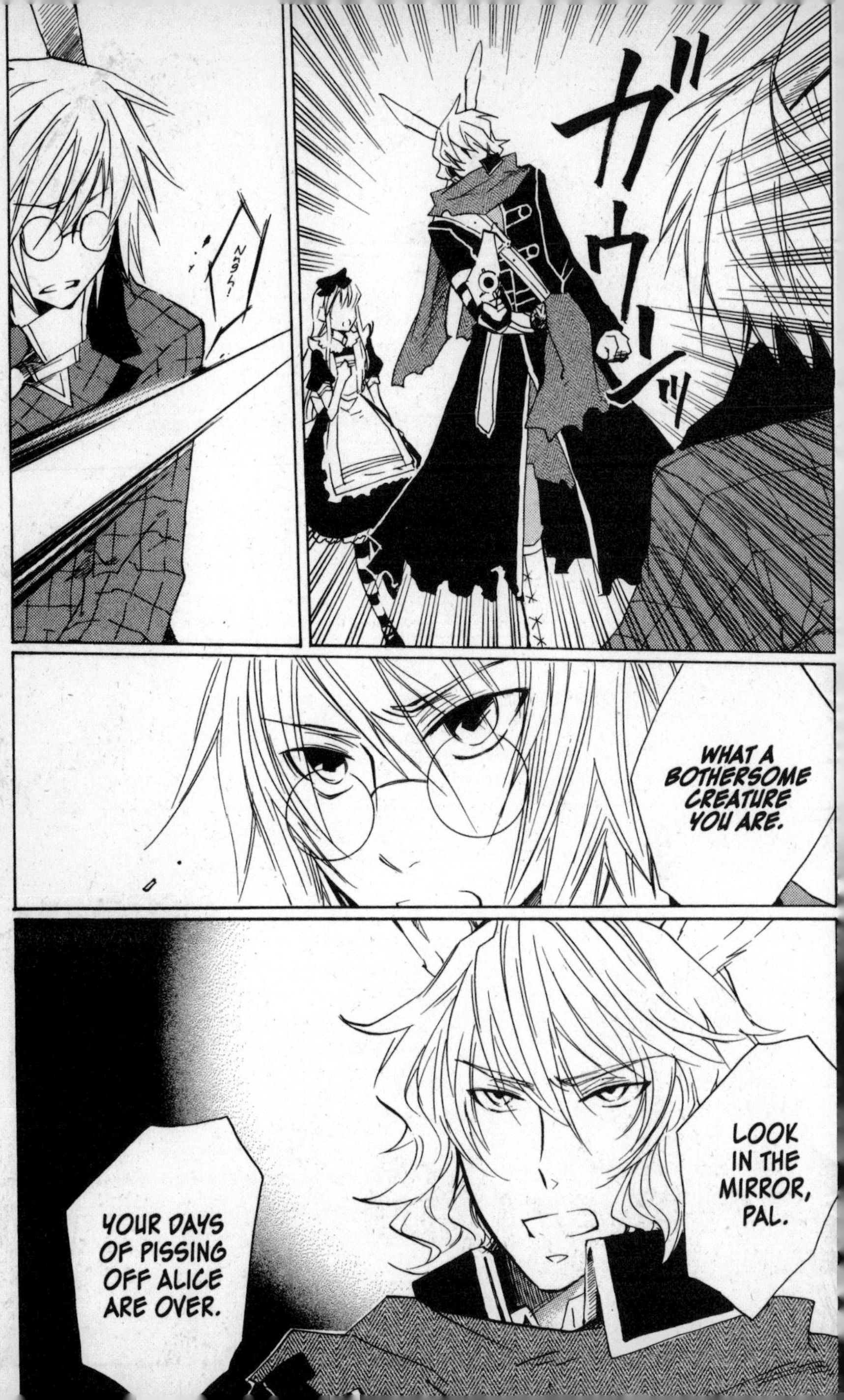
ガウンッ
Nggh!
WHAT A BOTHERSOME CREATURE YOU ARE.
LOOK IN THE MIRROR, PAL.
YOUR DAYS OF PISSING OFF ALICE ARE OVER.

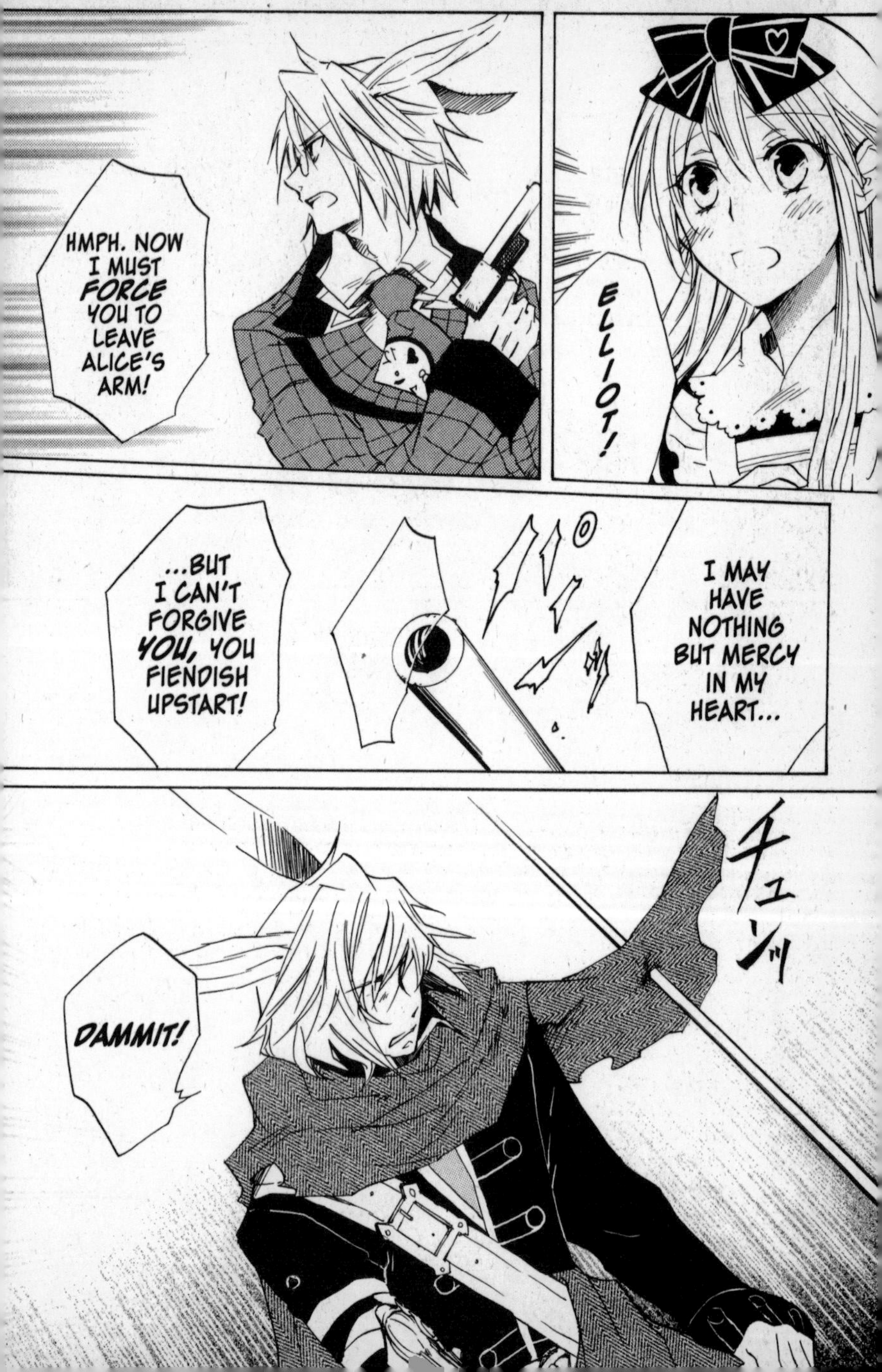
ELLIOT!
HMPH. NOW I MUST *FORCE* YOU TO LEAVE ALICE'S ARM!
I MAY HAVE NOTHING BUT MERCY IN MY HEART...
...BUT I CAN'T FORGIVE *YOU*, YOU FIENDISH UPSTART!
*DAMMIT!*

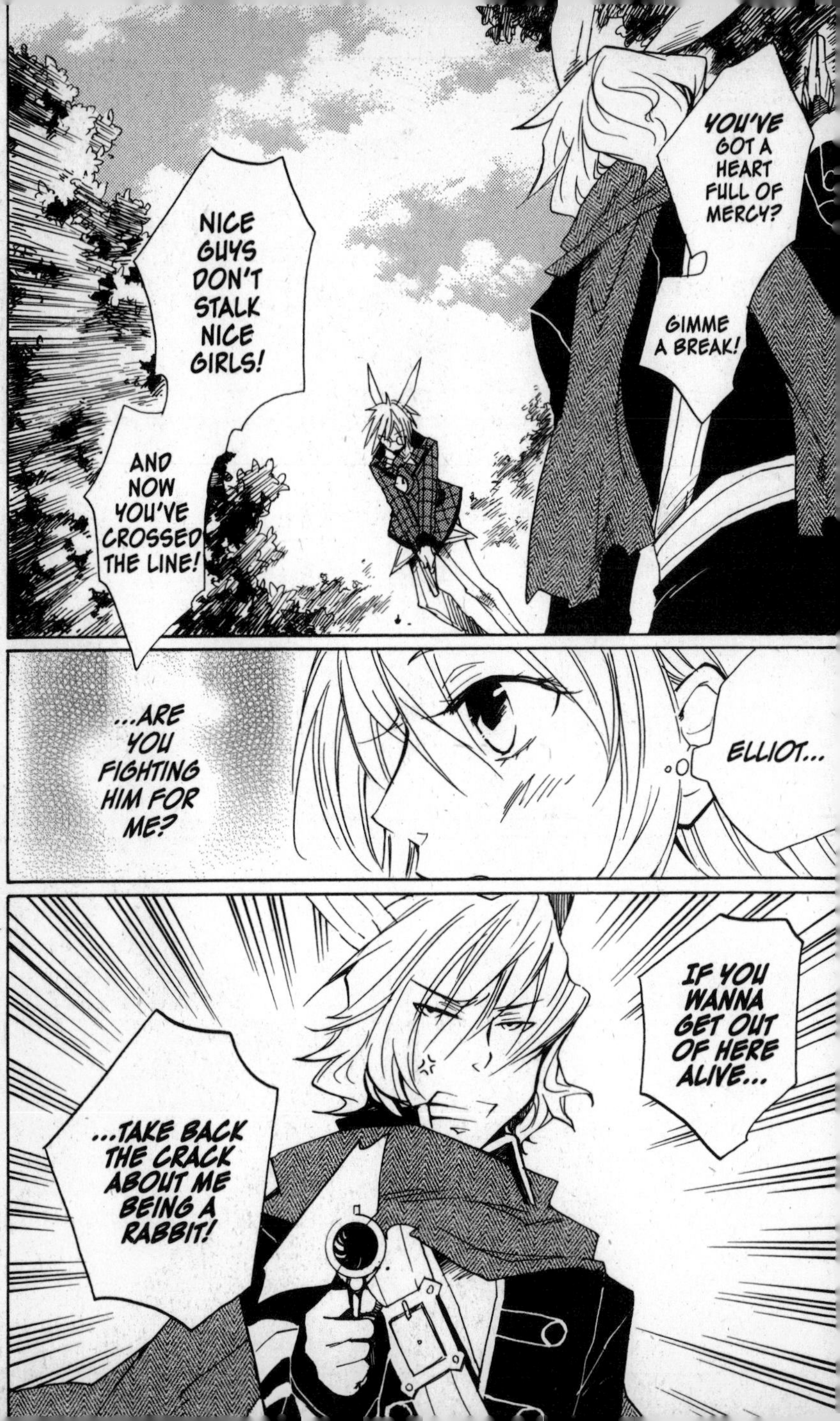
YOU'VE GOT A HEART FULL OF MERCY?
GIMME A BREAK!
NICE GUYS DON'T STALK NICE GIRLS!
AND NOW YOU'VE CROSSED THE LINE!
ELLIOT...
...ARE YOU FIGHTING HIM FOR ME?
IF YOU WANNA GET OUT OF HERE ALIVE...
...TAKE BACK THE CRACK ABOUT ME BEING A RABBIT!

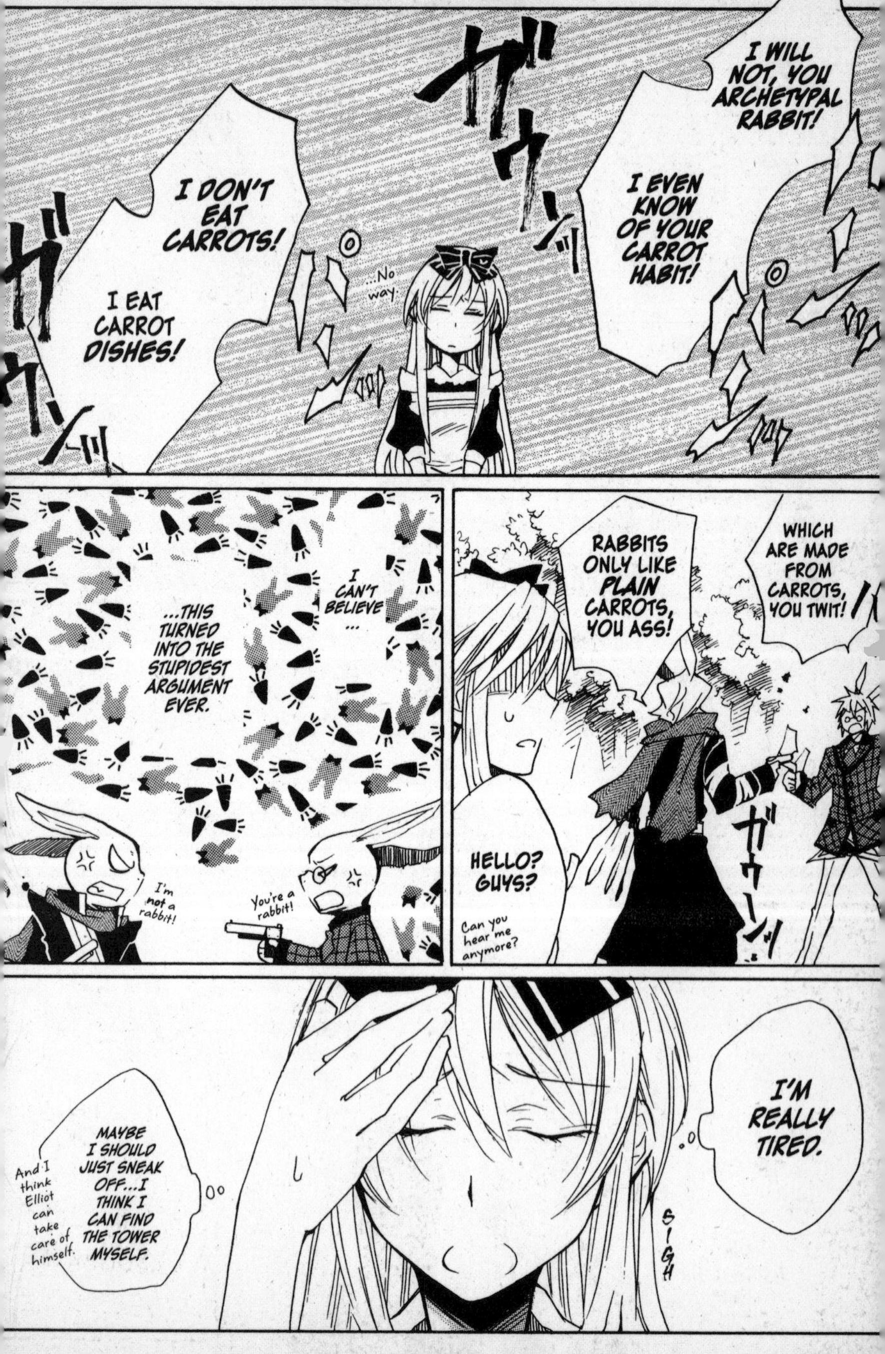
I WILL NOT, YOU ARCHETYPAL RABBIT!
I EVEN KNOW OF YOUR CARROT HABIT!
...No way.
I DON'T EAT CARROTS!
I EAT CARROT DISHES!
WHICH ARE MADE FROM CARROTS, YOU TWIT!
RABBITS ONLY LIKE PLAIN CARROTS, YOU ASS!
HELLO? GUYS?
Can you hear me anymore?
I CAN'T BELIEVE...
...THIS TURNED INTO THE STUPIDEST ARGUMENT EVER.
You're a rabbit!
I'm not a rabbit!
I'M REALLY TIRED.
SIGH
MAYBE I SHOULD JUST SNEAK OFF...I THINK I CAN FIND THE TOWER MYSELF.
And I think Elliot can take care of himself.

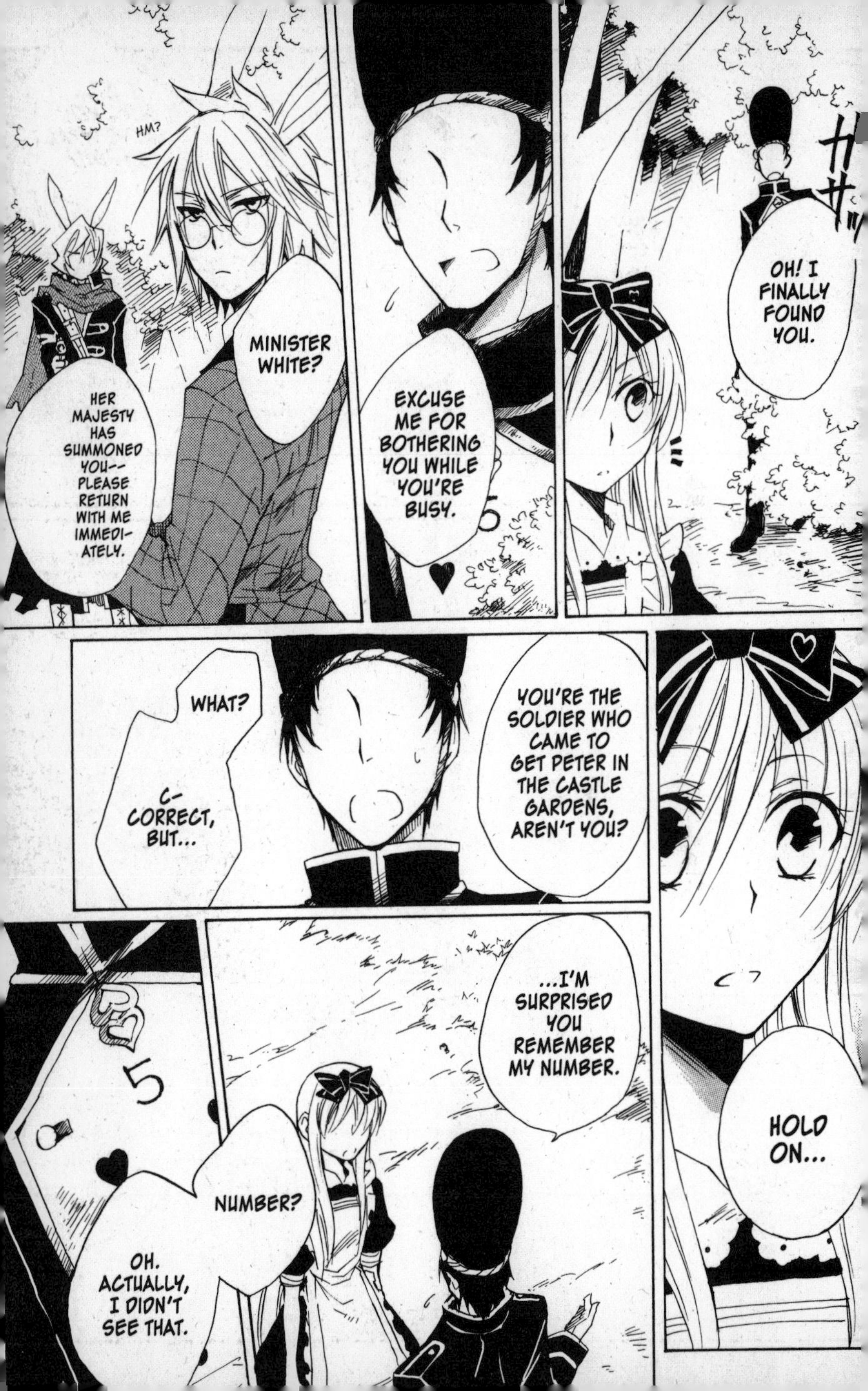
OH! I FINALLY FOUND YOU.
EXCUSE ME FOR BOTHERING YOU WHILE YOU'RE BUSY.
HM?
MINISTER WHITE?
HER MAJESTY HAS SUMMONED YOU--PLEASE RETURN WITH ME IMMEDIATELY.
HOLD ON...
YOU'RE THE SOLDIER WHO CAME TO GET PETER IN THE CASTLE GARDENS, AREN'T YOU?
WHAT?
C-CORRECT, BUT...
...I'M SURPRISED YOU REMEMBER MY NUMBER.
NUMBER?
OH. ACTUALLY, I DIDN'T SEE THAT.

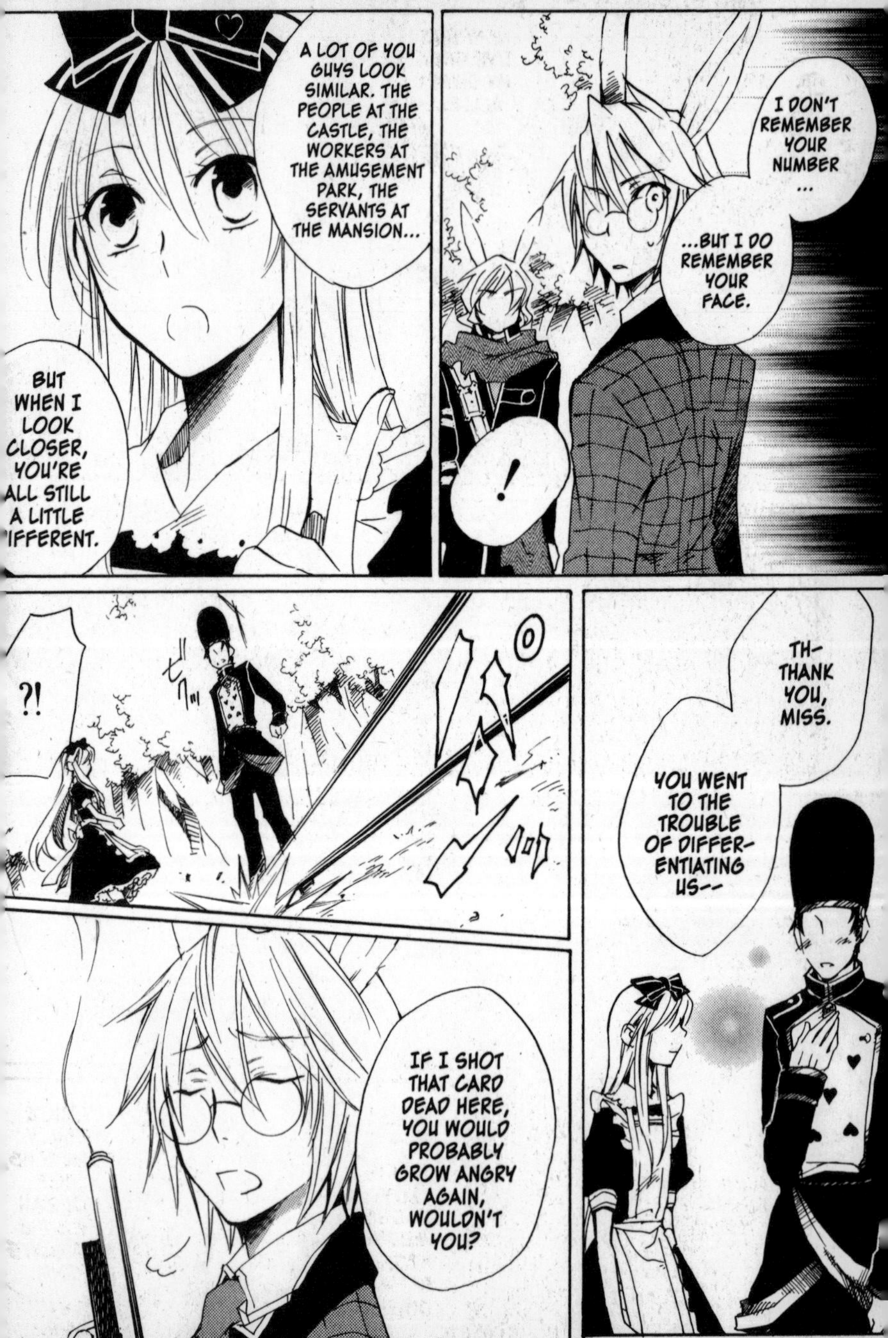
I DON'T REMEMBER YOUR NUMBER ...
...BUT I DO REMEMBER YOUR FACE.
!
A LOT OF YOU GUYS LOOK SIMILAR. THE PEOPLE AT THE CASTLE, THE WORKERS AT THE AMUSEMENT PARK, THE SERVANTS AT THE MANSION...
BUT WHEN I LOOK CLOSER, YOU'RE ALL STILL A LITTLE IFFERENT.
TH-THANK YOU, MISS.
YOU WENT TO THE TROUBLE OF DIFFER-ENTIATING US--
?!
IF I SHOT THAT CARD DEAD HERE, YOU WOULD PROBABLY GROW ANGRY AGAIN, WOULDN'T YOU?

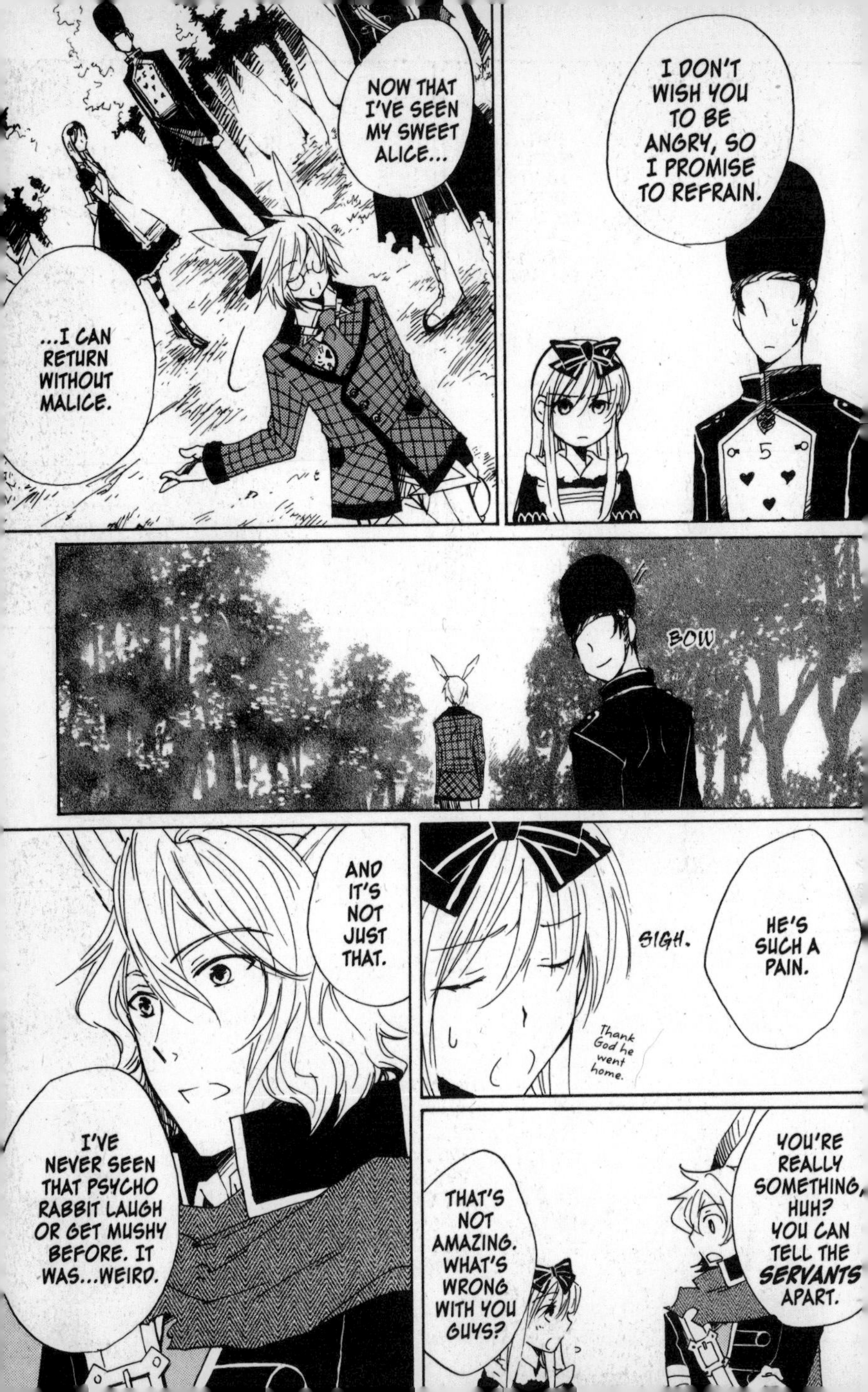
I DON'T WISH YOU TO BE ANGRY, SO I PROMISE TO REFRAIN.
NOW THAT I'VE SEEN MY SWEET ALICE...
...I CAN RETURN WITHOUT MALICE.
BOW
HE'S SUCH A PAIN.
SIGH.
Thank God he went home.
YOU'RE REALLY SOMETHING, HUH? YOU CAN TELL THE SERVANTS APART.
THAT'S NOT AMAZING. WHAT'S WRONG WITH YOU GUYS?
AND IT'S NOT JUST THAT.
I'VE NEVER SEEN THAT PSYCHO RABBIT LAUGH OR GET MUSHY BEFORE. IT WAS...WEIRD.

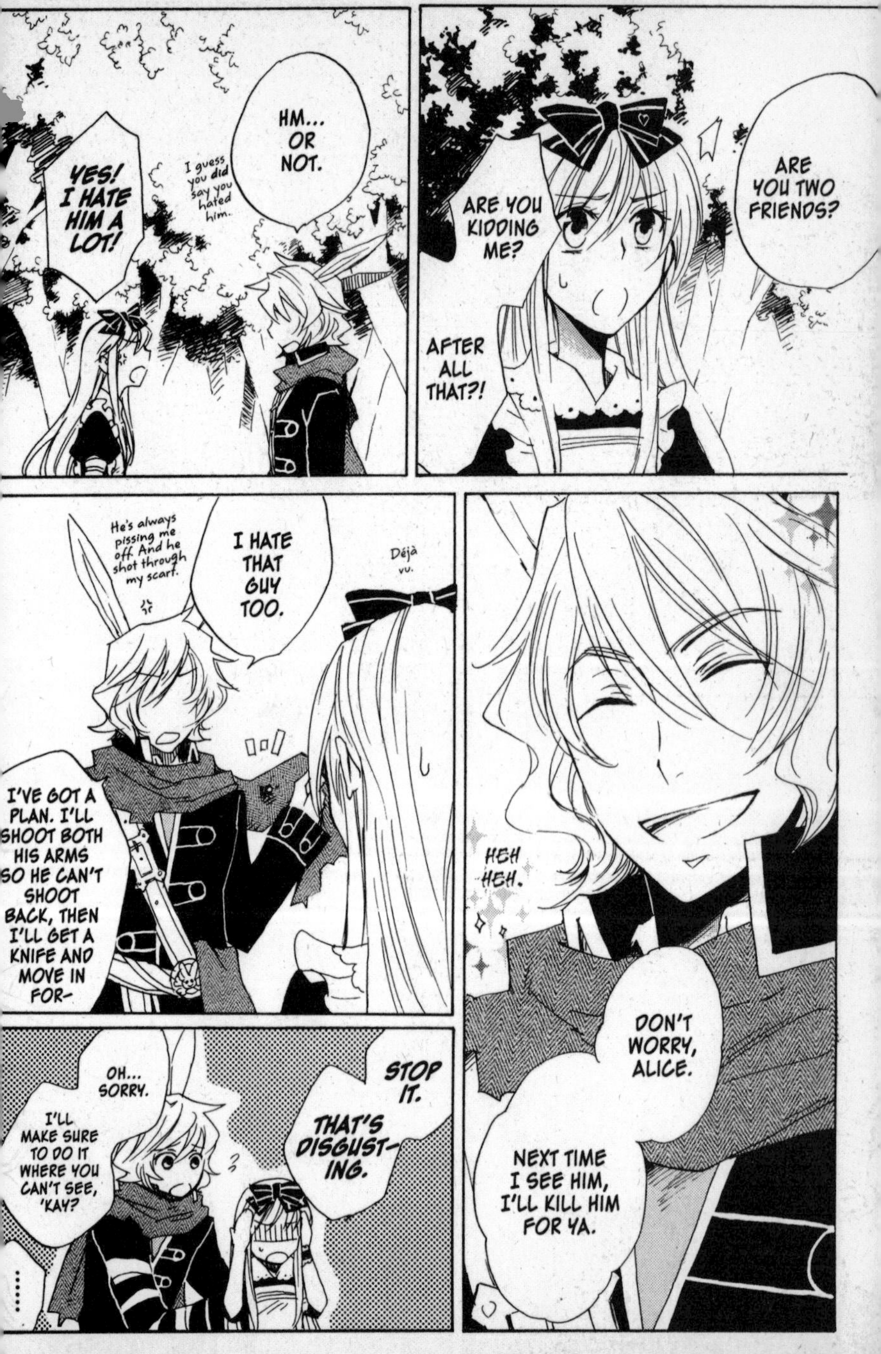
ARE YOU TWO FRIENDS?
ARE YOU KIDDING ME?
AFTER ALL THAT?!
HM... OR NOT.
I guess you did say you hated him.
YES! I HATE HIM A LOT!
HEH HEH.
DON'T WORRY, ALICE.
NEXT TIME I SEE HIM, I'LL KILL HIM FOR YA.
Déjà vu.
I HATE THAT GUY TOO.
He's always pissing me off. And he shot through my scarf.
I'VE GOT A PLAN. I'LL SHOOT BOTH HIS ARMS SO HE CAN'T SHOOT BACK, THEN I'LL GET A KNIFE AND MOVE IN FOR-
STOP IT.
THAT'S DISGUSTING.
OH... SORRY.
I'LL MAKE SURE TO DO IT WHERE YOU CAN'T SEE, 'KAY?
......

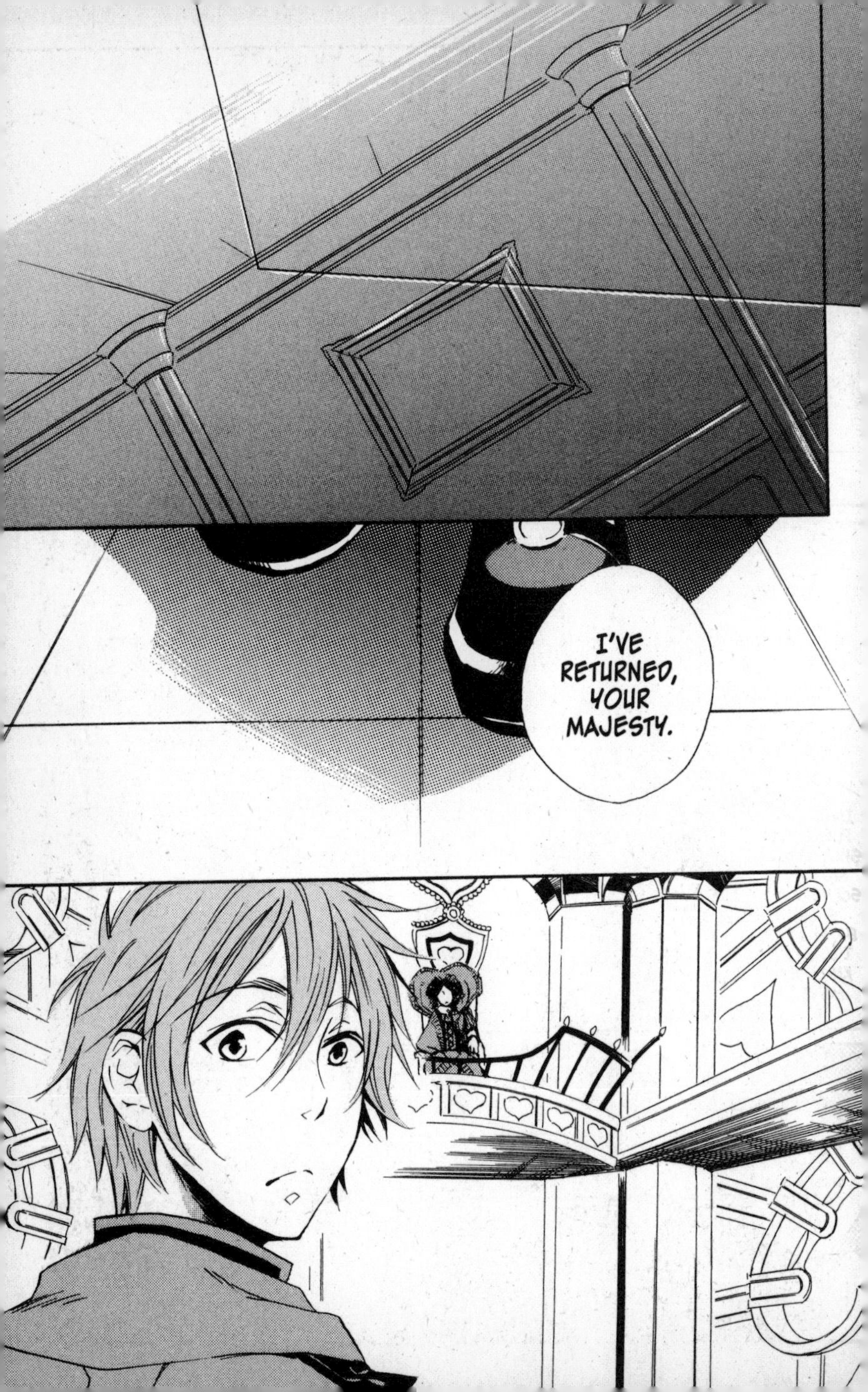
I'VE RETURNED, YOUR MAJESTY.

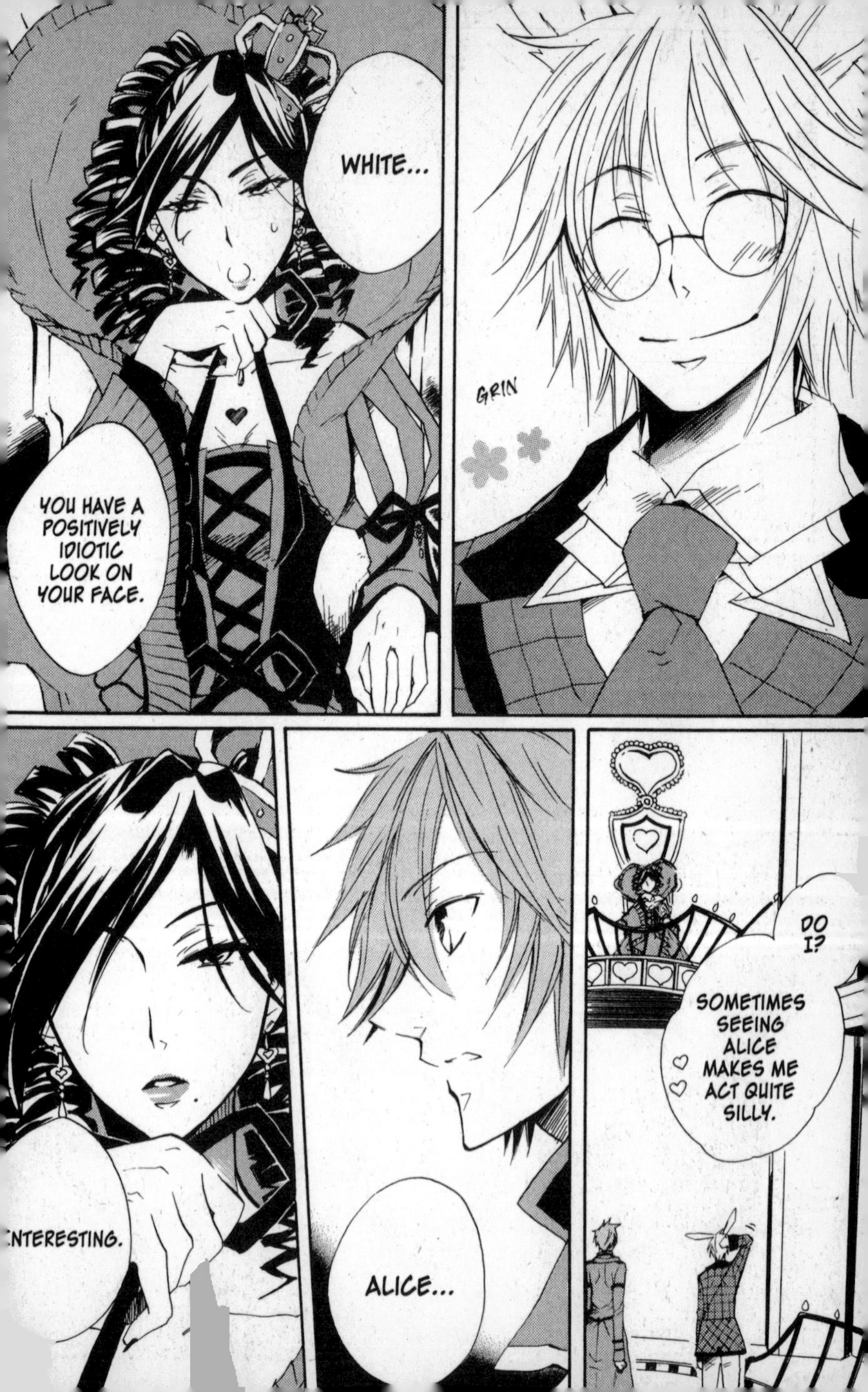
GRIN
WHITE...
YOU HAVE A POSITIVELY IDIOTIC LOOK ON YOUR FACE.
DO I?
SOMETIMES SEEING ALICE MAKES ME ACT QUITE SILLY.
ALICE...
NTERESTING.

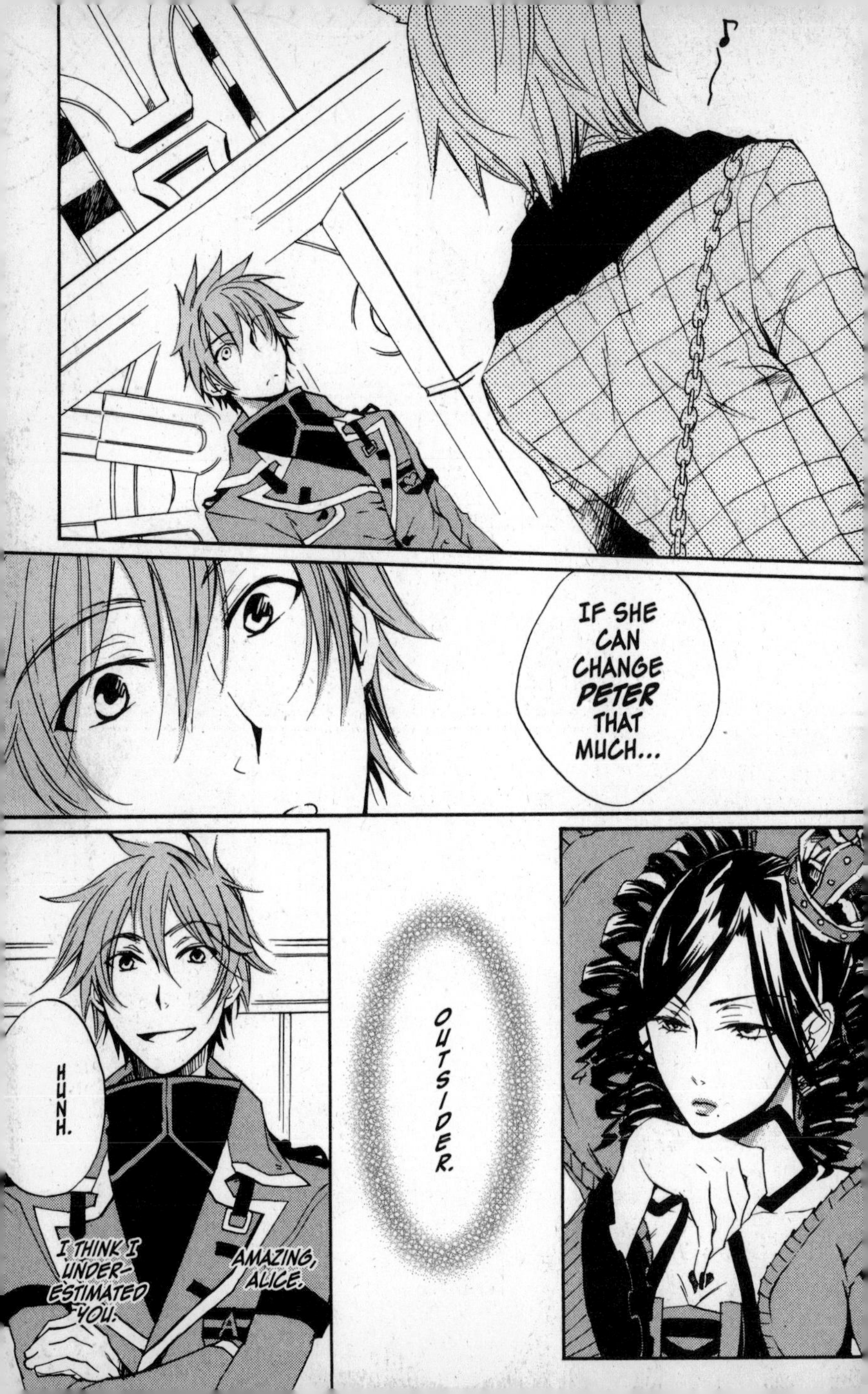
IF SHE CAN CHANGE PETER THAT MUCH...
OUTSIDER.
HUNH.
AMAZING, ALICE.
I THINK I UNDER-ESTIMATED YOU.

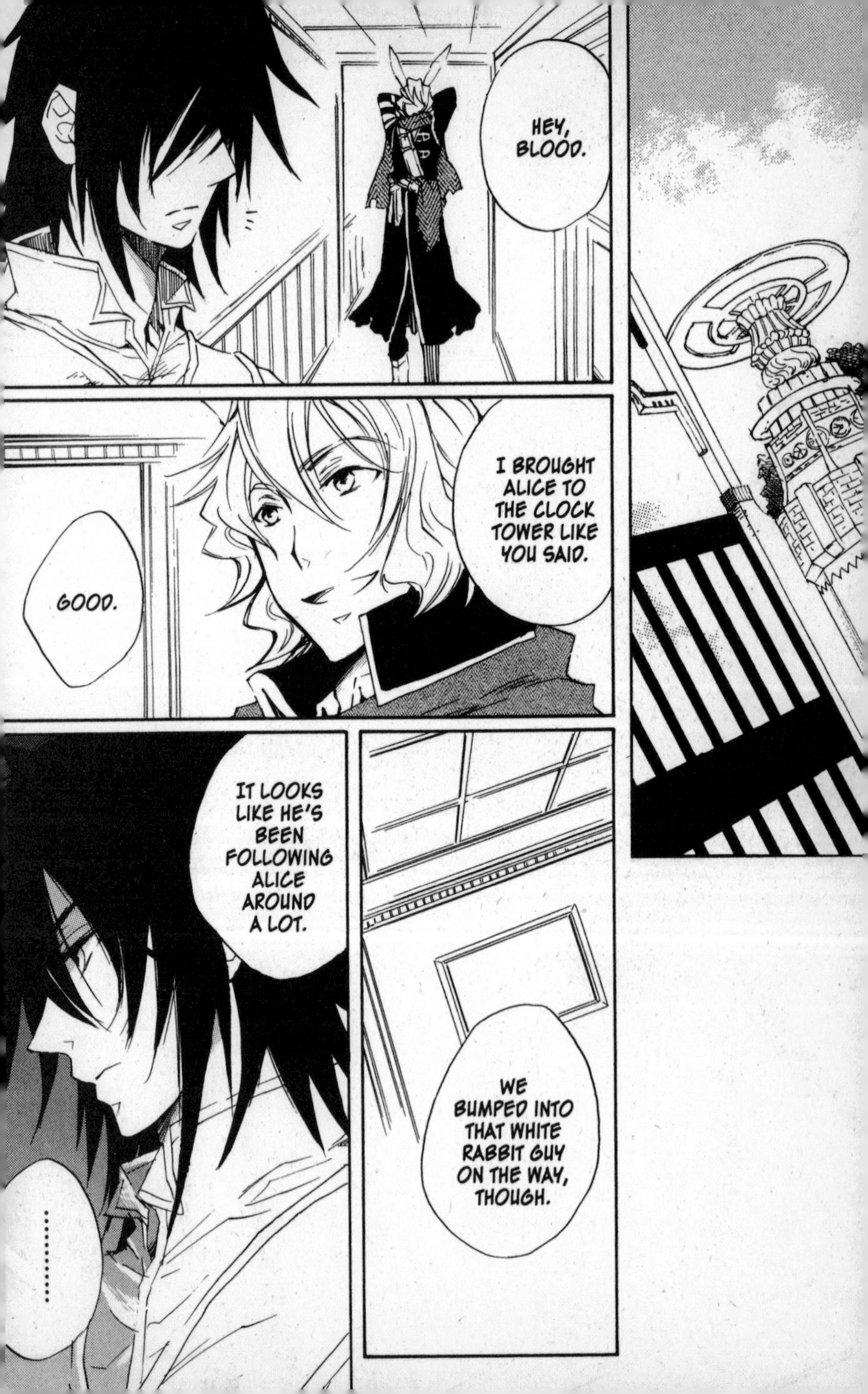
HEY, BLOOD.
I BROUGHT ALICE TO THE CLOCK TOWER LIKE YOU SAID.
GOOD.
WE BUMPED INTO THAT WHITE RABBIT GUY ON THE WAY, THOUGH.
IT LOOKS LIKE HE'S BEEN FOLLOWING ALICE AROUND A LOT.
......

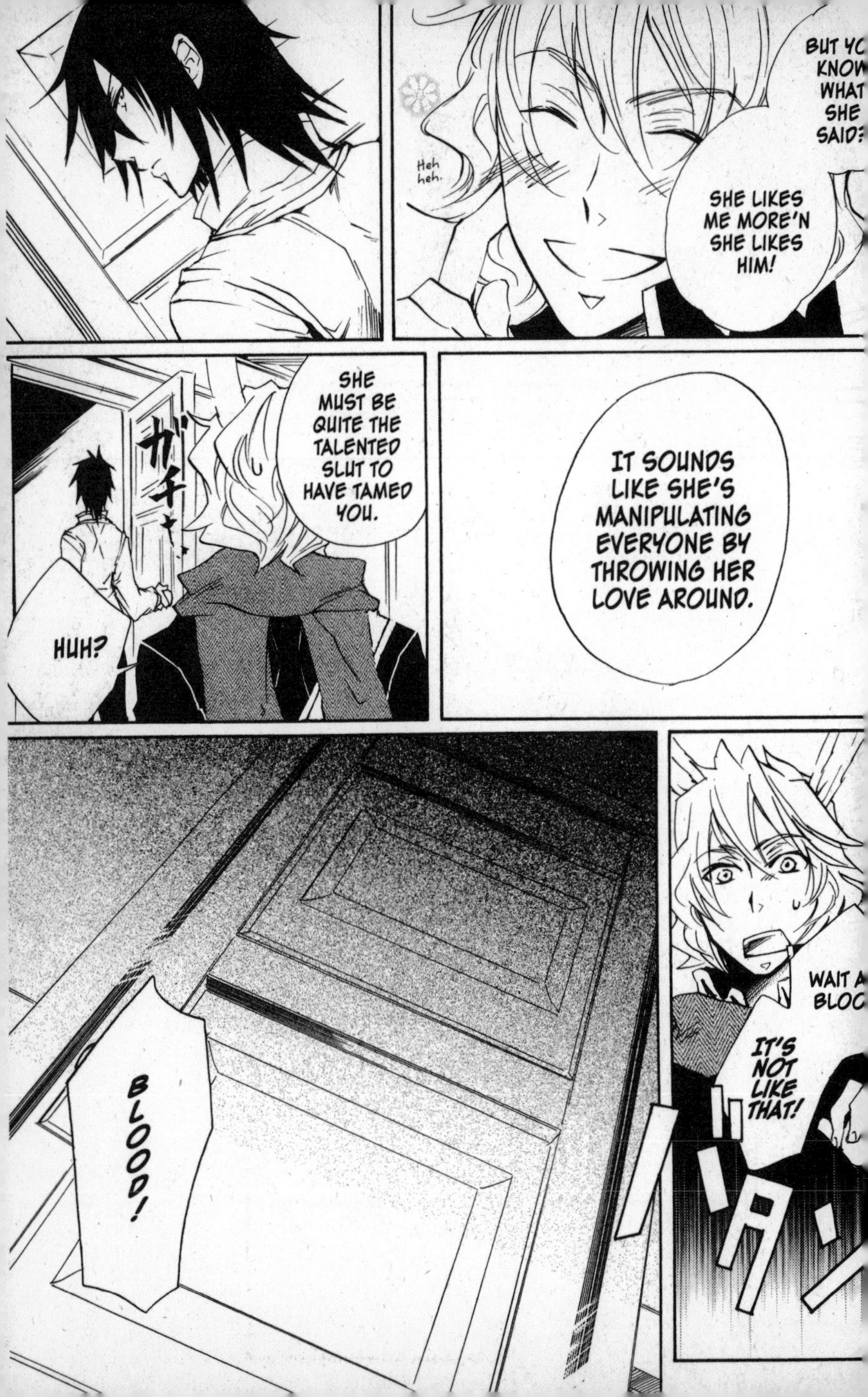
BUT Y
KNOW
WHAT
SHE
SAID?
Heh heh.
SHE LIKES ME MORE'N SHE LIKES HIM!
IT SOUNDS LIKE SHE'S MANIPULATING EVERYONE BY THROWING HER LOVE AROUND.
SHE MUST BE QUITE THE TALENTED SLUT TO HAVE TAMED YOU.
ガチャ
HUH?
WAIT A
BLO
IT'S NOT LIKE THAT!
バタン
BLOOD!

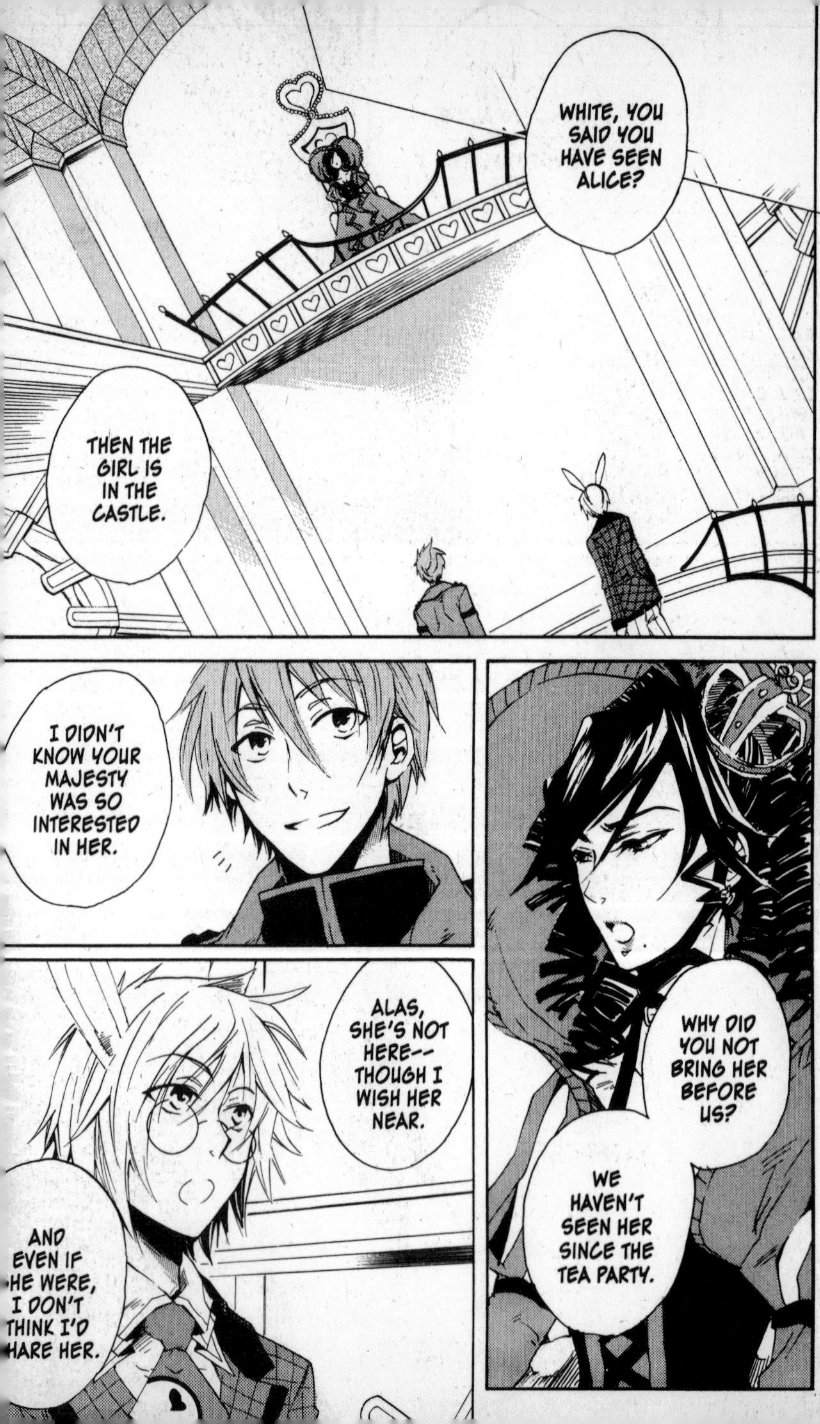
WHITE, YOU SAID YOU HAVE SEEN ALICE?
THEN THE GIRL IS IN THE CASTLE.
WHY DID YOU NOT BRING HER BEFORE US?
WE HAVEN'T SEEN HER SINCE THE TEA PARTY.
I DIDN'T KNOW YOUR MAJESTY WAS SO INTERESTED IN HER.
ALAS, SHE'S NOT HERE--THOUGH I WISH HER NEAR.
AND EVEN IF HE WERE, I DON'T THINK I'D HARE HER.

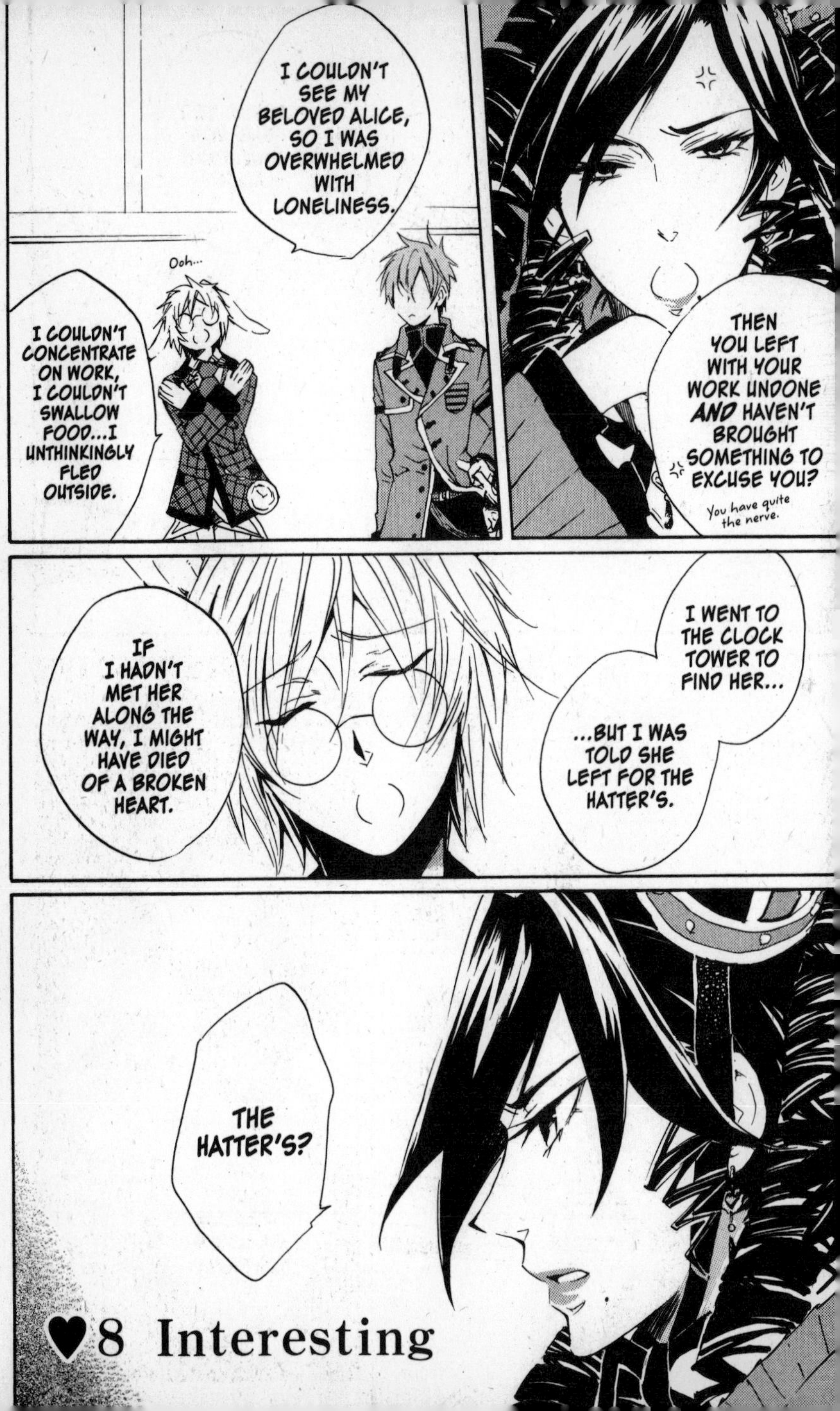
THEN YOU LEFT WITH YOUR WORK UNDONE AND HAVEN'T BROUGHT SOMETHING TO EXCUSE YOU?
You have quite the nerve.
I COULDN'T SEE MY BELOVED ALICE, SO I WAS OVERWHELMED WITH LONELINESS.
Ooh...
I COULDN'T CONCENTRATE ON WORK, I COULDN'T SWALLOW FOOD...I UNTHINKINGLY FLED OUTSIDE.
I WENT TO THE CLOCK TOWER TO FIND HER...
...BUT I WAS TOLD SHE LEFT FOR THE HATTER'S.
IF I HADN'T MET HER ALONG THE WAY, I MIGHT HAVE DIED OF A BROKEN HEART.
THE HATTER'S?
♥8 Interesting

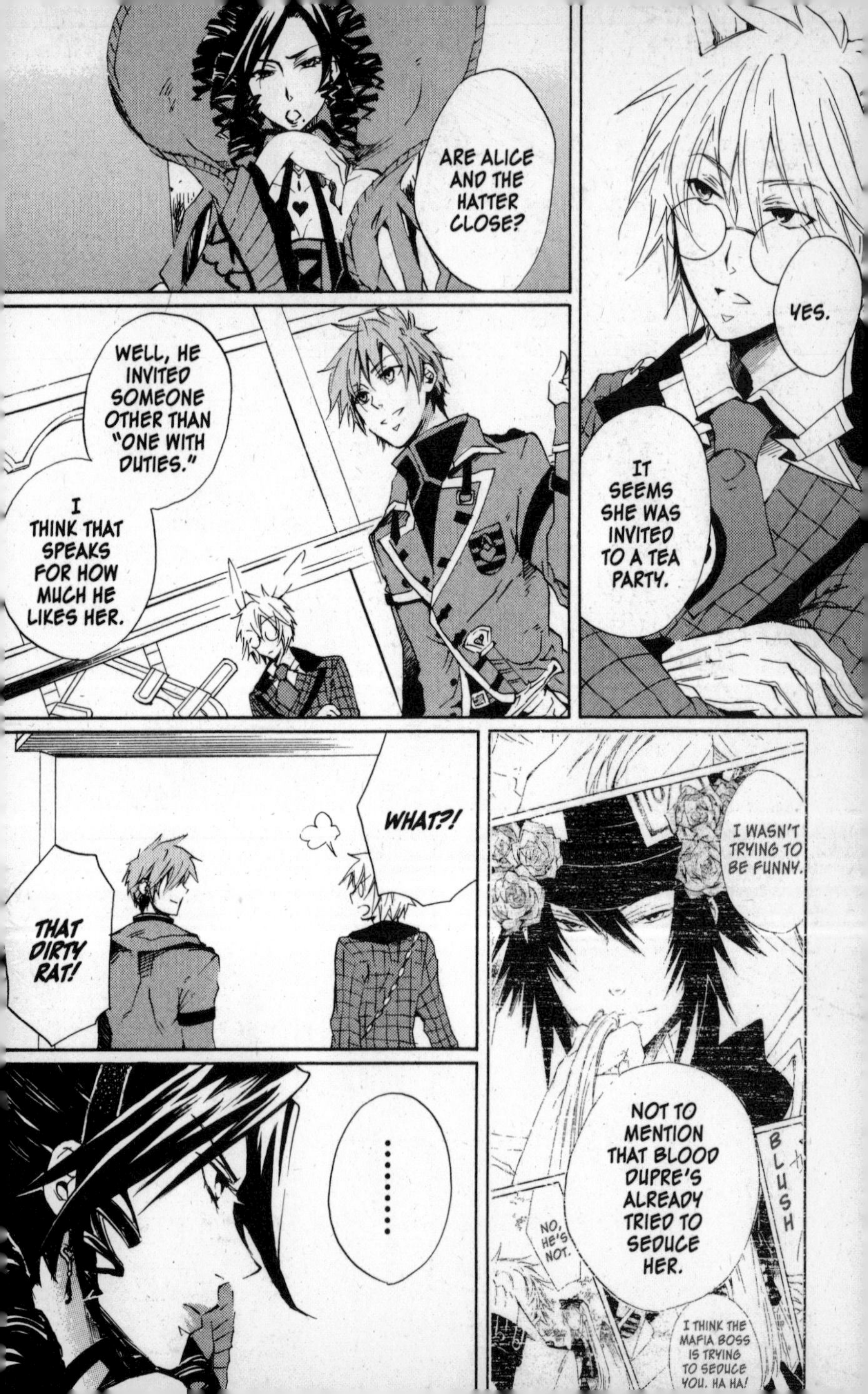
ARE ALICE AND THE HATTER CLOSE?
YES.
IT SEEMS SHE WAS INVITED TO A TEA PARTY.
WELL, HE INVITED SOMEONE OTHER THAN "ONE WITH DUTIES."
I THINK THAT SPEAKS FOR HOW MUCH HE LIKES HER.
NOT TO MENTION THAT BLOOD DUPRE'S ALREADY TRIED TO SEDUCE HER.
I THINK THE MAFIA BOSS IS TRYING TO SEDUCE YOU. HA HA!
NO, HE'S NOT.
I WASN'T TRYING TO BE FUNNY.
BLUSH
WHAT?!
THAT DIRTY RAT!
........

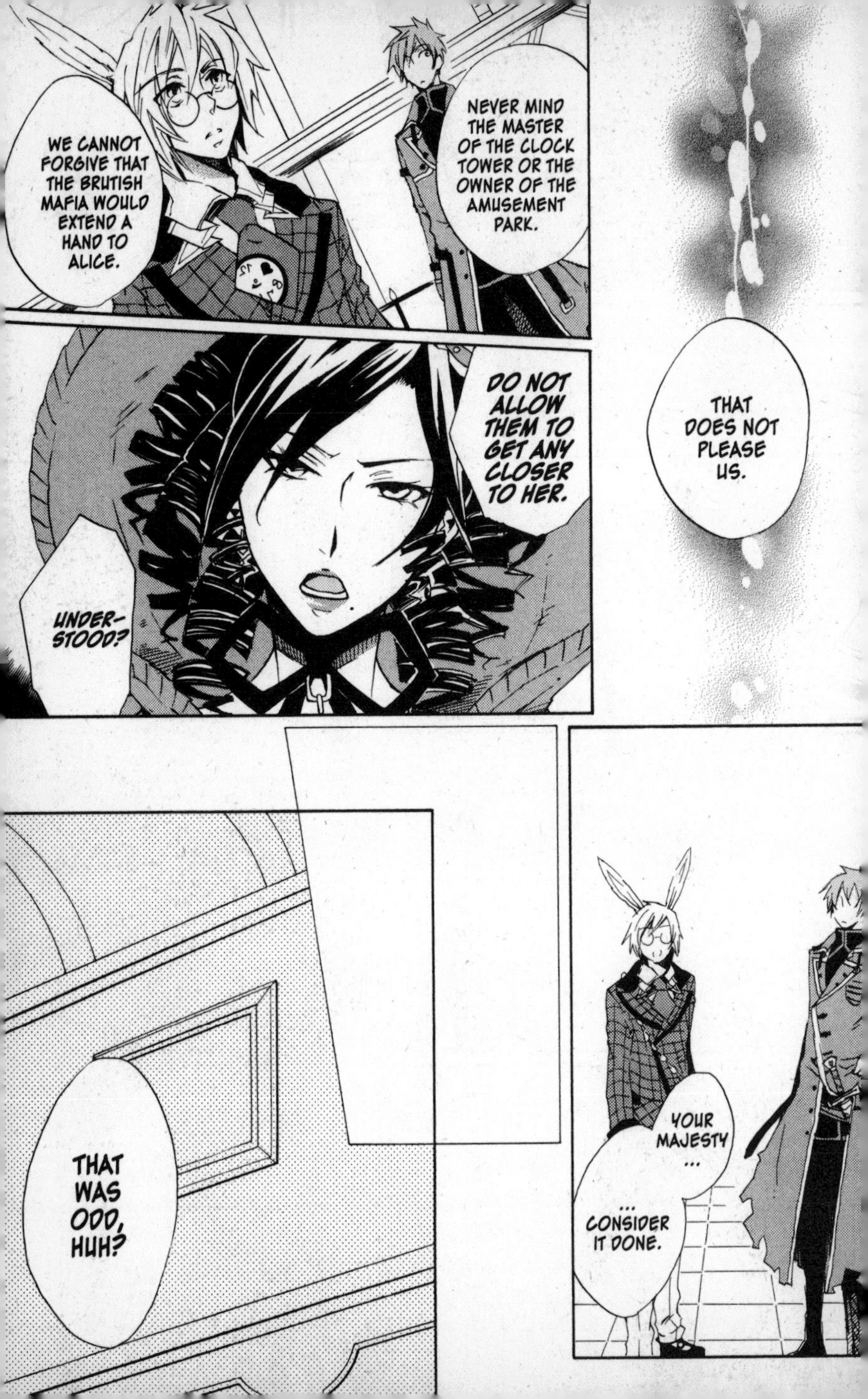
THAT DOES NOT PLEASE US.
NEVER MIND THE MASTER OF THE CLOCK TOWER OR THE OWNER OF THE AMUSEMENT PARK.
WE CANNOT FORGIVE THAT THE BRUTISH MAFIA WOULD EXTEND A HAND TO ALICE.
DO NOT ALLOW THEM TO GET ANY CLOSER TO HER.
UNDER-STOOD?
YOUR MAJESTY ...
... CONSIDER IT DONE.
THAT WAS ODD, HUH?

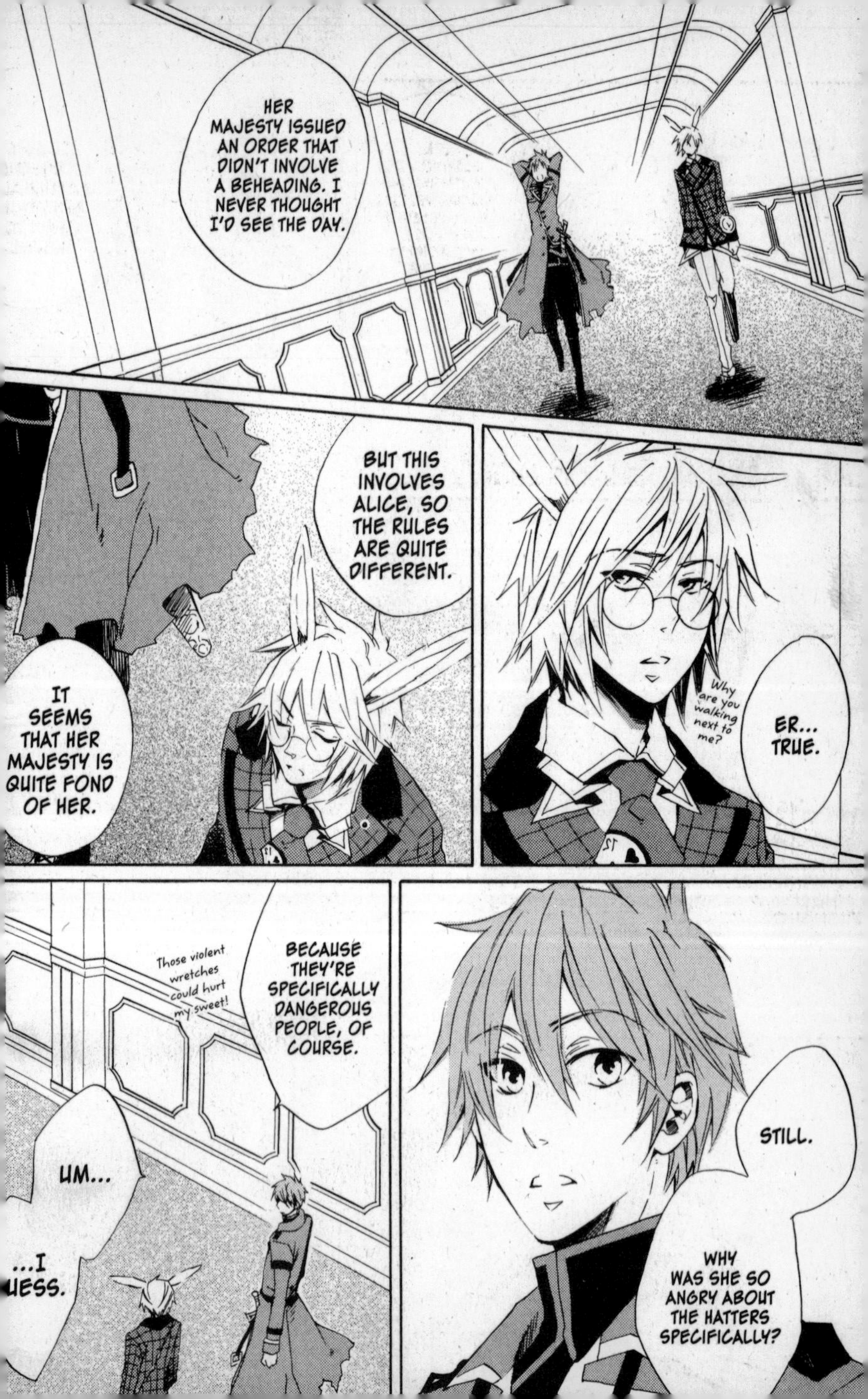
HER MAJESTY ISSUED AN ORDER THAT DIDN'T INVOLVE A BEHEADING. I NEVER THOUGHT I'D SEE THE DAY.
ER... TRUE.
Why are you walking next to me?
BUT THIS INVOLVES ALICE, SO THE RULES ARE QUITE DIFFERENT.
IT SEEMS THAT HER MAJESTY IS QUITE FOND OF HER.
STILL.
WHY WAS SHE SO ANGRY ABOUT THE HATTERS SPECIFICALLY?
BECAUSE THEY'RE SPECIFICALLY DANGEROUS PEOPLE, OF COURSE.
Those violent wretches could hurt my sweet!
UM...
...I UESS.

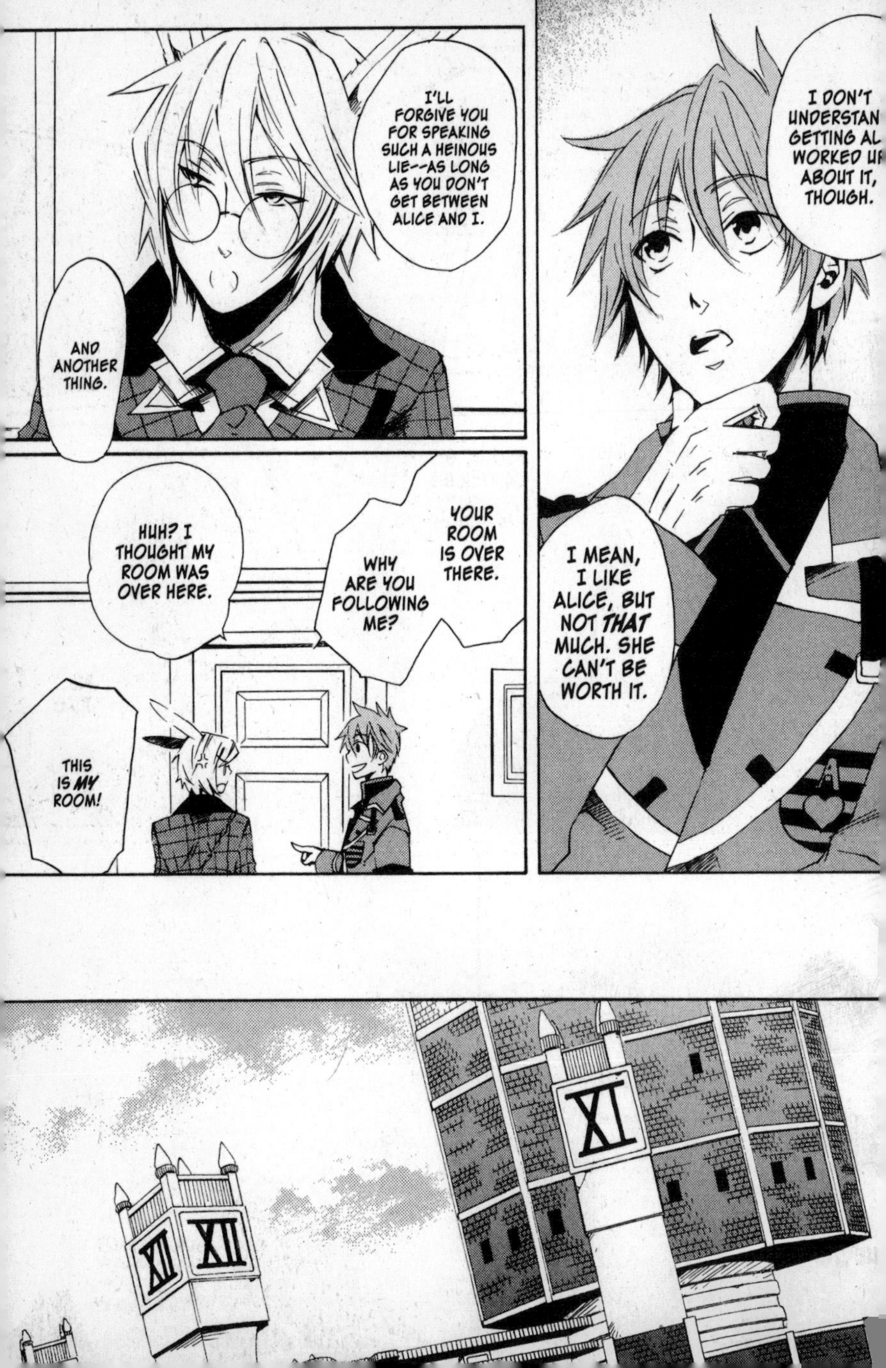
I DON'T UNDERSTAN GETTING AL WORKED UP ABOUT IT, THOUGH.
I MEAN, I LIKE ALICE, BUT NOT *THAT* MUCH. SHE CAN'T BE WORTH IT.
I'LL FORGIVE YOU FOR SPEAKING SUCH A HEINOUS LIE--AS LONG AS YOU DON'T GET BETWEEN ALICE AND I.
AND ANOTHER THING.
YOUR ROOM IS OVER THERE.
WHY ARE YOU FOLLOWING ME?
HUH? I THOUGHT MY ROOM WAS OVER HERE.
THIS IS *MY* ROOM!

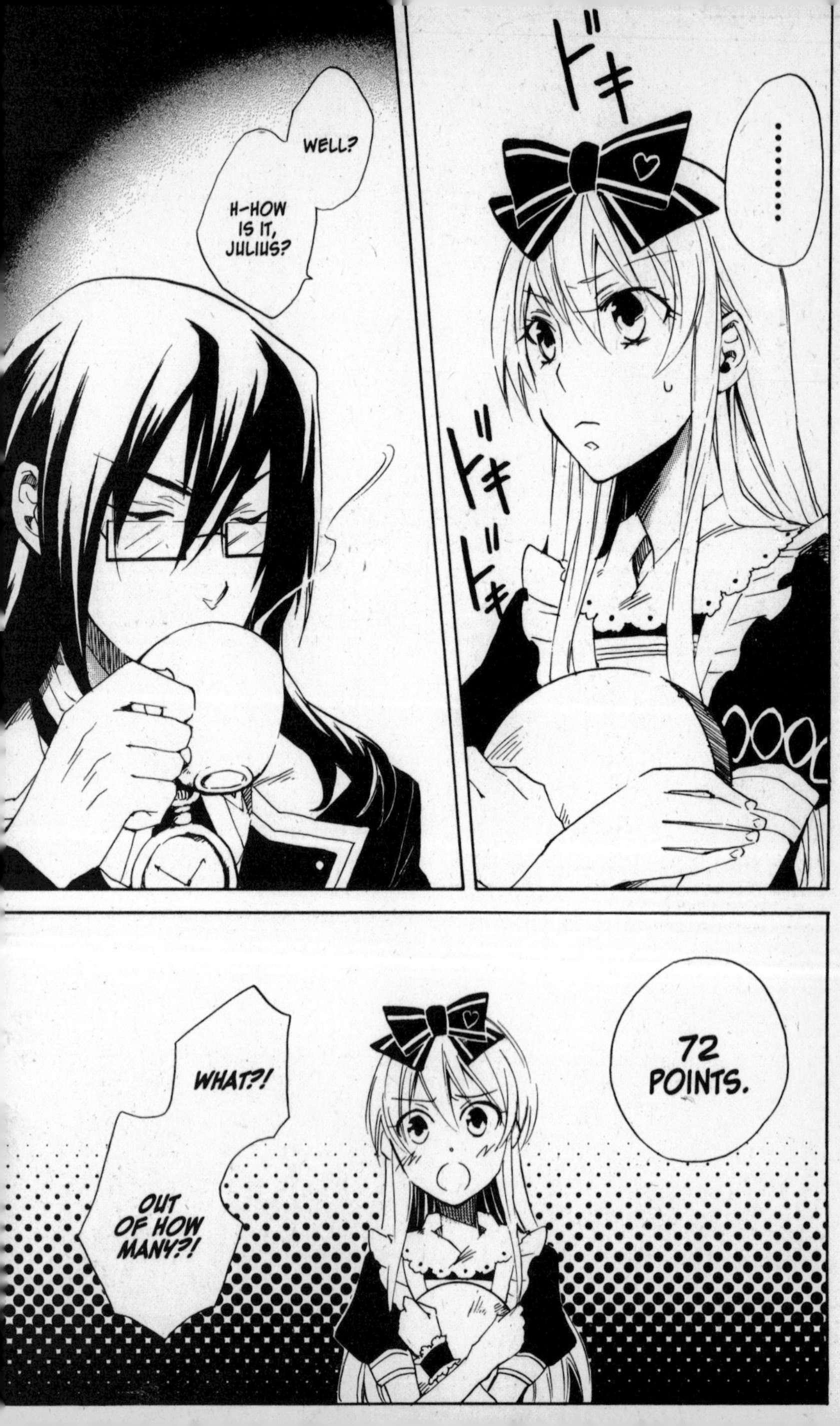
ドキ
......
ドキドキ
WELL?
H-HOW IS IT, JULIUS?
72 POINTS.
WHAT?!
OUT OF HOW MANY?!

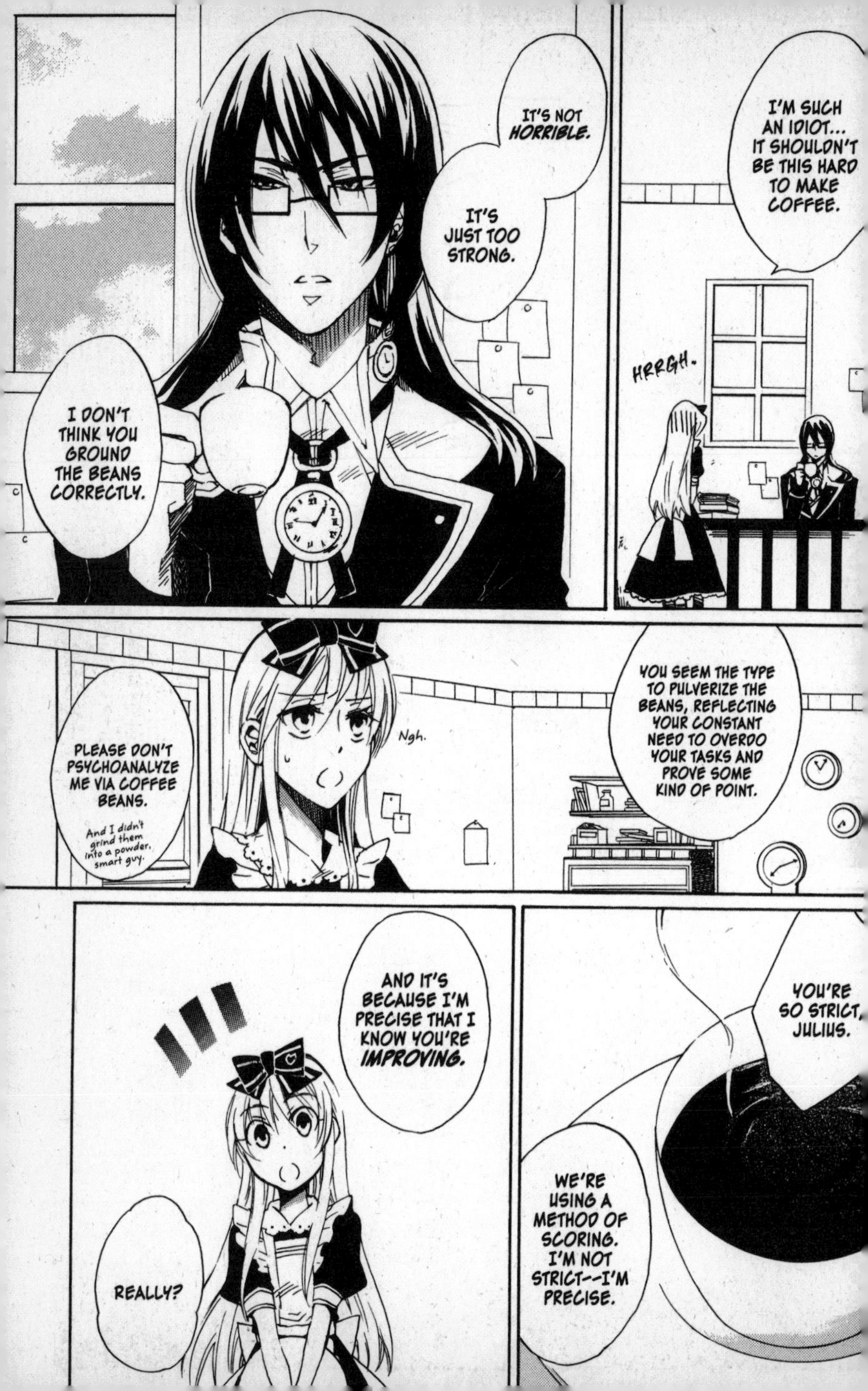
I'M SUCH AN IDIOT... IT SHOULDN'T BE THIS HARD TO MAKE COFFEE.
HRRGH.
IT'S NOT *HORRIBLE.*
IT'S JUST TOO STRONG.
I DON'T THINK YOU GROUND THE BEANS CORRECTLY.
YOU SEEM THE TYPE TO PULVERIZE THE BEANS, REFLECTING YOUR CONSTANT NEED TO OVERDO YOUR TASKS AND PROVE SOME KIND OF POINT.
Ngh.
PLEASE DON'T PSYCHOANALYZE ME VIA COFFEE BEANS.
And I didn't grind them into a powder, smart guy.
YOU'RE SO STRICT, JULIUS.
WE'RE USING A METHOD OF SCORING. I'M NOT STRICT--I'M PRECISE.
AND IT'S BECAUSE I'M PRECISE THAT I KNOW YOU'RE *IMPROVING.*
REALLY?

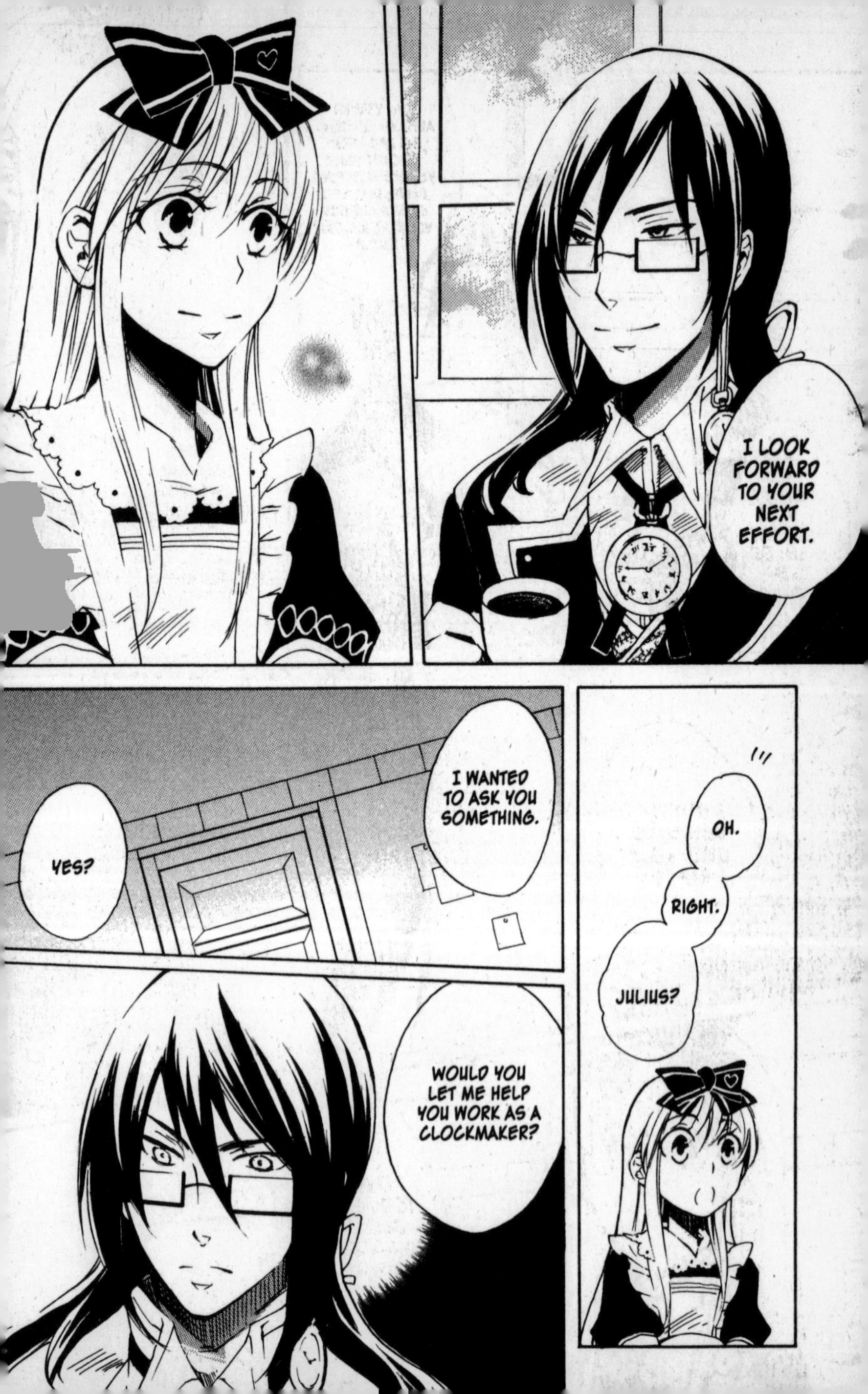
I LOOK FORWARD TO YOUR NEXT EFFORT.
OH.
RIGHT.
JULIUS?
I WANTED TO ASK YOU SOMETHING.
YES?
WOULD YOU LET ME HELP YOU WORK AS A CLOCKMAKER?

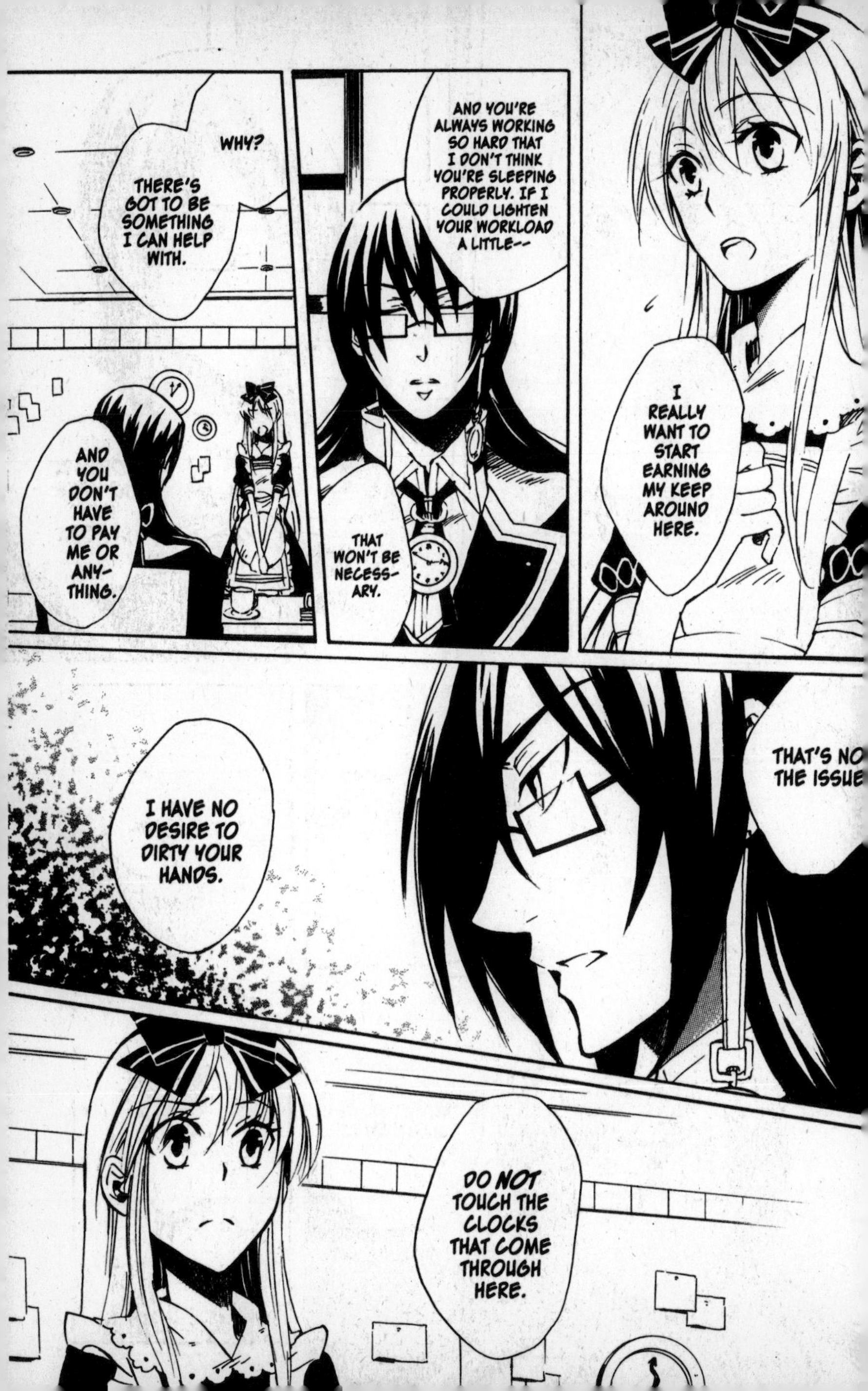
I REALLY WANT TO START EARNING MY KEEP AROUND HERE.
AND YOU'RE ALWAYS WORKING SO HARD THAT I DON'T THINK YOU'RE SLEEPING PROPERLY. IF I COULD LIGHTEN YOUR WORKLOAD A LITTLE--
THAT WON'T BE NECESSARY.
WHY?
THERE'S GOT TO BE SOMETHING I CAN HELP WITH.
AND YOU DON'T HAVE TO PAY ME OR ANYTHING.
THAT'S NO THE ISSUE
I HAVE NO DESIRE TO DIRTY YOUR HANDS.
DO *NOT* TOUCH THE CLOCKS THAT COME THROUGH HERE.

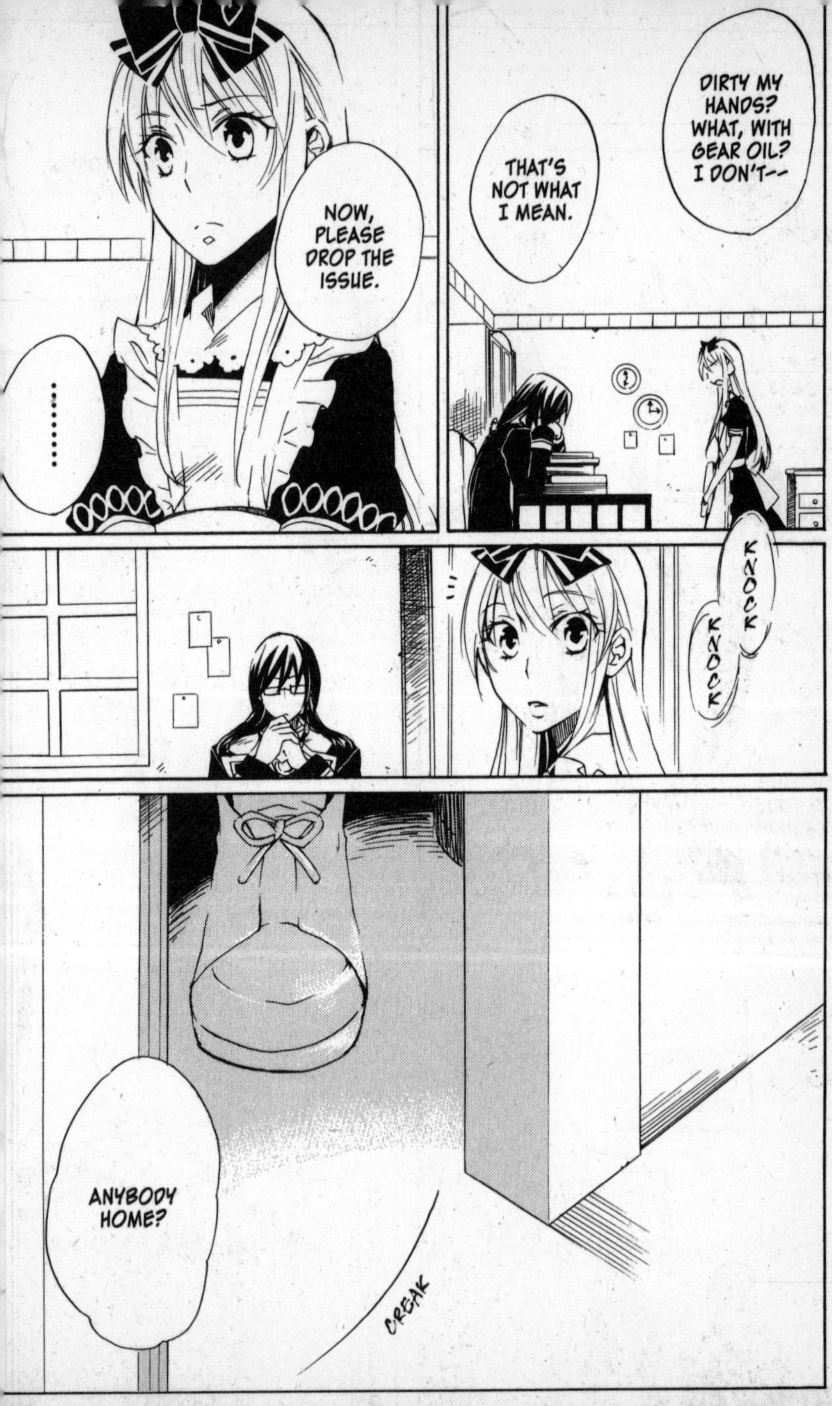
DIRTY MY HANDS? WHAT, WITH GEAR OIL? I DON'T--
THAT'S NOT WHAT I MEAN.
NOW, PLEASE DROP THE ISSUE.
........
KNOCK
KNOCK
CREAK
ANYBODY HOME?

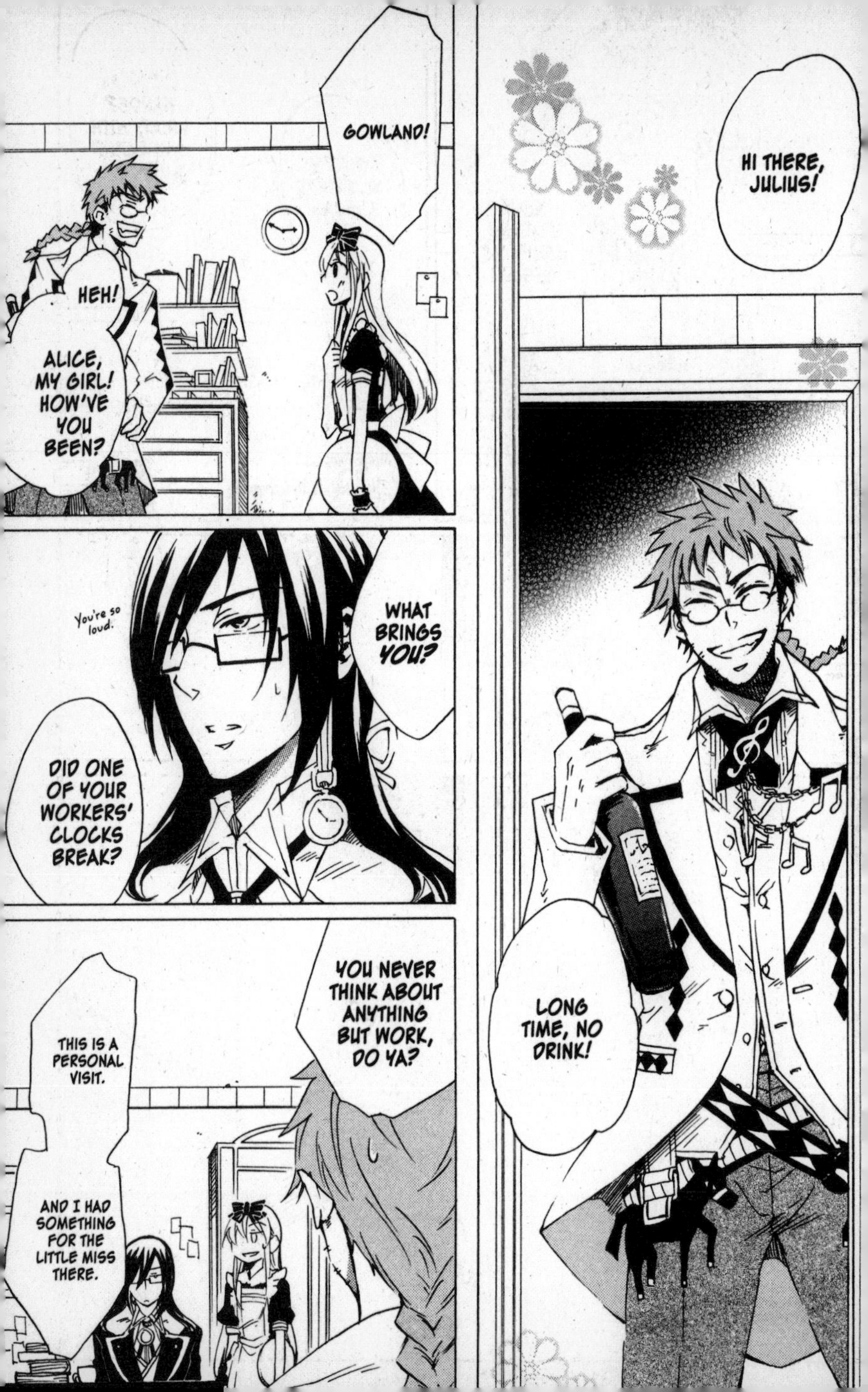
HI THERE, JULIUS!
LONG TIME, NO DRINK!
GOWLAND!
HEH!
ALICE, MY GIRL! HOW'VE YOU BEEN?
WHAT BRINGS YOU?
You're so loud.
DID ONE OF YOUR WORKERS' CLOCKS BREAK?
YOU NEVER THINK ABOUT ANYTHING BUT WORK, DO YA?
THIS IS A PERSONAL VISIT.
AND I HAD SOMETHING FOR THE LITTLE MISS THERE.

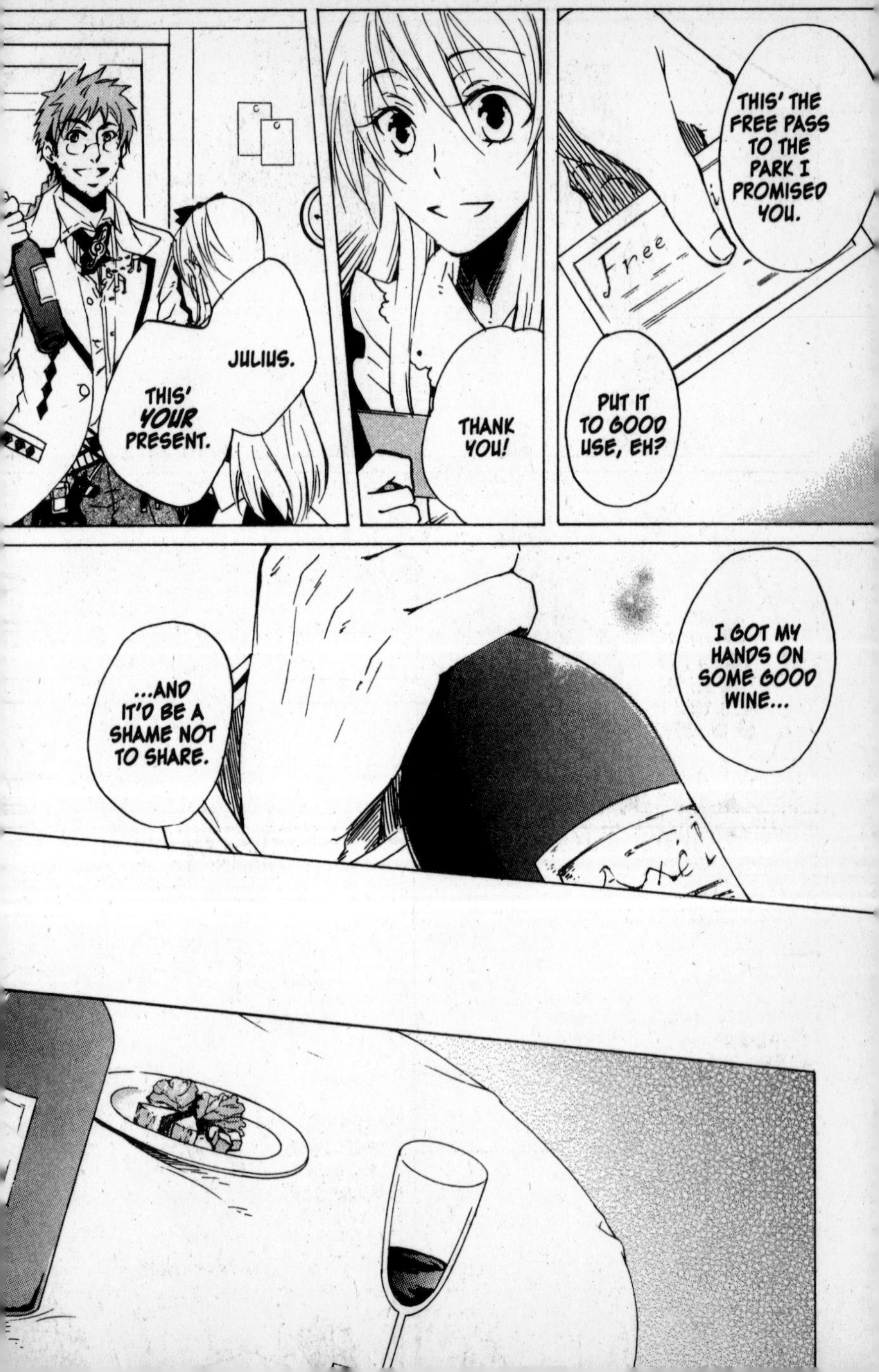
THIS' THE FREE PASS TO THE PARK I PROMISED YOU.
Free
PUT IT TO GOOD USE, EH?
THANK YOU!
JULIUS.
THIS' *YOUR* PRESENT.
I GOT MY HANDS ON SOME GOOD WINE...
...AND IT'D BE A SHAME NOT TO SHARE.

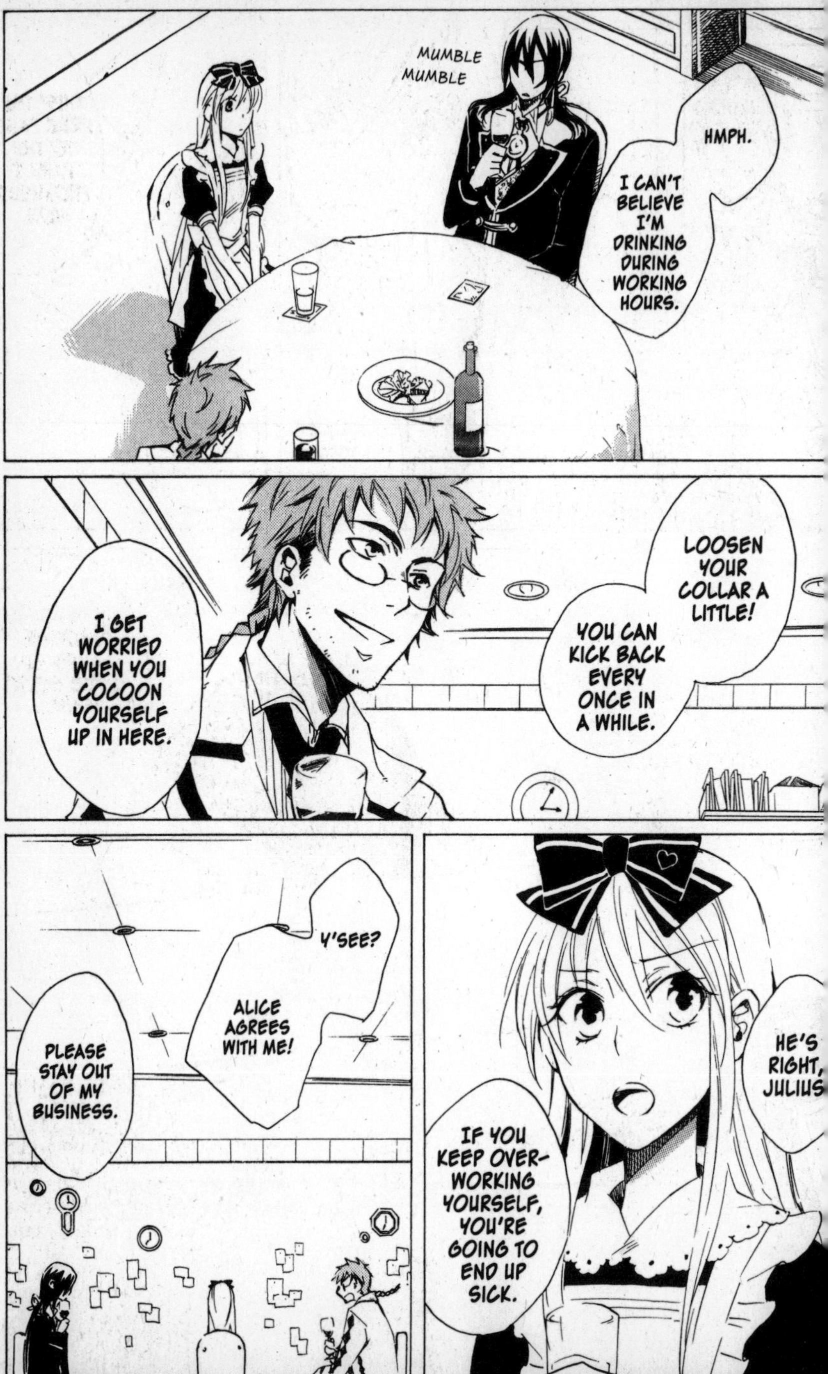
HMPH.
I CAN'T BELIEVE I'M DRINKING DURING WORKING HOURS.
MUMBLE MUMBLE
LOOSEN YOUR COLLAR A LITTLE!
YOU CAN KICK BACK EVERY ONCE IN A WHILE.
I GET WORRIED WHEN YOU COCOON YOURSELF UP IN HERE.
HE'S RIGHT, JULIUS
IF YOU KEEP OVER-WORKING YOURSELF, YOU'RE GOING TO END UP SICK.
Y'SEE?
ALICE AGREES WITH ME!
PLEASE STAY OUT OF MY BUSINESS.

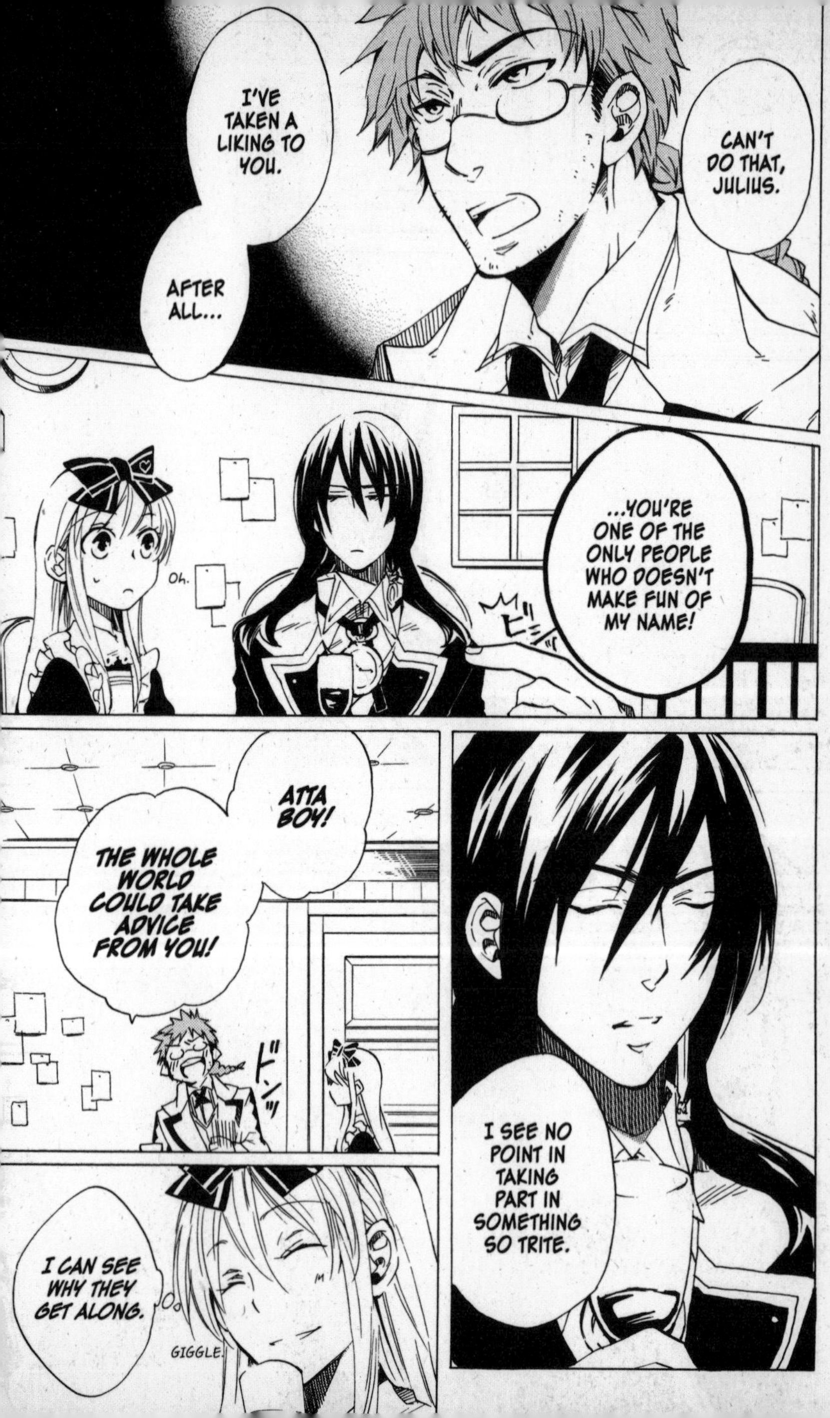
CAN'T DO THAT, JULIUS.
I'VE TAKEN A LIKING TO YOU.
AFTER ALL...
...YOU'RE ONE OF THE ONLY PEOPLE WHO DOESN'T MAKE FUN OF MY NAME!
Oh.
I SEE NO POINT IN TAKING PART IN SOMETHING SO TRITE.
ATTA BOY!
THE WHOLE WORLD COULD TAKE ADVICE FROM YOU!
I CAN SEE WHY THEY GET ALONG.
GIGGLE.

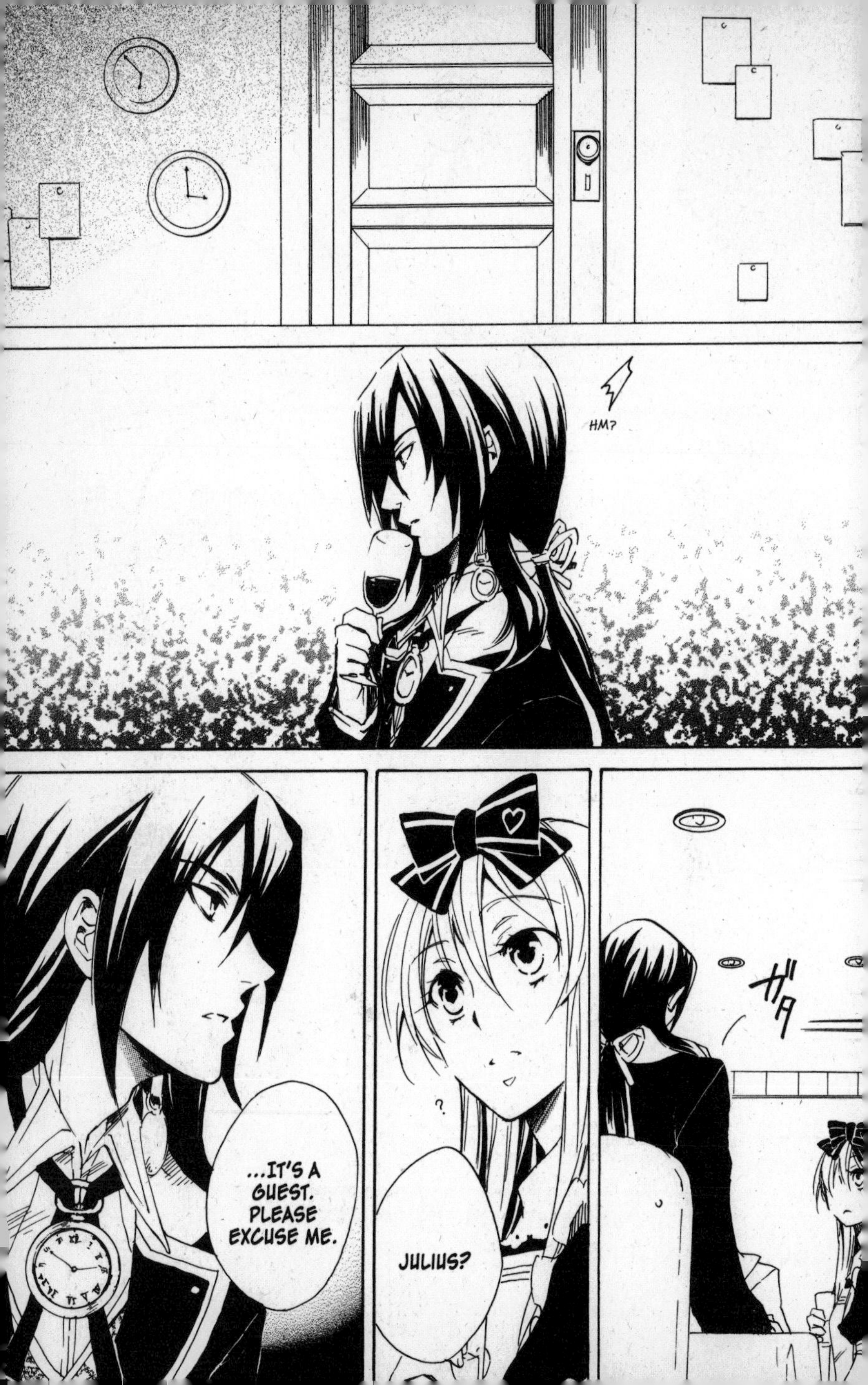
HM?
ガタ
?
JULIUS?
...IT'S A GUEST. PLEASE EXCUSE ME.

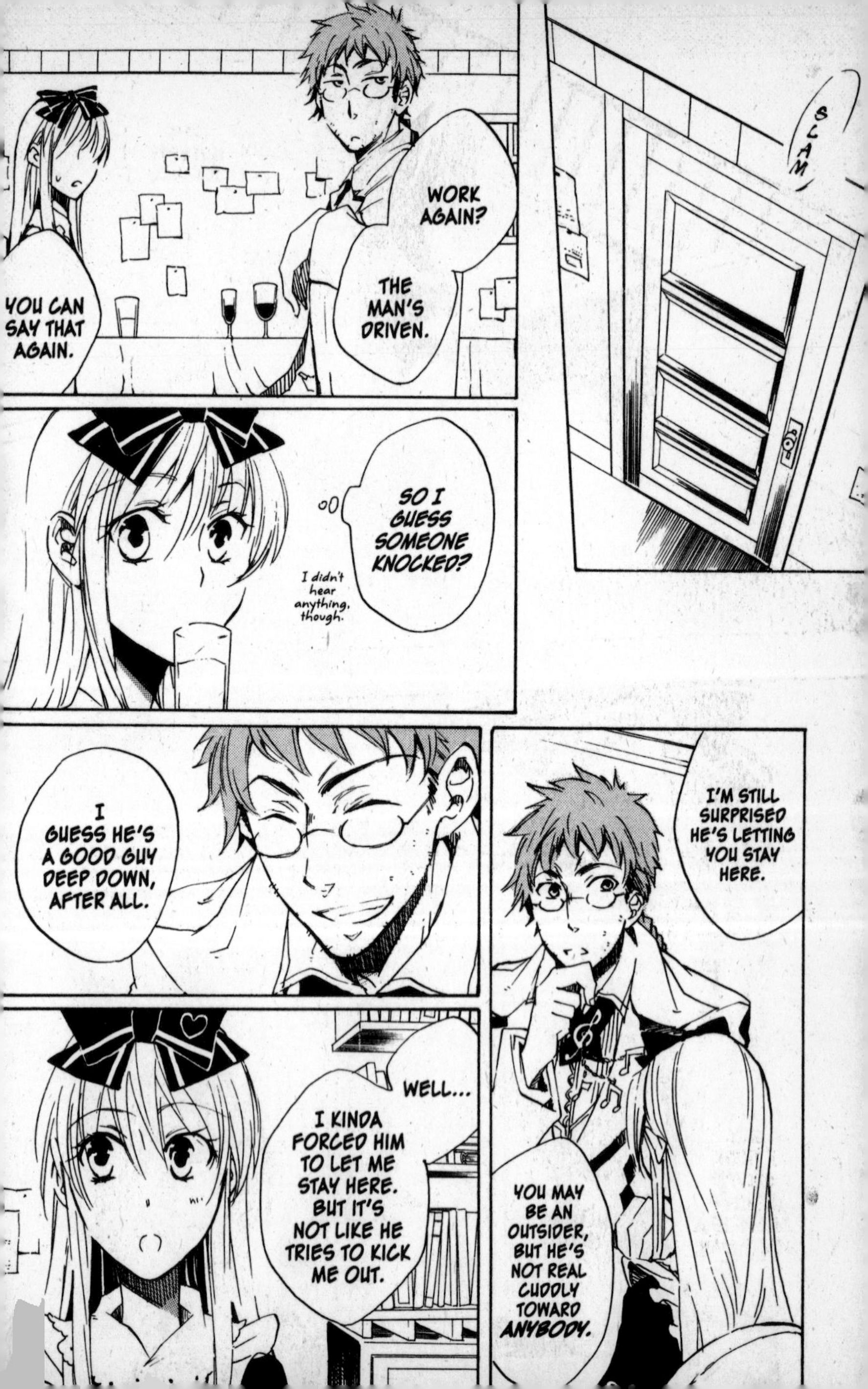
SLAM
WORK AGAIN?
THE MAN'S DRIVEN.
YOU CAN SAY THAT AGAIN.
SO I GUESS SOMEONE KNOCKED?
I didn't hear anything, though.
I'M STILL SURPRISED HE'S LETTING YOU STAY HERE.
YOU MAY BE AN OUTSIDER, BUT HE'S NOT REAL CUDDLY TOWARD ANYBODY.
I GUESS HE'S A GOOD GUY DEEP DOWN, AFTER ALL.
WELL...
I KINDA FORCED HIM TO LET ME STAY HERE. BUT IT'S NOT LIKE HE TRIES TO KICK ME OUT.

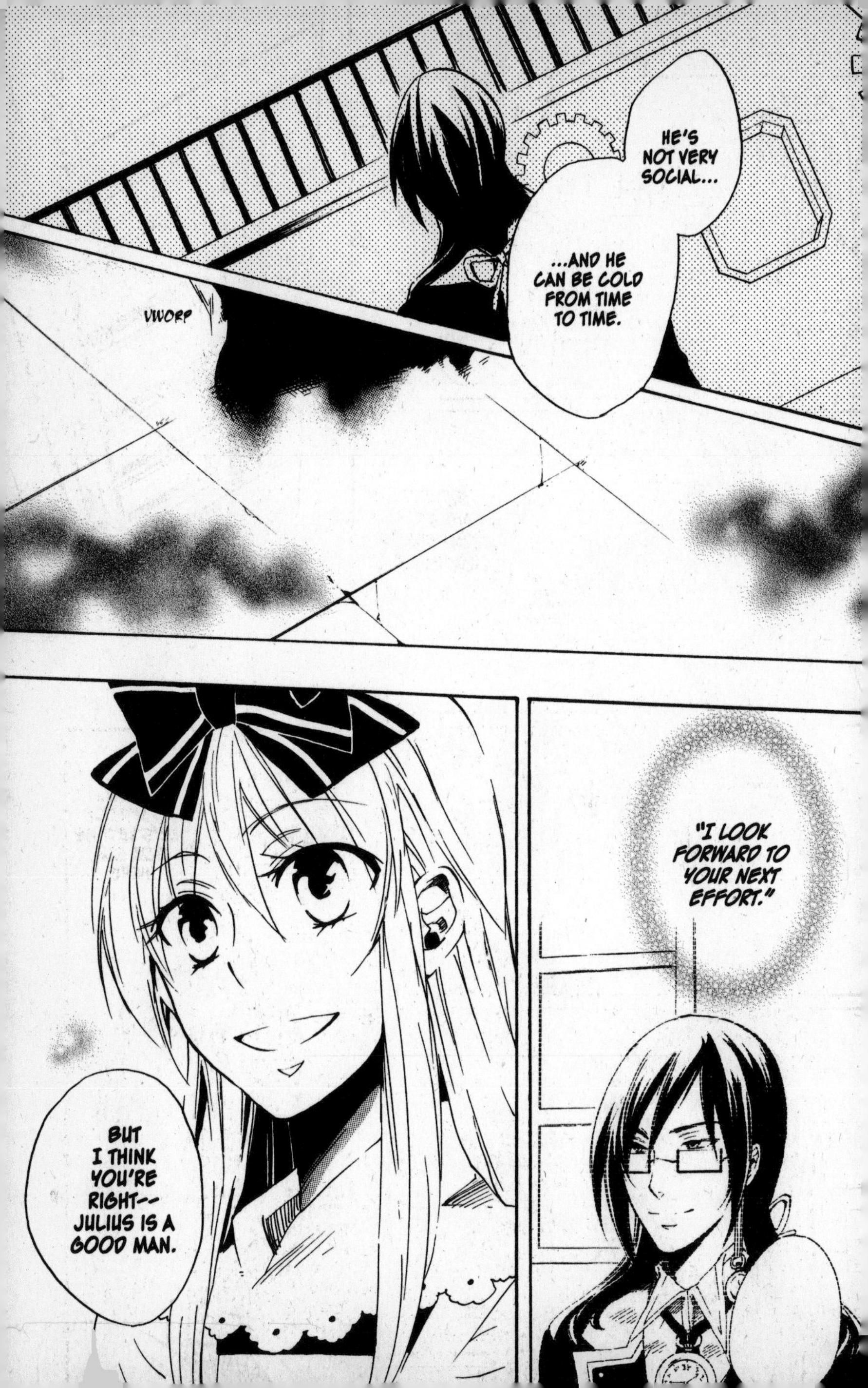
HE'S NOT VERY SOCIAL...
...AND HE CAN BE COLD FROM TIME TO TIME.
VWORP
"I LOOK FORWARD TO YOUR NEXT EFFORT."
BUT I THINK YOU'RE RIGHT--JULIUS IS A GOOD MAN.

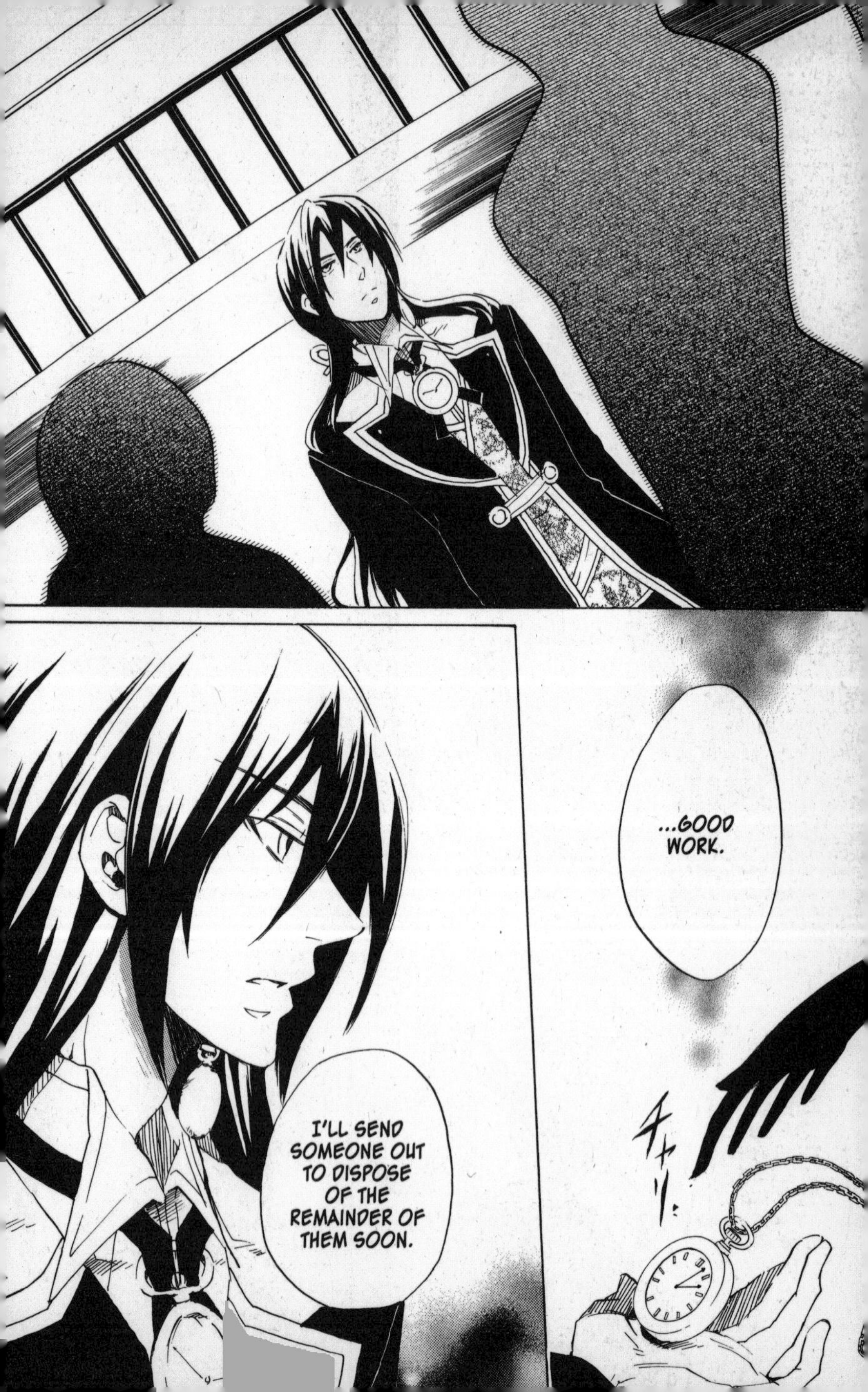
...GOOD WORK.
チャリ
I'LL SEND SOMEONE OUT TO DISPOSE OF THE REMAINDER OF THEM SOON.

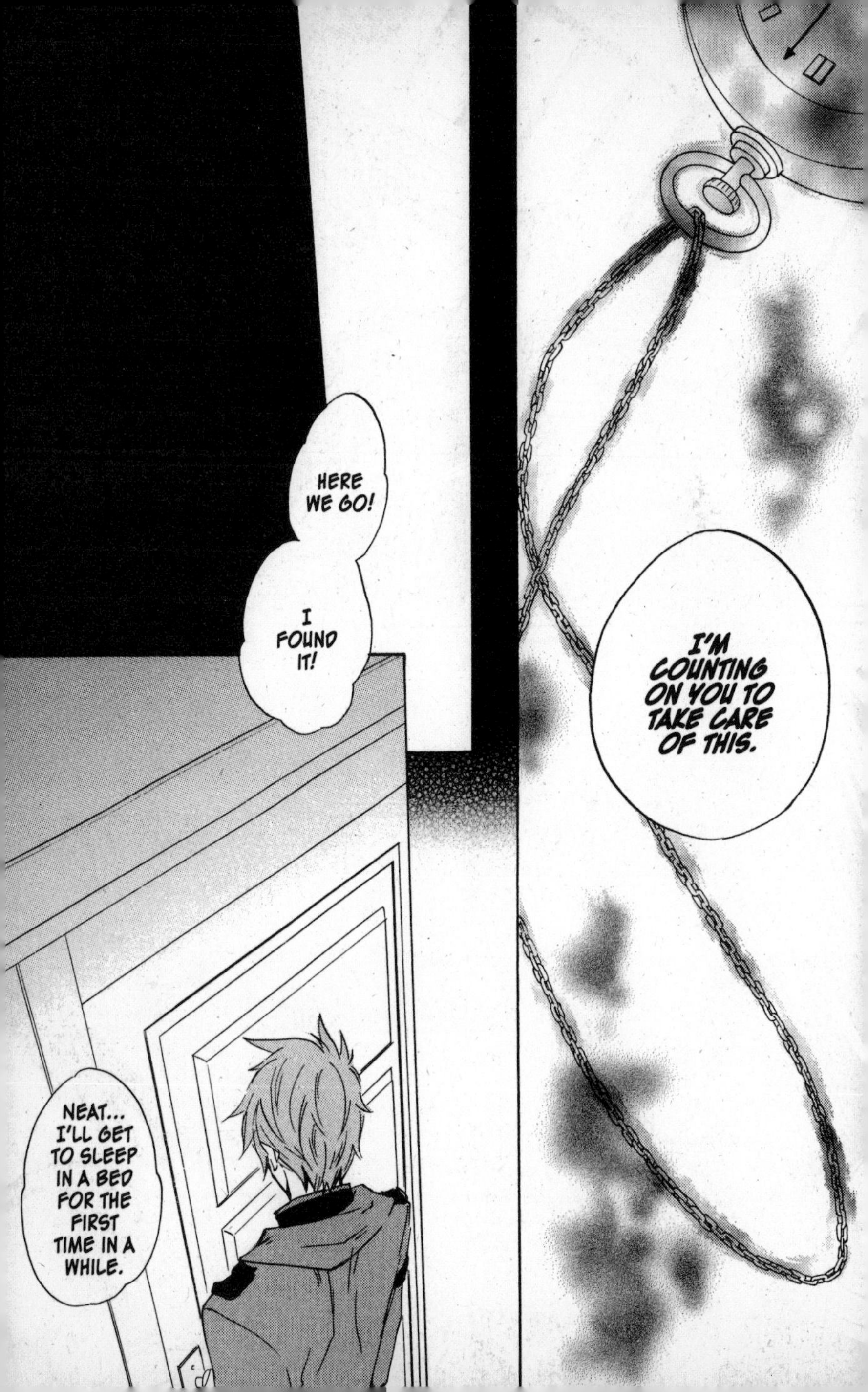
I'M COUNTING ON YOU TO TAKE CARE OF THIS.
HERE WE GO!
I FOUND IT!
NEAT... I'LL GET TO SLEEP IN A BED FOR THE FIRST TIME IN A WHILE.

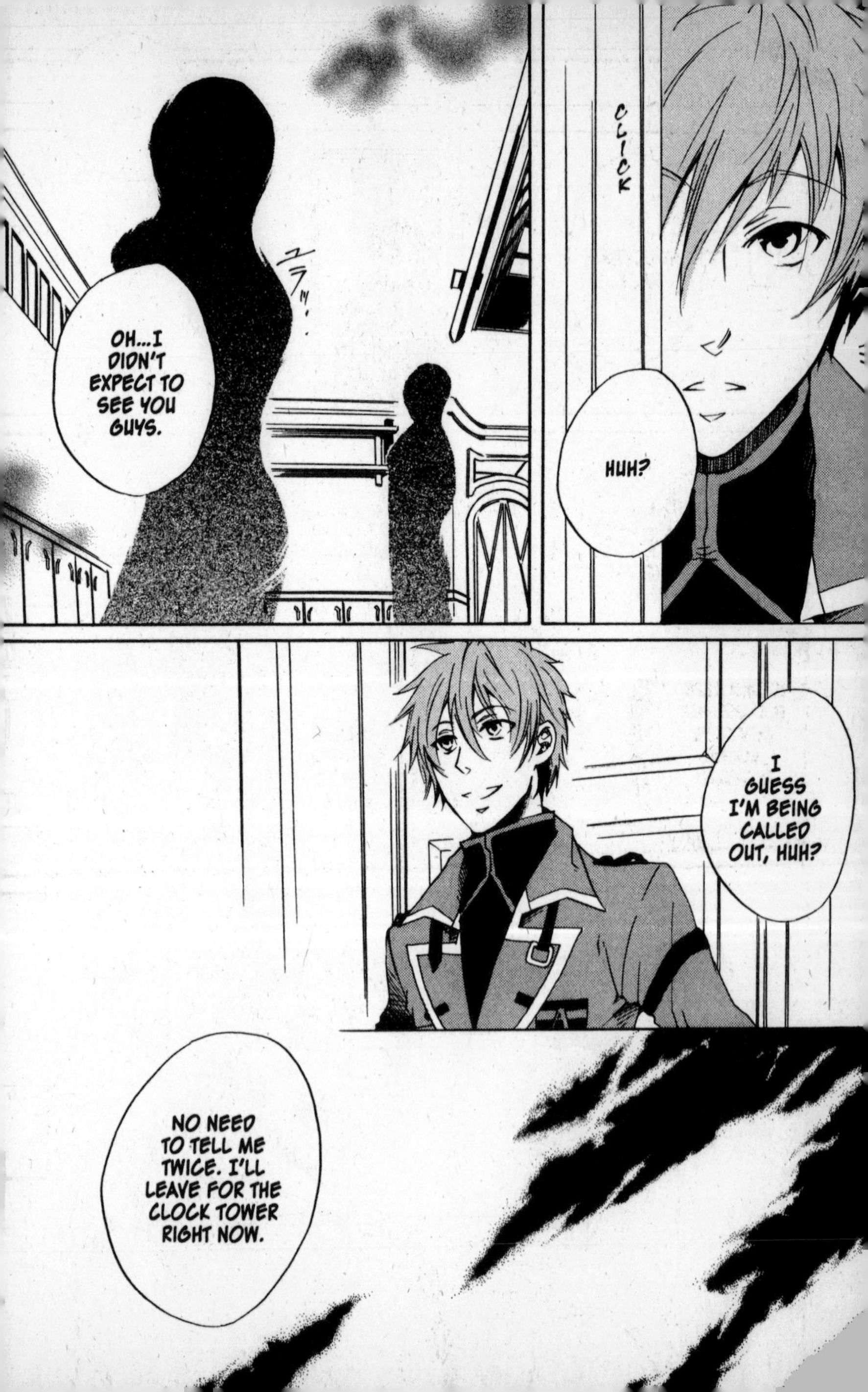
CLICK
HUH?
ユラッ
OH...I DIDN'T EXPECT TO SEE YOU GUYS.
I GUESS I'M BEING CALLED OUT, HUH?
NO NEED TO TELL ME TWICE. I'LL LEAVE FOR THE CLOCK TOWER RIGHT NOW.

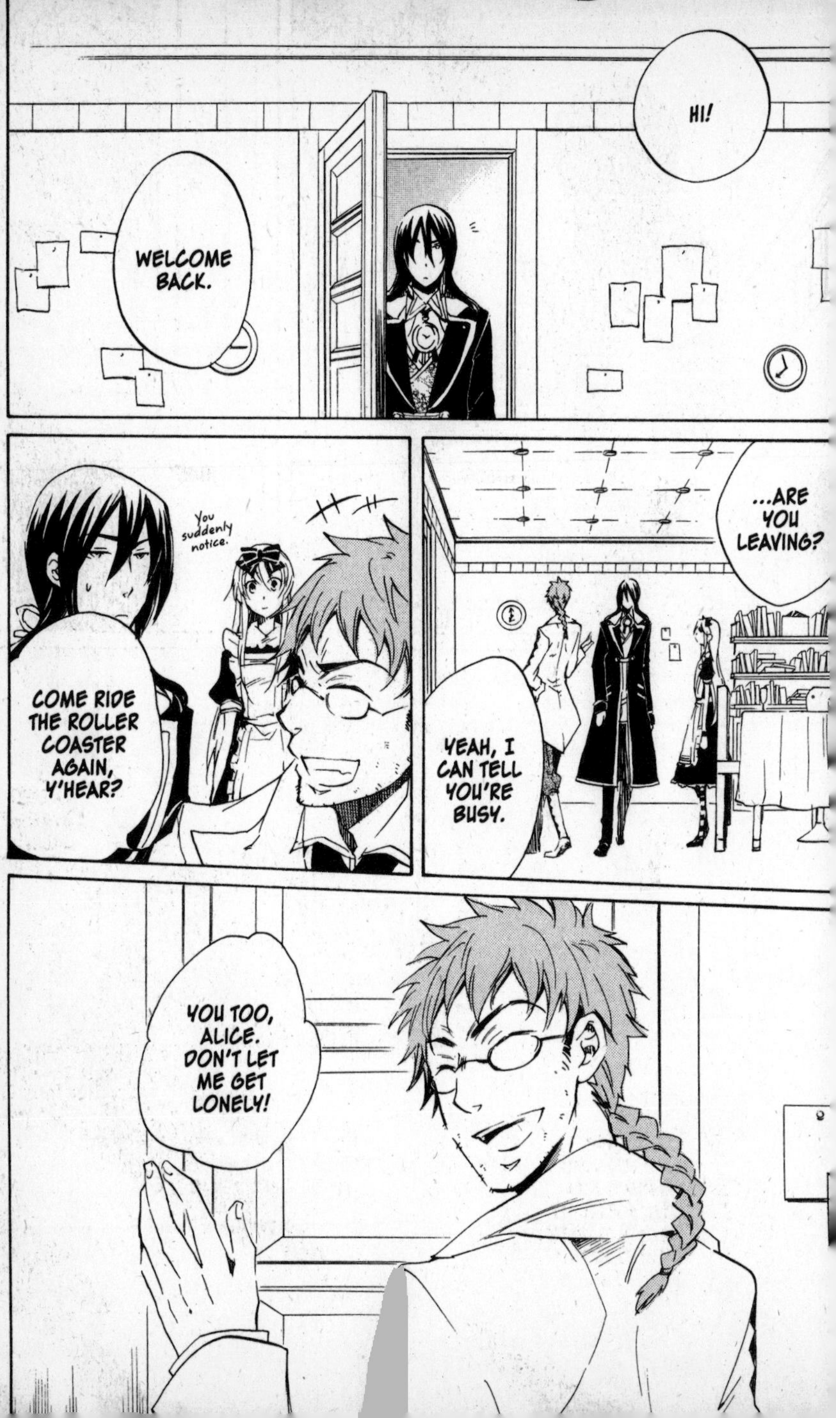
HI!
WELCOME BACK.
...ARE YOU LEAVING?
YEAH, I CAN TELL YOU'RE BUSY.
You suddenly notice.
COME RIDE THE ROLLER COASTER AGAIN, Y'HEAR?
YOU TOO, ALICE. DON'T LET ME GET LONELY!

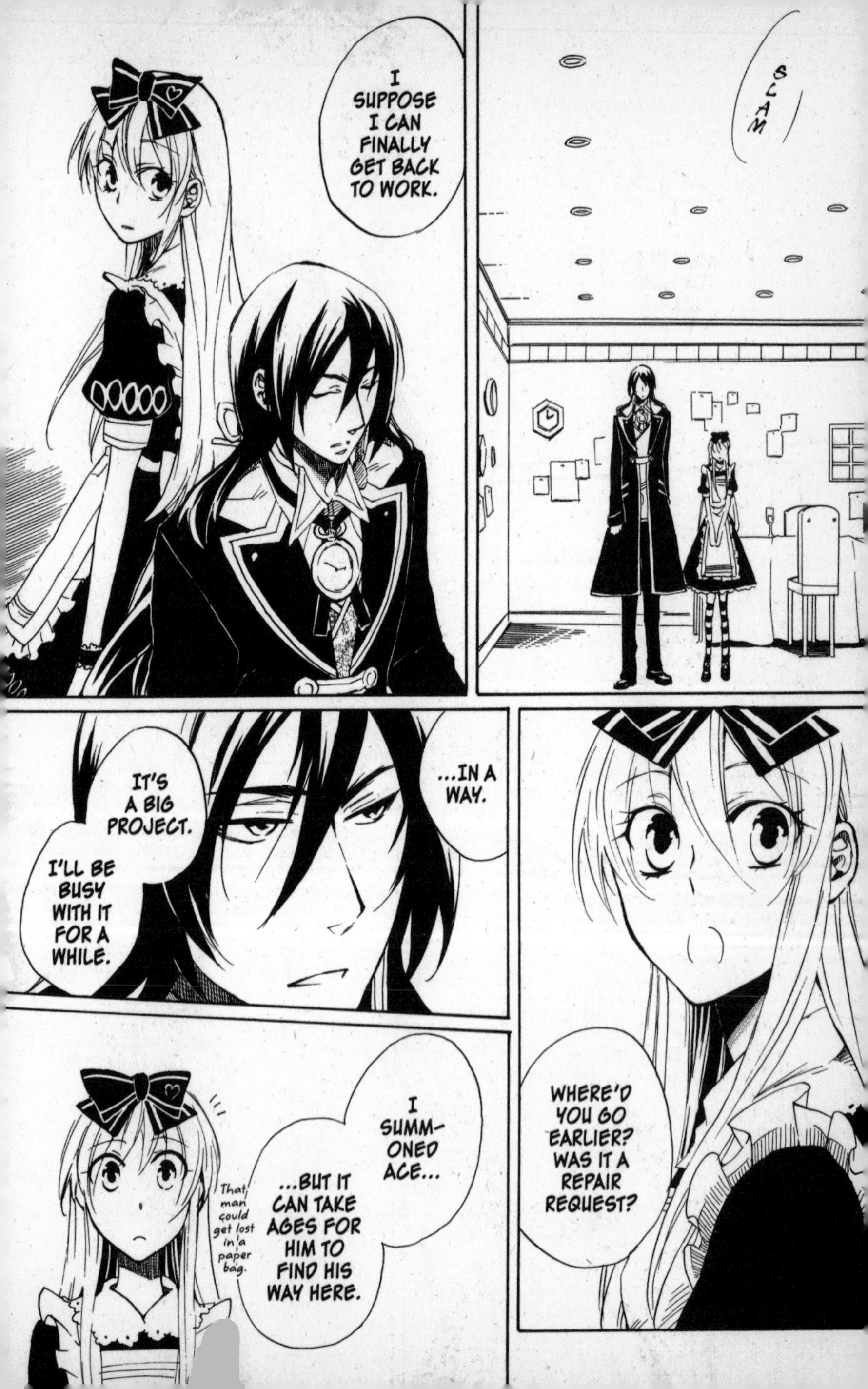
SLAM
I SUPPOSE I CAN FINALLY GET BACK TO WORK.
WHERE'D YOU GO EARLIER? WAS IT A REPAIR REQUEST?
IT'S A BIG PROJECT.
I'LL BE BUSY WITH IT FOR A WHILE.
...IN A WAY.
I SUMMONED ACE...
...BUT IT CAN TAKE AGES FOR HIM TO FIND HIS WAY HERE.
That man could get lost in a paper bag.

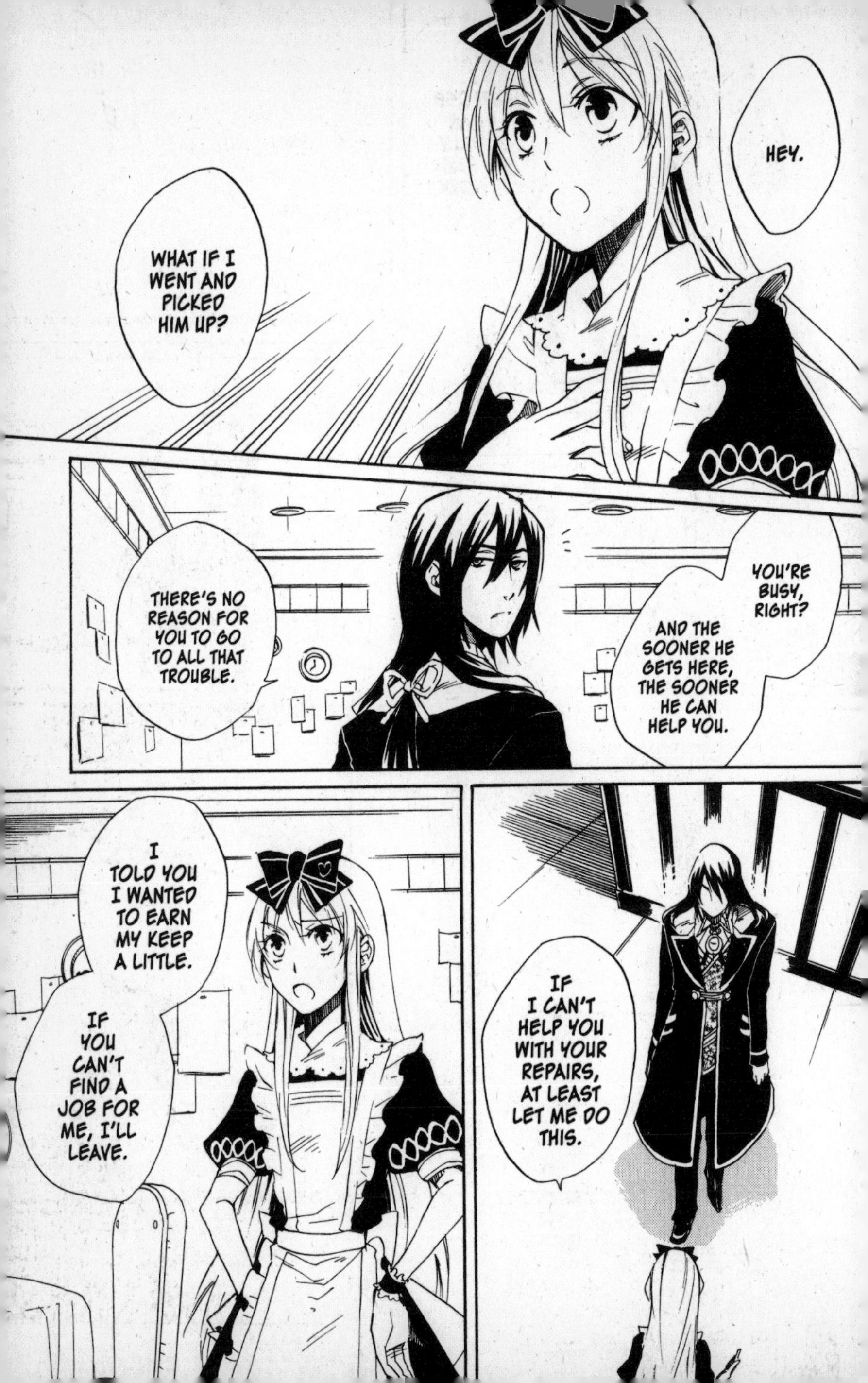
HEY.
WHAT IF I WENT AND PICKED HIM UP?
YOU'RE BUSY, RIGHT?
AND THE SOONER HE GETS HERE, THE SOONER HE CAN HELP YOU.
THERE'S NO REASON FOR YOU TO GO TO ALL THAT TROUBLE.
IF I CAN'T HELP YOU WITH YOUR REPAIRS, AT LEAST LET ME DO THIS.
I TOLD YOU I WANTED TO EARN MY KEEP A LITTLE.
IF YOU CAN'T FIND A JOB FOR ME, I'LL LEAVE.

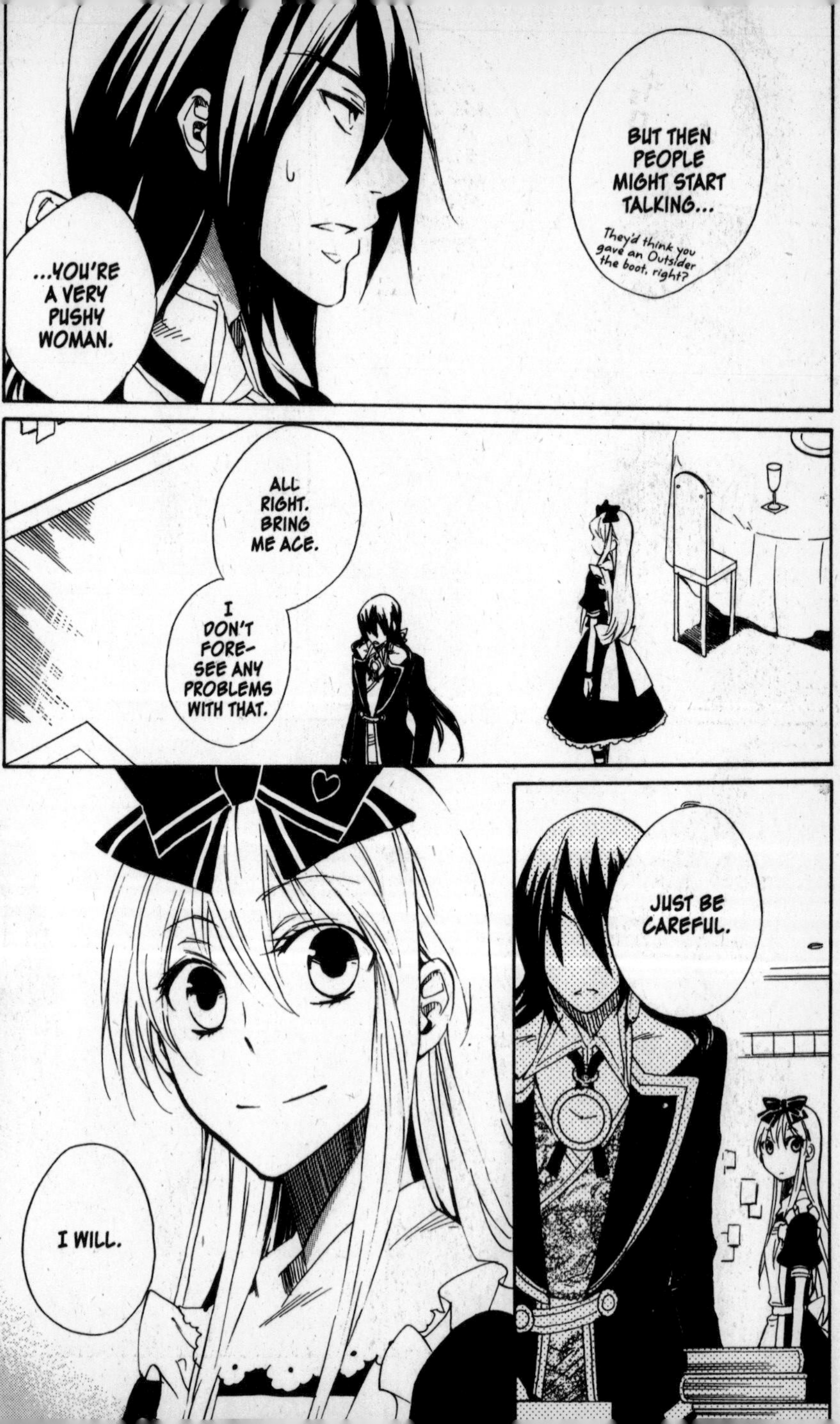
BUT THEN PEOPLE MIGHT START TALKING...
They'd think you gave an Outsider the boot, right?
...YOU'RE A VERY PUSHY WOMAN.
ALL RIGHT. BRING ME ACE.
I DON'T FORESEE ANY PROBLEMS WITH THAT.
JUST BE CAREFUL.
I WILL.

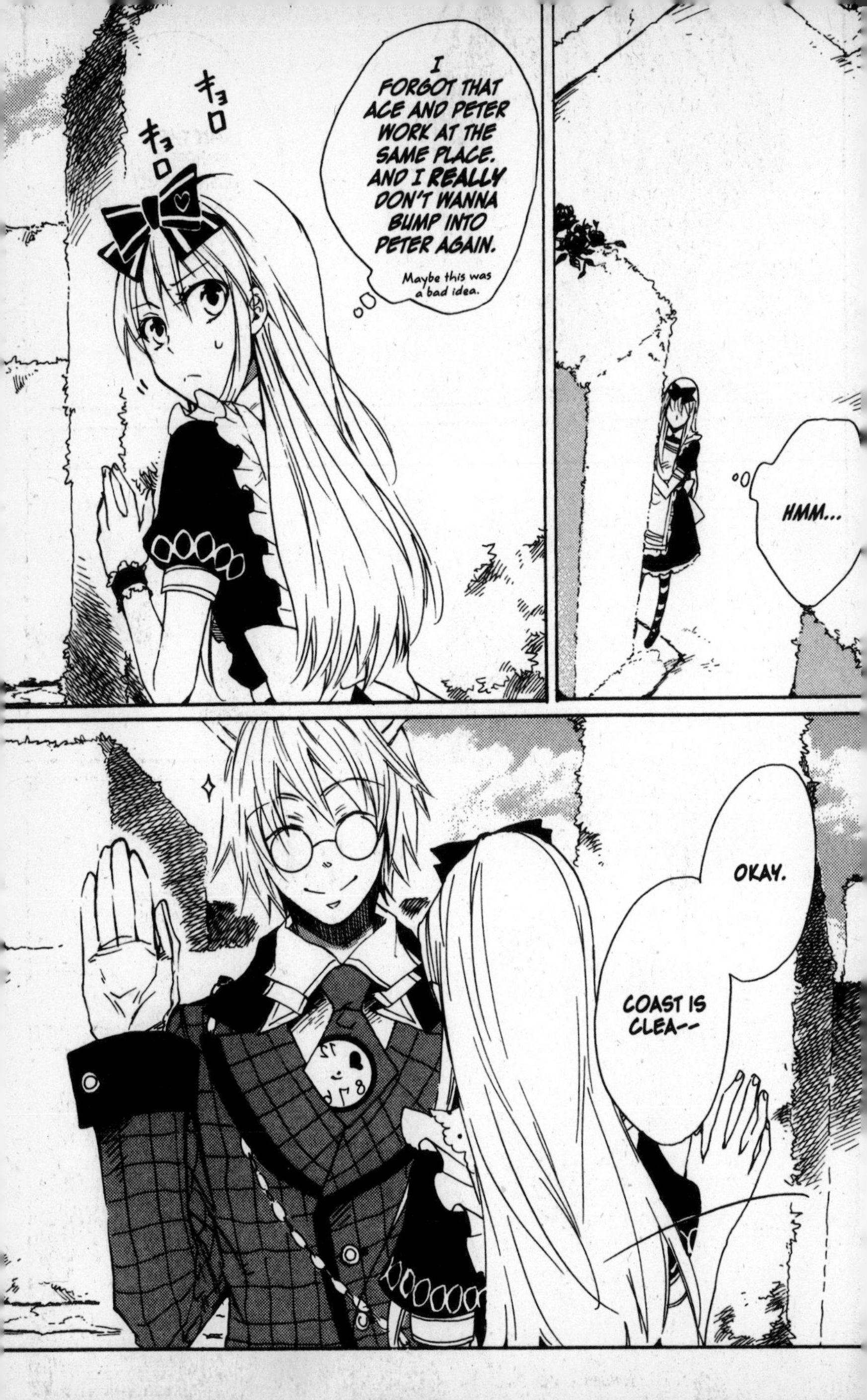
HMM...
I FORGOT THAT ACE AND PETER WORK AT THE SAME PLACE. AND I REALLY DON'T WANNA BUMP INTO PETER AGAIN.
Maybe this was a bad idea.
キョロ
キョロ
OKAY.
COAST IS CLEA--

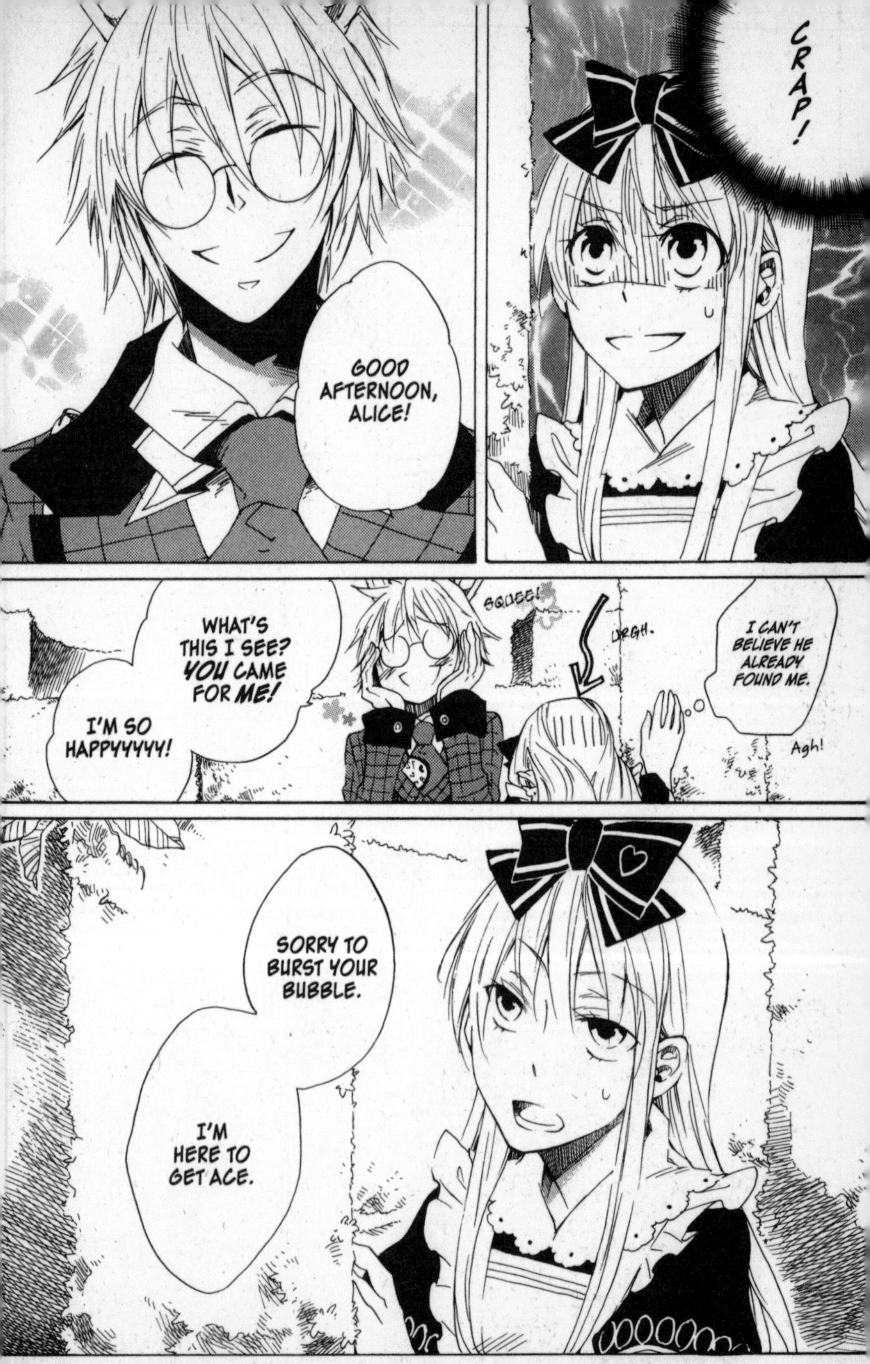
CRAP!
GOOD AFTERNOON, ALICE!
I CAN'T BELIEVE HE ALREADY FOUND ME.
Agh!
URGH.
SQUEE!
WHAT'S THIS I SEE? YOU CAME FOR ME!
I'M SO HAPPYYYYY!
SORRY TO BURST YOUR BUBBLE.
I'M HERE TO GET ACE.

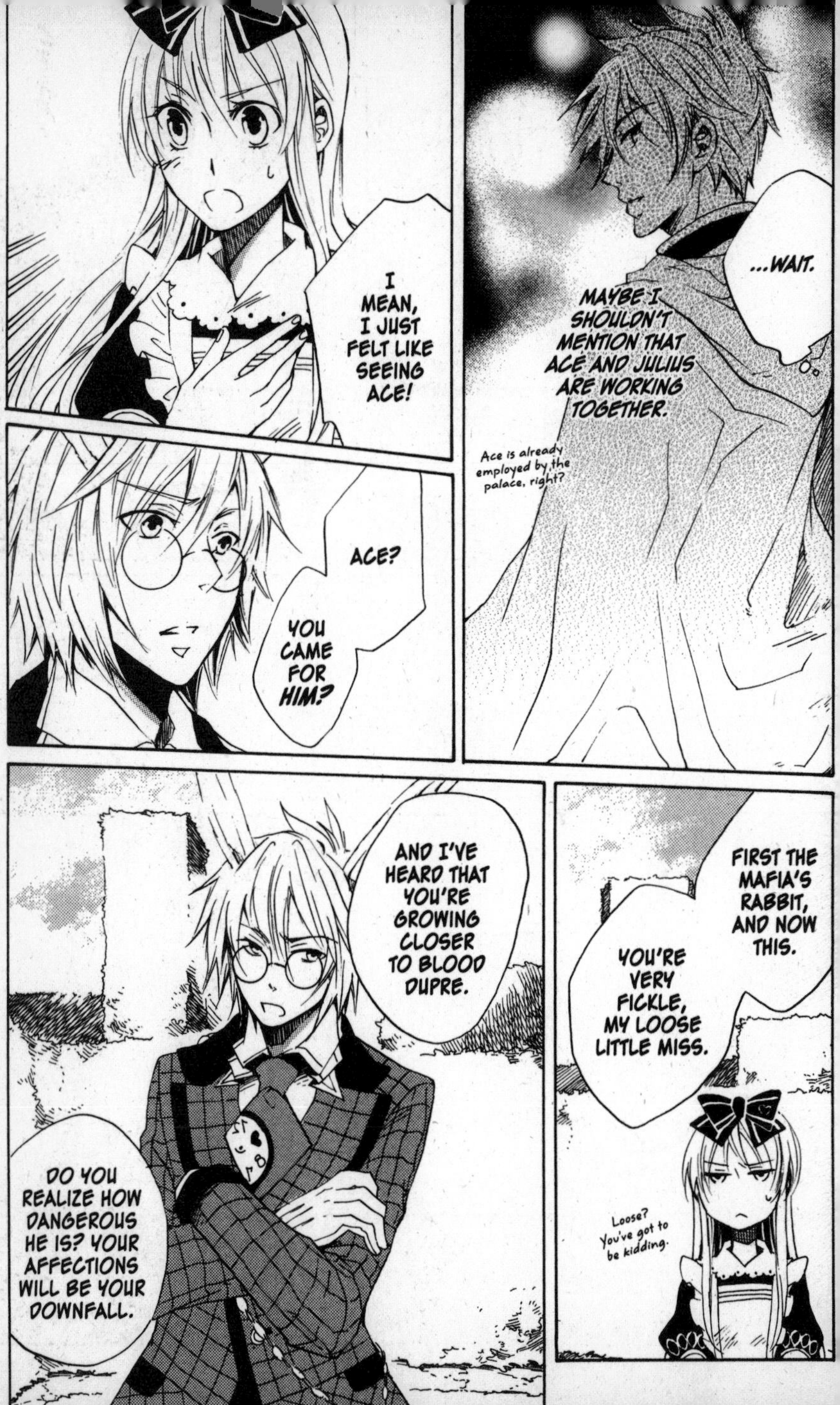
I MEAN, I JUST FELT LIKE SEEING ACE!
ACE?
YOU CAME FOR HIM?
...WAIT.
MAYBE I SHOULDN'T MENTION THAT ACE AND JULIUS ARE WORKING TOGETHER.
Ace is already employed by the palace, right?
AND I'VE HEARD THAT YOU'RE GROWING CLOSER TO BLOOD DUPRE.
DO YOU REALIZE HOW DANGEROUS HE IS? YOUR AFFECTIONS WILL BE YOUR DOWNFALL.
FIRST THE MAFIA'S RABBIT, AND NOW THIS.
YOU'RE VERY FICKLE, MY LOOSE LITTLE MISS.
Loose? You've got to be kidding.

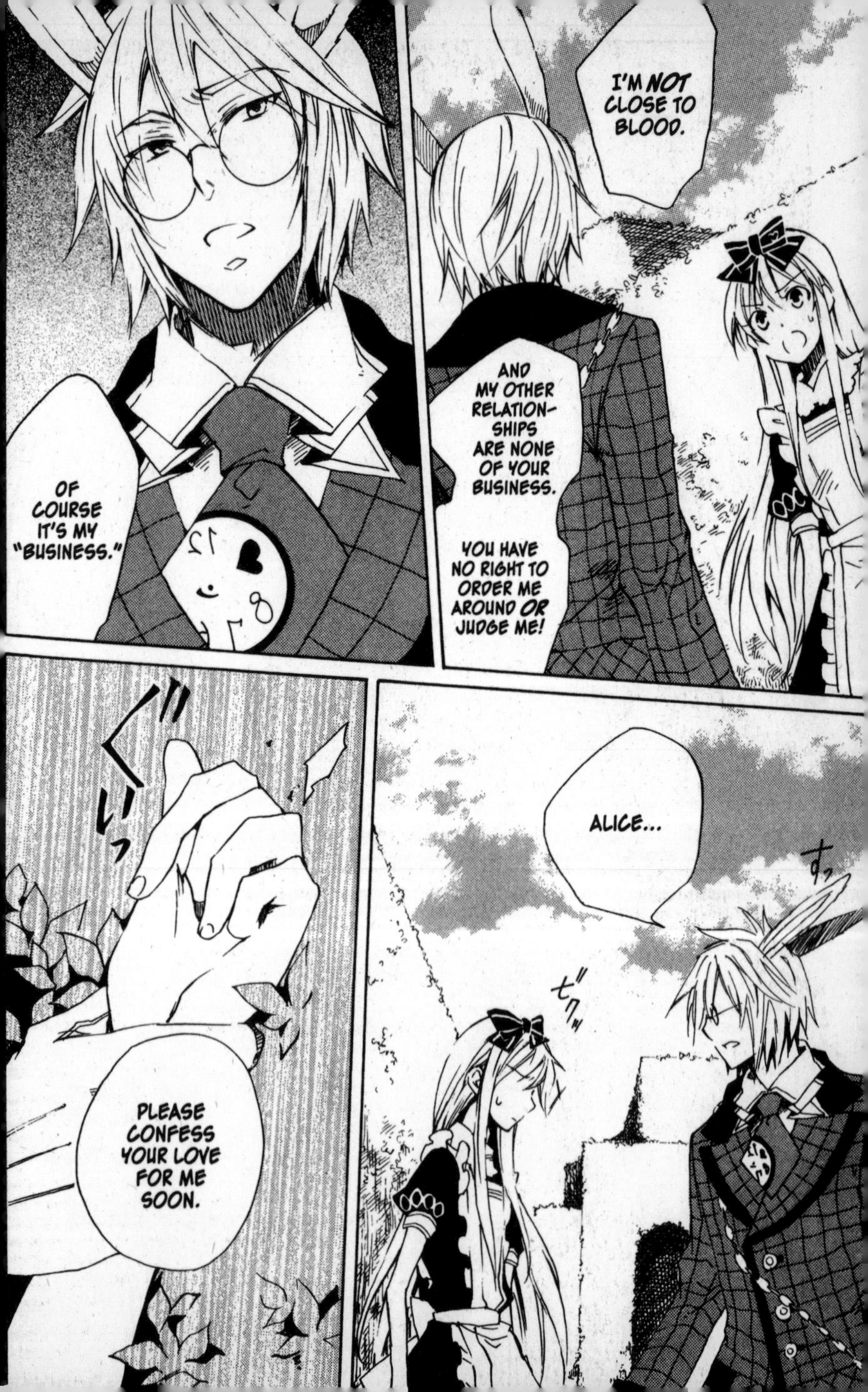
I'M *NOT* CLOSE TO BLOOD.
AND MY OTHER RELATION-SHIPS ARE NONE OF YOUR BUSINESS.
YOU HAVE NO RIGHT TO ORDER ME AROUND *OR* JUDGE ME!
OF COURSE IT'S MY "BUSINESS."
ALICE...
すっ
ビクッ
ぐいっ
PLEASE CONFESS YOUR LOVE FOR ME SOON.

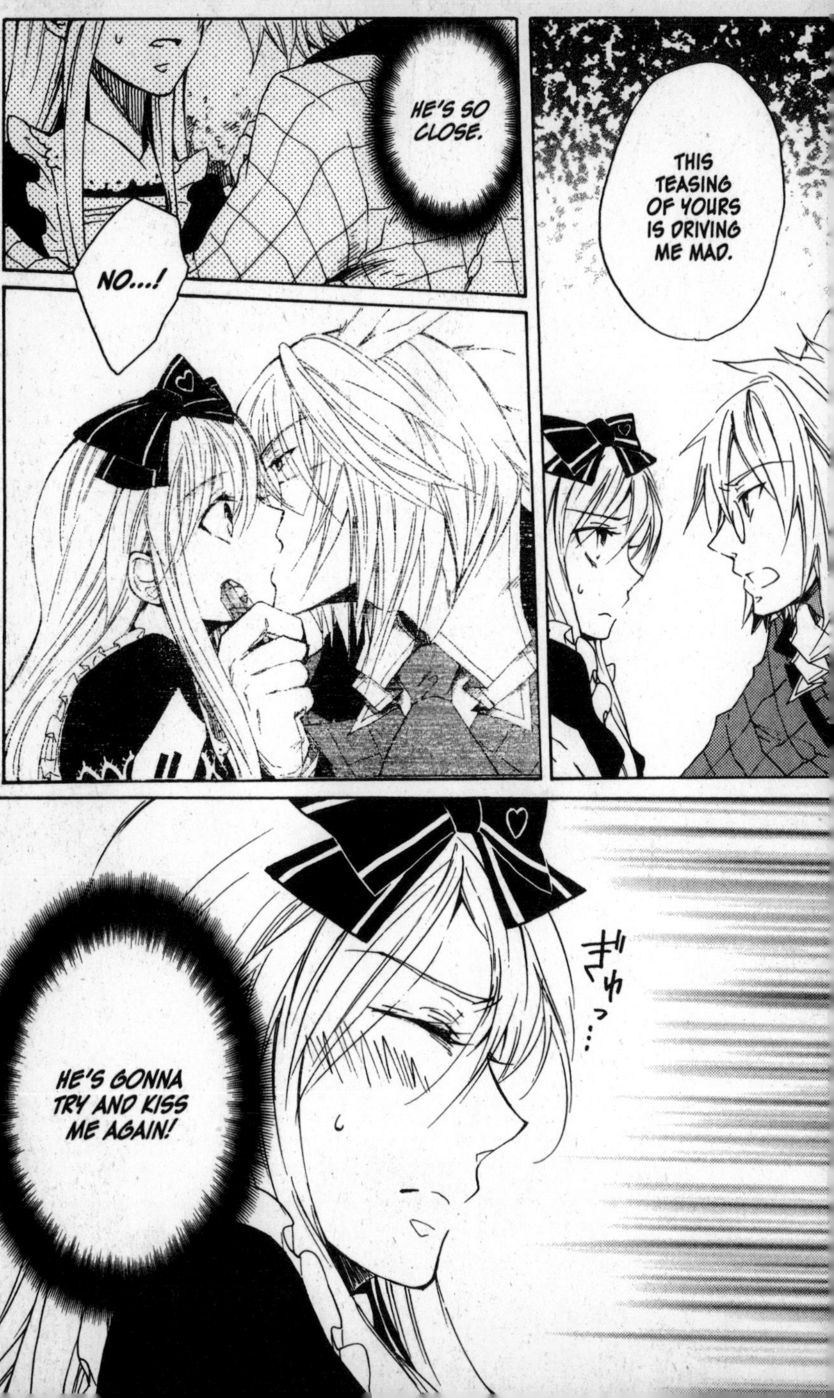
THIS TEASING OF YOURS IS DRIVING ME MAD.
HE'S SO CLOSE.
NO...!
ぎゅっ…
HE'S GONNA TRY AND KISS ME AGAIN!

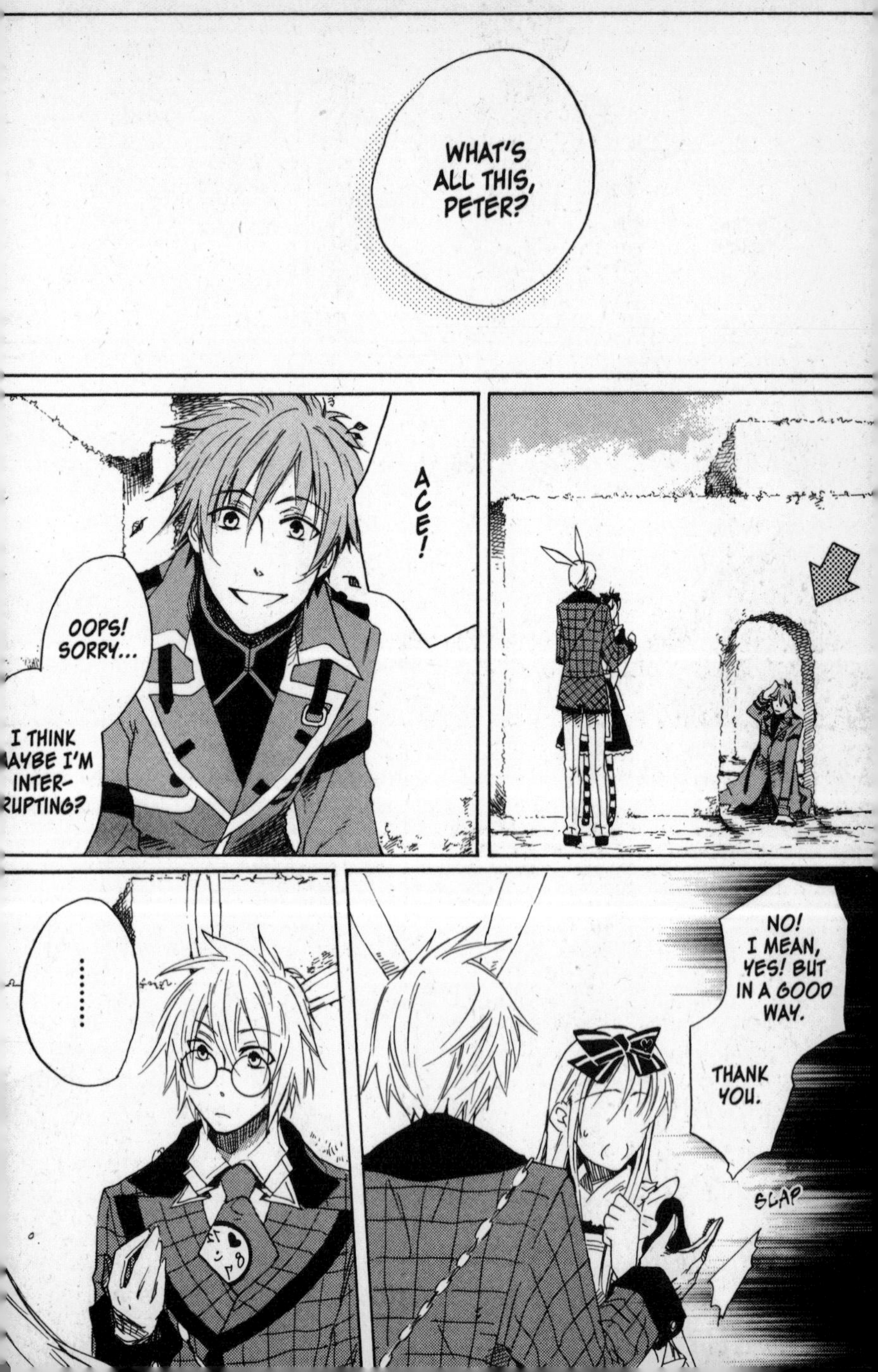
WHAT'S ALL THIS, PETER?
ACE!
OOPS! SORRY...
I THINK AYBE I'M INTER-RUPTING?
NO! I MEAN, YES! BUT IN A GOOD WAY.
THANK YOU.
SLAP
........

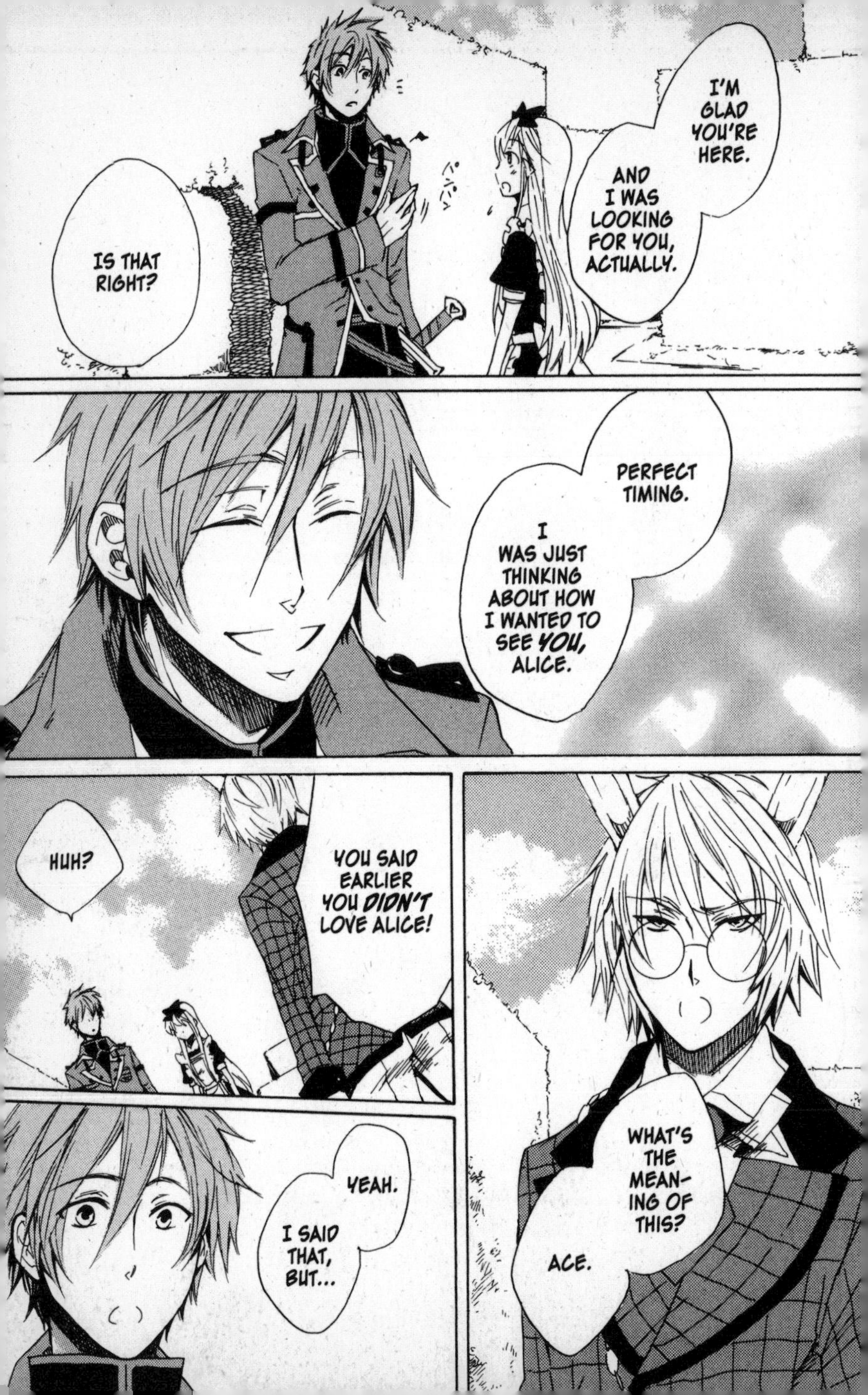

I'M GLAD YOU'RE HERE.
AND I WAS LOOKING FOR YOU, ACTUALLY.
IS THAT RIGHT?
PERFECT TIMING.
I WAS JUST THINKING ABOUT HOW I WANTED TO SEE *YOU*, ALICE.
WHAT'S THE MEAN-ING OF THIS?
ACE.
YOU SAID EARLIER YOU *DIDN'T* LOVE ALICE!
HUH?
YEAH.
I SAID THAT, BUT...

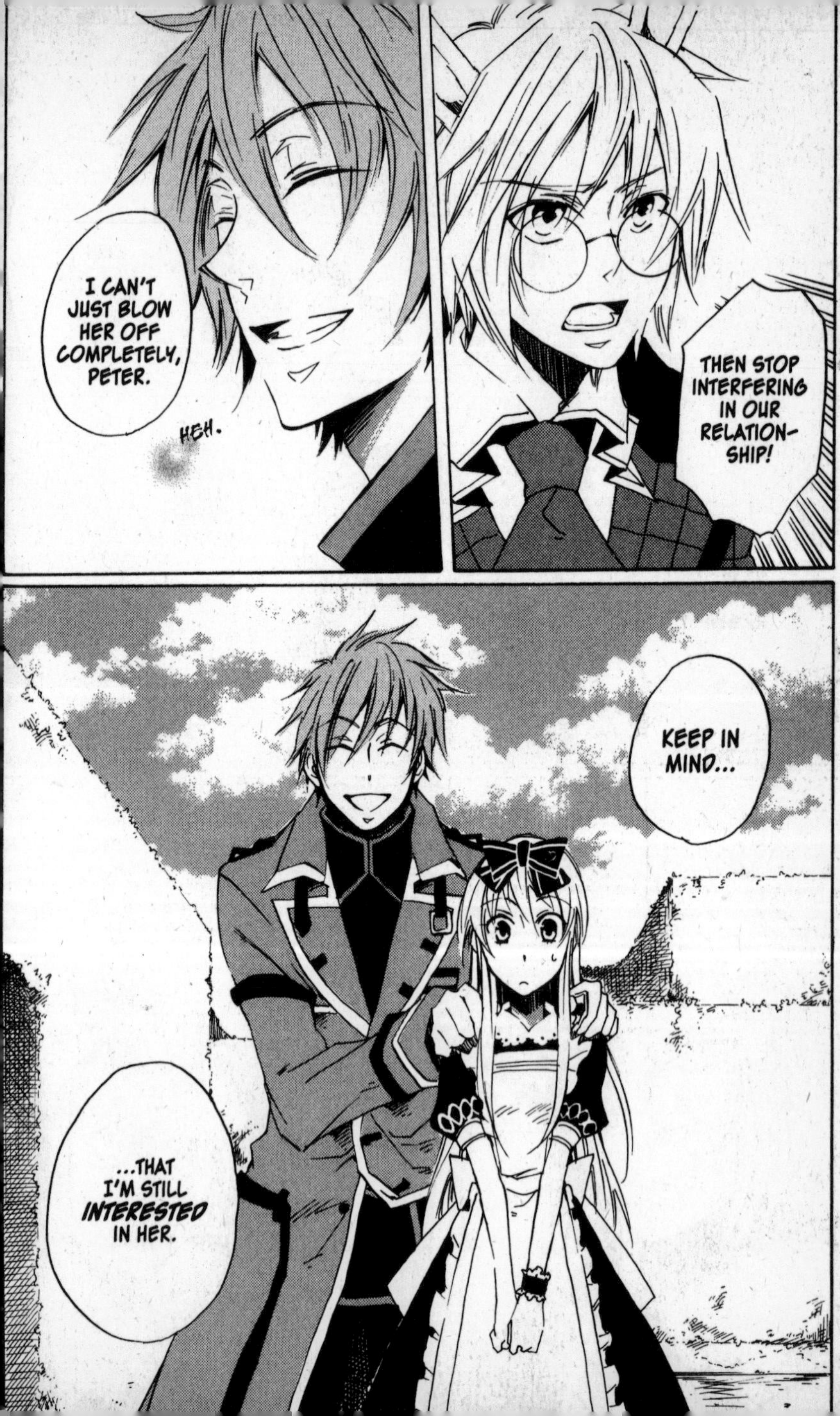
THEN STOP INTERFERING IN OUR RELATION-SHIP!
I CAN'T JUST BLOW HER OFF COMPLETELY, PETER.
HEH.
KEEP IN MIND...
...THAT I'M STILL *INTERESTED* IN HER.

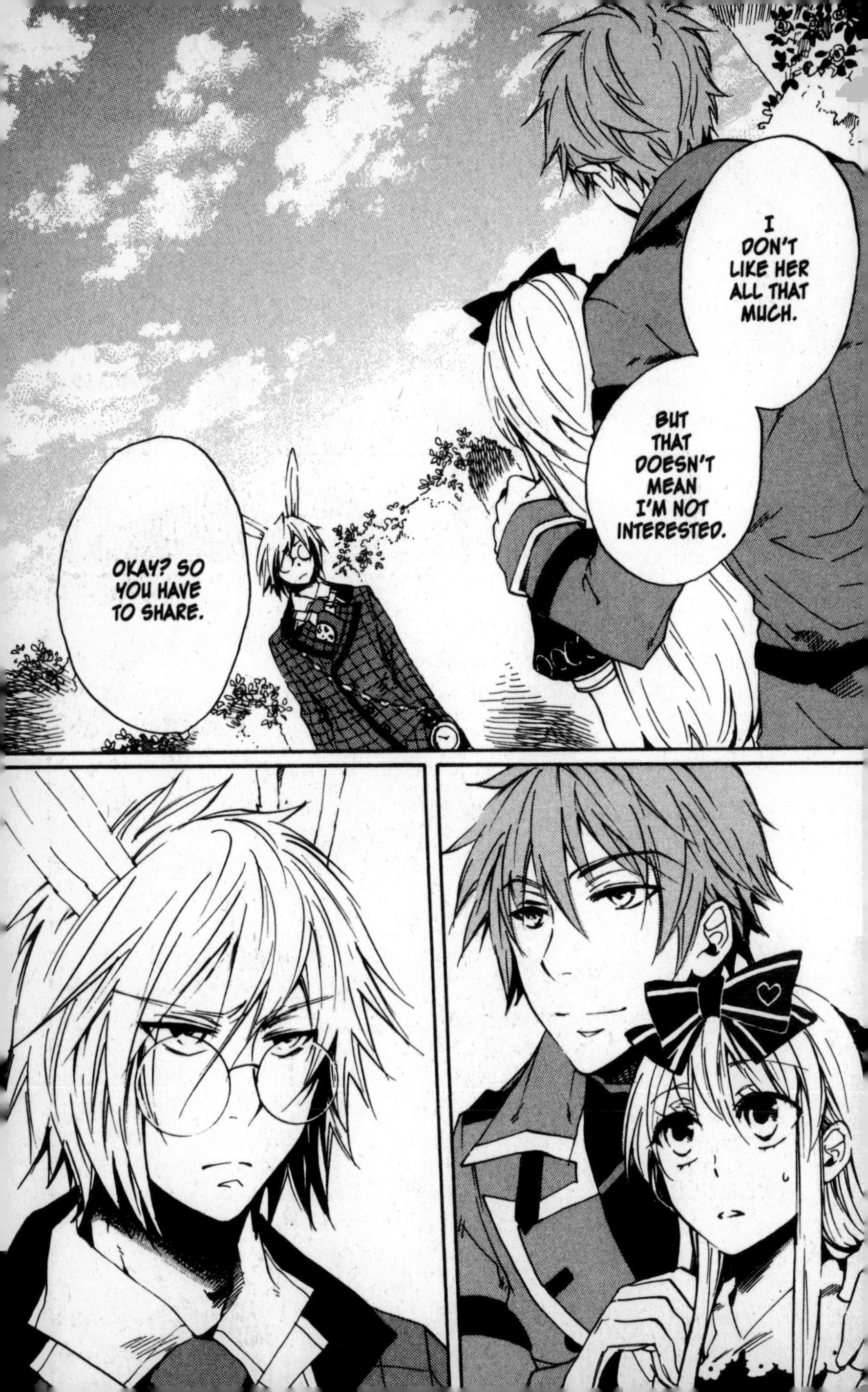
I DON'T LIKE HER ALL THAT MUCH.
BUT THAT DOESN'T MEAN I'M NOT INTERESTED.
OKAY? SO YOU HAVE TO SHARE.

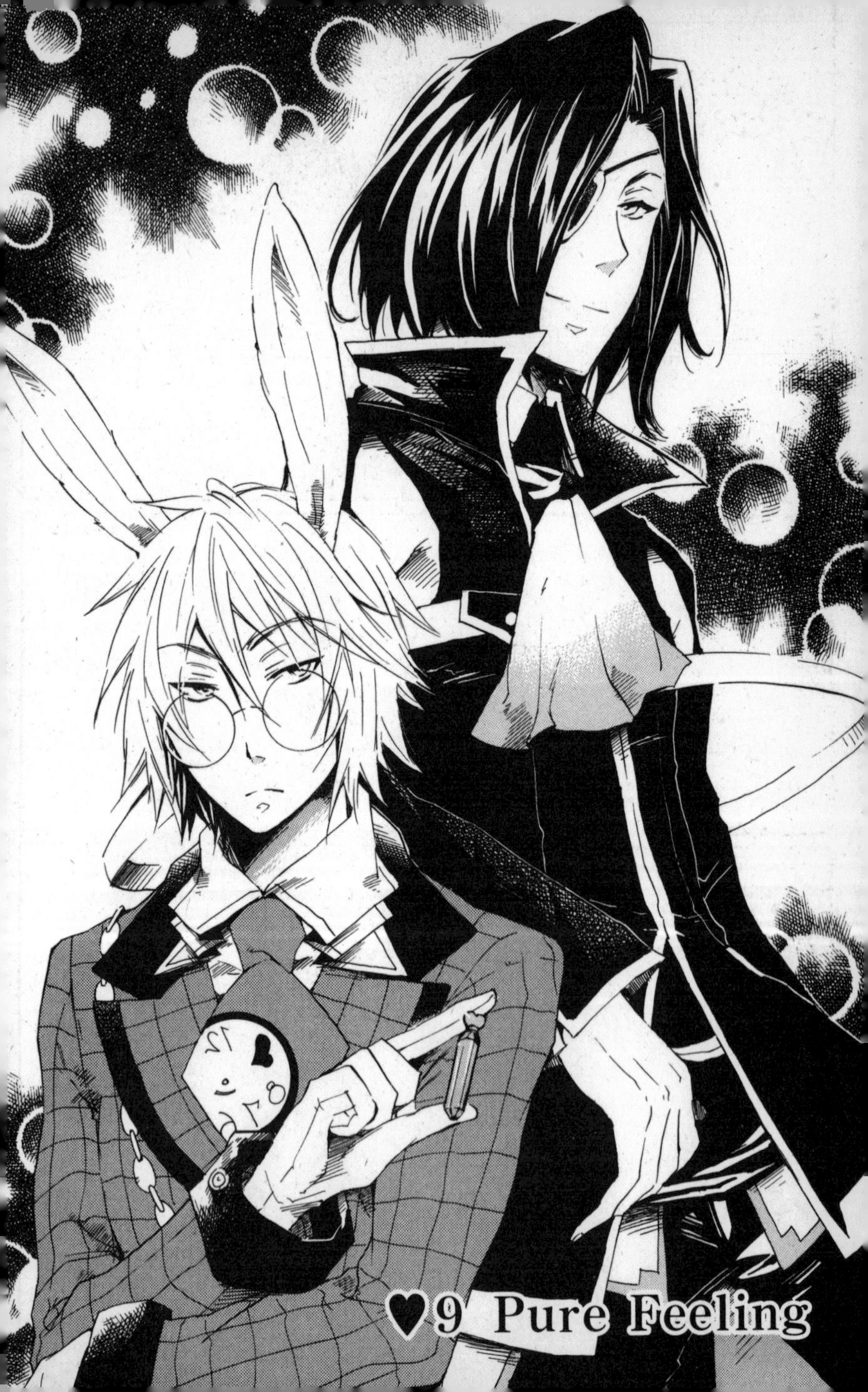
♥9 Pure Feeling

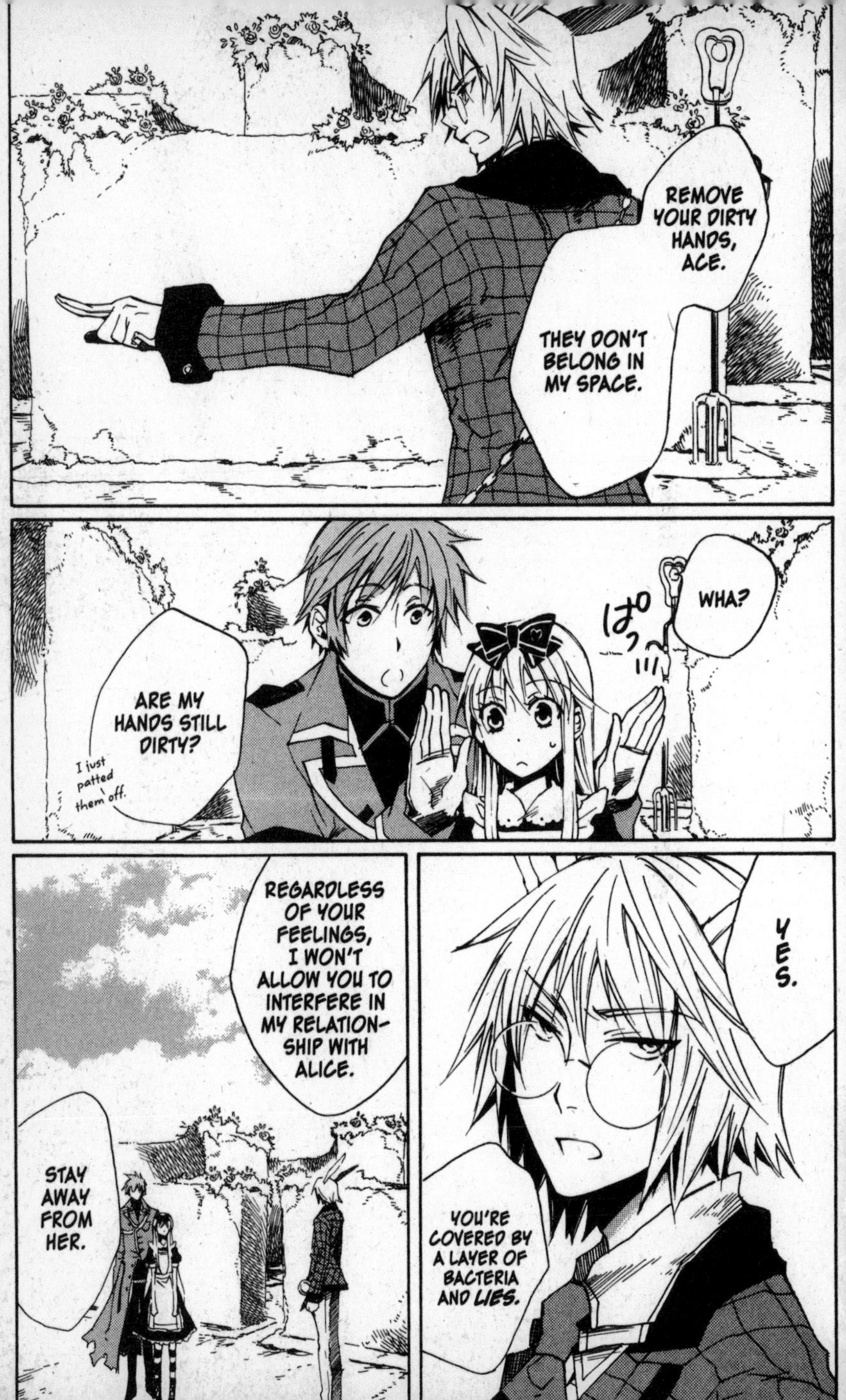
REMOVE YOUR DIRTY HANDS, ACE.
THEY DON'T BELONG IN MY SPACE.
WHA?
ぱっ
ARE MY HANDS STILL DIRTY?
I just patted them off.
YES.
YOU'RE COVERED BY A LAYER OF BACTERIA AND LIES.
REGARDLESS OF YOUR FEELINGS, I WON'T ALLOW YOU TO INTERFERE IN MY RELATIONSHIP WITH ALICE.
STAY AWAY FROM HER.

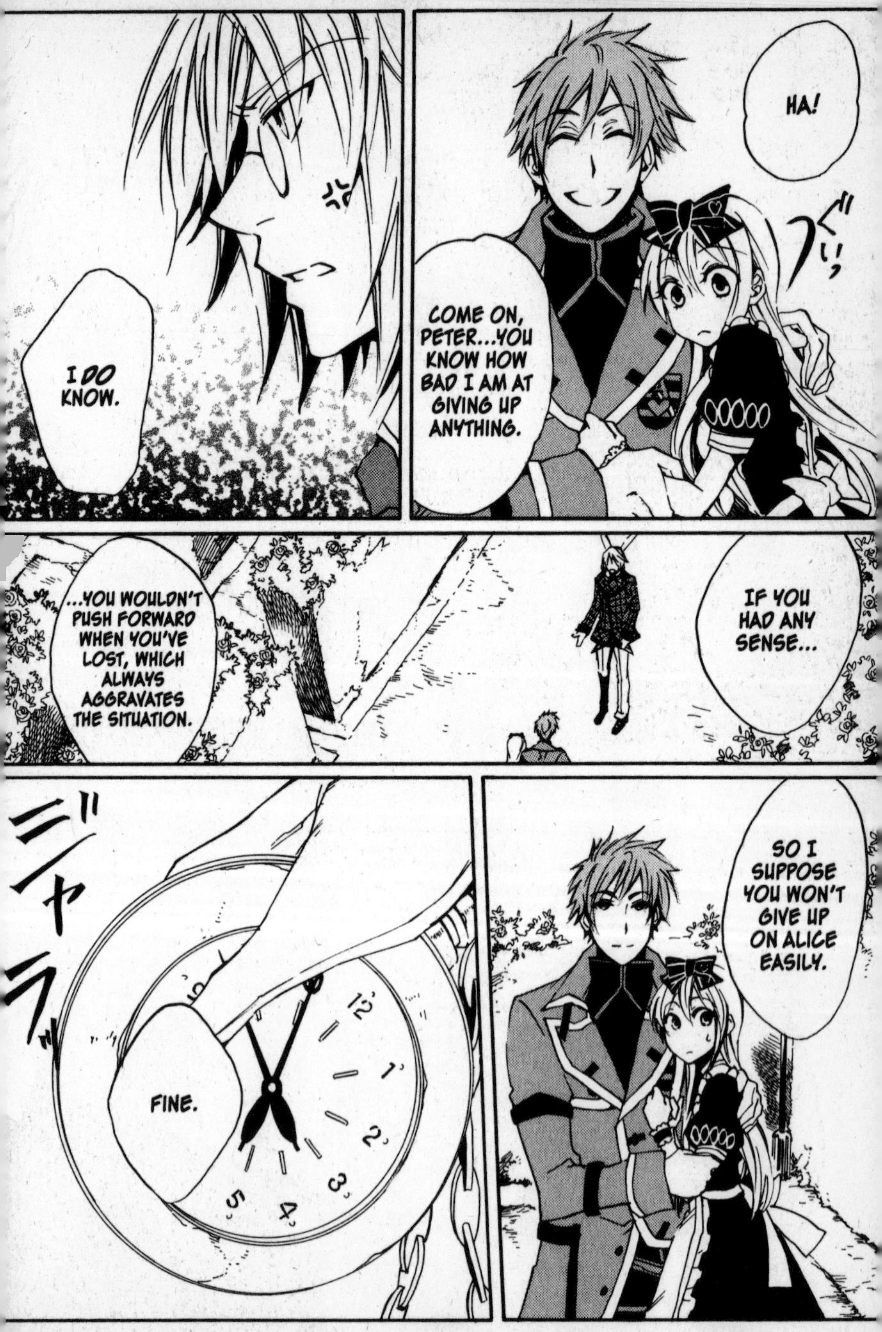
HA!
ぐい
COME ON, PETER...YOU KNOW HOW BAD I AM AT GIVING UP ANYTHING.
I DO KNOW.
IF YOU HAD ANY SENSE...
...YOU WOULDN'T PUSH FORWARD WHEN YOU'VE LOST, WHICH ALWAYS AGGRAVATES THE SITUATION.
SO I SUPPOSE YOU WON'T GIVE UP ON ALICE EASILY.
FINE.
ジャラ

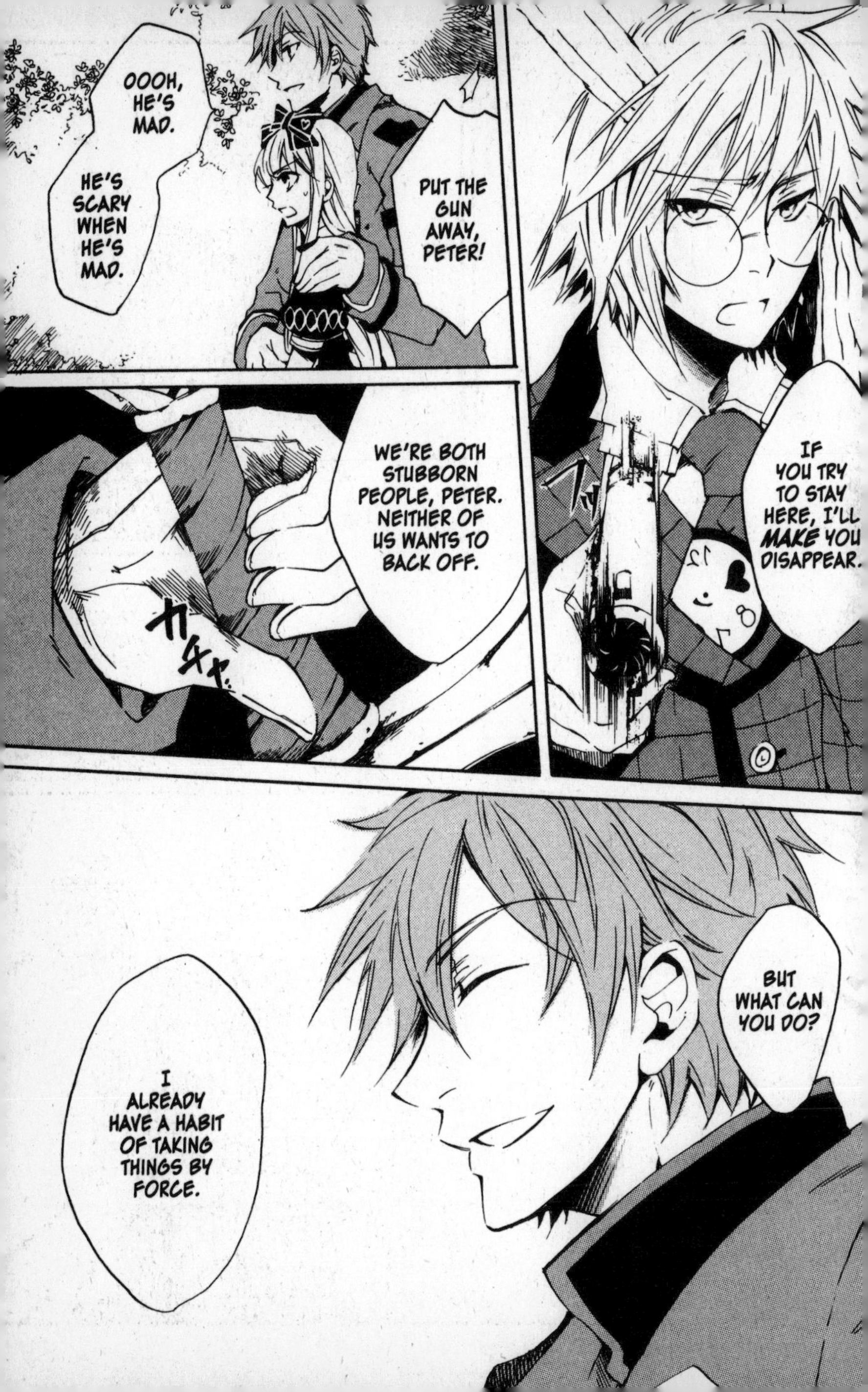
IF YOU TRY TO STAY HERE, I'LL *MAKE* YOU DISAPPEAR.
PUT THE GUN AWAY, PETER!
OOOH, HE'S MAD.
HE'S SCARY WHEN HE'S MAD.
WE'RE BOTH STUBBORN PEOPLE, PETER. NEITHER OF US WANTS TO BACK OFF.
カチャ.
BUT WHAT CAN YOU DO?
I ALREADY HAVE A HABIT OF TAKING THINGS BY FORCE.

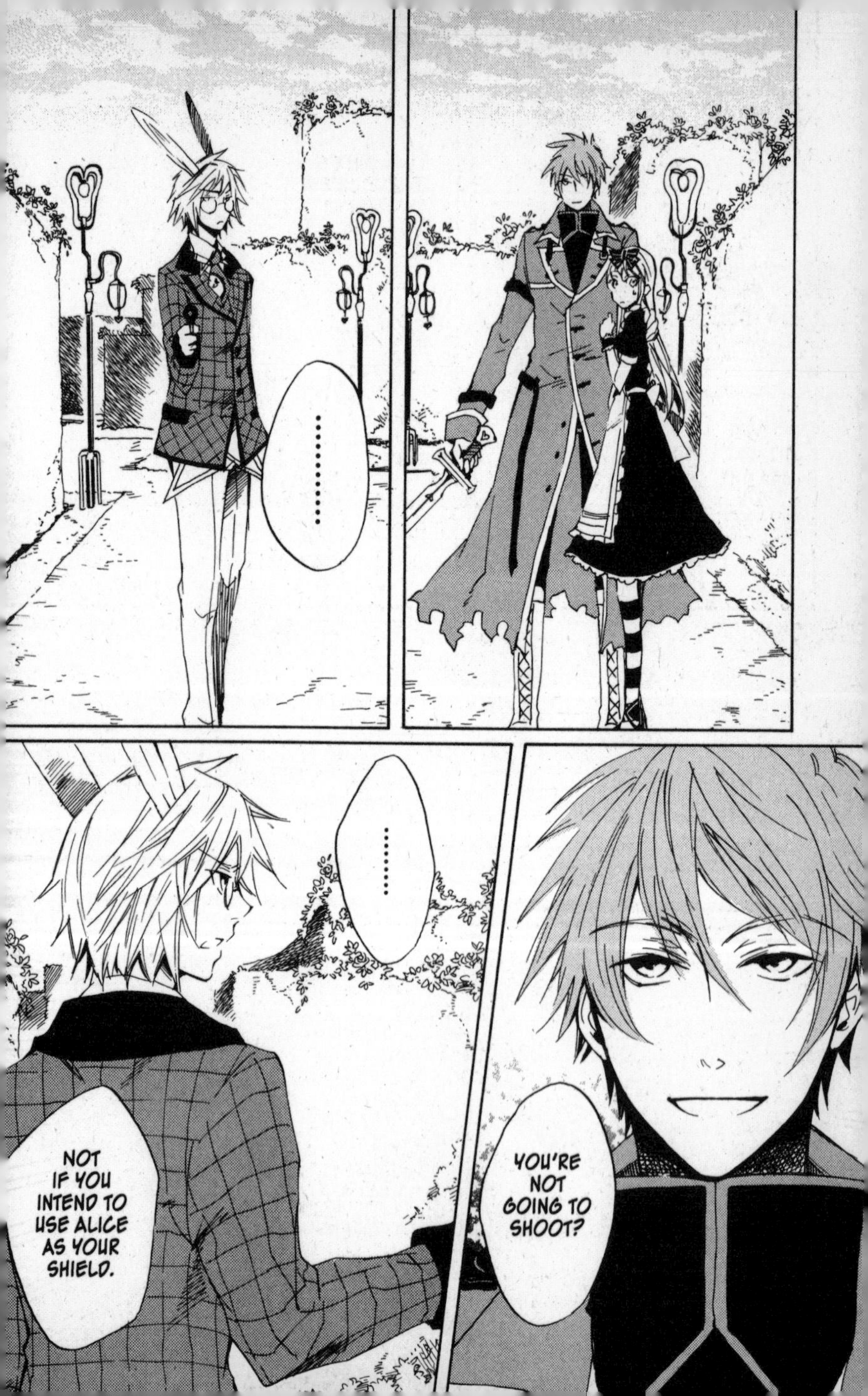
......
......
YOU'RE NOT GOING TO SHOOT?
NOT IF YOU INTEND TO USE ALICE AS YOUR SHIELD.

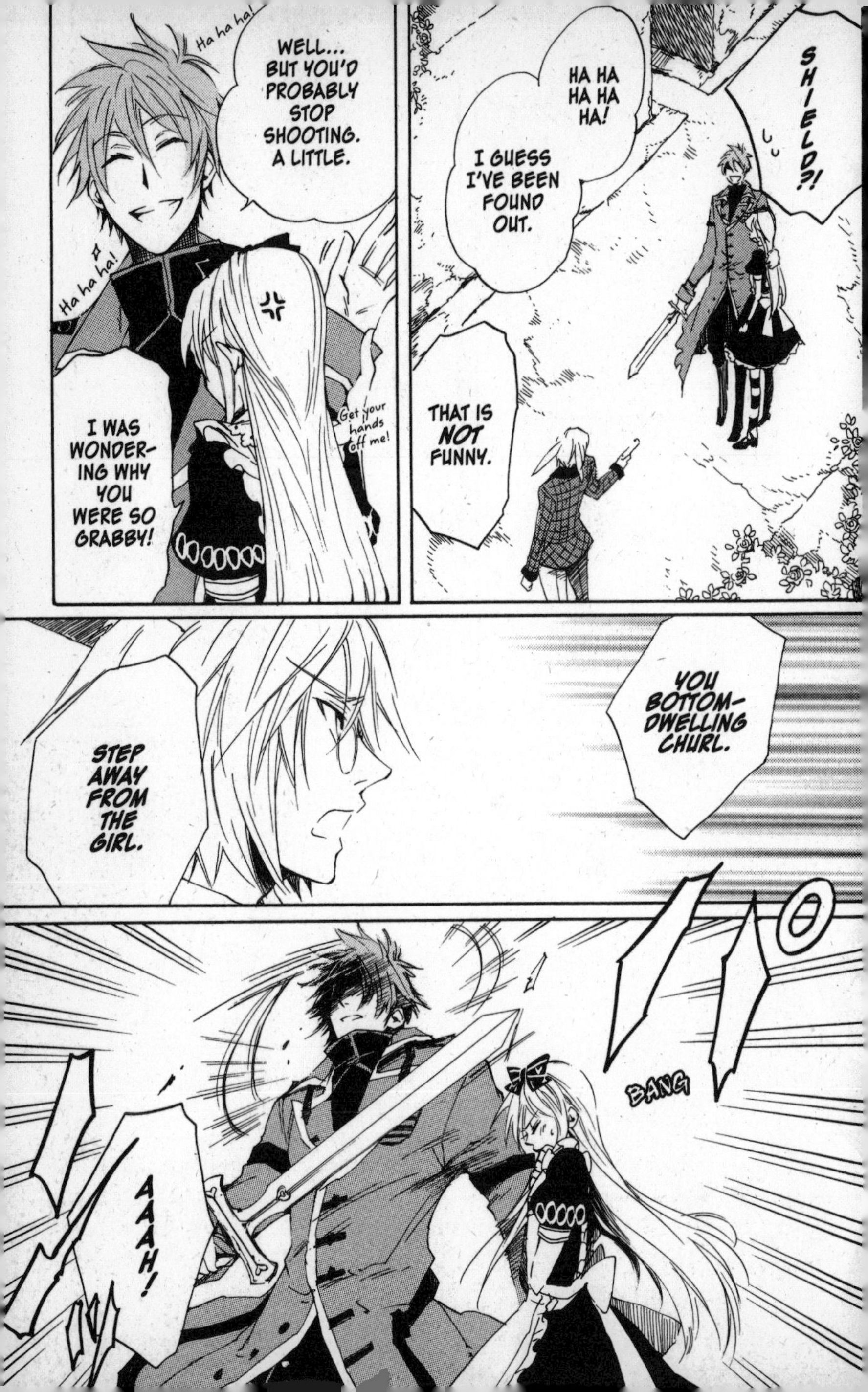

SHIELD?!
HA HA HA HA HA!
I GUESS I'VE BEEN FOUND OUT.
THAT IS NOT FUNNY.
Ha ha ha!
WELL... BUT YOU'D PROBABLY STOP SHOOTING. A LITTLE.
Ha ha ha!
Get your hands off me!
I WAS WONDERING WHY YOU WERE SO GRABBY!
YOU BOTTOM-DWELLING CHURL.
STEP AWAY FROM THE GIRL.
BANG
AAAH!

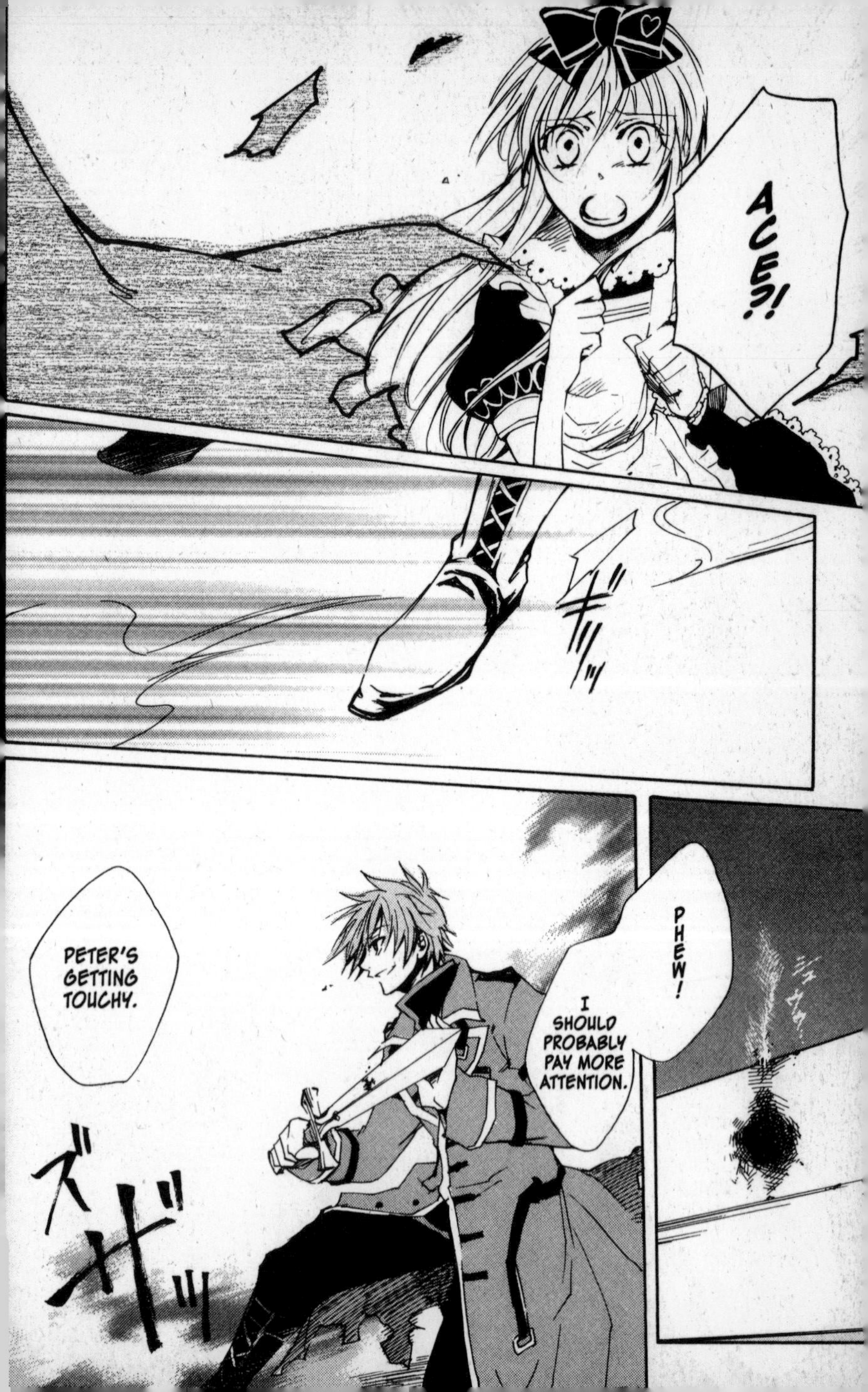
ACES?!
PHEW!
I SHOULD PROBABLY PAY MORE ATTENTION.
PETER'S GETTING TOUCHY.

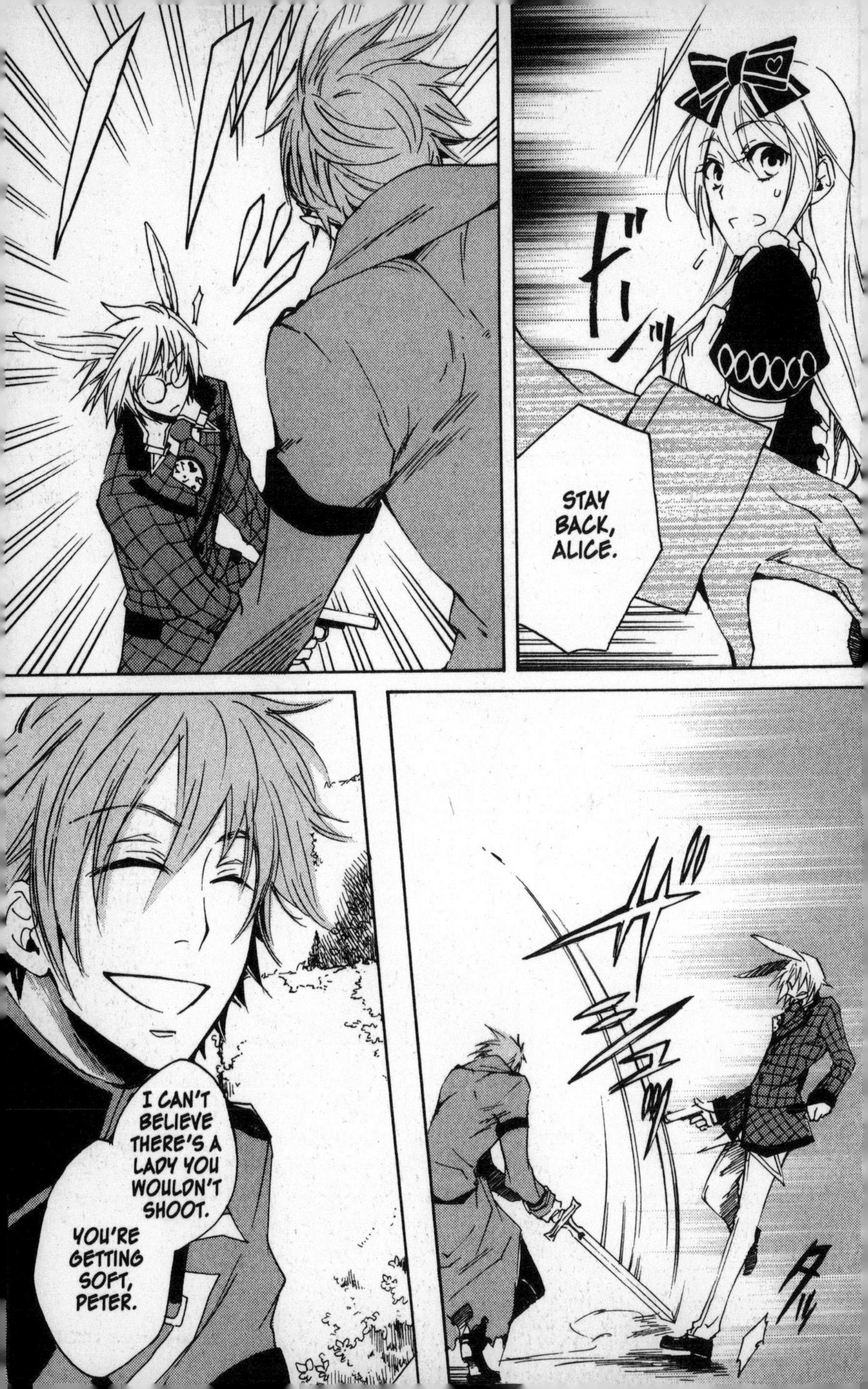
STAY BACK, ALICE.
I CAN'T BELIEVE THERE'S A LADY YOU WOULDN'T SHOOT.
YOU'RE GETTING SOFT, PETER.

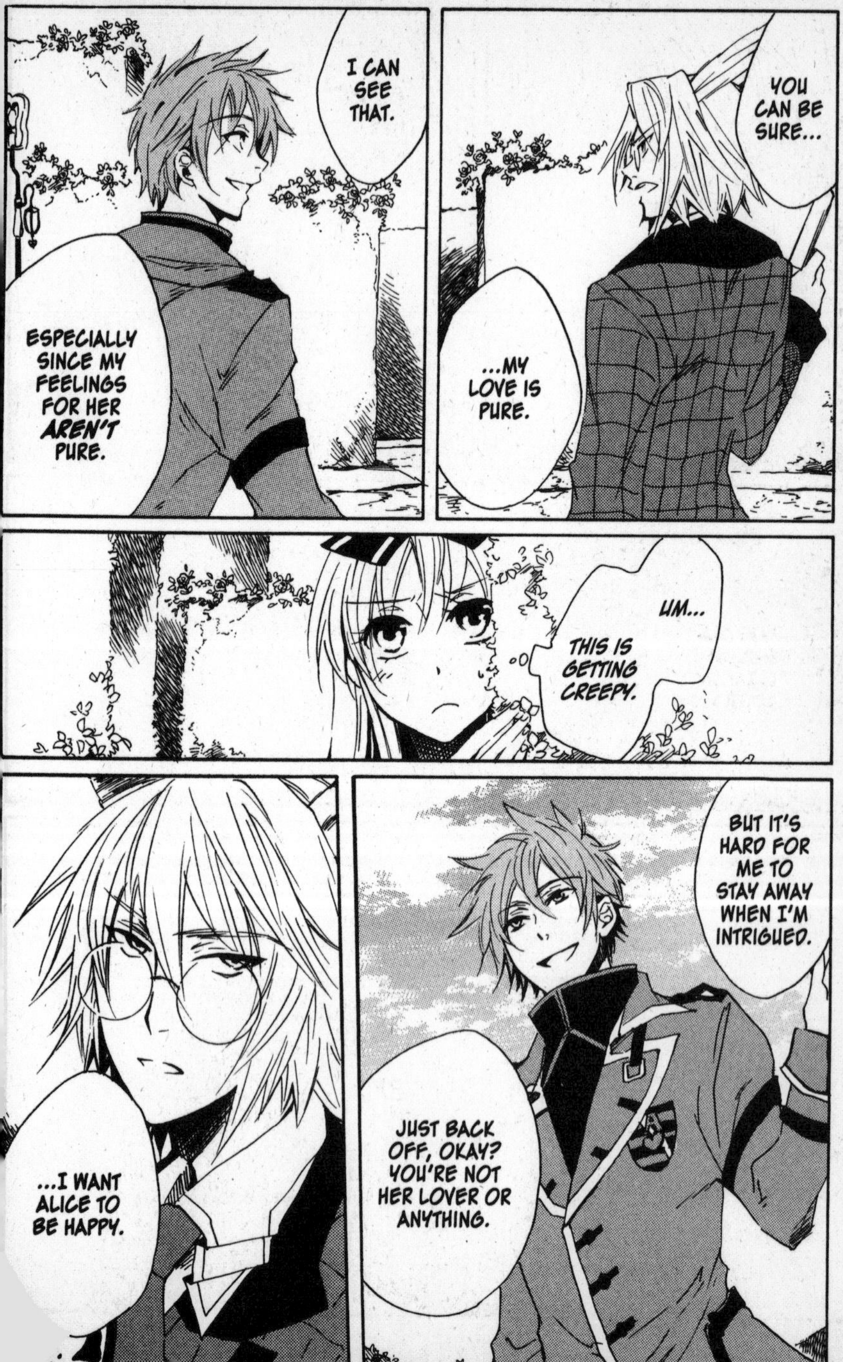
YOU CAN BE SURE...
...MY LOVE IS PURE.
I CAN SEE THAT.
ESPECIALLY SINCE MY FEELINGS FOR HER *AREN'T* PURE.
UM... THIS IS GETTING CREEPY.
BUT IT'S HARD FOR ME TO STAY AWAY WHEN I'M INTRIGUED.
JUST BACK OFF, OKAY? YOU'RE NOT HER LOVER OR ANYTHING.
...I WANT ALICE TO BE HAPPY.

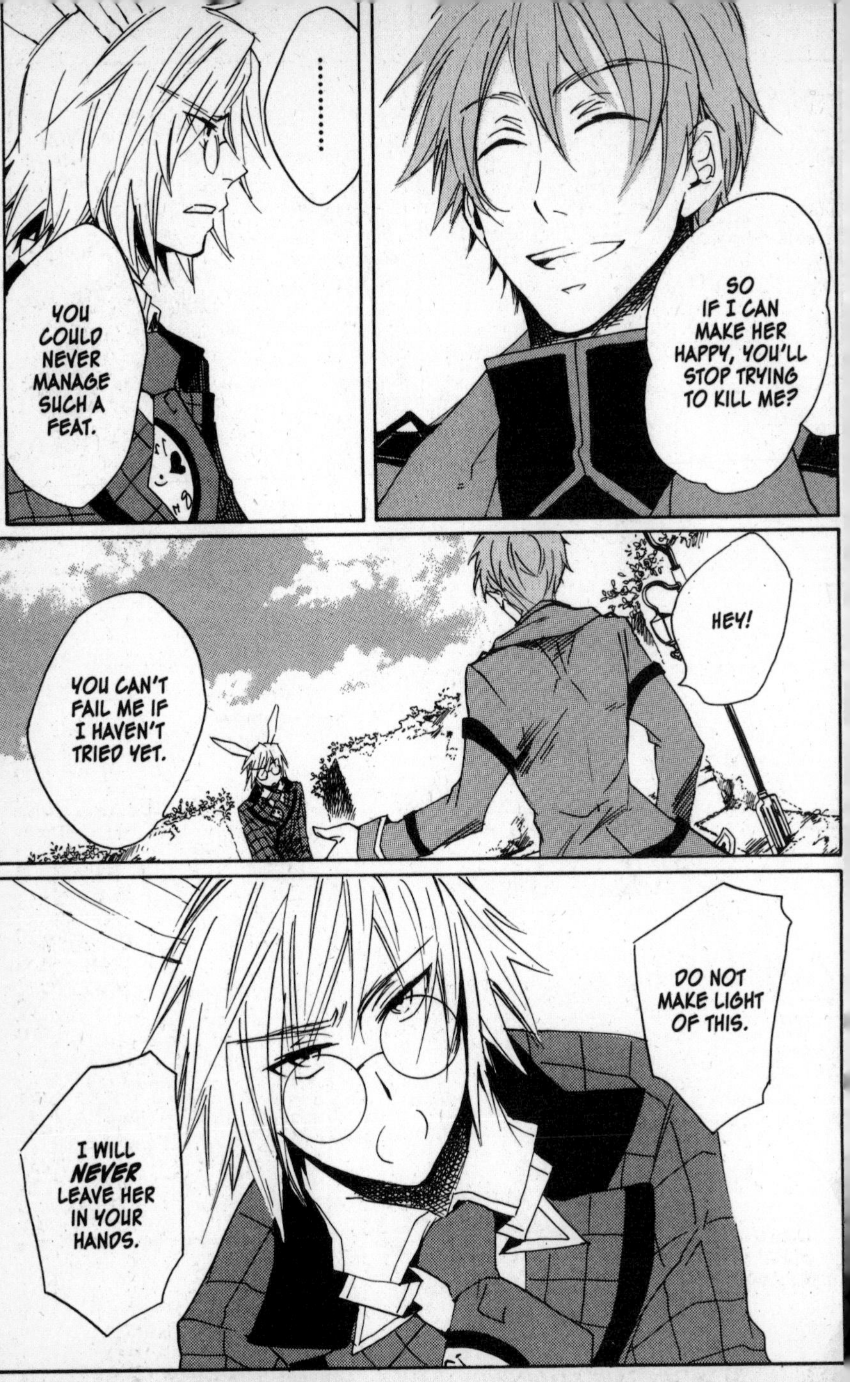
SO IF I CAN MAKE HER HAPPY, YOU'LL STOP TRYING TO KILL ME?
......
YOU COULD NEVER MANAGE SUCH A FEAT.
HEY!
YOU CAN'T FAIL ME IF I HAVEN'T TRIED YET.
DO NOT MAKE LIGHT OF THIS.
I WILL *NEVER* LEAVE HER IN YOUR HANDS.

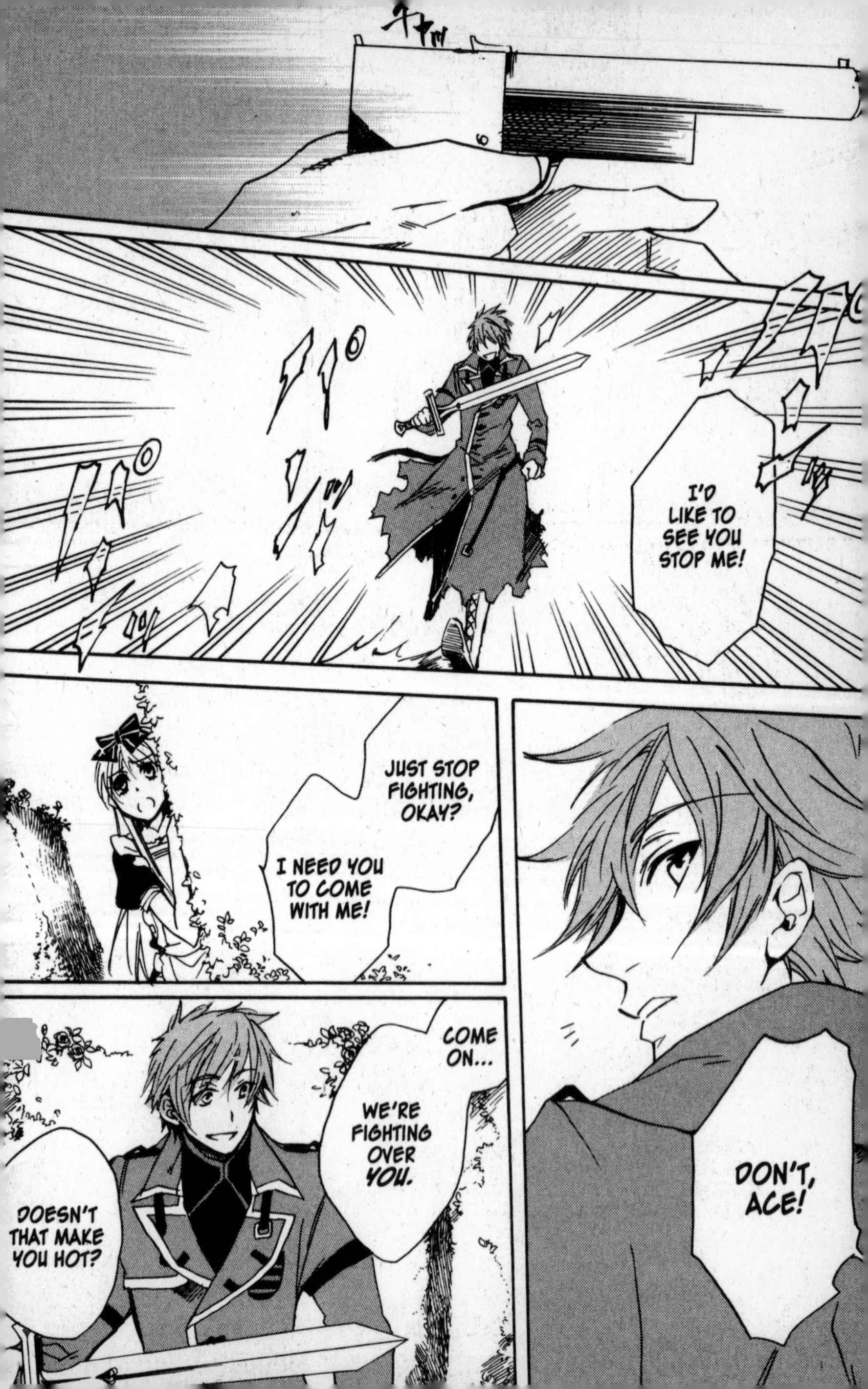
I'D LIKE TO SEE YOU STOP ME!
DON'T, ACE!
JUST STOP FIGHTING, OKAY?
I NEED YOU TO COME WITH ME!
COME ON...
WE'RE FIGHTING OVER YOU.
DOESN'T THAT MAKE YOU HOT?

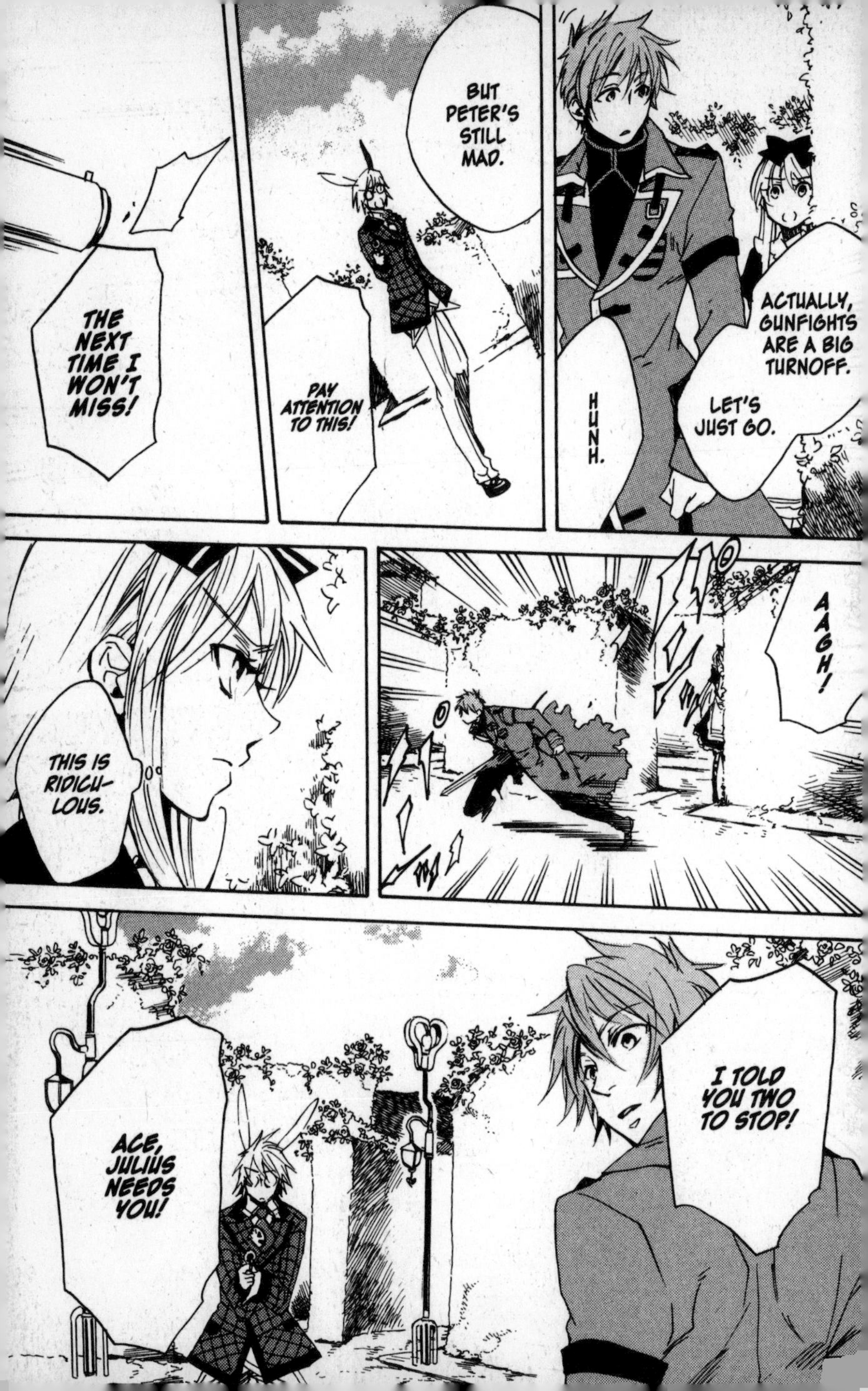
ACTUALLY, GUNFIGHTS ARE A BIG TURNOFF.
LET'S JUST GO.
HUNH.
BUT PETER'S STILL MAD.
PAY ATTENTION TO THIS!
THE NEXT TIME I WON'T MISS!
AAGH!
THIS IS RIDICULOUS.
I TOLD YOU TWO TO STOP!
ACE, JULIUS NEEDS YOU!

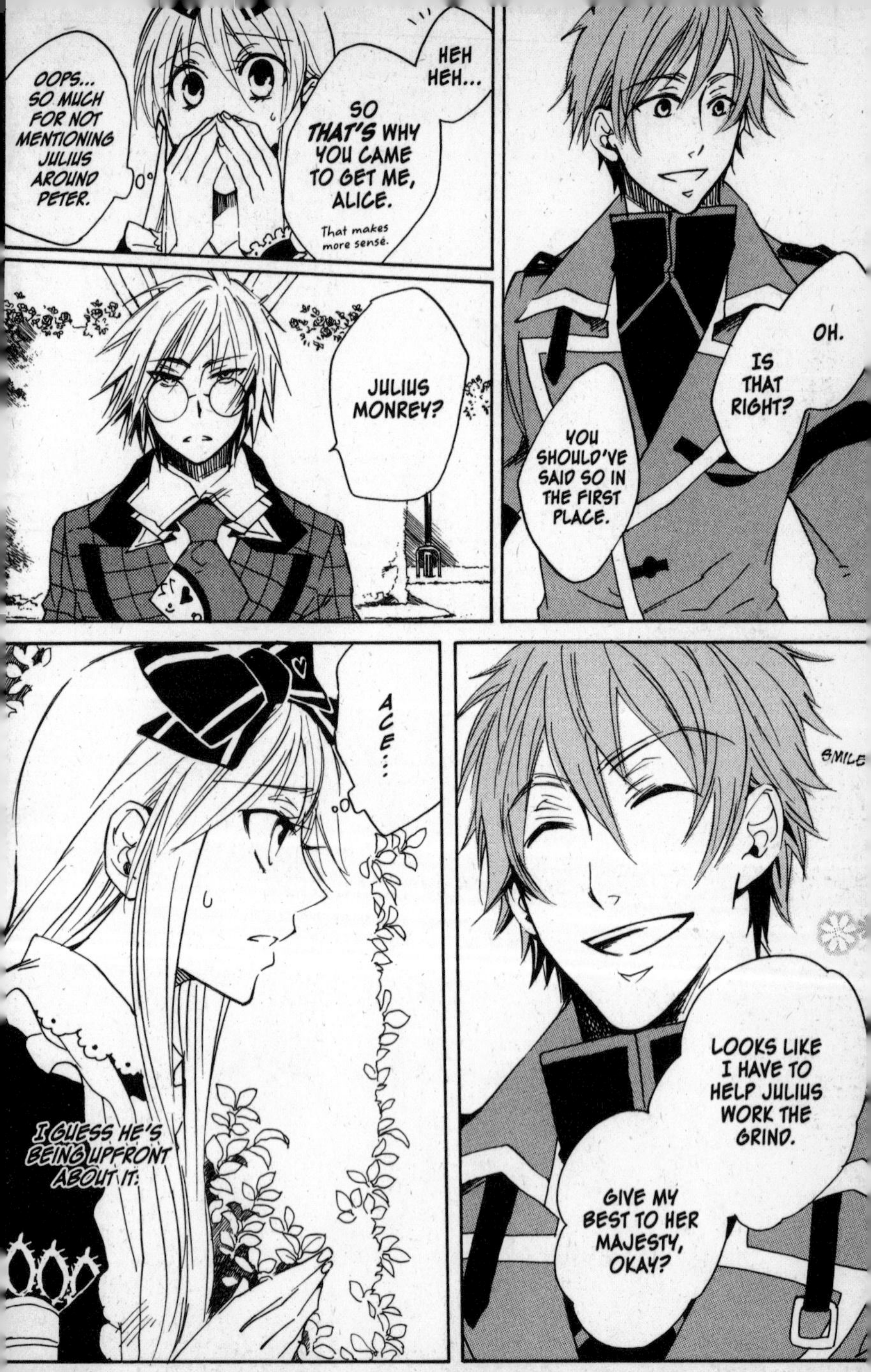
OH.
IS THAT RIGHT?
YOU SHOULD'VE SAID SO IN THE FIRST PLACE.
HEH HEH...
SO THAT'S WHY YOU CAME TO GET ME, ALICE.
That makes more sense.
OOPS... SO MUCH FOR NOT MENTIONING JULIUS AROUND PETER.
JULIUS MONREY?
SMILE
LOOKS LIKE I HAVE TO HELP JULIUS WORK THE GRIND.
GIVE MY BEST TO HER MAJESTY, OKAY?
ACE...
I GUESS HE'S BEING UPFRONT ABOUT IT.

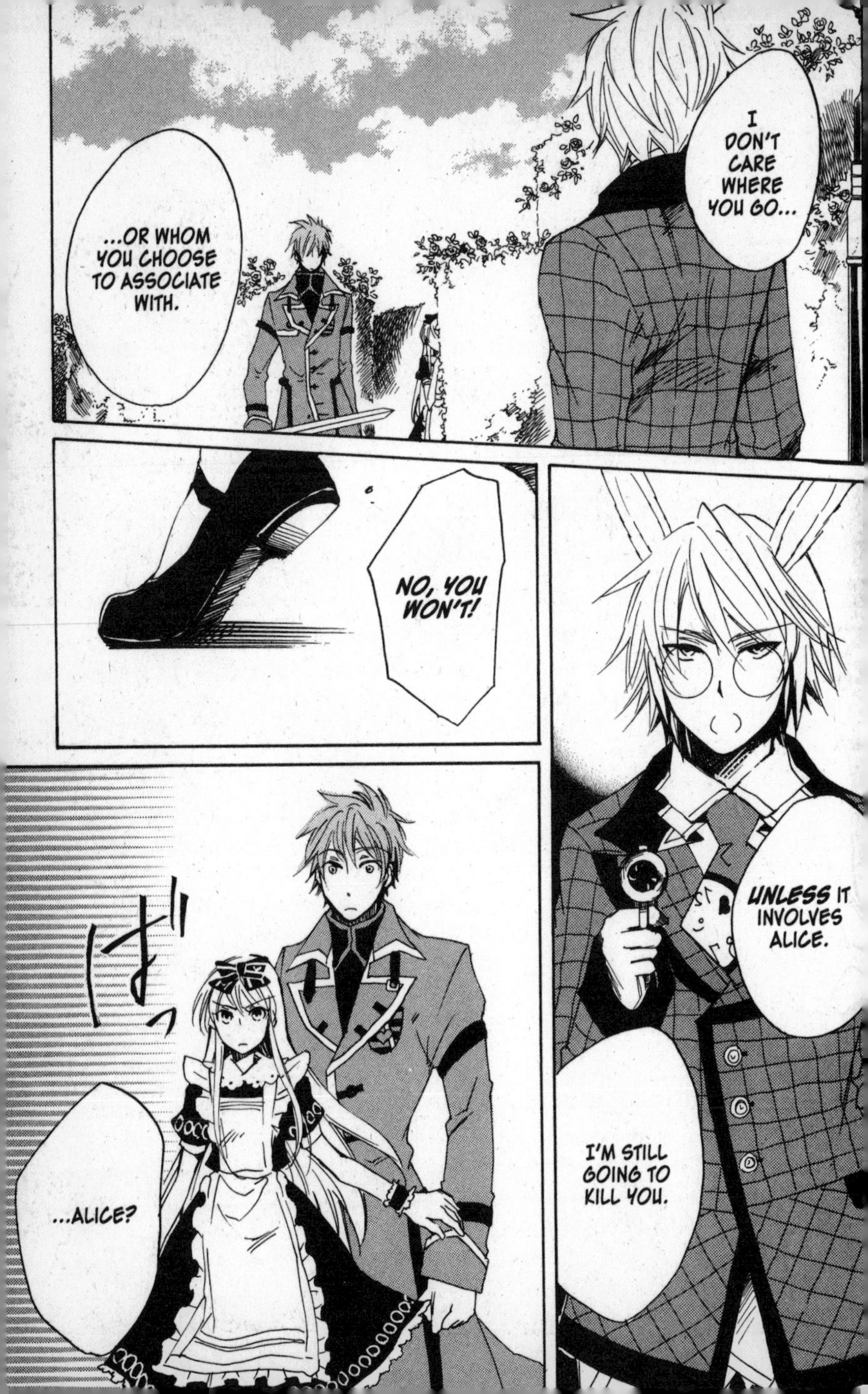
I DON'T CARE WHERE YOU GO...
...OR WHOM YOU CHOOSE TO ASSOCIATE WITH.
UNLESS IT INVOLVES ALICE.
I'M STILL GOING TO KILL YOU.
NO, YOU WON'T!
ばっ
...ALICE?

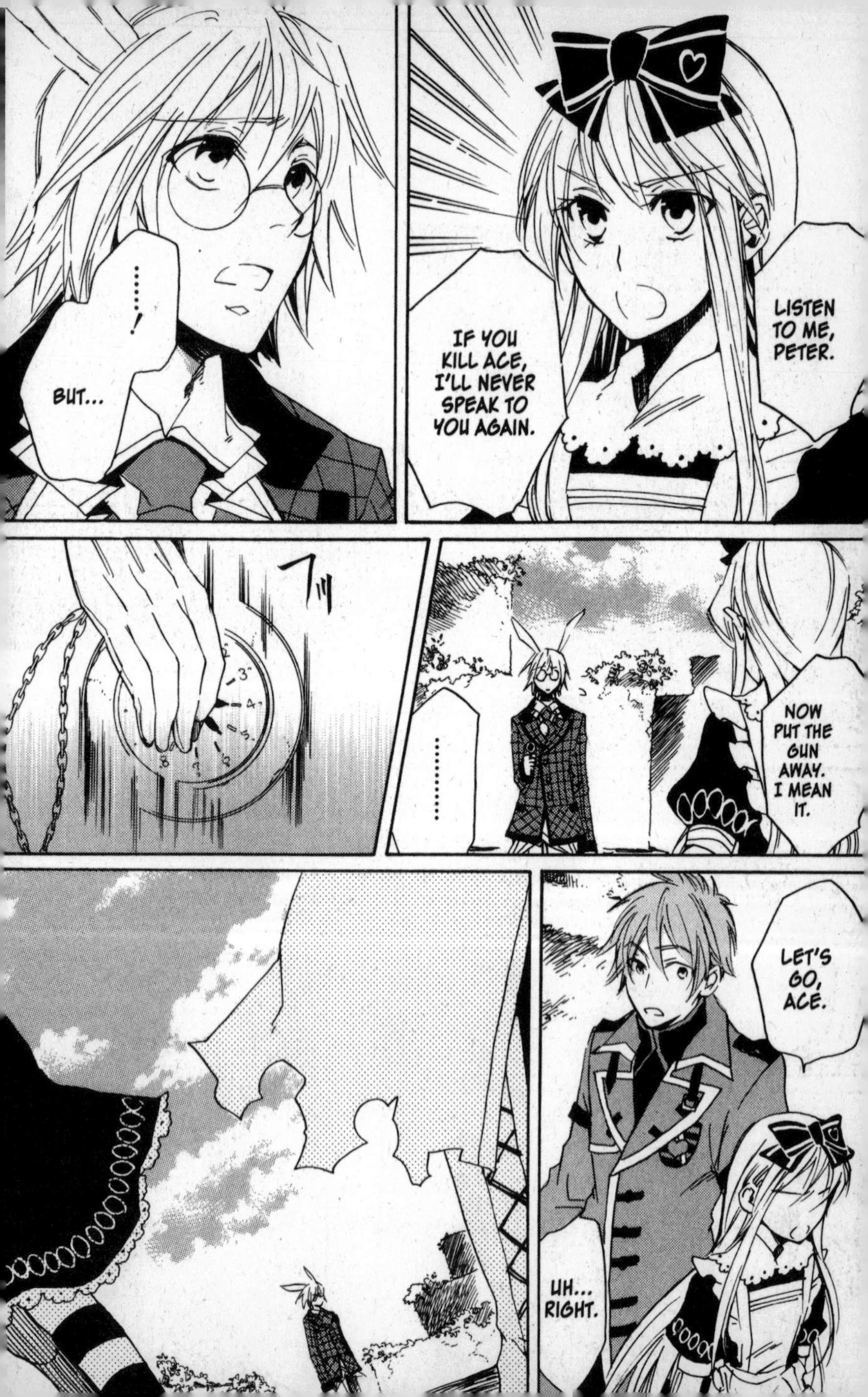
LISTEN TO ME, PETER.
IF YOU KILL ACE, I'LL NEVER SPEAK TO YOU AGAIN.
......!
BUT...
NOW PUT THE GUN AWAY. I MEAN IT.
.........
フッ
LET'S GO, ACE.
UH... RIGHT.

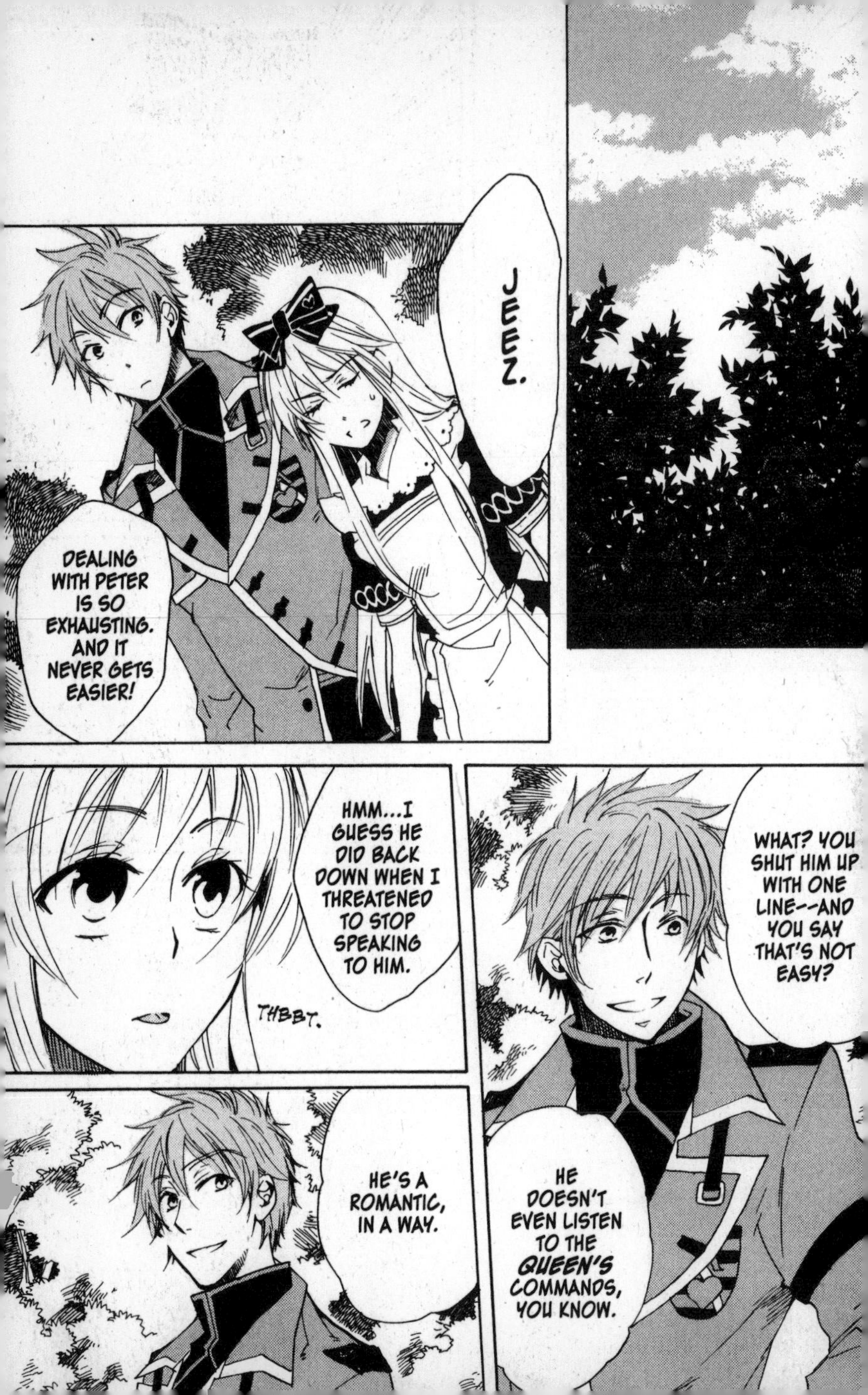
JEEZ.
DEALING WITH PETER IS SO EXHAUSTING. AND IT NEVER GETS EASIER!
WHAT? YOU SHUT HIM UP WITH ONE LINE--AND YOU SAY THAT'S NOT EASY?
HE DOESN'T EVEN LISTEN TO THE *QUEEN'S* COMMANDS, YOU KNOW.
HMM...I GUESS HE DID BACK DOWN WHEN I THREATENED TO STOP SPEAKING TO HIM.
THBBT.
HE'S A ROMANTIC, IN A WAY.

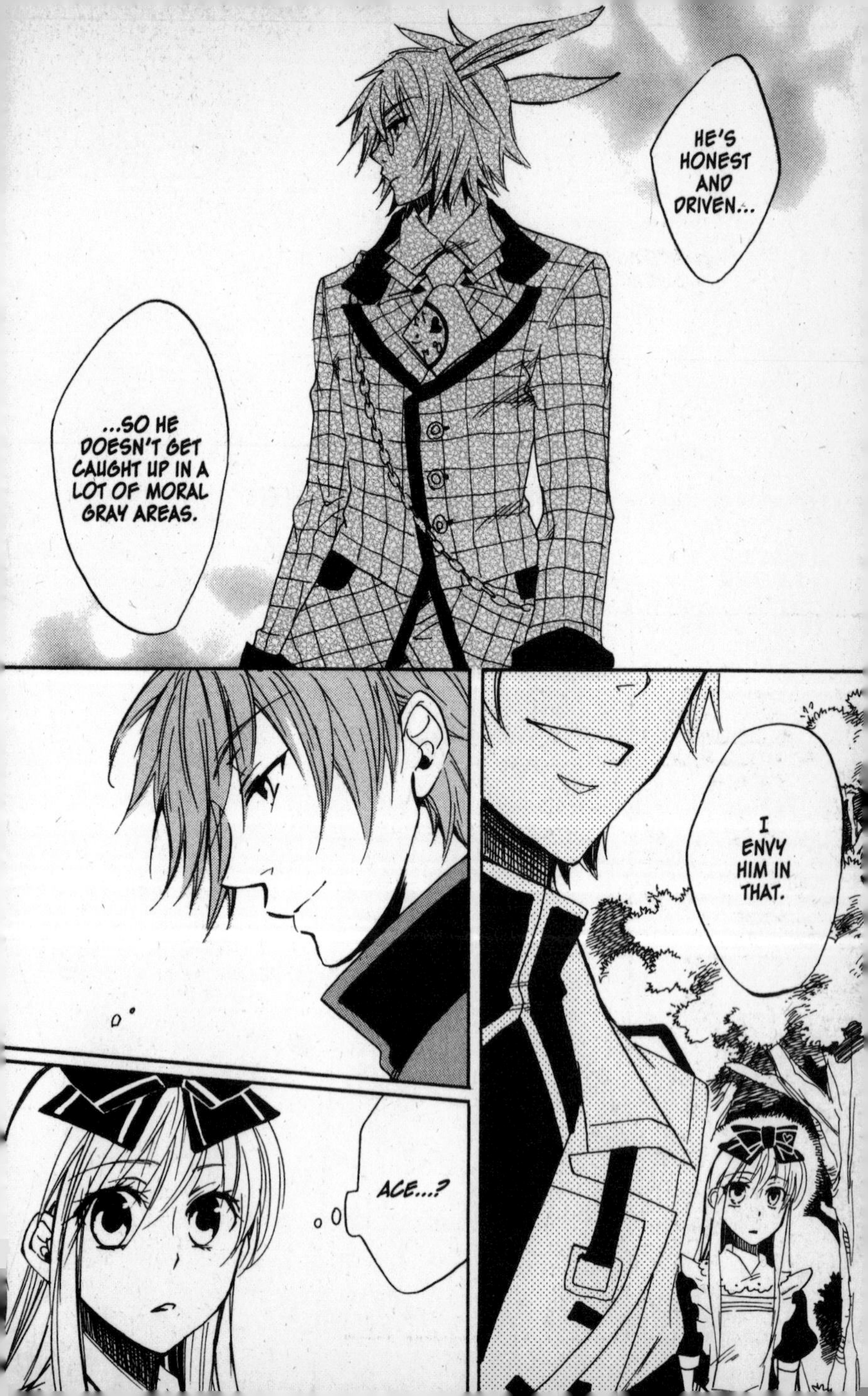
HE'S HONEST AND DRIVEN...
...SO HE DOESN'T GET CAUGHT UP IN A LOT OF MORAL GRAY AREAS.
I ENVY HIM IN THAT.
ACE...?

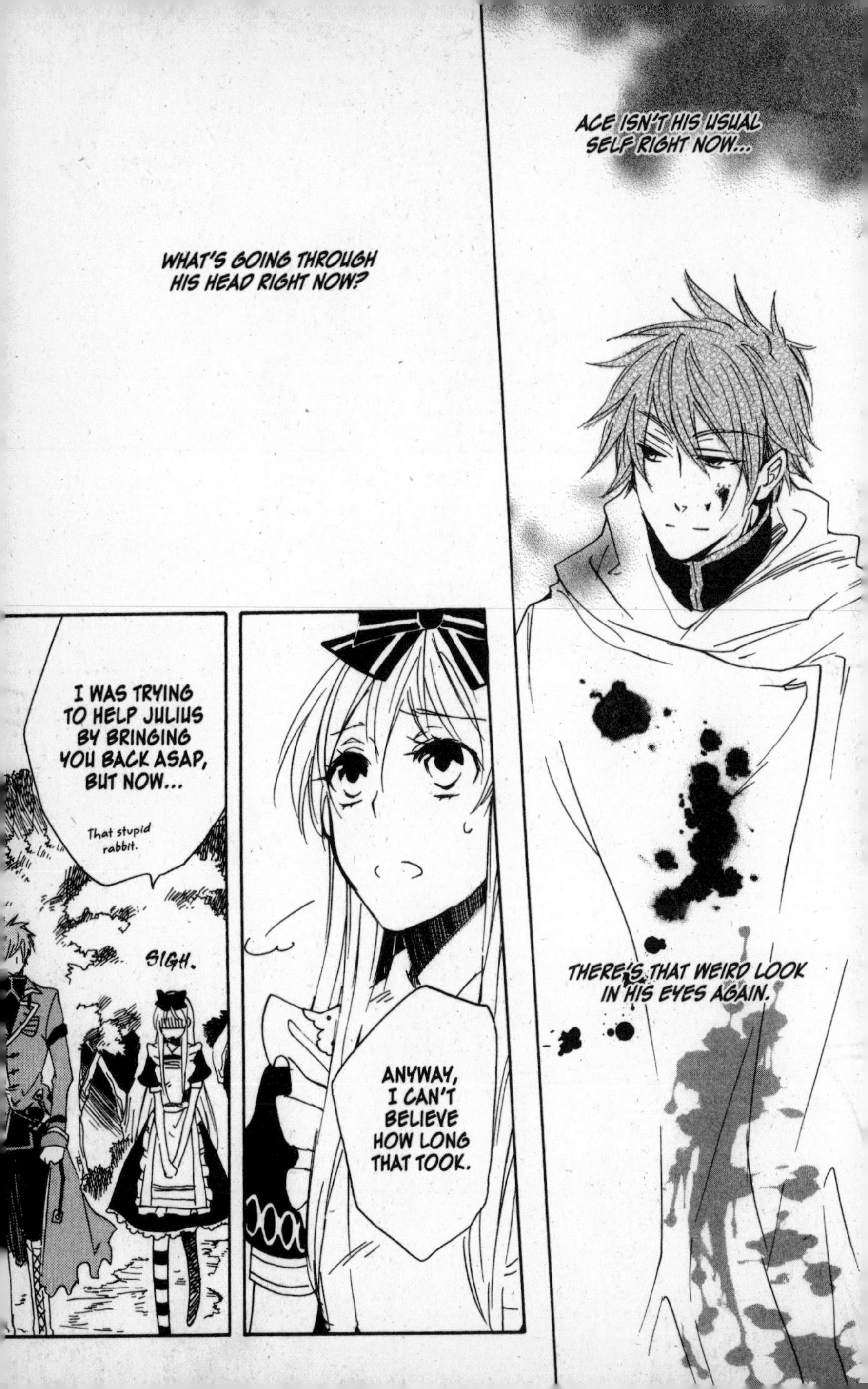
ACE ISN'T HIS USUAL SELF RIGHT NOW...
THERE'S THAT WEIRD LOOK IN HIS EYES AGAIN.
WHAT'S GOING THROUGH HIS HEAD RIGHT NOW?
ANYWAY, I CAN'T BELIEVE HOW LONG THAT TOOK.
I WAS TRYING TO HELP JULIUS BY BRINGING YOU BACK ASAP, BUT NOW...
That stupid rabbit.
SIGH.

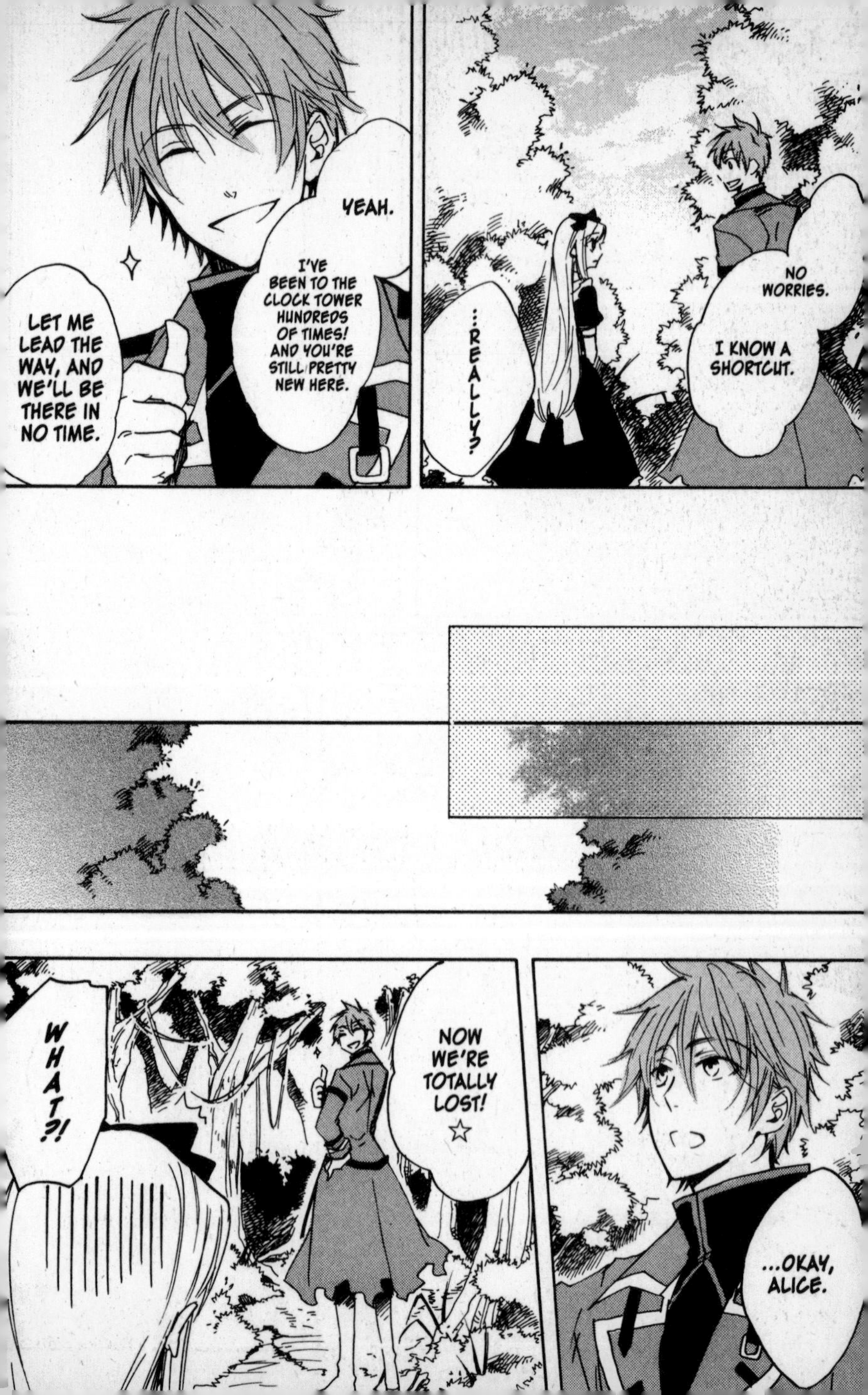
NO WORRIES.
I KNOW A SHORTCUT.
...REALLY?
YEAH.
I'VE BEEN TO THE CLOCK TOWER HUNDREDS OF TIMES! AND YOU'RE STILL PRETTY NEW HERE.
LET ME LEAD THE WAY, AND WE'LL BE THERE IN NO TIME.
...OKAY, ALICE.
NOW WE'RE TOTALLY LOST! ☆
WHAT?!

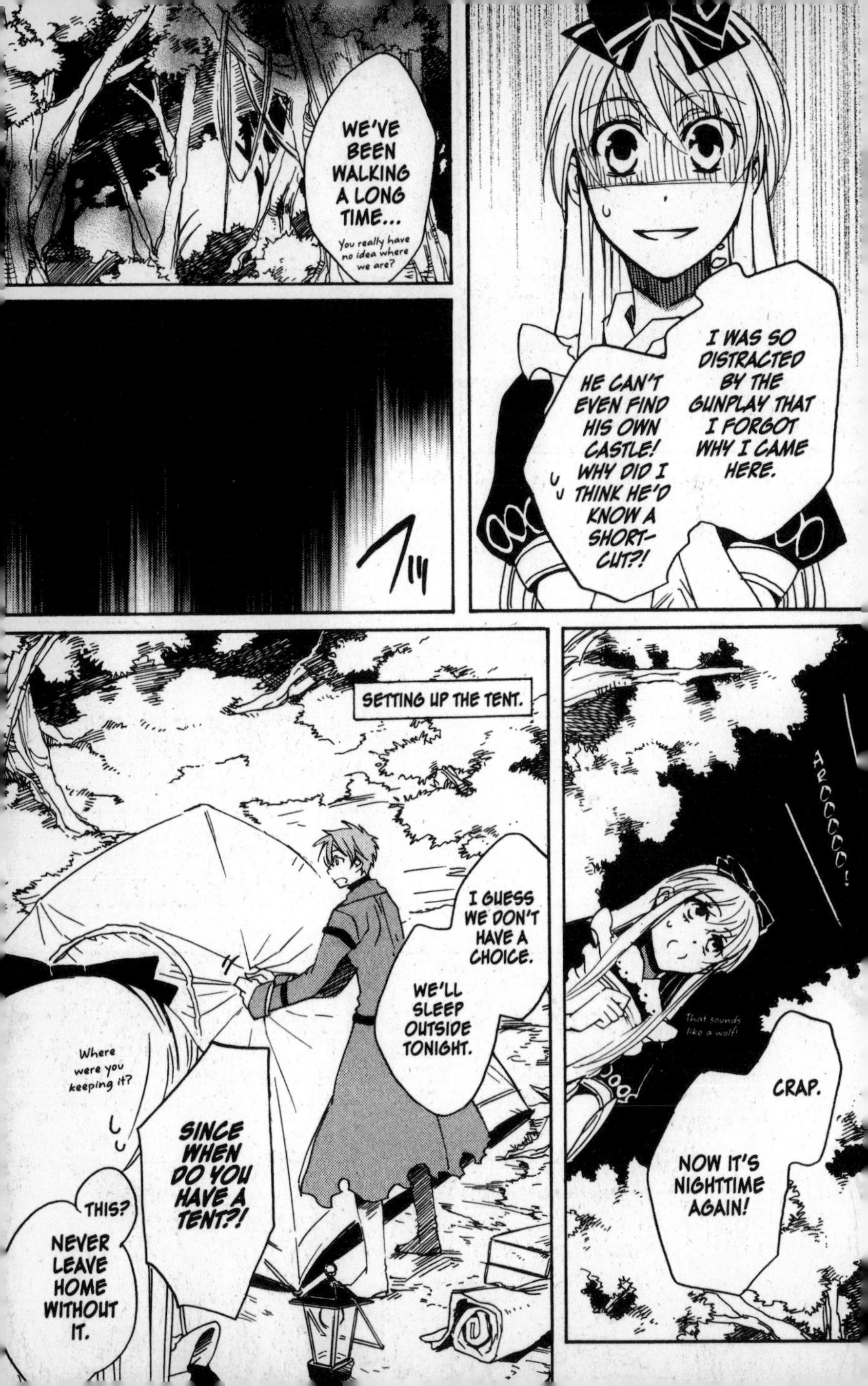
I WAS SO DISTRACTED BY THE GUNPLAY THAT I FORGOT WHY I CAME HERE.
HE CAN'T EVEN FIND HIS OWN CASTLE! WHY DID I THINK HE'D KNOW A SHORTCUT?!
WE'VE BEEN WALKING A LONG TIME...
You really have no idea where we are?
AROOOOO!
That sounds like a wolf!
CRAP.
NOW IT'S NIGHTTIME AGAIN!
SETTING UP THE TENT.
I GUESS WE DON'T HAVE A CHOICE.
WE'LL SLEEP OUTSIDE TONIGHT.
SINCE WHEN DO YOU HAVE A TENT?!
Where were you keeping it?
THIS? NEVER LEAVE HOME WITHOUT IT.

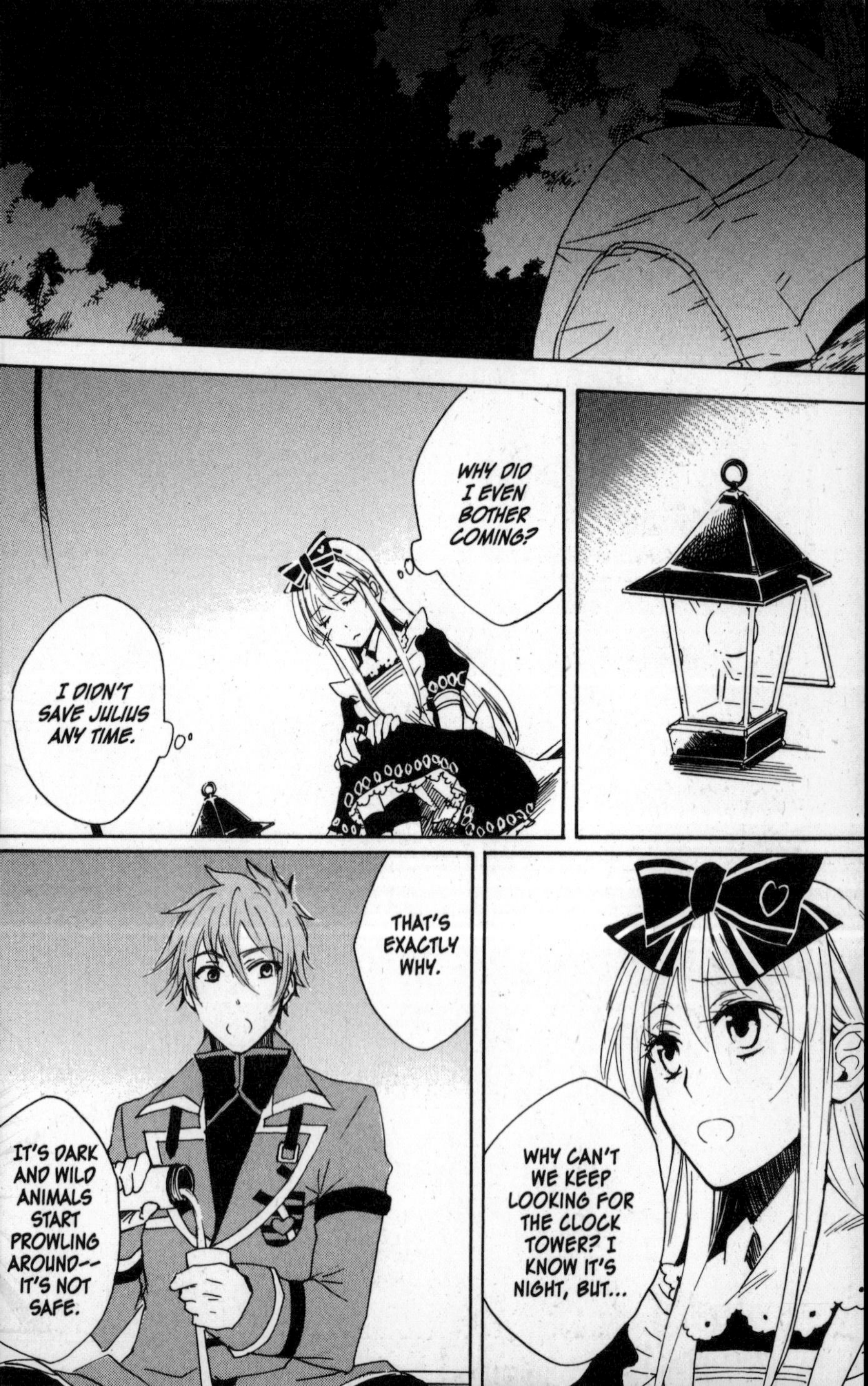
WHY DID I EVEN BOTHER COMING?
I DIDN'T SAVE JULIUS ANY TIME.
WHY CAN'T WE KEEP LOOKING FOR THE CLOCK TOWER? I KNOW IT'S NIGHT, BUT...
THAT'S EXACTLY WHY.
IT'S DARK AND WILD ANIMALS START PROWLING AROUND--IT'S NOT SAFE.

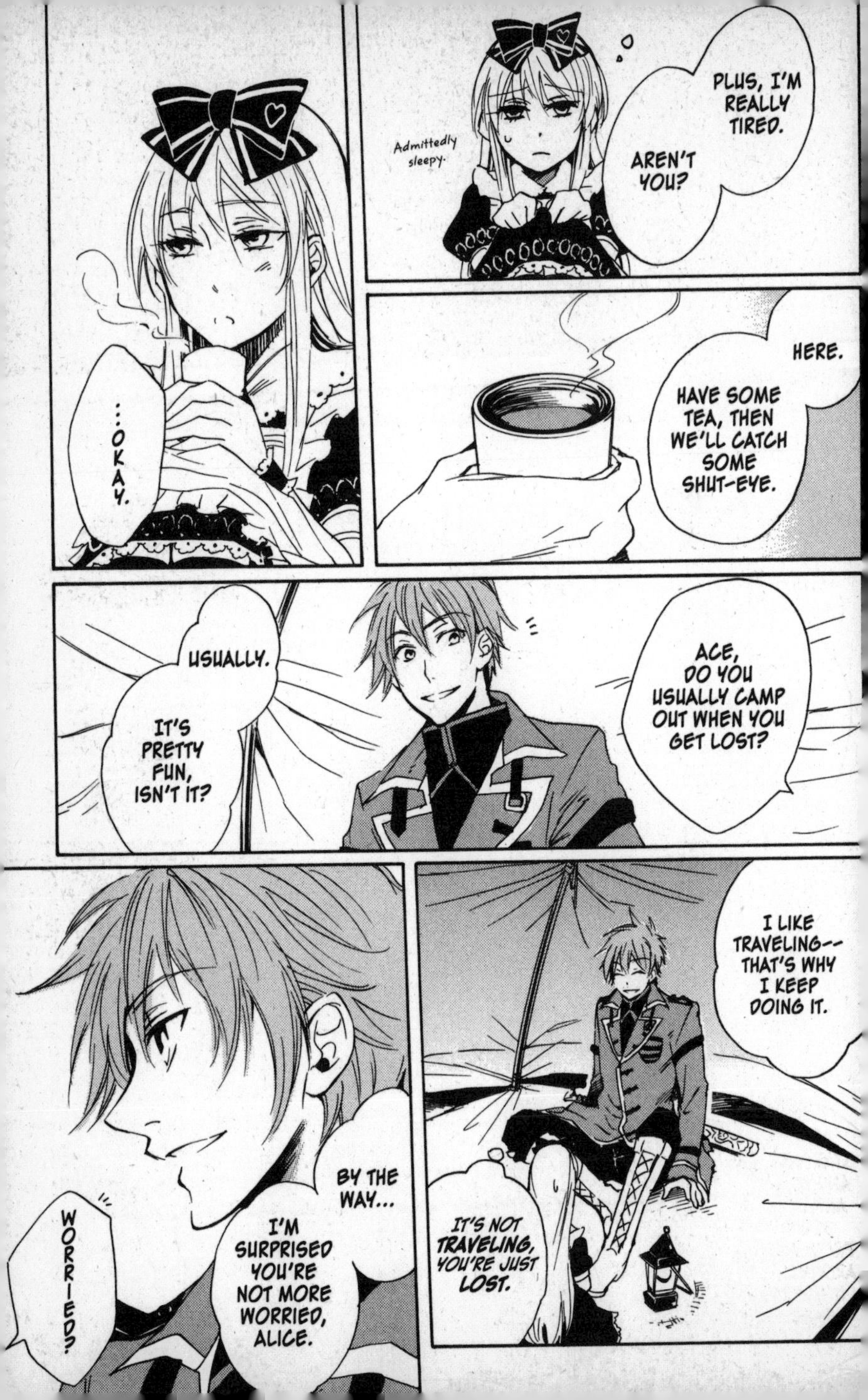
PLUS, I'M REALLY TIRED.
AREN'T YOU?
Admittedly sleepy.
HERE.
HAVE SOME TEA, THEN WE'LL CATCH SOME SHUT-EYE.
...OKAY.
ACE, DO YOU USUALLY CAMP OUT WHEN YOU GET LOST?
USUALLY.
IT'S PRETTY FUN, ISN'T IT?
I LIKE TRAVELING--THAT'S WHY I KEEP DOING IT.
IT'S NOT TRAVELING, YOU'RE JUST LOST.
BY THE WAY...
I'M SURPRISED YOU'RE NOT MORE WORRIED, ALICE.
WORRIED?

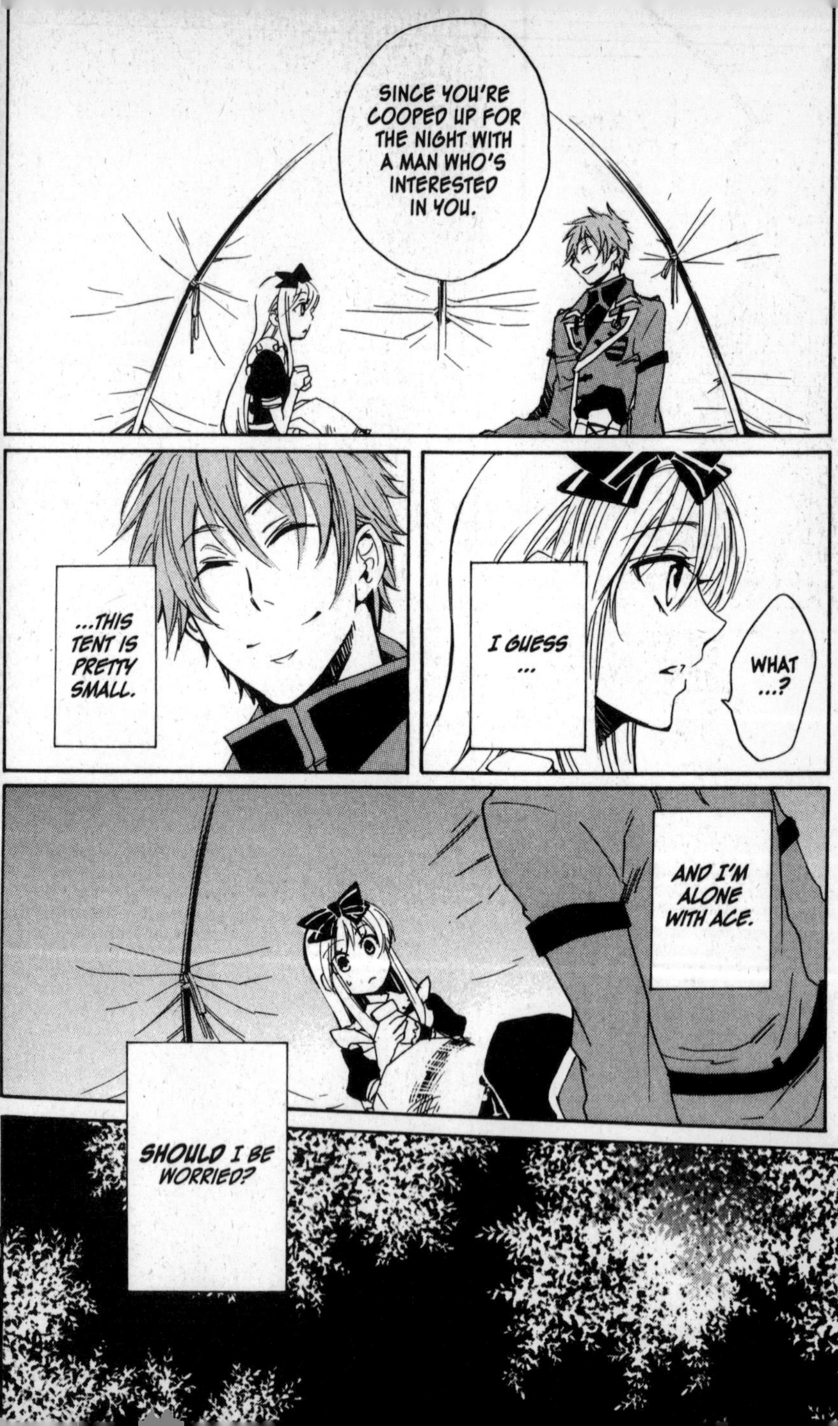
SINCE YOU'RE COOPED UP FOR THE NIGHT WITH A MAN WHO'S INTERESTED IN YOU.
WHAT ...?
I GUESS ...
...THIS TENT IS PRETTY SMALL.
AND I'M ALONE WITH ACE.
SHOULD I BE WORRIED?

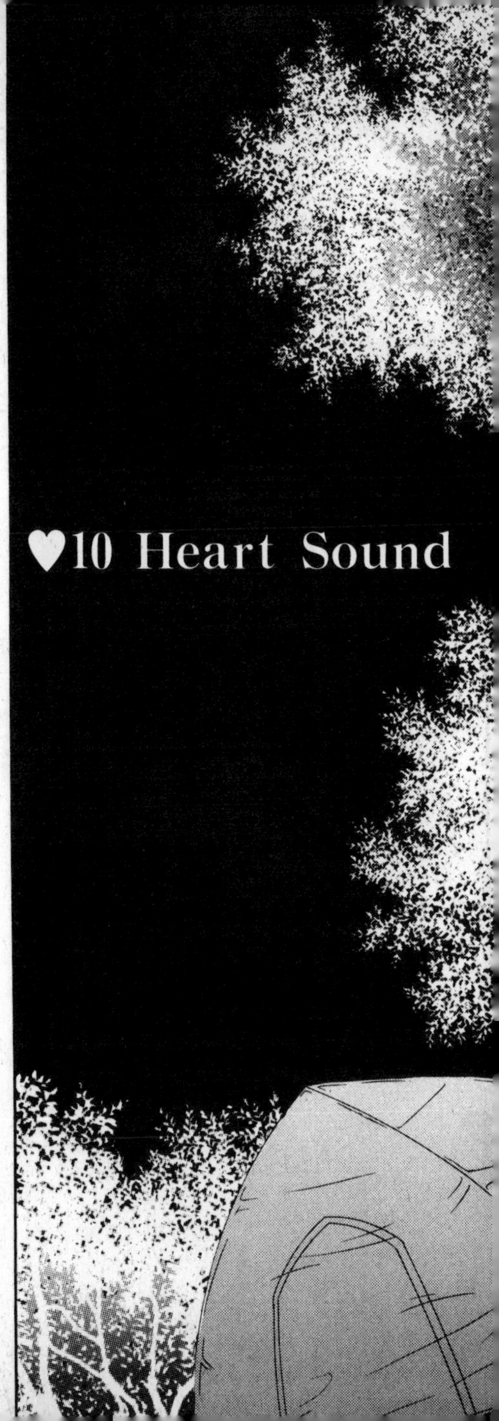
♥10 Heart Sound

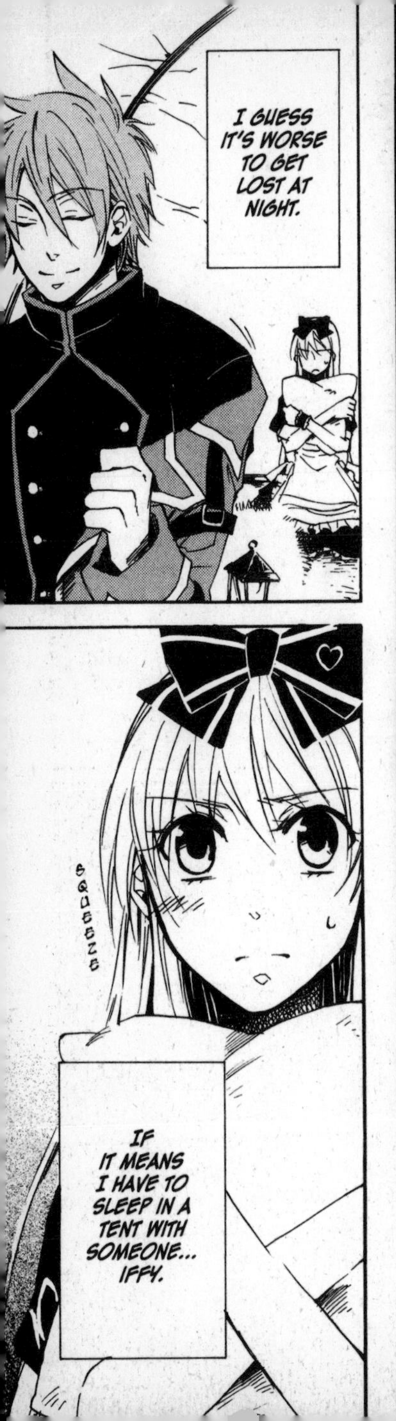
I GUESS IT'S WORSE TO GET LOST AT NIGHT.
SQUEEZE
IF IT MEANS I HAVE TO SLEEP IN A TENT WITH SOMEONE... IFFY.

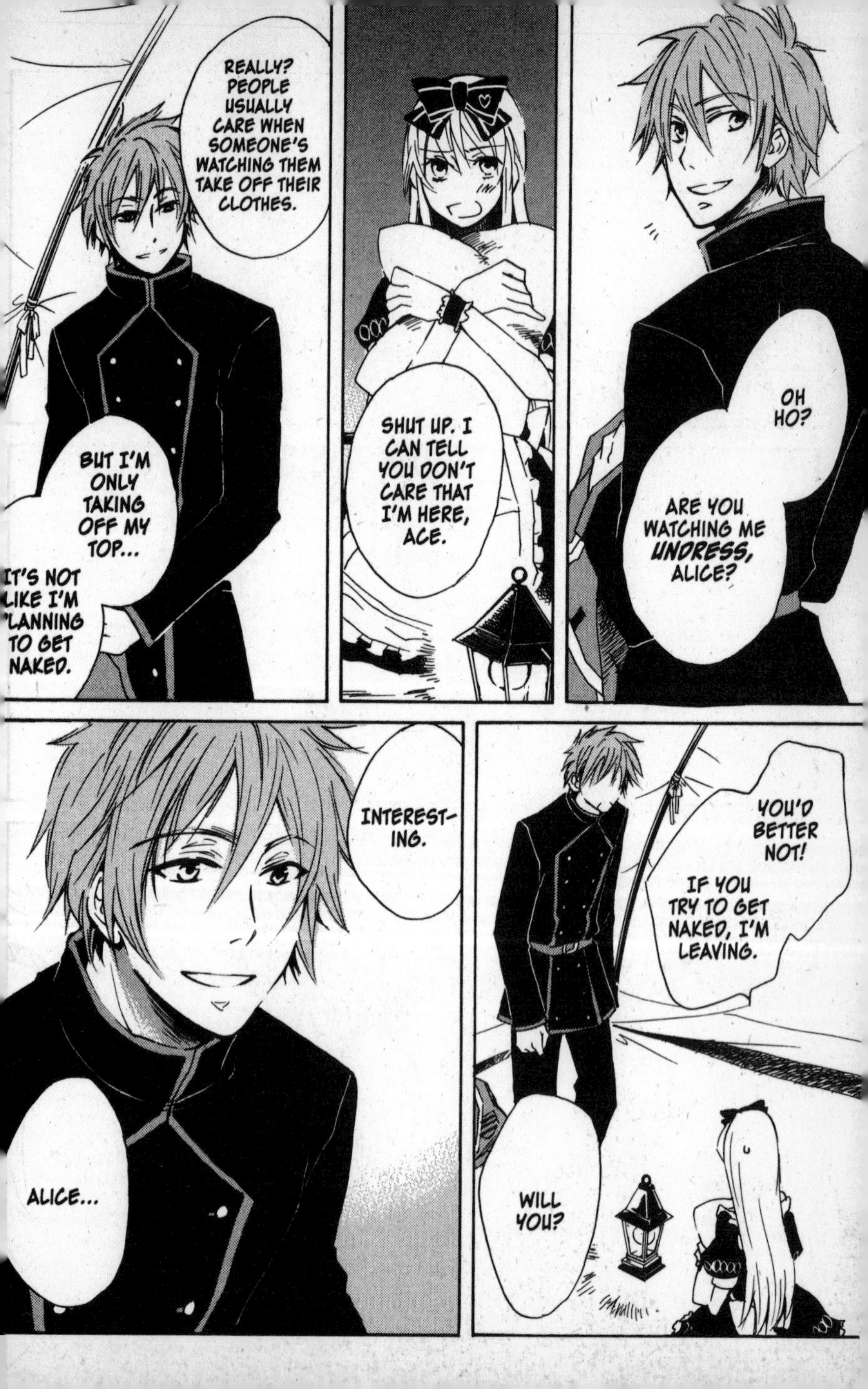
OH HO?
ARE YOU WATCHING ME UNDRESS, ALICE?
SHUT UP. I CAN TELL YOU DON'T CARE THAT I'M HERE, ACE.
REALLY? PEOPLE USUALLY CARE WHEN SOMEONE'S WATCHING THEM TAKE OFF THEIR CLOTHES.
BUT I'M ONLY TAKING OFF MY TOP...
IT'S NOT LIKE I'M PLANNING TO GET NAKED.
YOU'D BETTER NOT!
IF YOU TRY TO GET NAKED, I'M LEAVING.
WILL YOU?
INTEREST-ING.
ALICE...

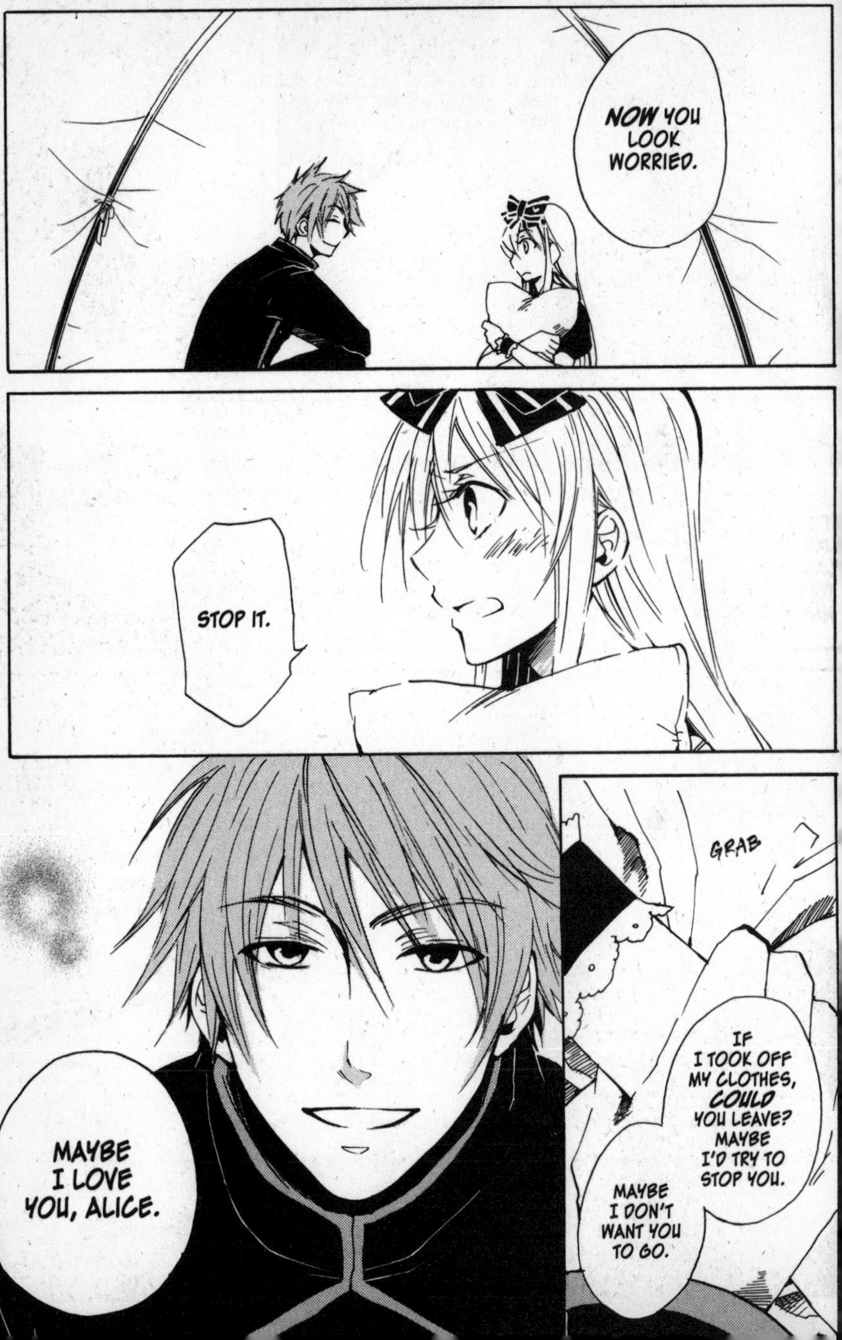
NOW YOU LOOK WORRIED.
STOP IT.
GRAB
IF I TOOK OFF MY CLOTHES, COULD YOU LEAVE? MAYBE I'D TRY TO STOP YOU.
MAYBE I DON'T WANT YOU TO GO.
MAYBE I LOVE YOU, ALICE.

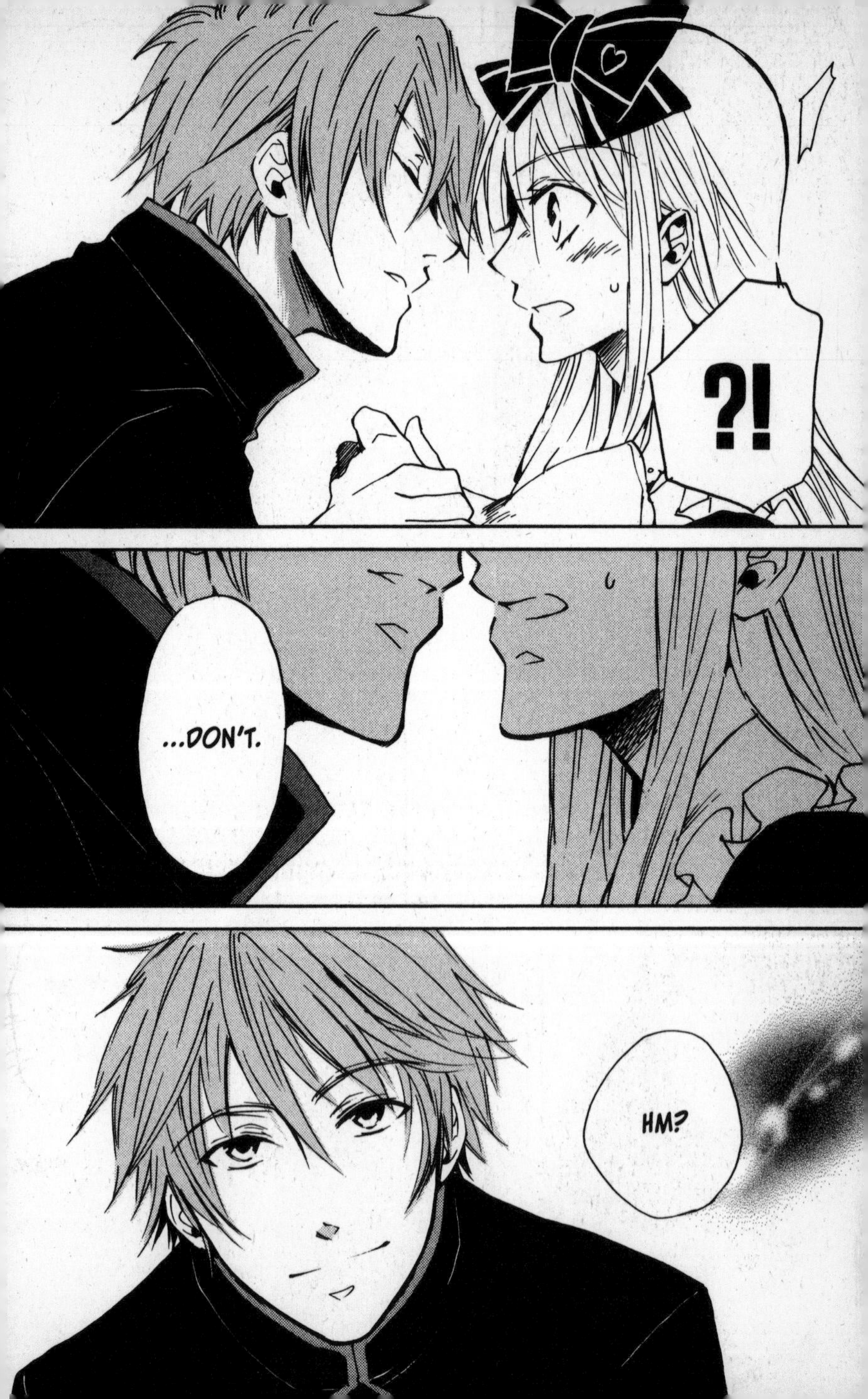
?!
...DON'T.
HM?

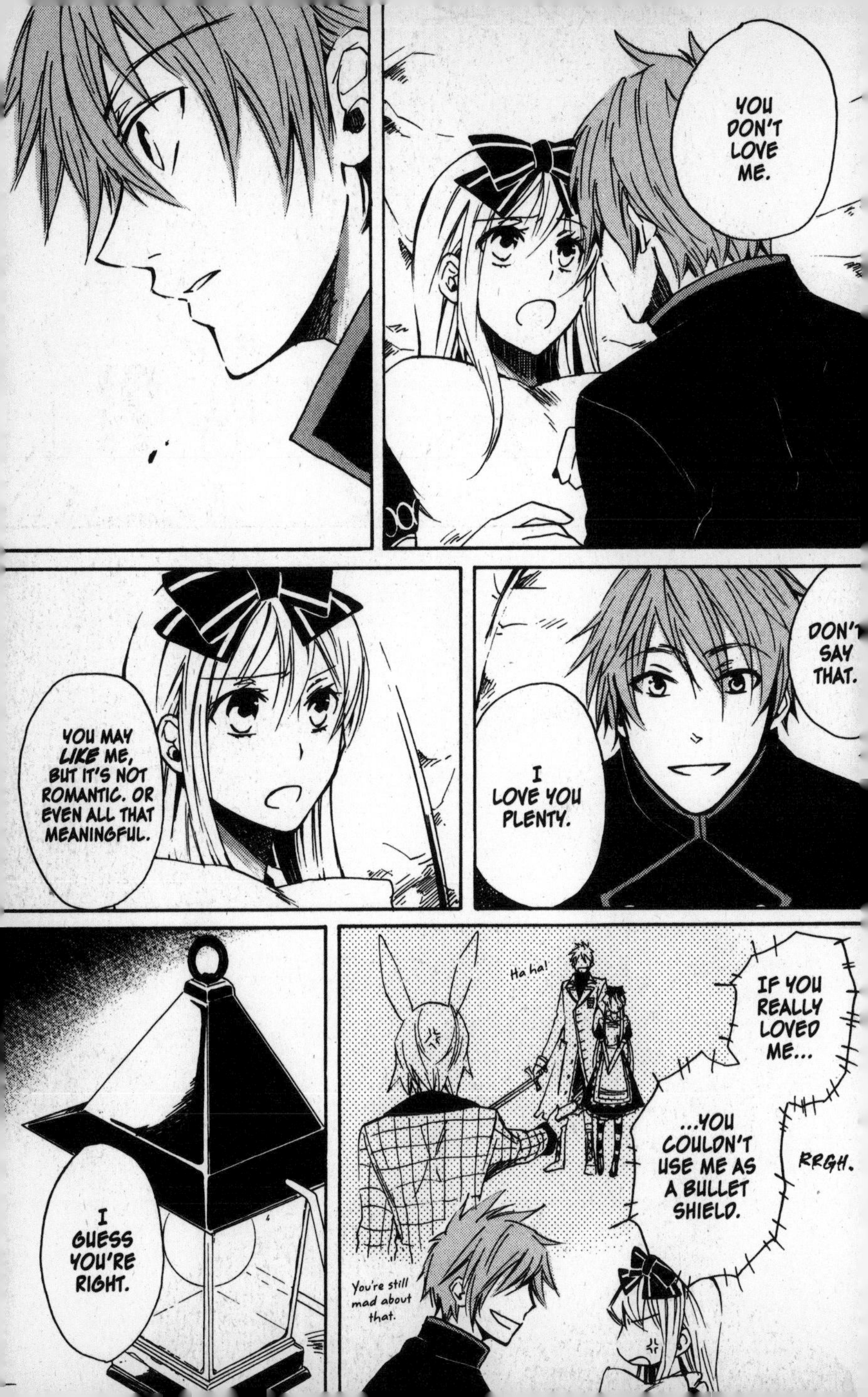
YOU DON'T LOVE ME.
DON'T SAY THAT.
I LOVE YOU PLENTY.
YOU MAY *LIKE* ME, BUT IT'S NOT ROMANTIC. OR EVEN ALL THAT MEANINGFUL.
IF YOU REALLY LOVED ME...
...YOU COULDN'T USE ME AS A BULLET SHIELD.
Ha ha!
RRGH.
You're still mad about that.
I GUESS YOU'RE RIGHT.

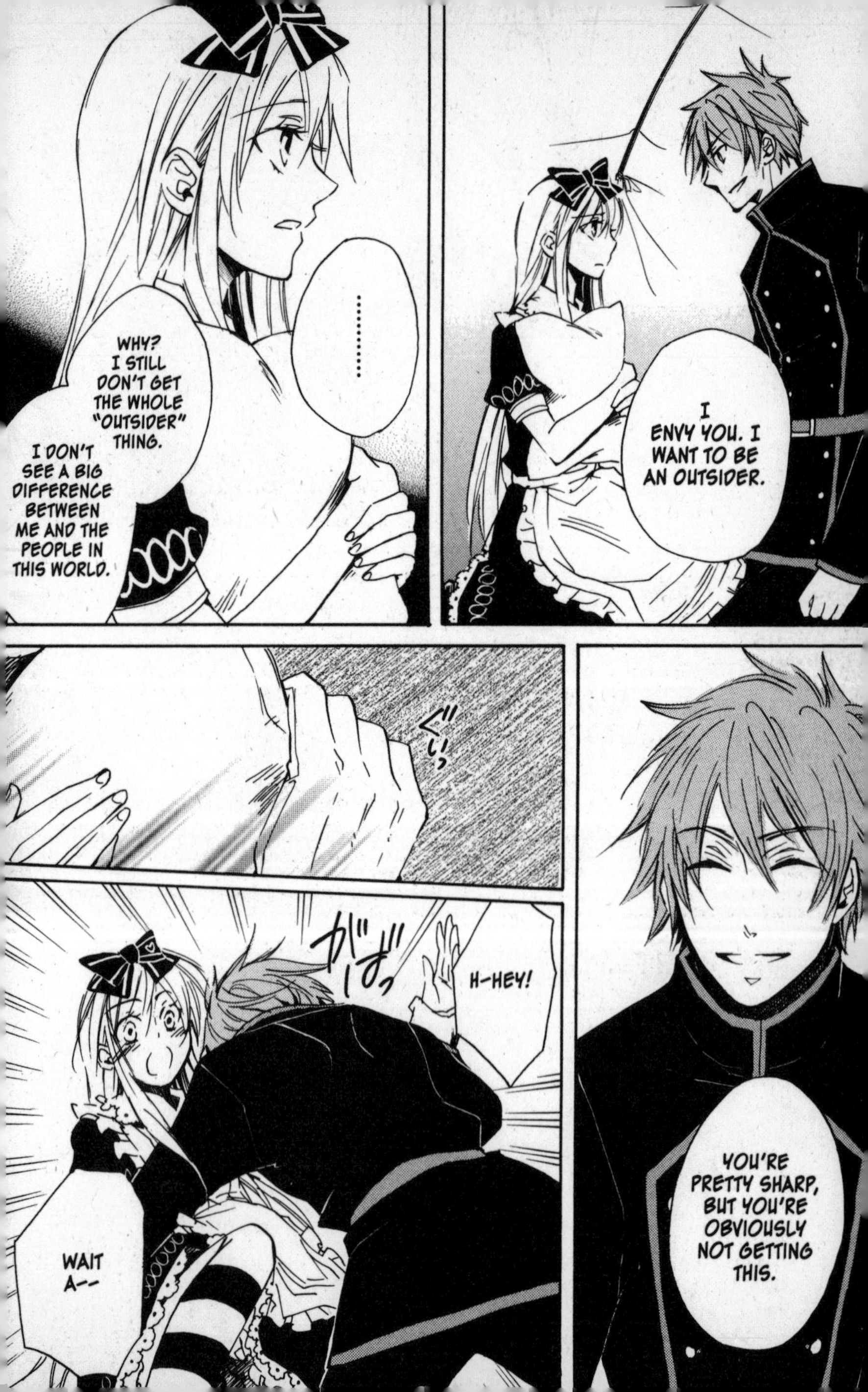
I ENVY YOU. I WANT TO BE AN OUTSIDER.
......
WHY? I STILL DON'T GET THE WHOLE "OUTSIDER" THING.
I DON'T SEE A BIG DIFFERENCE BETWEEN ME AND THE PEOPLE IN THIS WORLD.
YOU'RE PRETTY SHARP, BUT YOU'RE OBVIOUSLY NOT GETTING THIS.
ぐいっ
がばっ
H-HEY!
WAIT A--

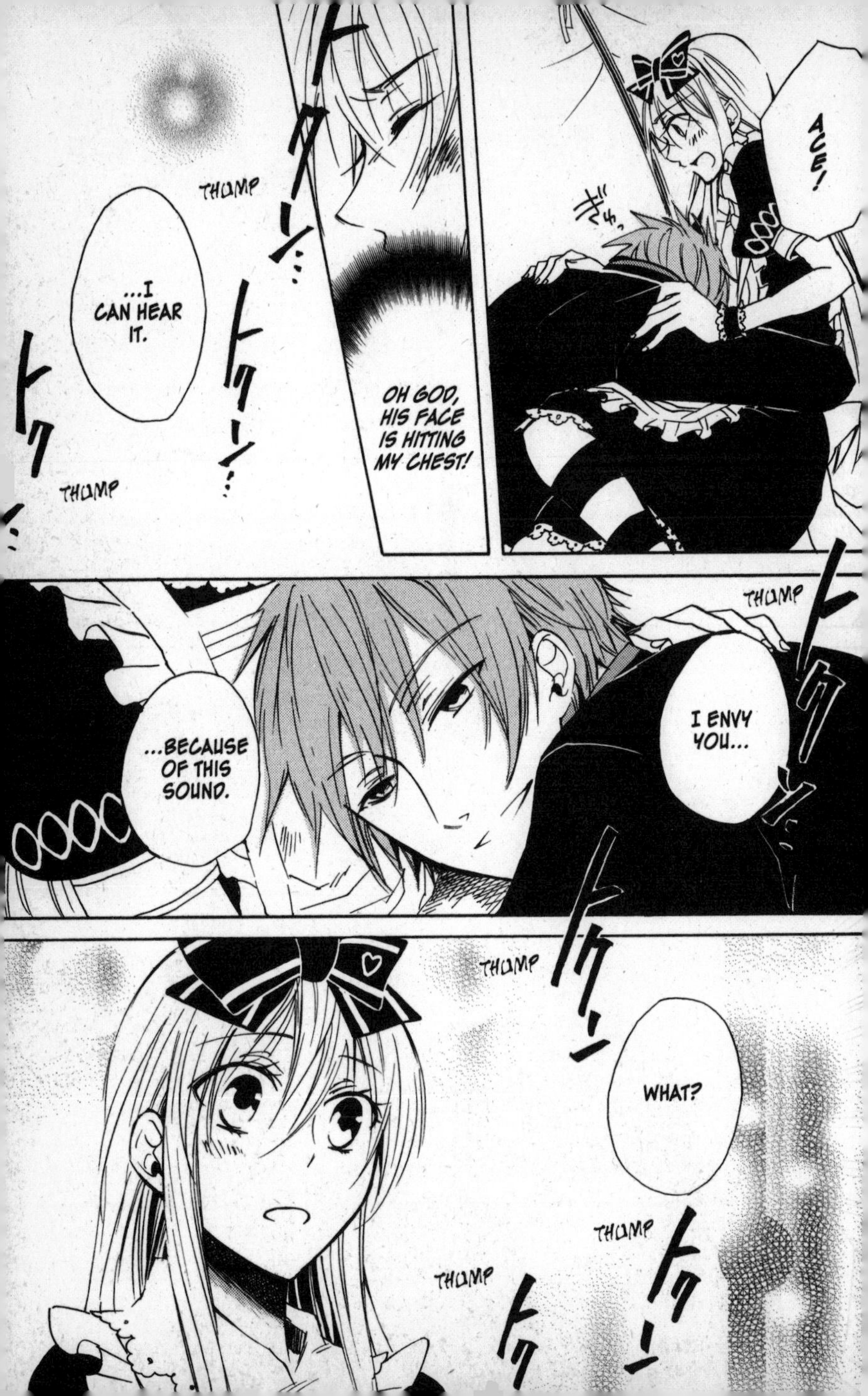
ACE!
ぎゅ
OH GOD, HIS FACE IS HITTING MY CHEST!
THUMP
...I CAN HEAR IT.
THUMP
THUMP
I ENVY YOU...
...BECAUSE OF THIS SOUND.
THUMP
WHAT?
THUMP
THUMP

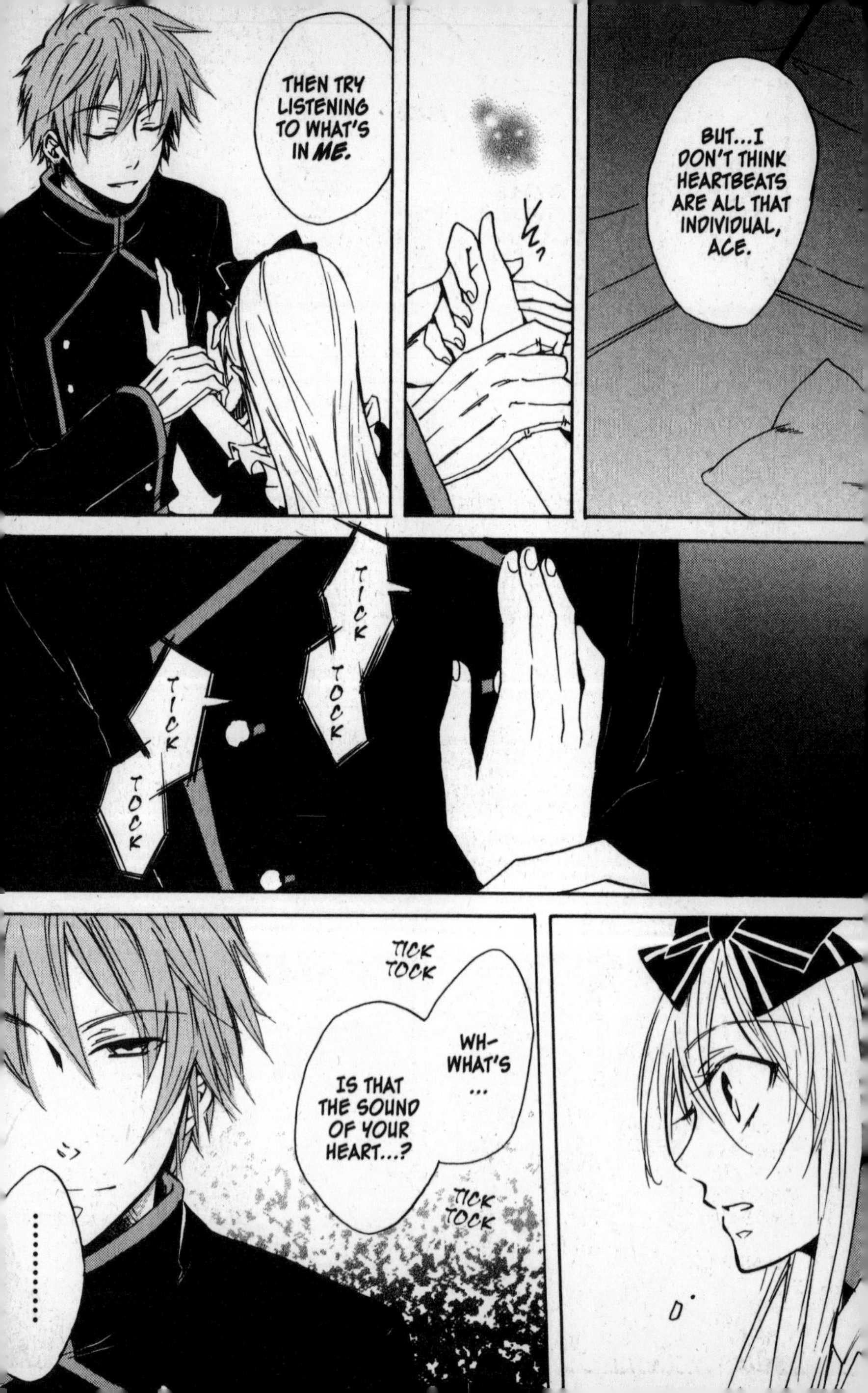
BUT...I DON'T THINK HEARTBEATS ARE ALL THAT INDIVIDUAL, ACE.
THEN TRY LISTENING TO WHAT'S IN ME.
TICK TOCK
TICK TOCK
TICK TOCK
WH- WHAT'S ...
IS THAT THE SOUND OF YOUR HEART...?
TICK TOCK
........

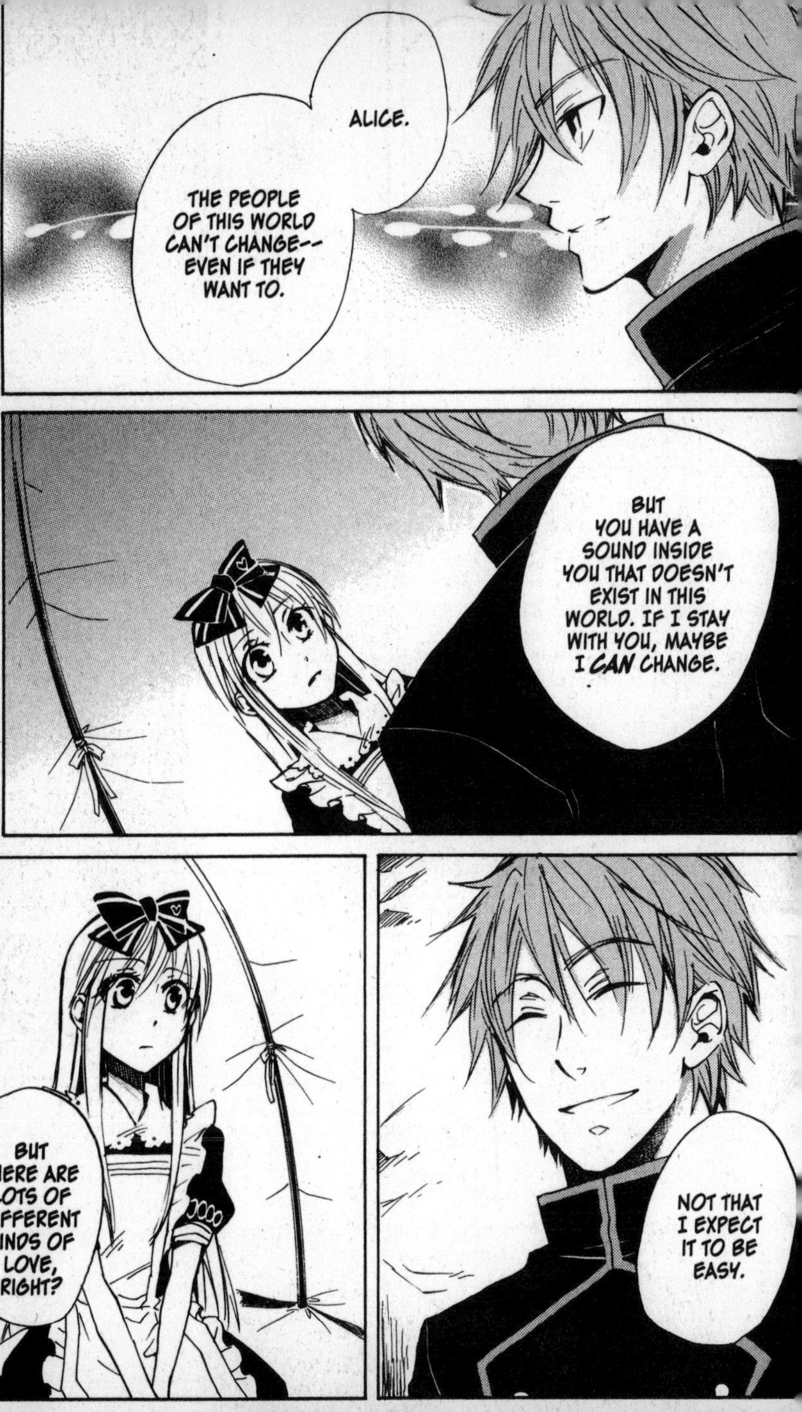
ALICE.
THE PEOPLE OF THIS WORLD CAN'T CHANGE-- EVEN IF THEY WANT TO.
BUT YOU HAVE A SOUND INSIDE YOU THAT DOESN'T EXIST IN THIS WORLD. IF I STAY WITH YOU, MAYBE I CAN CHANGE.
NOT THAT I EXPECT IT TO BE EASY.
BUT THERE ARE LOTS OF DIFFERENT KINDS OF LOVE, RIGHT?

UH... THANKS?

MY FEELINGS FOR YOU MAY NOT BE ROMANTIC NOW...

...BUT I DO LOVE YOU.

AND HE SAID "NOW."

HUNH.

NOT SURE WHY THE LIGHT WENT OUT.

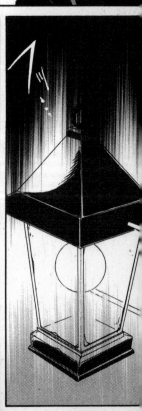

MAYBE THAT'S A SIGN THAT WE SHOULD GET SOME SLEEP.

YAAWN.

How long have those blankets been there?

ALICE, YOU CAN TAKE THAT ONE.

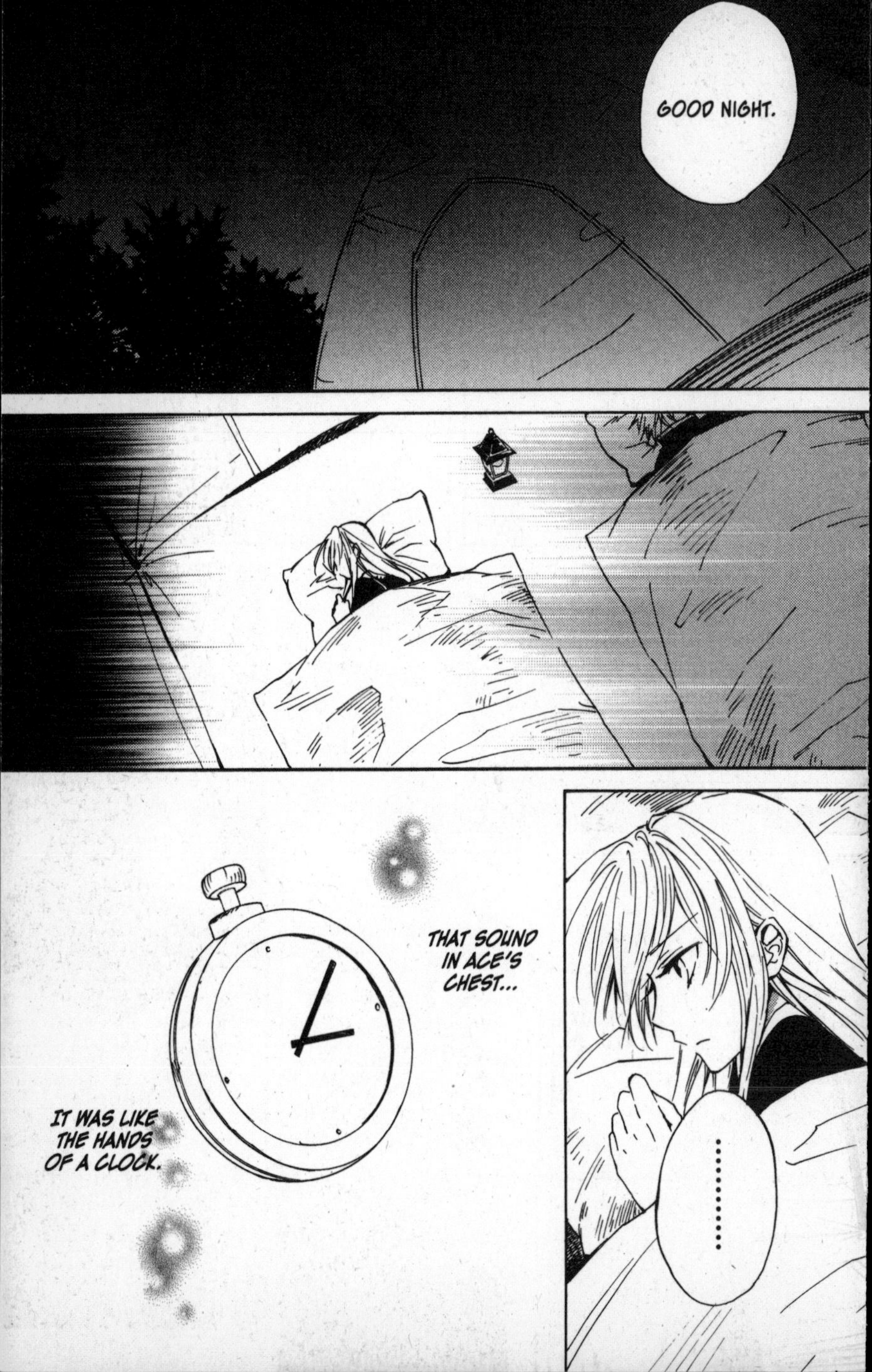
GOOD NIGHT.
..........
THAT SOUND IN ACE'S CHEST...
IT WAS LIKE THE HANDS OF A CLOCK.

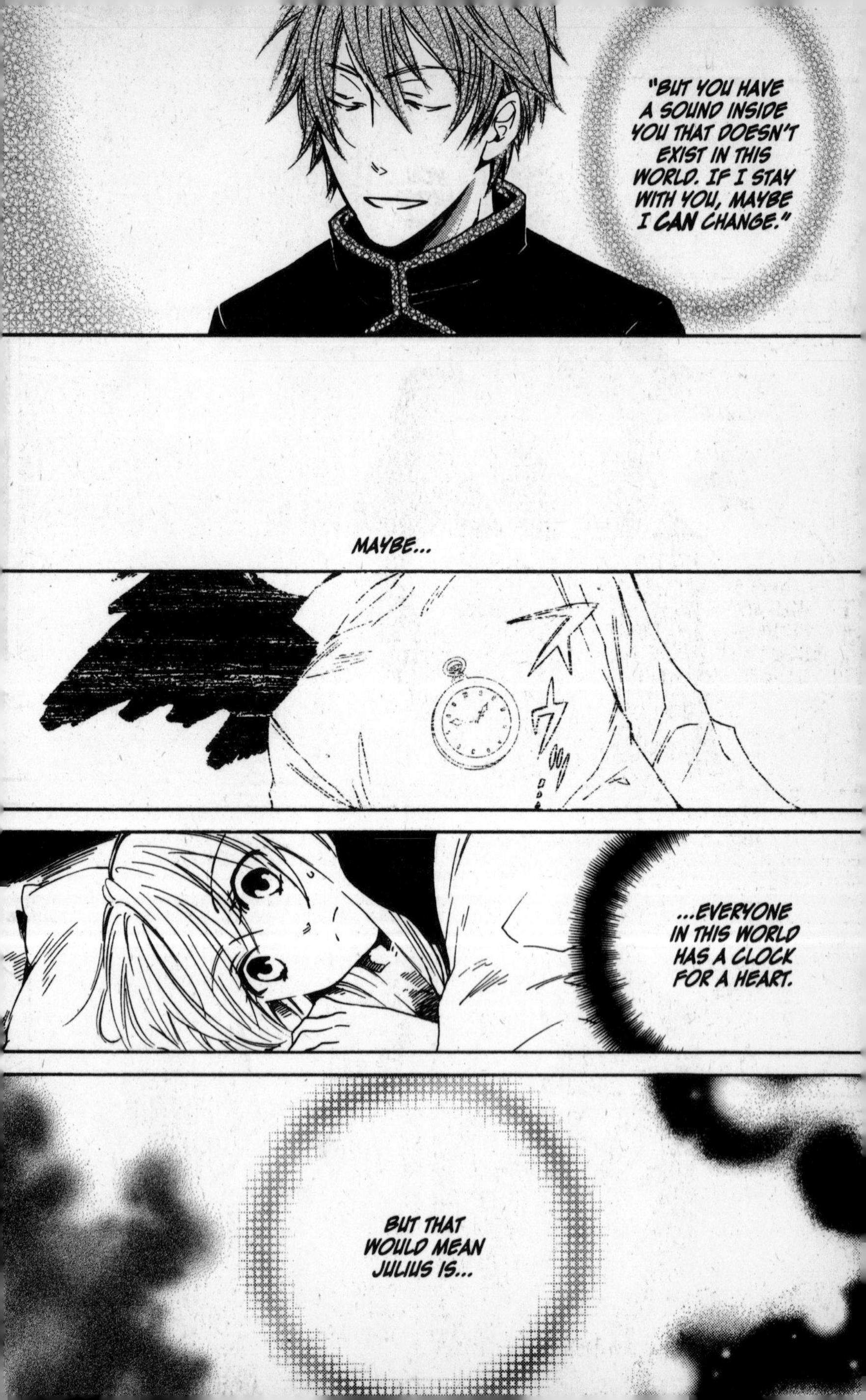
"BUT YOU HAVE A SOUND INSIDE YOU THAT DOESN'T EXIST IN THIS WORLD. IF I STAY WITH YOU, MAYBE I CAN CHANGE."
MAYBE...
...EVERYONE IN THIS WORLD HAS A CLOCK FOR A HEART.
BUT THAT WOULD MEAN JULIUS IS...

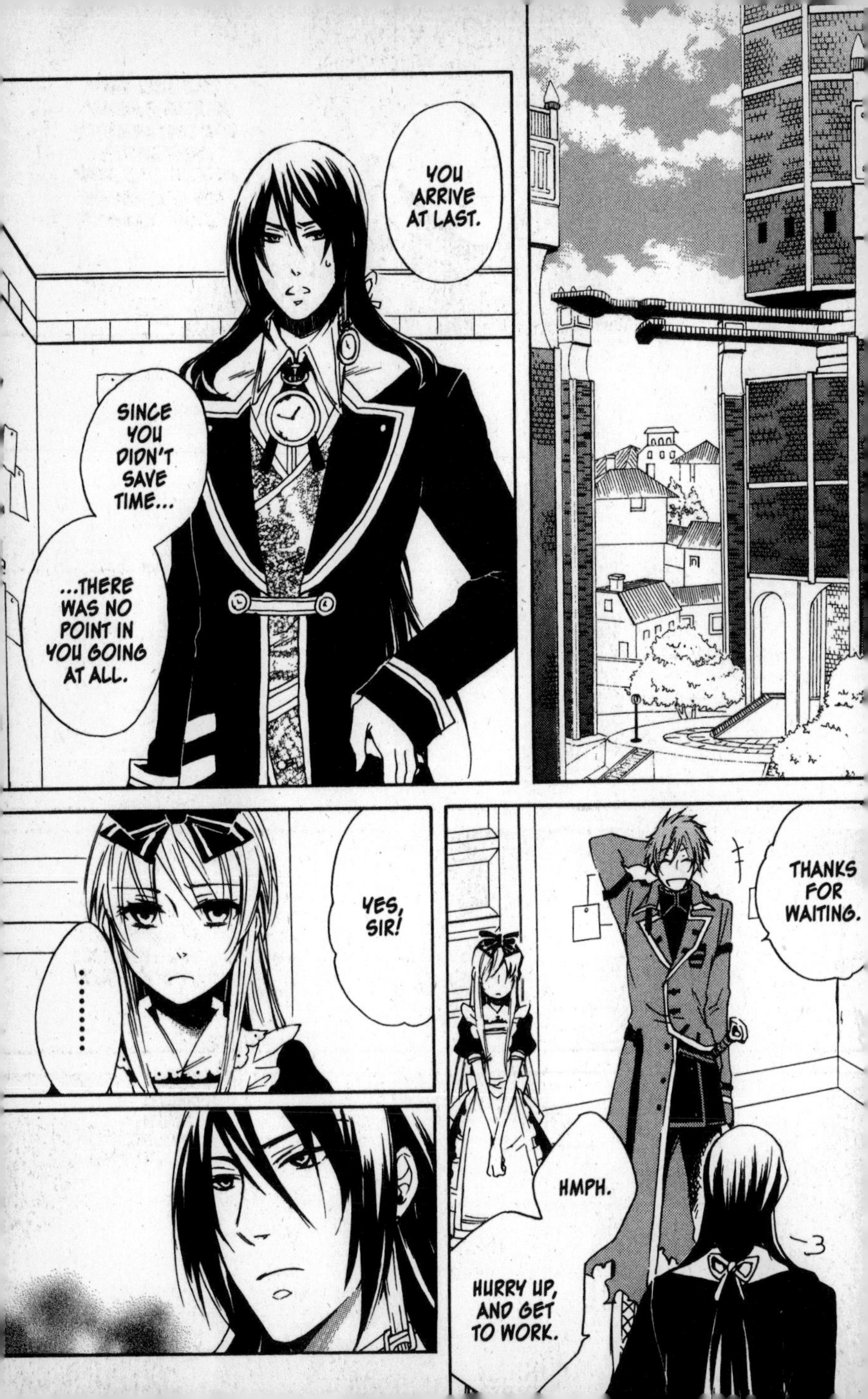
YOU ARRIVE AT LAST.
SINCE YOU DIDN'T SAVE TIME...
...THERE WAS NO POINT IN YOU GOING AT ALL.
THANKS FOR WAITING.
HMPH.
HURRY UP, AND GET TO WORK.
YES, SIR!
........

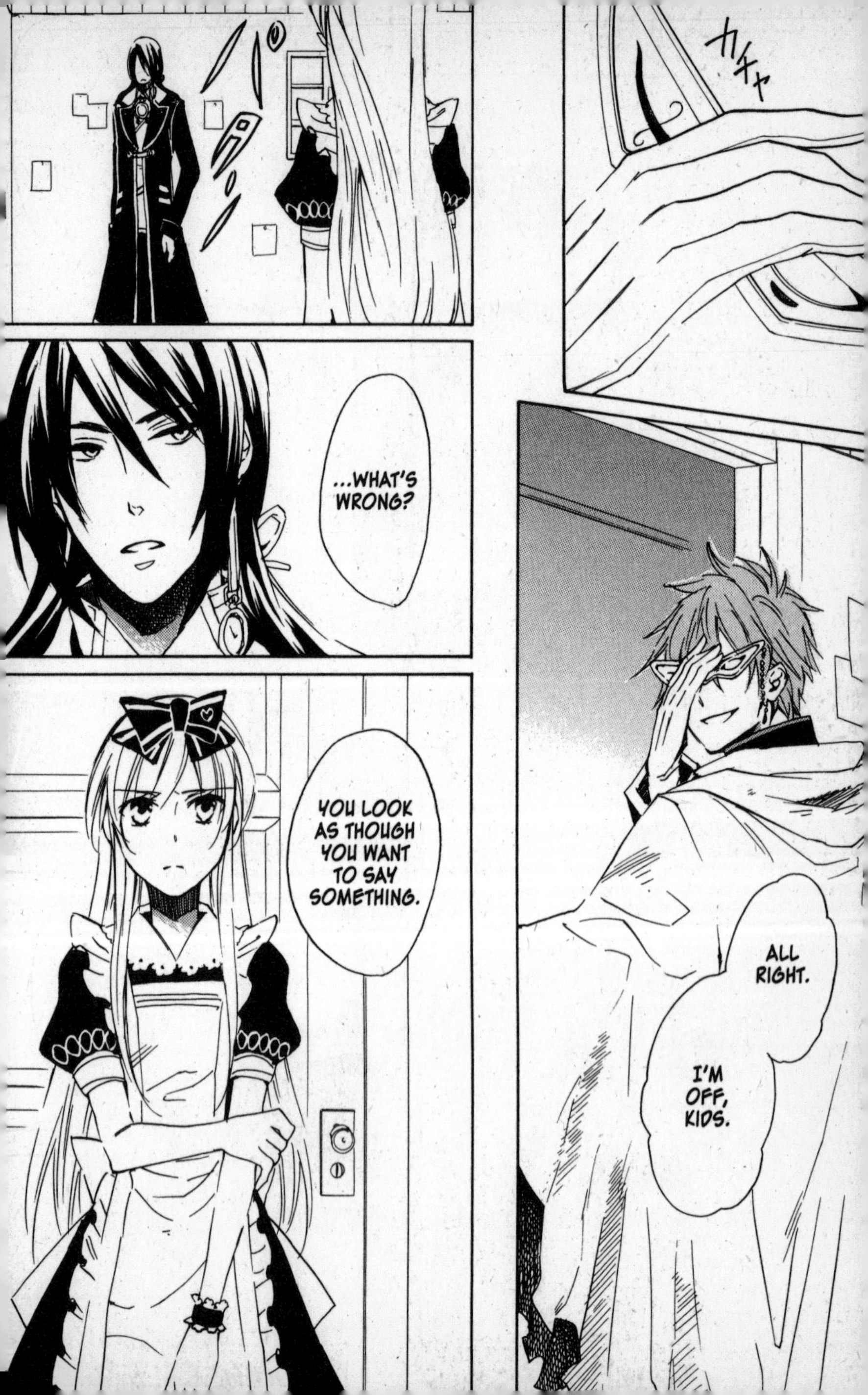
カチャ
ALL RIGHT.
I'M OFF, KIDS.
...WHAT'S WRONG?
YOU LOOK AS THOUGH YOU WANT TO SAY SOMETHING.

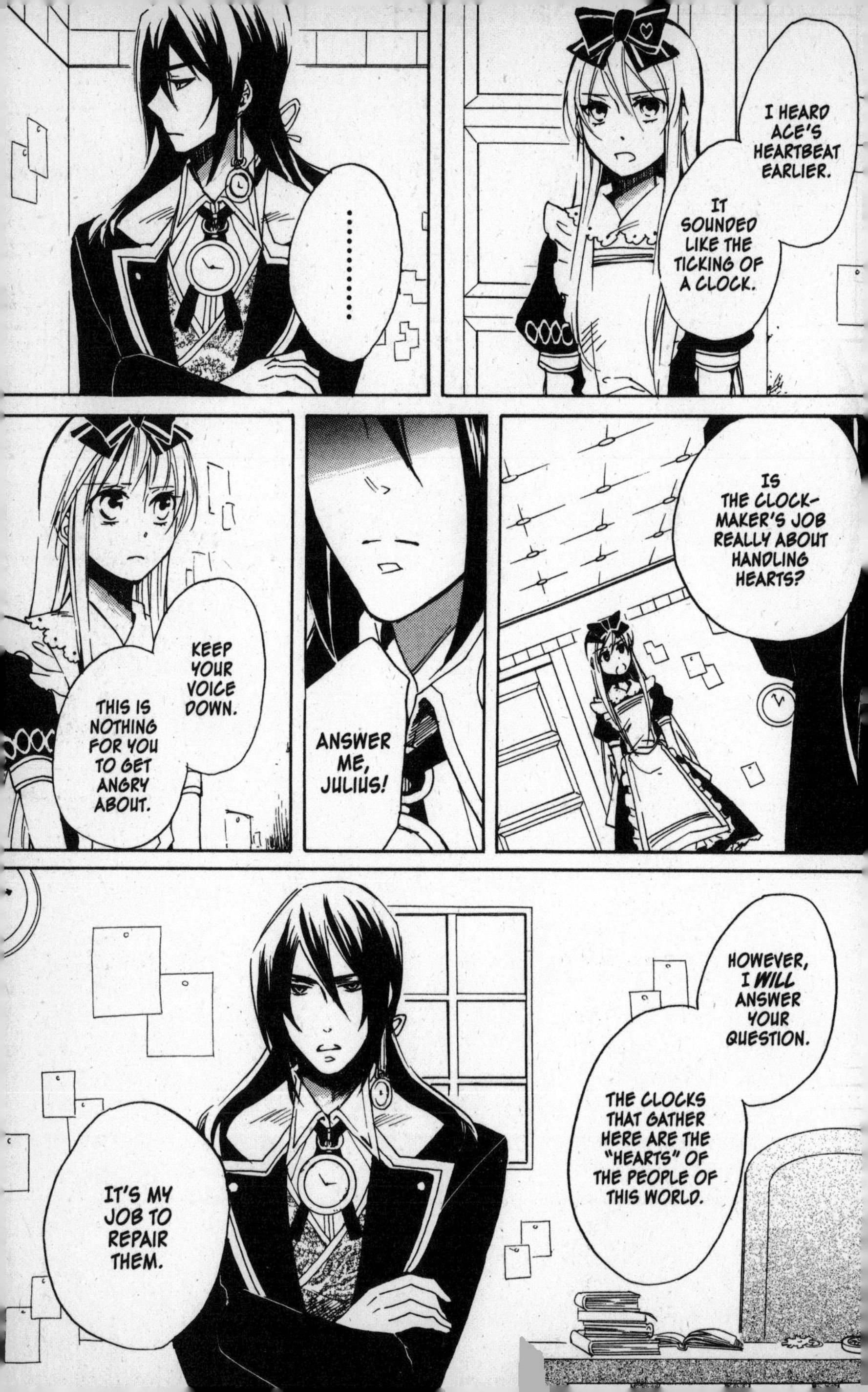
I HEARD ACE'S HEARTBEAT EARLIER.
IT SOUNDED LIKE THE TICKING OF A CLOCK.
........
IS THE CLOCK-MAKER'S JOB REALLY ABOUT HANDLING HEARTS?
ANSWER ME, JULIUS!
KEEP YOUR VOICE DOWN.
THIS IS NOTHING FOR YOU TO GET ANGRY ABOUT.
HOWEVER, I *WILL* ANSWER YOUR QUESTION.
THE CLOCKS THAT GATHER HERE ARE THE "HEARTS" OF THE PEOPLE OF THIS WORLD.
IT'S MY JOB TO REPAIR THEM.

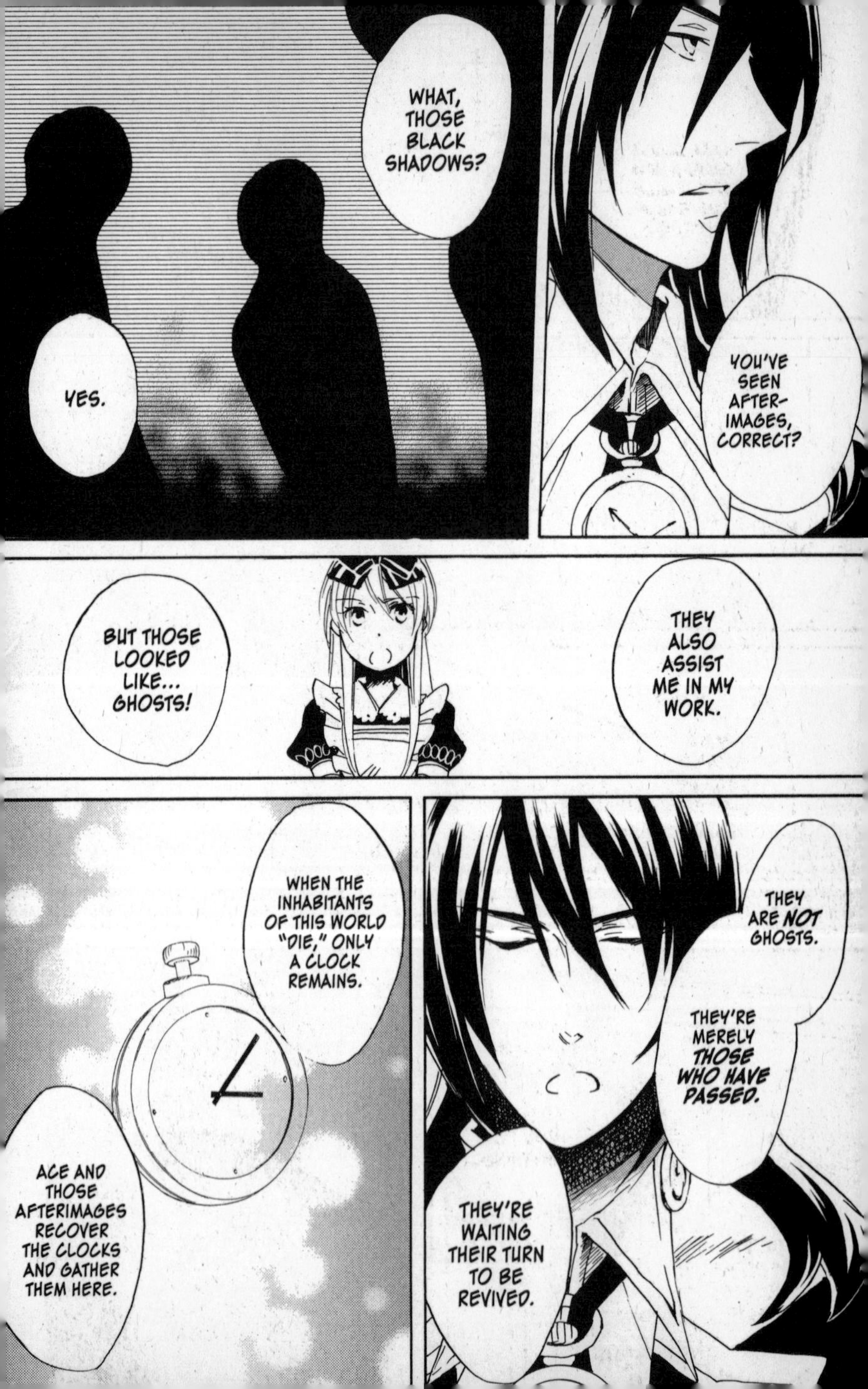
YOU'VE SEEN AFTER-IMAGES, CORRECT?
WHAT, THOSE BLACK SHADOWS?
YES.
THEY ALSO ASSIST ME IN MY WORK.
BUT THOSE LOOKED LIKE... GHOSTS!
THEY ARE *NOT* GHOSTS.
THEY'RE MERELY *THOSE WHO HAVE PASSED.*
THEY'RE WAITING THEIR TURN TO BE REVIVED.
WHEN THE INHABITANTS OF THIS WORLD "DIE," ONLY A CLOCK REMAINS.
ACE AND THOSE AFTERIMAGES RECOVER THE CLOCKS AND GATHER THEM HERE.

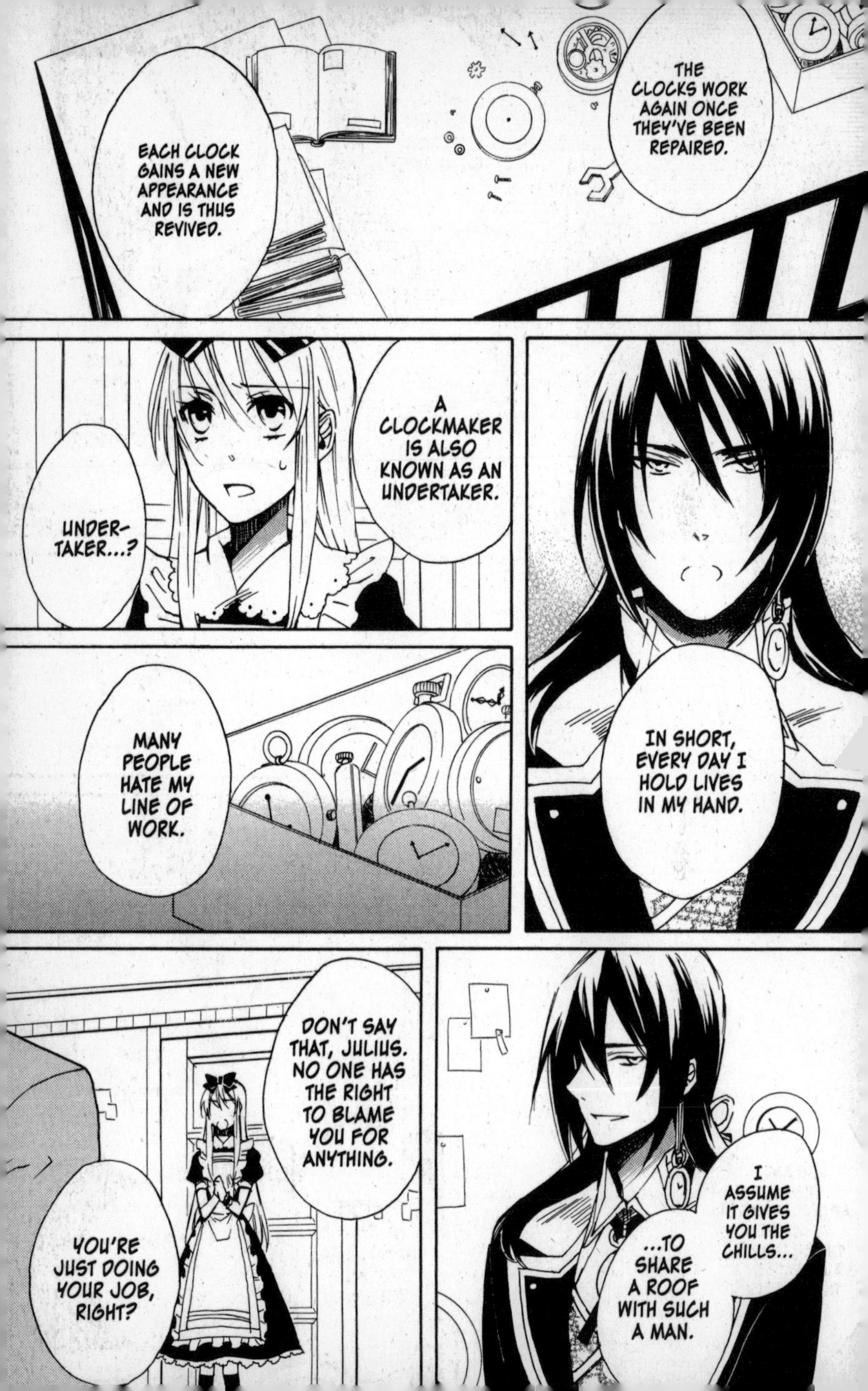
THE CLOCKS WORK AGAIN ONCE THEY'VE BEEN REPAIRED.
EACH CLOCK GAINS A NEW APPEARANCE AND IS THUS REVIVED.
IN SHORT, EVERY DAY I HOLD LIVES IN MY HAND.
A CLOCKMAKER IS ALSO KNOWN AS AN UNDERTAKER.
UNDER-TAKER...?
MANY PEOPLE HATE MY LINE OF WORK.
I ASSUME IT GIVES YOU THE CHILLS...
...TO SHARE A ROOF WITH SUCH A MAN.
DON'T SAY THAT, JULIUS. NO ONE HAS THE RIGHT TO BLAME YOU FOR ANYTHING.
YOU'RE JUST DOING YOUR JOB, RIGHT?

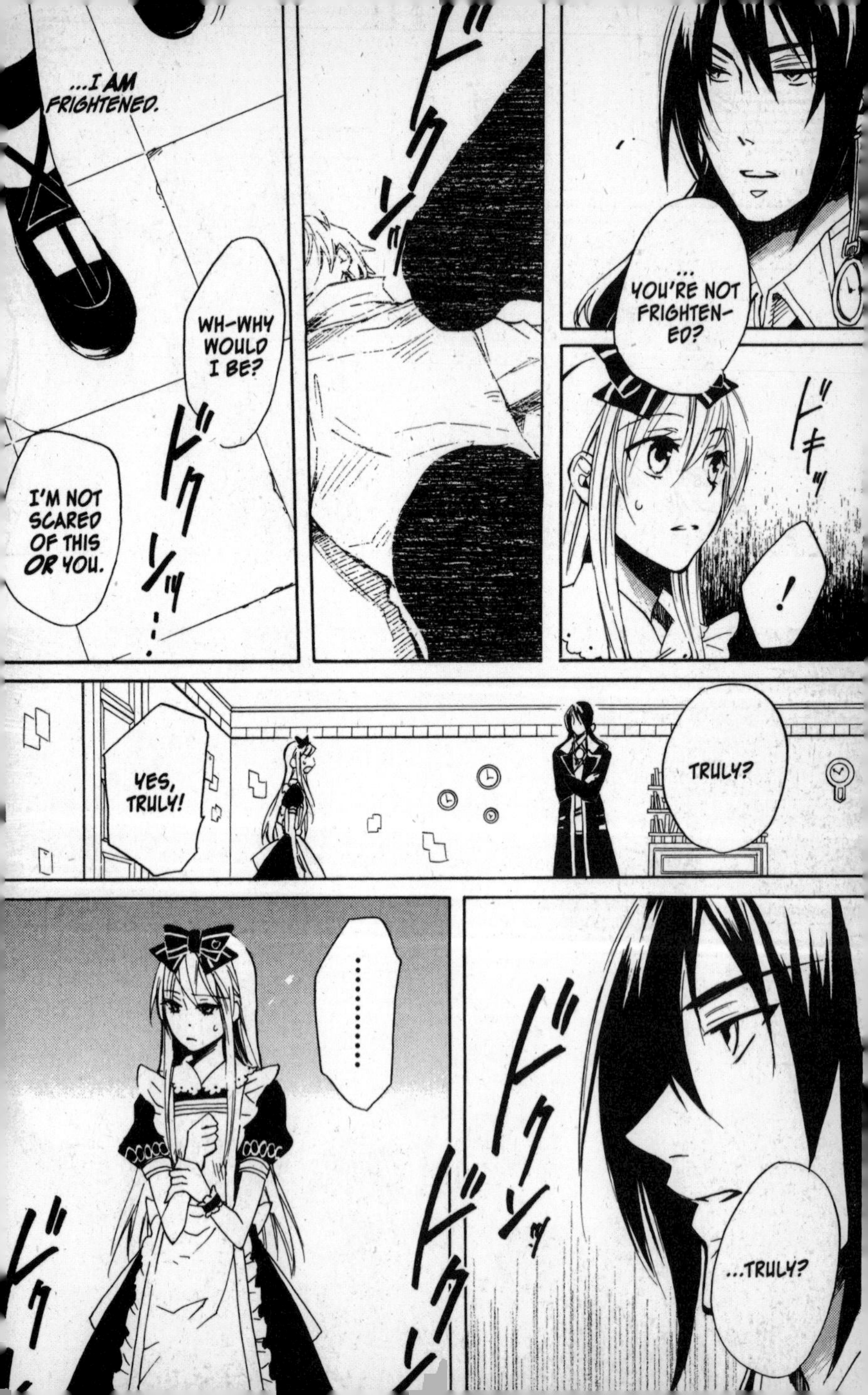
...
YOU'RE NOT FRIGHTENED?
ドキッ
!
ドクンッ
...I AM FRIGHTENED.
WH-WHY WOULD I BE?
ドクンッ
I'M NOT SCARED OF THIS OR YOU.
TRULY?
YES, TRULY!
ドクンッ
ドクンッ
...TRULY?
......

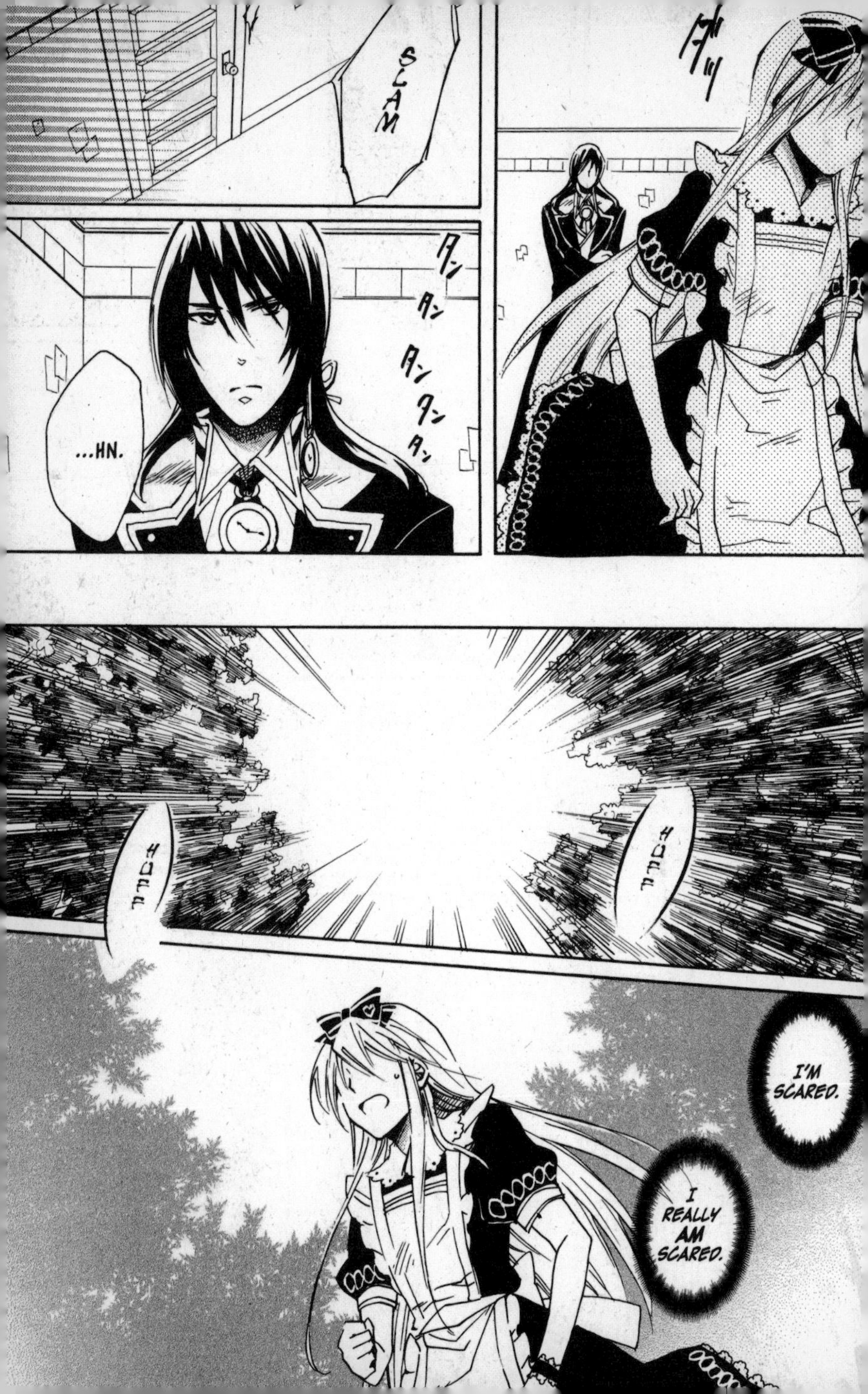
ダッ
SLAM
タン
タン
タン
タン
タン
...HN.
HUFF
HUFF
I'M SCARED.
I REALLY AM SCARED.

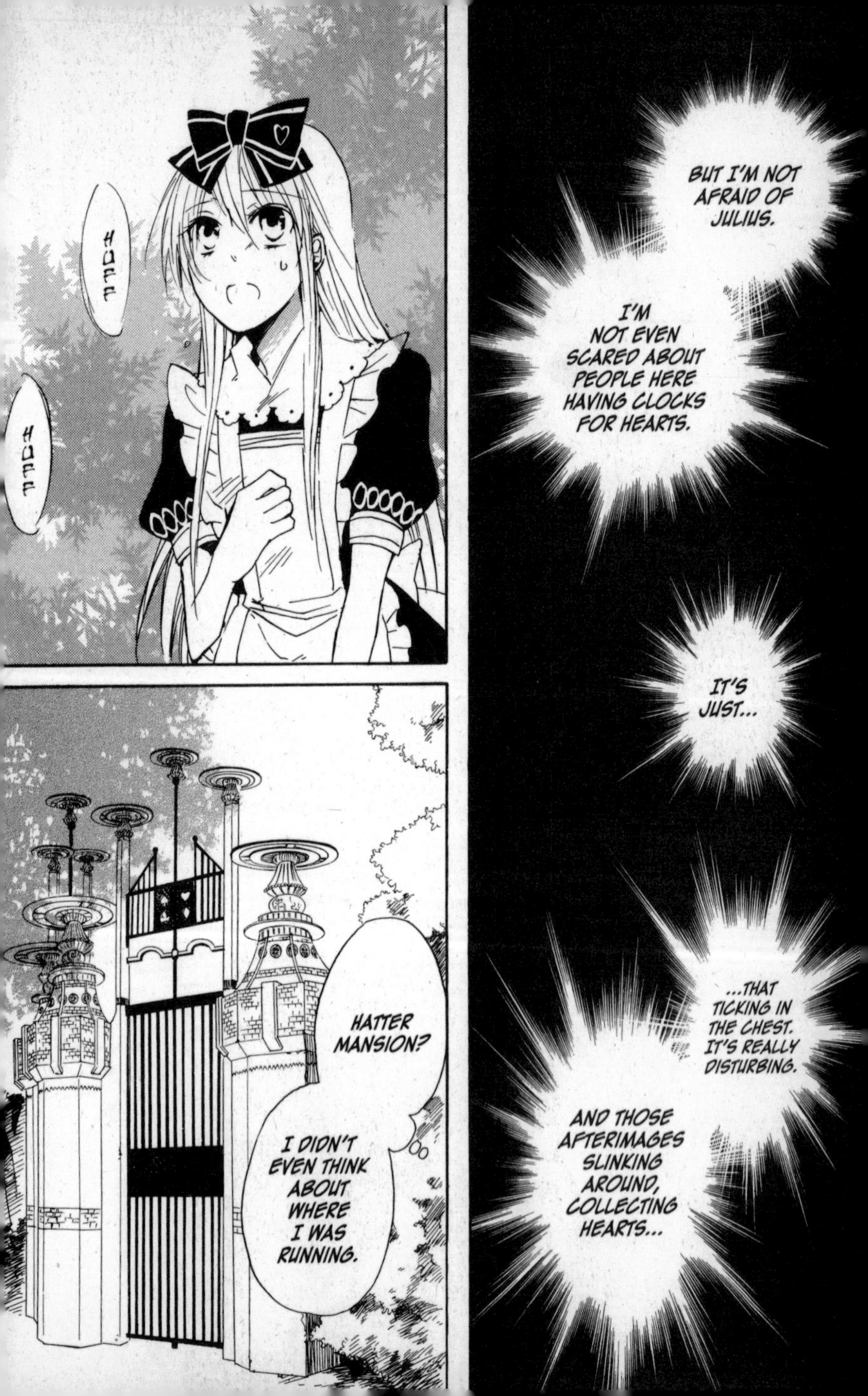
BUT I'M NOT AFRAID OF JULIUS.
I'M NOT EVEN SCARED ABOUT PEOPLE HERE HAVING CLOCKS FOR HEARTS.
IT'S JUST...
...THAT TICKING IN THE CHEST. IT'S REALLY DISTURBING.
AND THOSE AFTERIMAGES SLINKING AROUND, COLLECTING HEARTS...
HUFF
HUFF
HATTER MANSION?
I DIDN'T EVEN THINK ABOUT WHERE I WAS RUNNING.

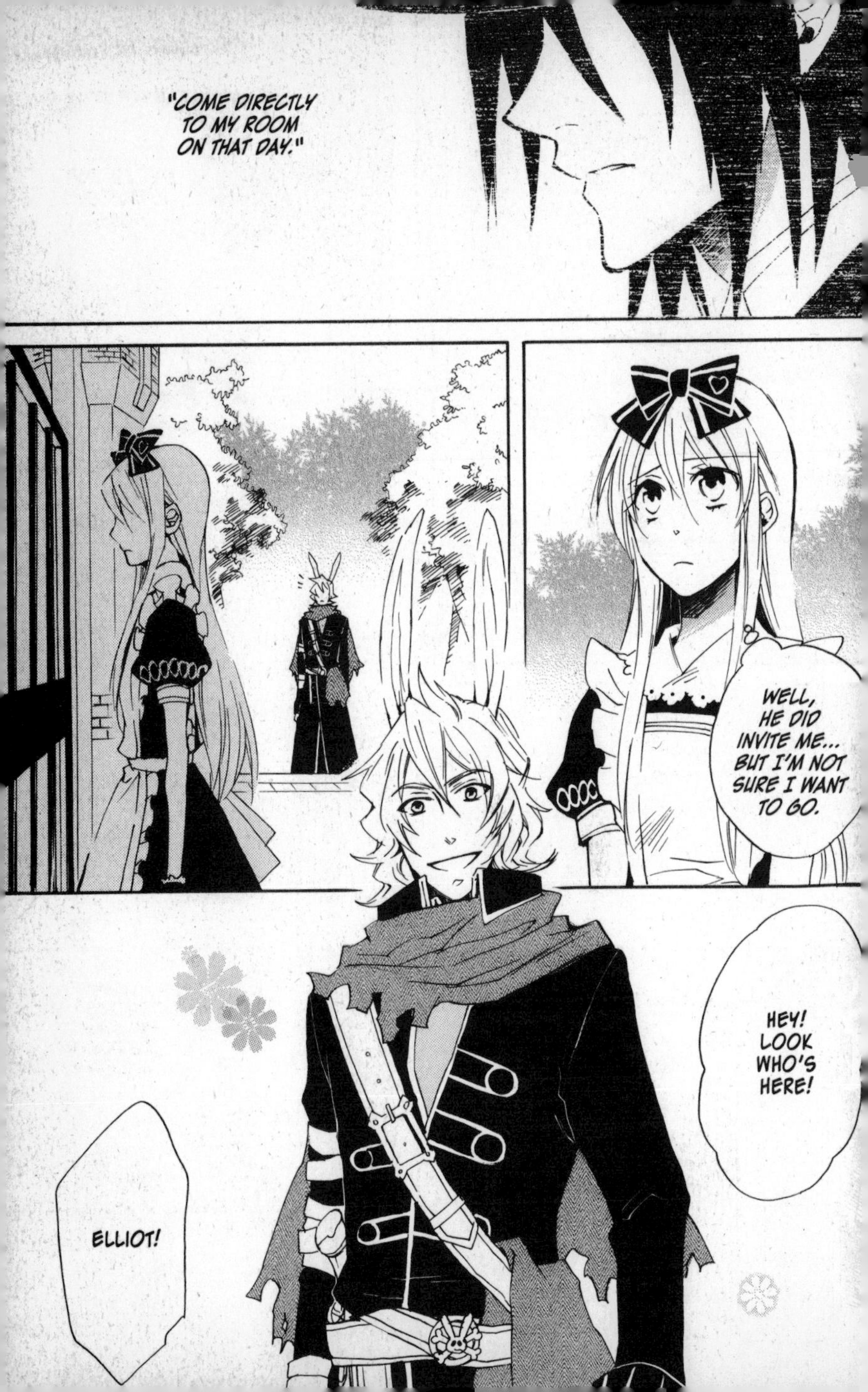
"COME DIRECTLY TO MY ROOM ON THAT DAY."
WELL, HE DID INVITE ME... BUT I'M NOT SURE I WANT TO GO.
HEY! LOOK WHO'S HERE!
ELLIOT!

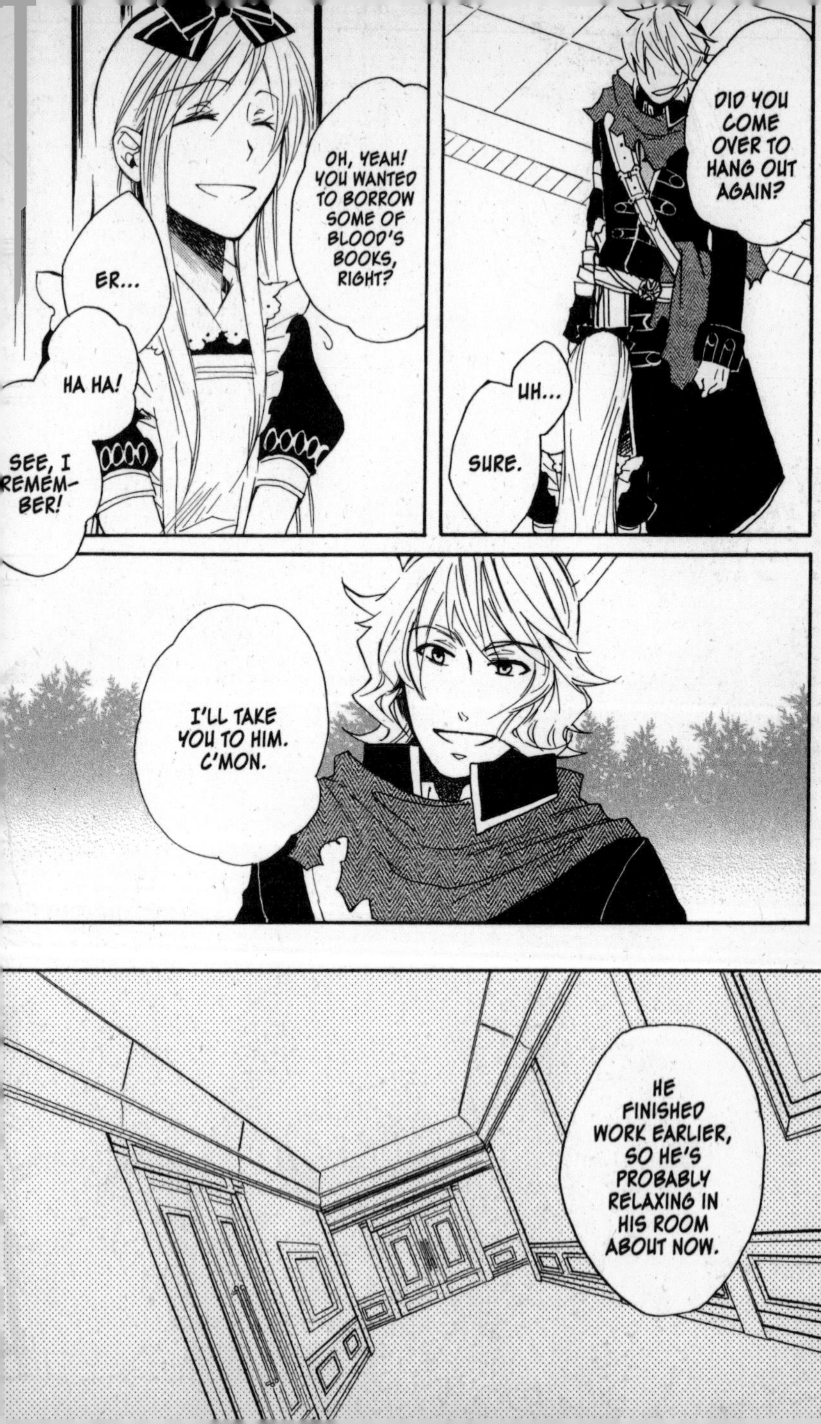
DID YOU COME OVER TO HANG OUT AGAIN?
UH...
SURE.
OH, YEAH! YOU WANTED TO BORROW SOME OF BLOOD'S BOOKS, RIGHT?
ER...
HA HA!
SEE, I REMEMBER!
I'LL TAKE YOU TO HIM. C'MON.
HE FINISHED WORK EARLIER, SO HE'S PROBABLY RELAXING IN HIS ROOM ABOUT NOW.

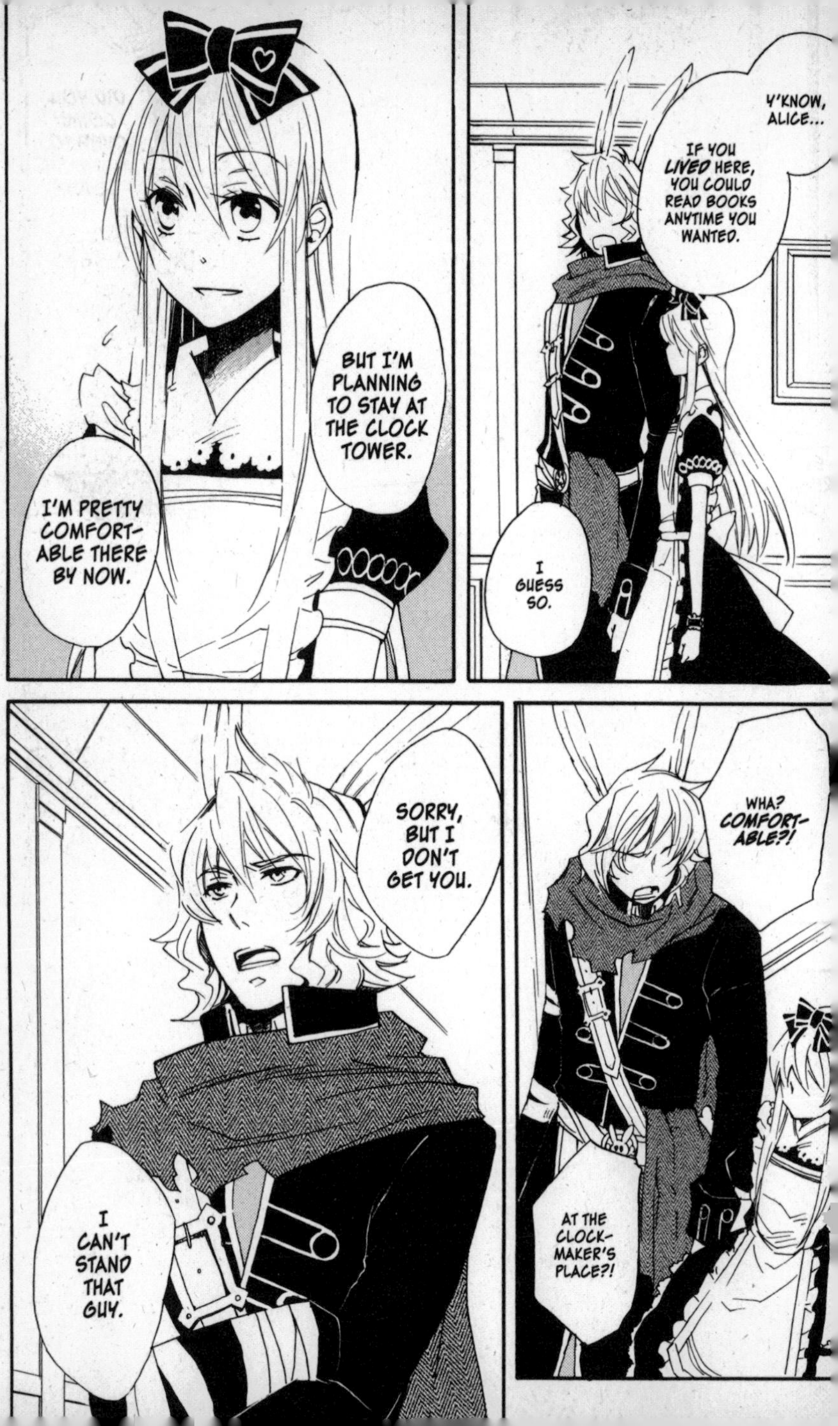
Y'KNOW, ALICE...
IF YOU LIVED HERE, YOU COULD READ BOOKS ANYTIME YOU WANTED.
I GUESS SO.
BUT I'M PLANNING TO STAY AT THE CLOCK TOWER.
I'M PRETTY COMFORT-ABLE THERE BY NOW.
WHA? COMFORT-ABLE?!
AT THE CLOCK-MAKER'S PLACE?!
SORRY, BUT I DON'T GET YOU.
I CAN'T STAND THAT GUY.

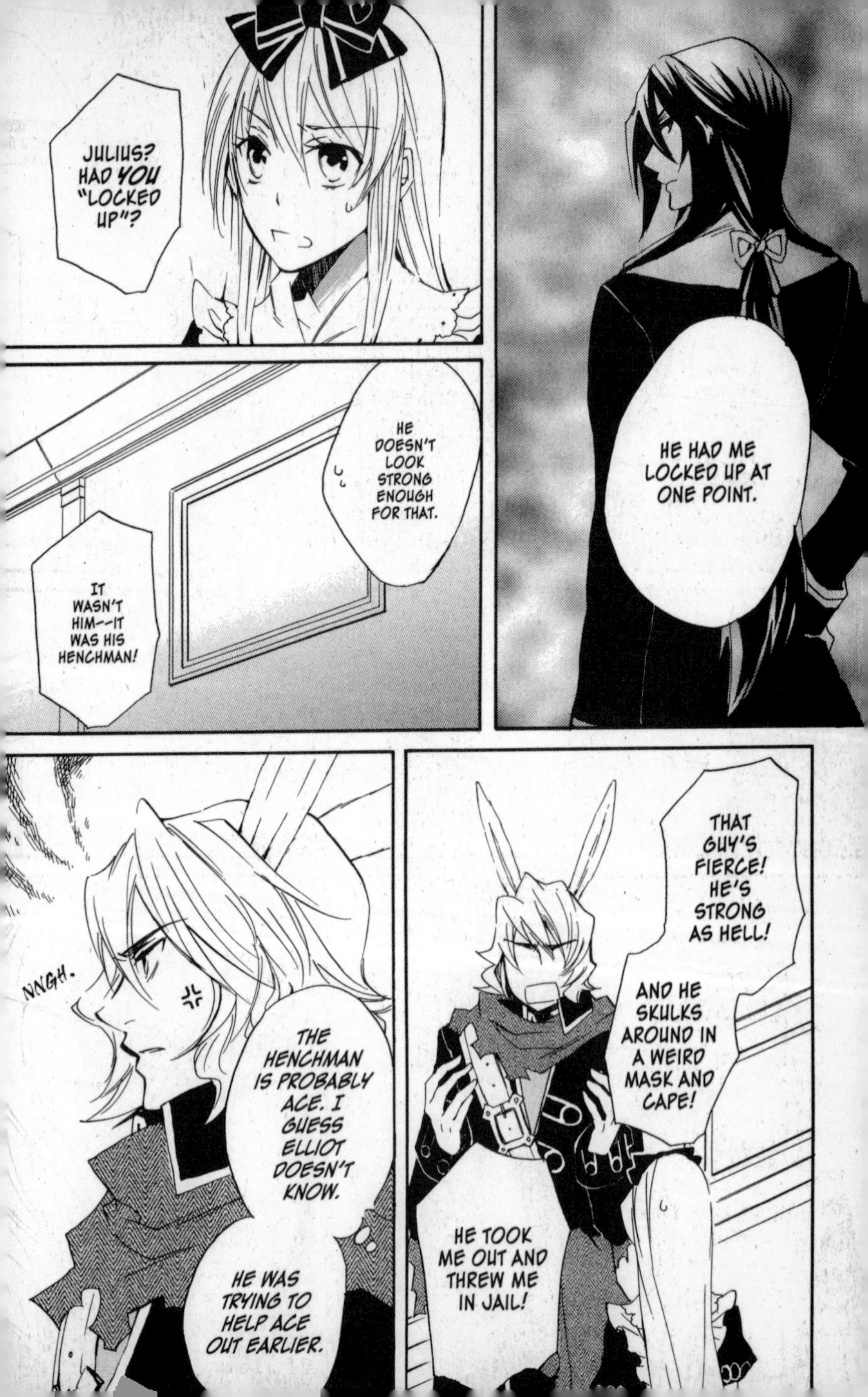
HE HAD ME LOCKED UP AT ONE POINT.
JULIUS? HAD YOU "LOCKED UP"?
HE DOESN'T LOOK STRONG ENOUGH FOR THAT.
IT WASN'T HIM--IT WAS HIS HENCHMAN!
THAT GUY'S FIERCE! HE'S STRONG AS HELL!
AND HE SKULKS AROUND IN A WEIRD MASK AND CAPE!
HE TOOK ME OUT AND THREW ME IN JAIL!
NNGH.
THE HENCHMAN IS PROBABLY ACE. I GUESS ELLIOT DOESN'T KNOW.
HE WAS TRYING TO HELP ACE OUT EARLIER.

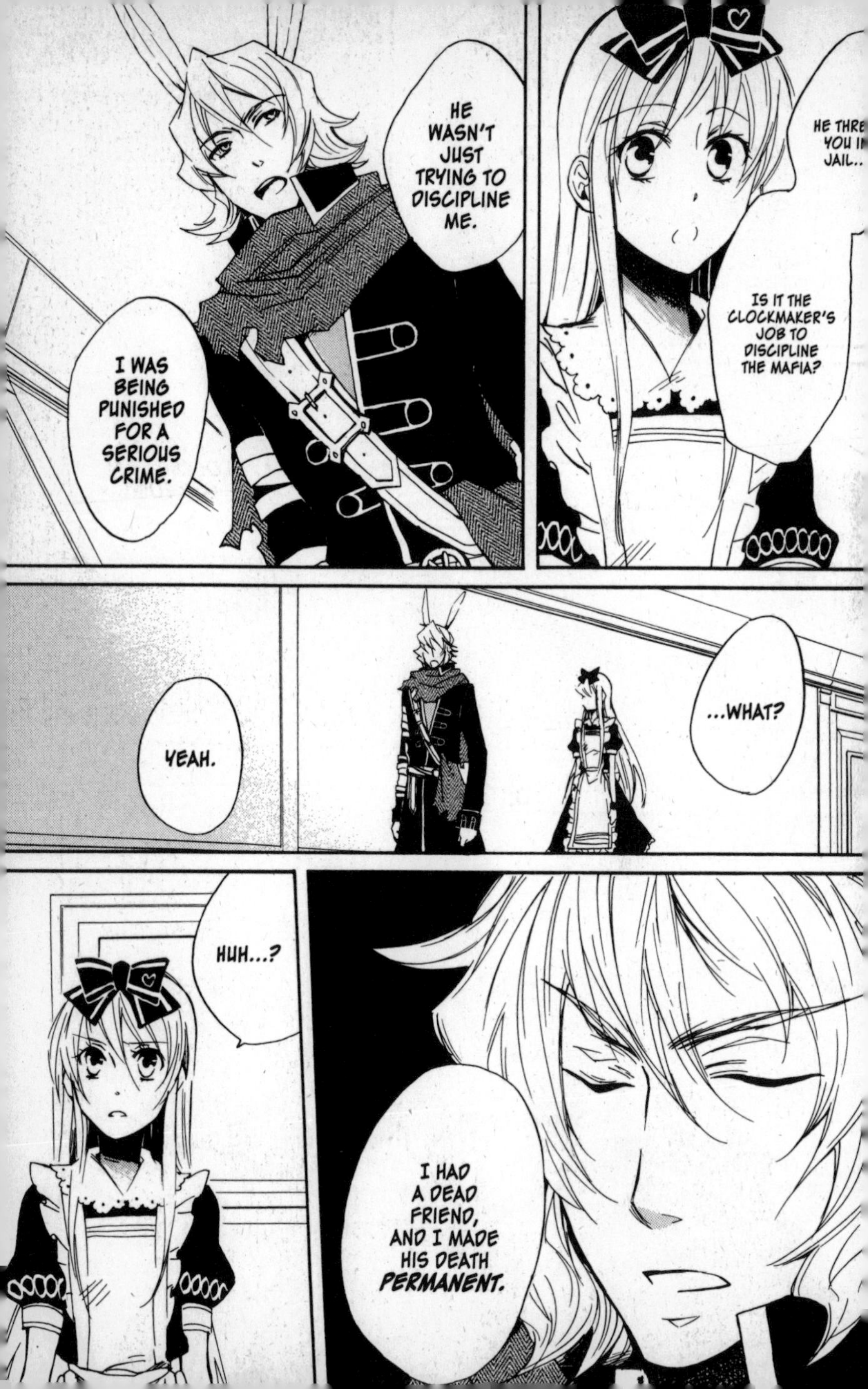
HE THRE YOU I JAIL...
IS IT THE CLOCKMAKER'S JOB TO DISCIPLINE THE MAFIA?
HE WASN'T JUST TRYING TO DISCIPLINE ME.
I WAS BEING PUNISHED FOR A SERIOUS CRIME.
...WHAT?
YEAH.
I HAD A DEAD FRIEND, AND I MADE HIS DEATH PERMANENT.
HUH...?

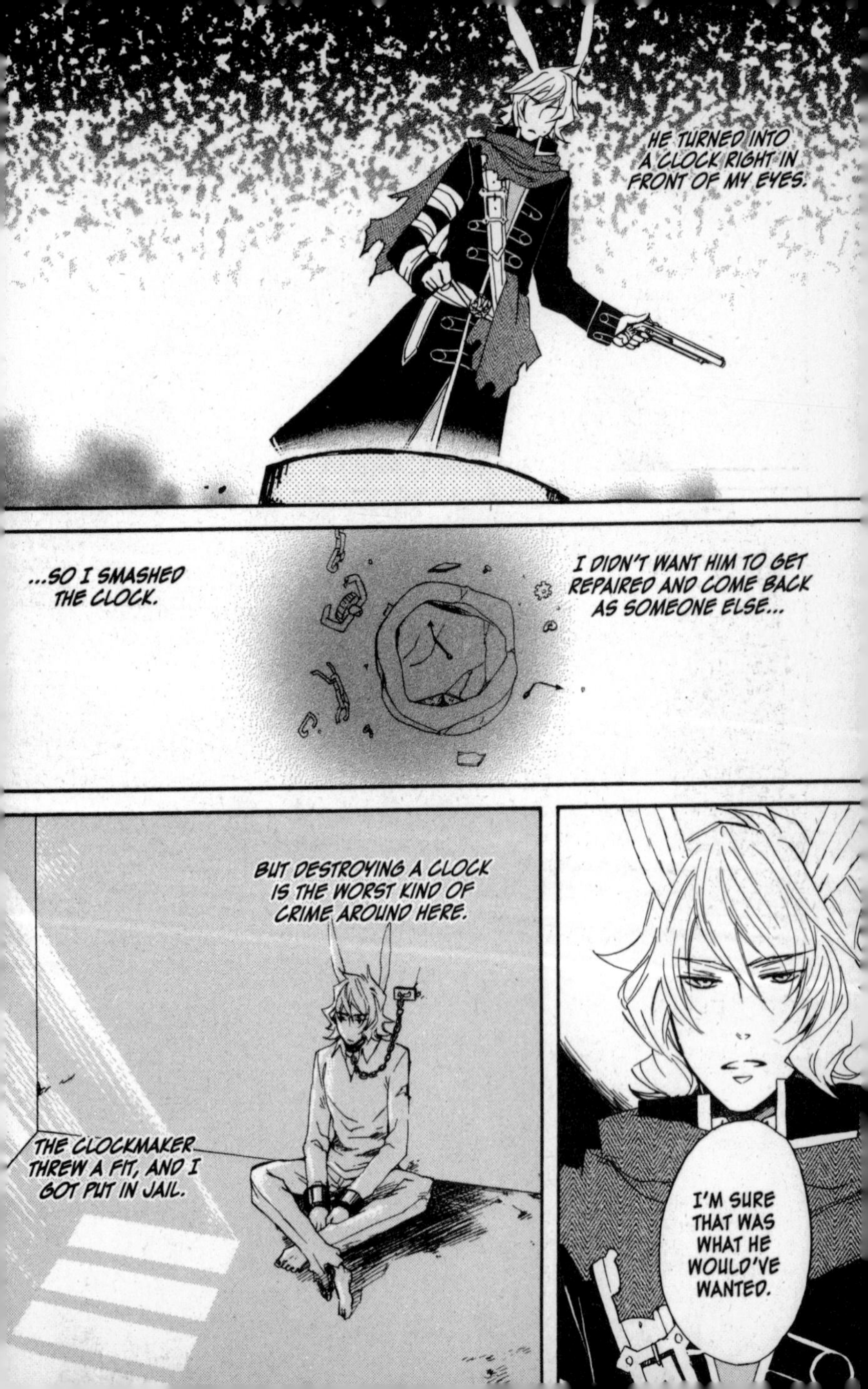
HE TURNED INTO A CLOCK RIGHT IN FRONT OF MY EYES.
I DIDN'T WANT HIM TO GET REPAIRED AND COME BACK AS SOMEONE ELSE...
...SO I SMASHED THE CLOCK.
I'M SURE THAT WAS WHAT HE WOULD'VE WANTED.
BUT DESTROYING A CLOCK IS THE WORST KIND OF CRIME AROUND HERE.
THE CLOCKMAKER THREW A FIT, AND I GOT PUT IN JAIL.

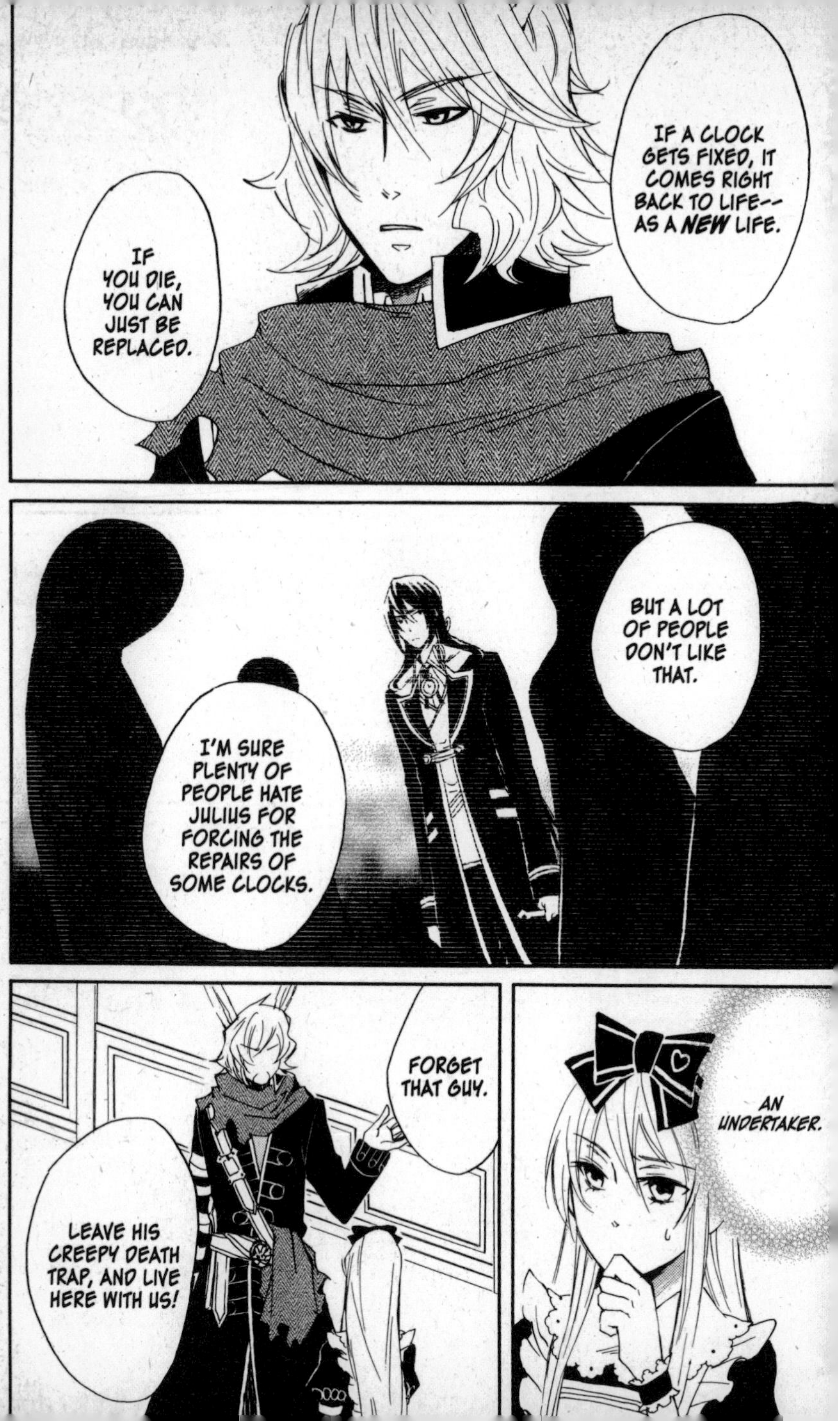
IF A CLOCK GETS FIXED, IT COMES RIGHT BACK TO LIFE-- AS A *NEW* LIFE.
IF YOU DIE, YOU CAN JUST BE REPLACED.
BUT A LOT OF PEOPLE DON'T LIKE THAT.
I'M SURE PLENTY OF PEOPLE HATE JULIUS FOR FORCING THE REPAIRS OF SOME CLOCKS.
AN UNDERTAKER.
FORGET THAT GUY.
LEAVE HIS CREEPY DEATH TRAP, AND LIVE HERE WITH US!

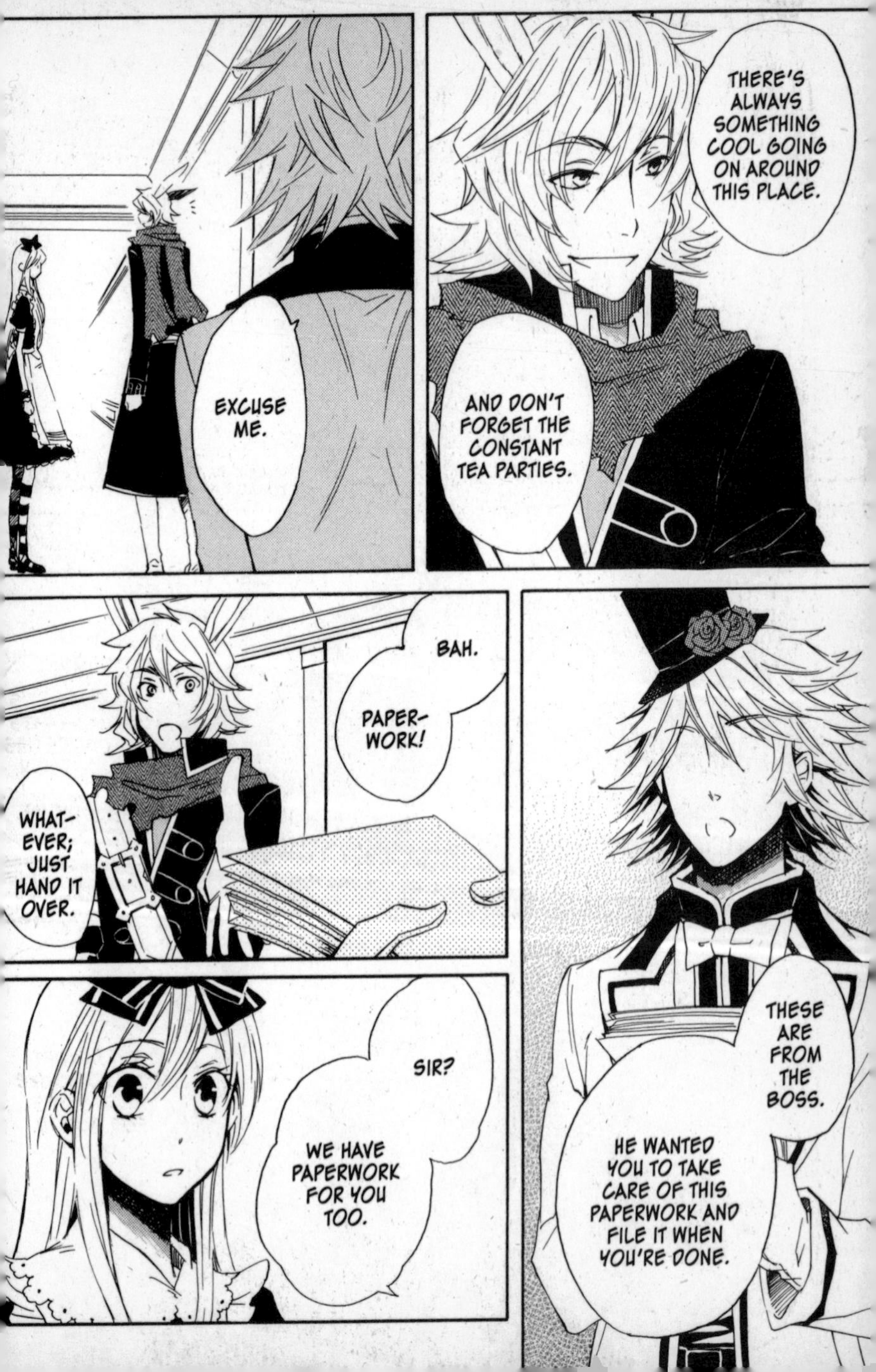
THERE'S ALWAYS SOMETHING COOL GOING ON AROUND THIS PLACE.
AND DON'T FORGET THE CONSTANT TEA PARTIES.
EXCUSE ME.
THESE ARE FROM THE BOSS.
HE WANTED YOU TO TAKE CARE OF THIS PAPERWORK AND FILE IT WHEN YOU'RE DONE.
BAH.
PAPER-WORK!
WHAT-EVER; JUST HAND IT OVER.
SIR?
WE HAVE PAPERWORK FOR YOU TOO.

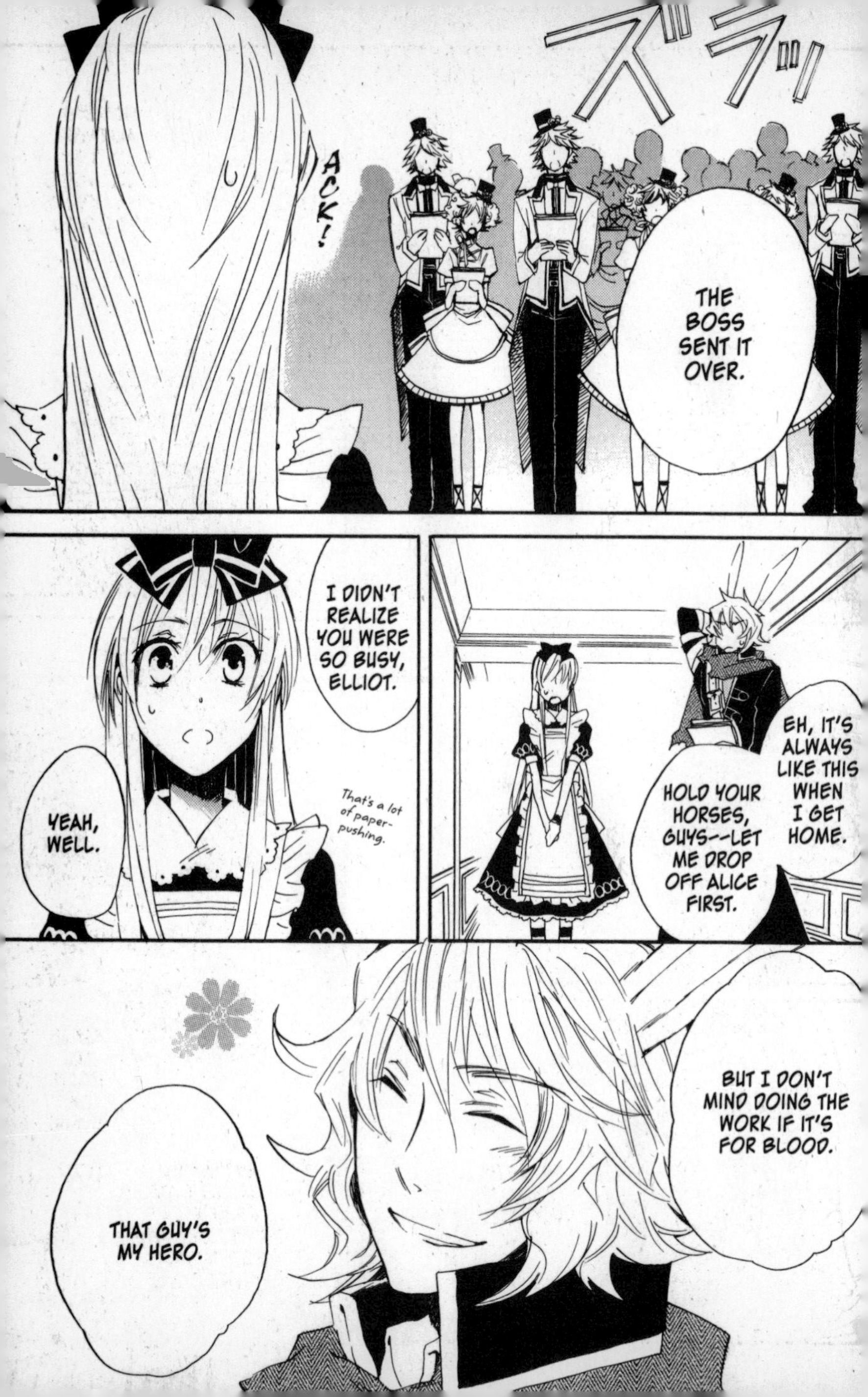
ズラッ!!
THE BOSS SENT IT OVER.
ACK!
EH, IT'S ALWAYS LIKE THIS WHEN I GET HOME.
HOLD YOUR HORSES, GUYS--LET ME DROP OFF ALICE FIRST.
I DIDN'T REALIZE YOU WERE SO BUSY, ELLIOT.
That's a lot of paper-pushing.
YEAH, WELL.
BUT I DON'T MIND DOING THE WORK IF IT'S FOR BLOOD.
THAT GUY'S MY HERO.

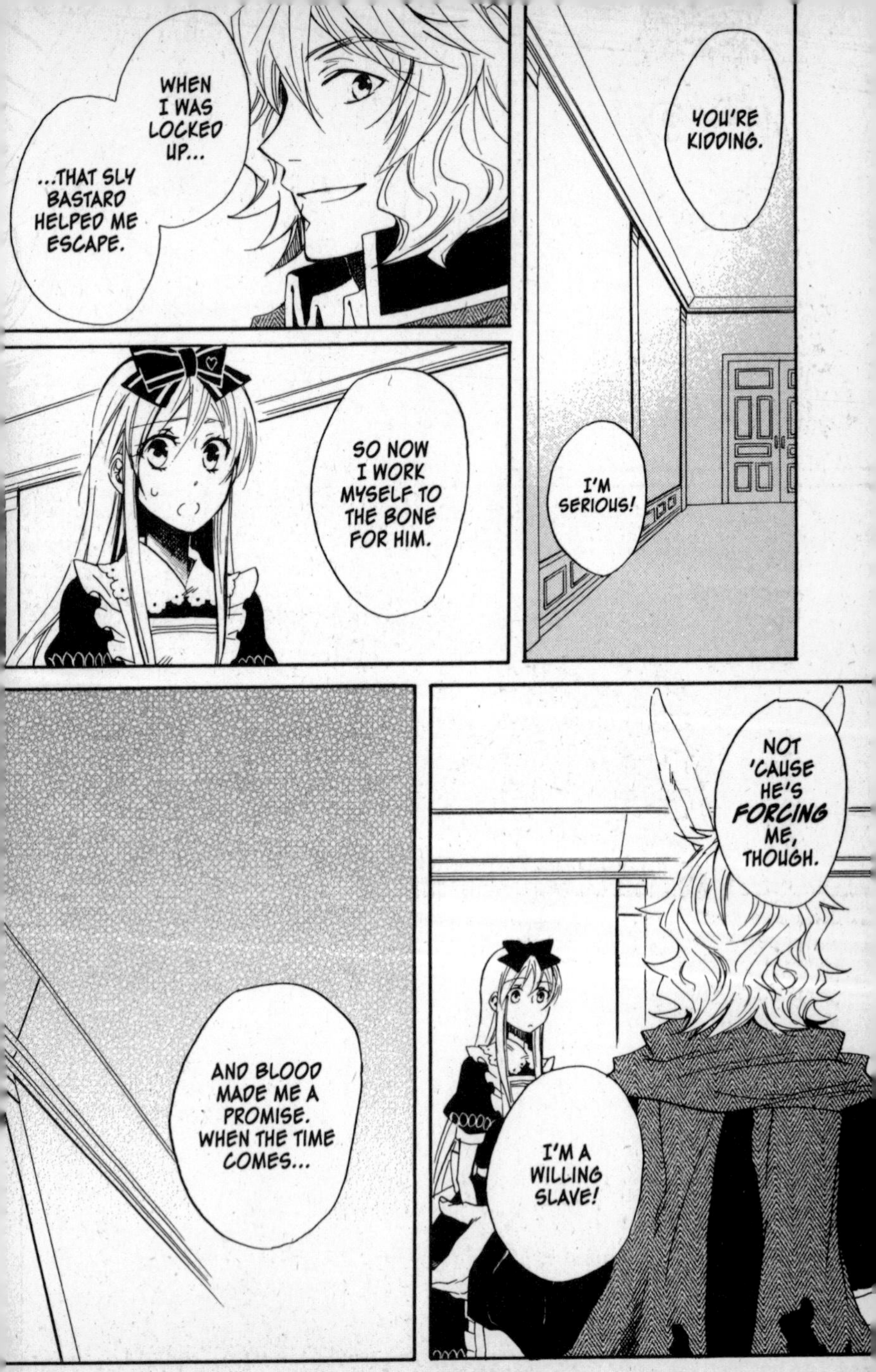
YOU'RE KIDDING.
I'M SERIOUS!
WHEN I WAS LOCKED UP...
...THAT SLY BASTARD HELPED ME ESCAPE.
SO NOW I WORK MYSELF TO THE BONE FOR HIM.
NOT 'CAUSE HE'S FORCING ME, THOUGH.
I'M A WILLING SLAVE!
AND BLOOD MADE ME A PROMISE. WHEN THE TIME COMES...

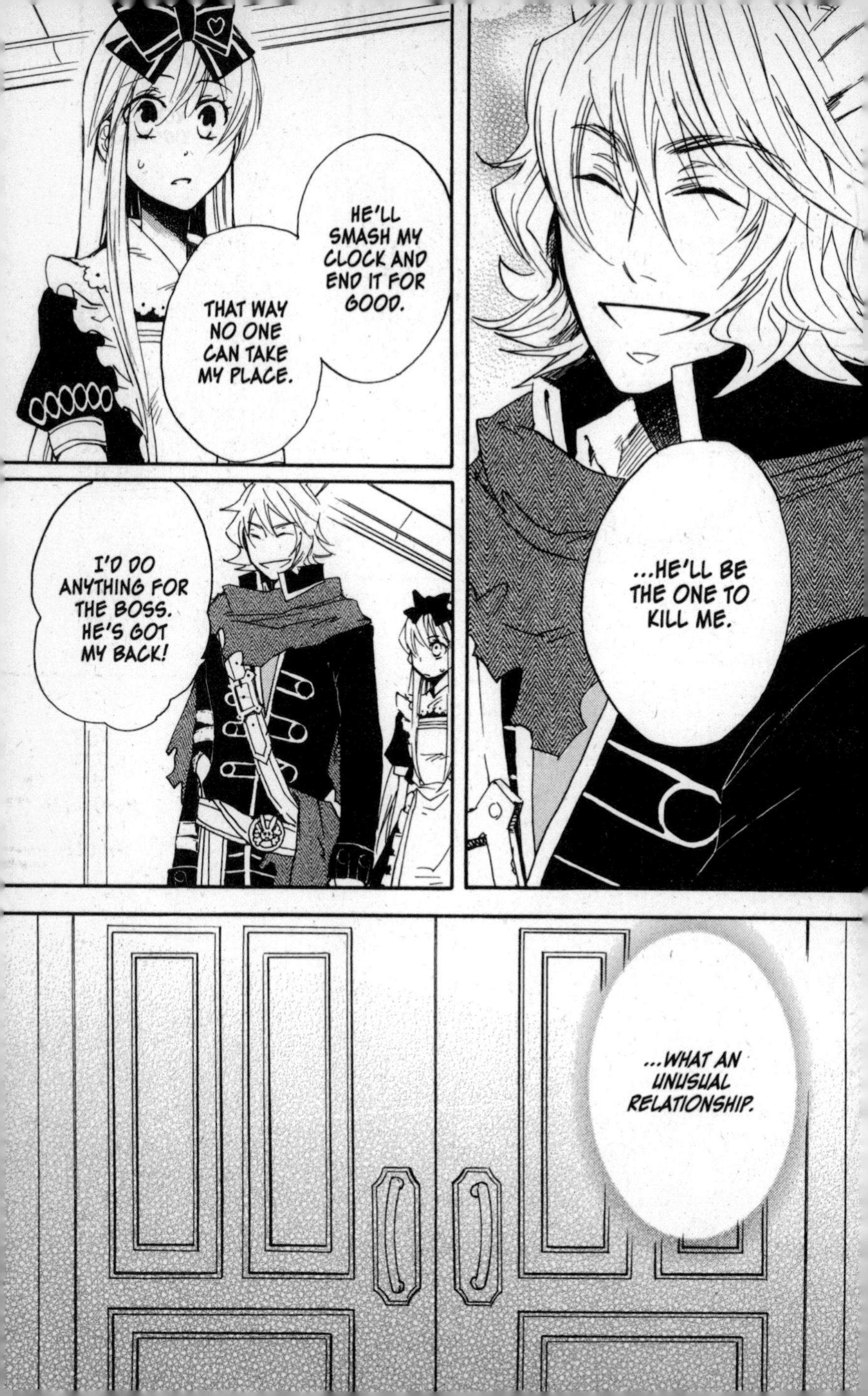
...HE'LL BE THE ONE TO KILL ME.
HE'LL SMASH MY CLOCK AND END IT FOR GOOD.
THAT WAY NO ONE CAN TAKE MY PLACE.
I'D DO ANYTHING FOR THE BOSS. HE'S GOT MY BACK!
...WHAT AN UNUSUAL RELATIONSHIP.

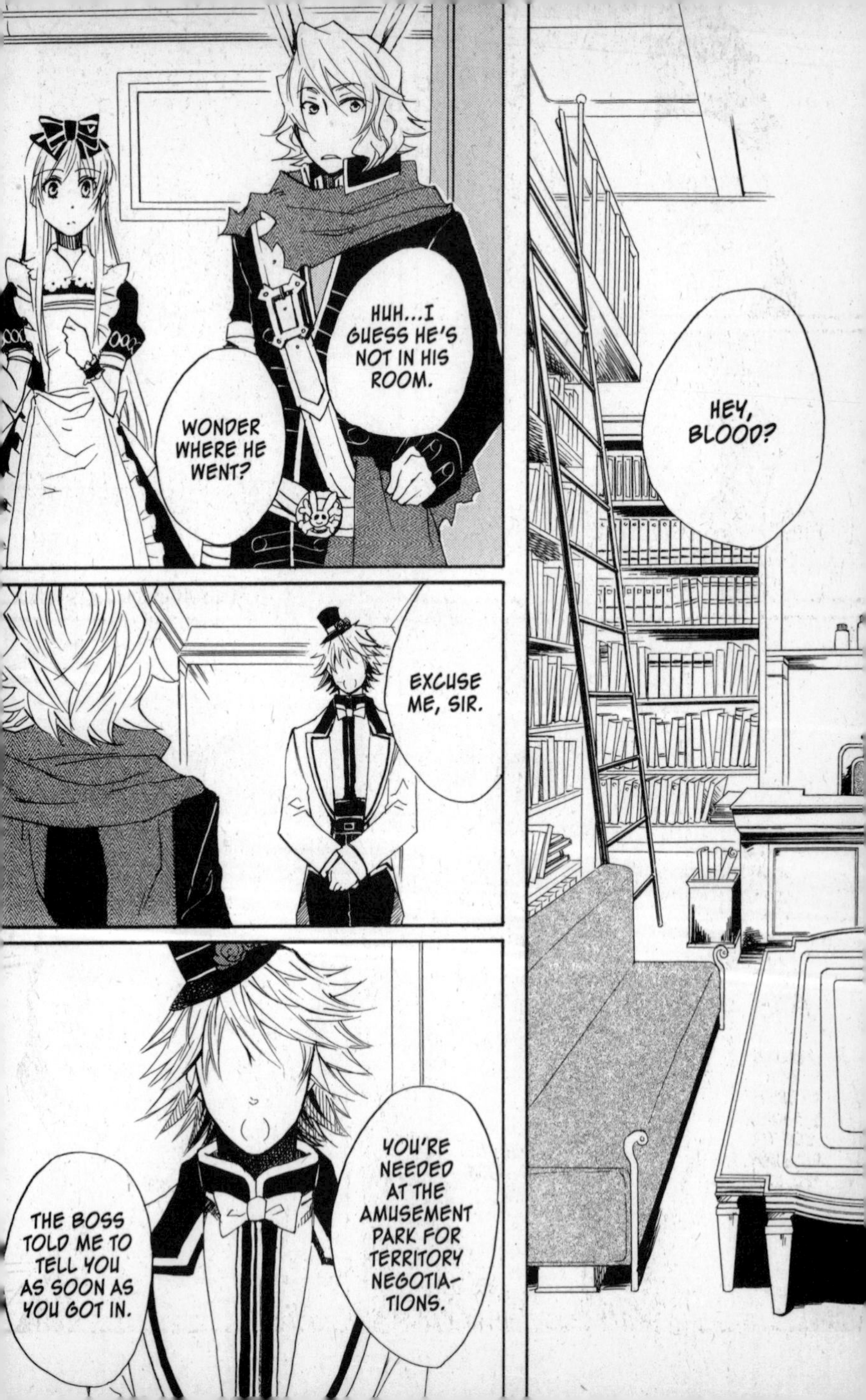
HEY, BLOOD?
HUH...I GUESS HE'S NOT IN HIS ROOM.
WONDER WHERE HE WENT?
EXCUSE ME, SIR.
YOU'RE NEEDED AT THE AMUSEMENT PARK FOR TERRITORY NEGOTIA-TIONS.
THE BOSS TOLD ME TO TELL YOU AS SOON AS YOU GOT IN.

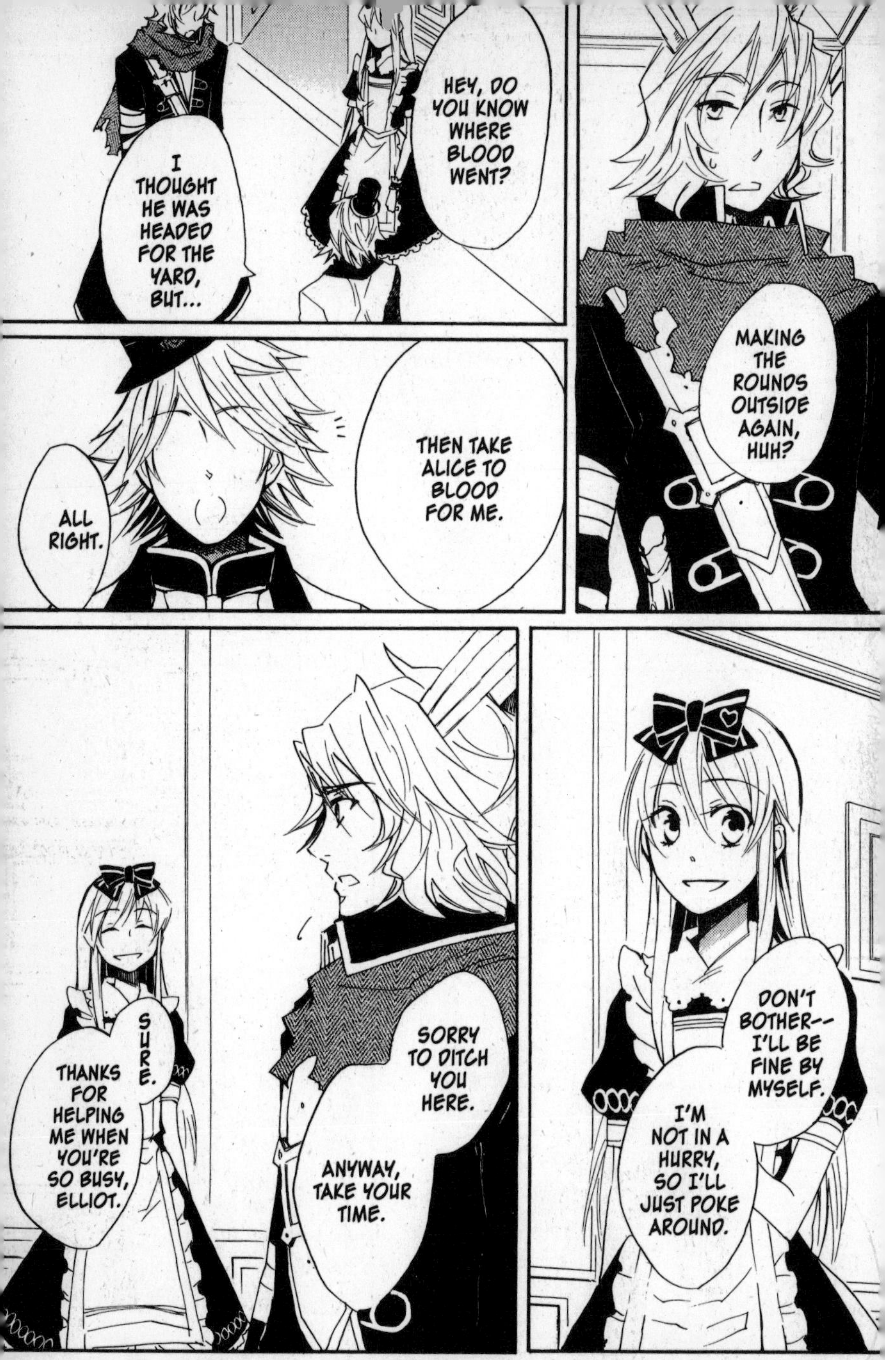
MAKING THE ROUNDS OUTSIDE AGAIN, HUH?
HEY, DO YOU KNOW WHERE BLOOD WENT?
I THOUGHT HE WAS HEADED FOR THE YARD, BUT...
THEN TAKE ALICE TO BLOOD FOR ME.
ALL RIGHT.
DON'T BOTHER-- I'LL BE FINE BY MYSELF.
I'M NOT IN A HURRY, SO I'LL JUST POKE AROUND.
SORRY TO DITCH YOU HERE.
ANYWAY, TAKE YOUR TIME.
SURE.
THANKS FOR HELPING ME WHEN YOU'RE SO BUSY, ELLIOT.

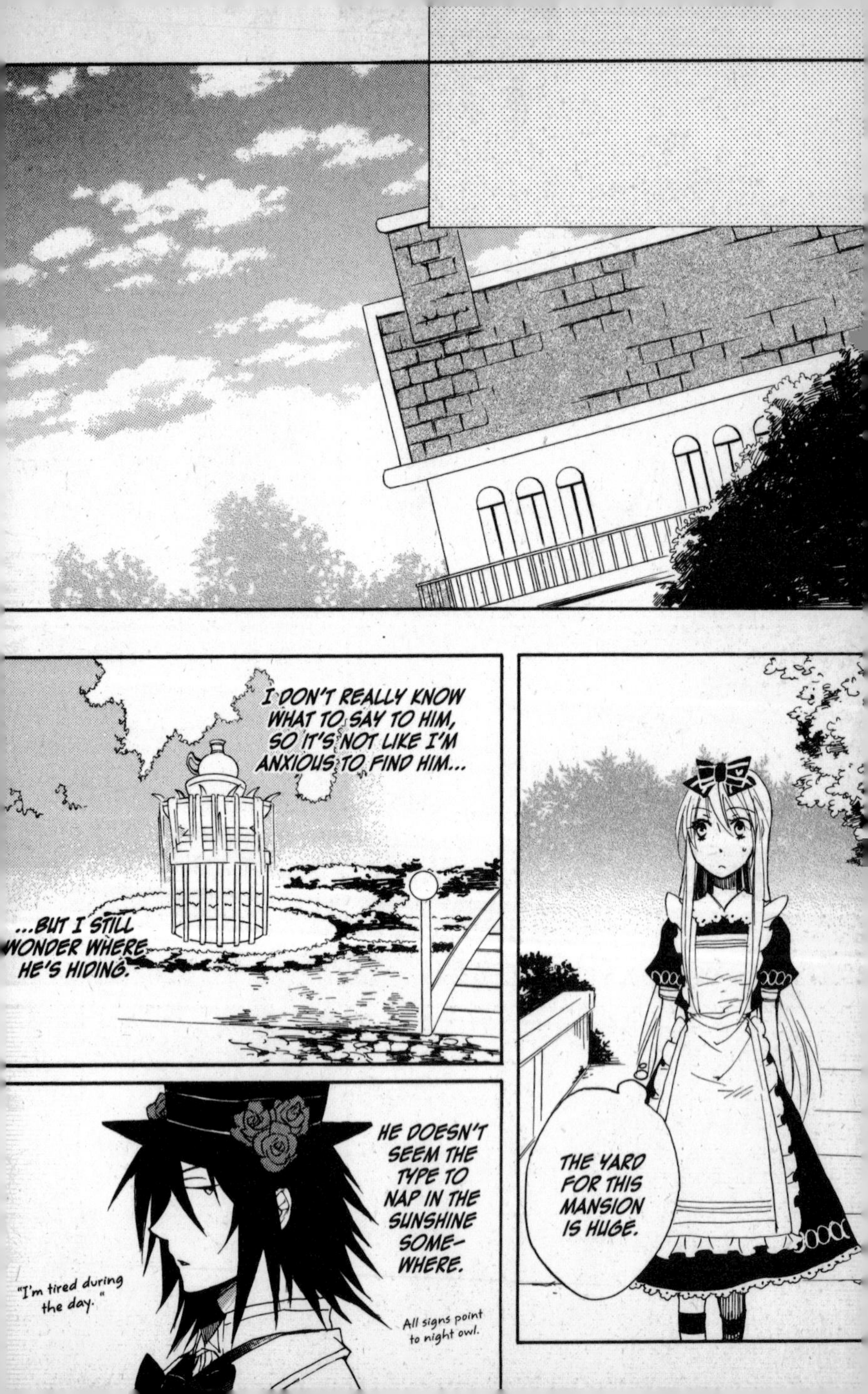
THE YARD FOR THIS MANSION IS HUGE.
I DON'T REALLY KNOW WHAT TO SAY TO HIM, SO IT'S NOT LIKE I'M ANXIOUS TO FIND HIM...
...BUT I STILL WONDER WHERE HE'S HIDING.
HE DOESN'T SEEM THE TYPE TO NAP IN THE SUNSHINE SOME-WHERE.
All signs point to night owl.
"I'm tired during the day."

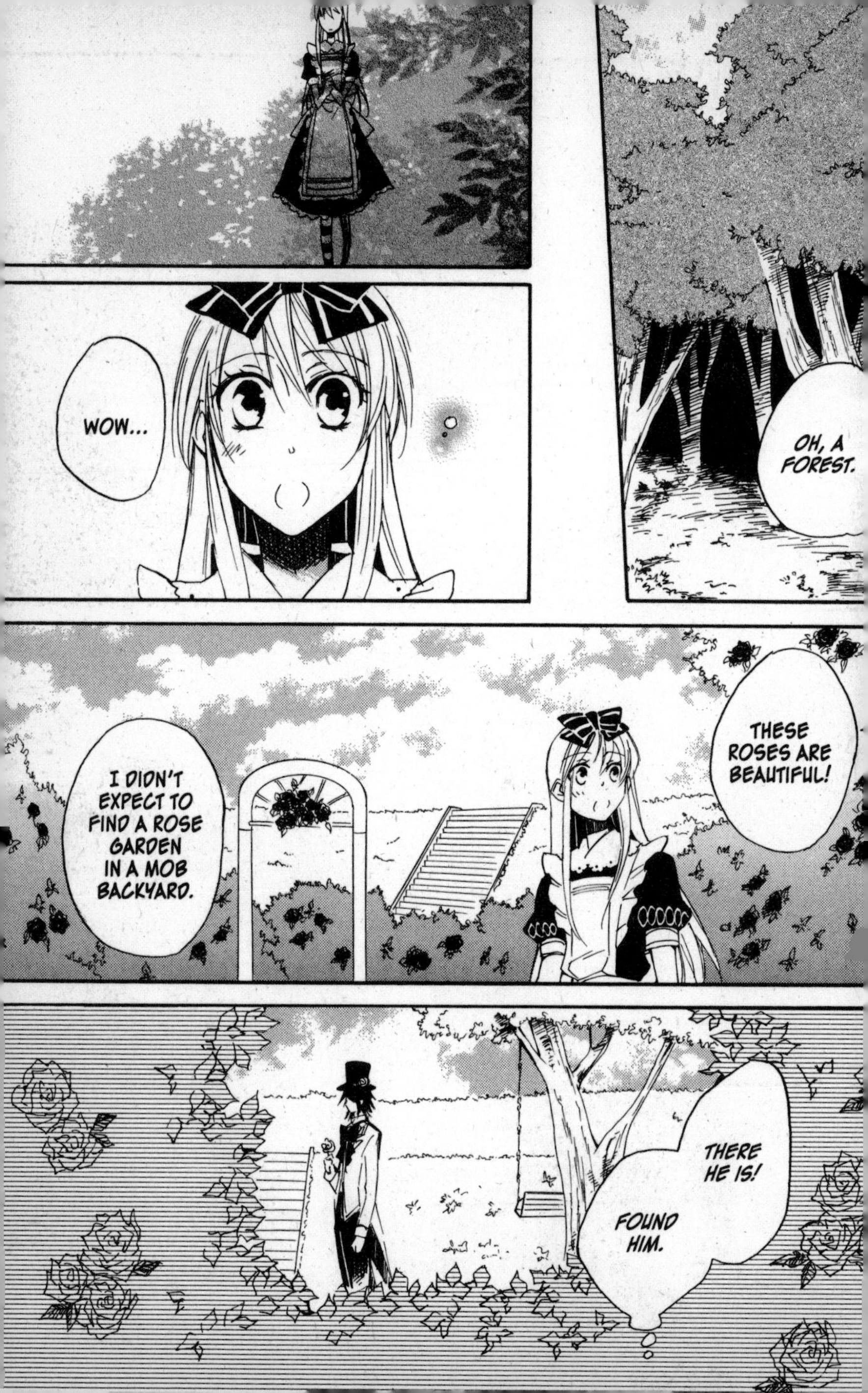
OH, A FOREST.
WOW...
THESE ROSES ARE BEAUTIFUL!
I DIDN'T EXPECT TO FIND A ROSE GARDEN IN A MOB BACKYARD.
THERE HE IS!
FOUND HIM.

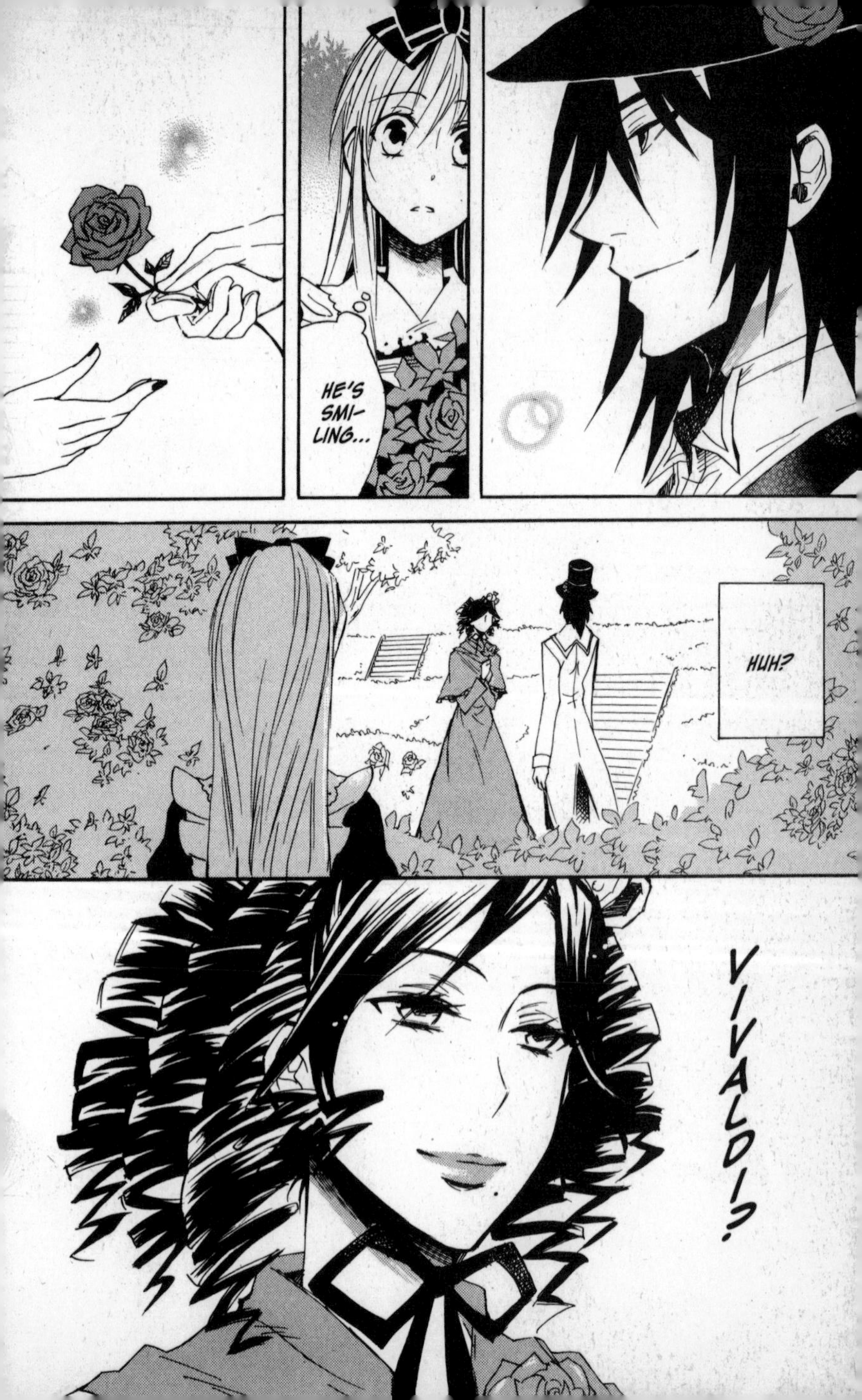
HE'S SMI-LING...
HUH?
VIVALDI!?

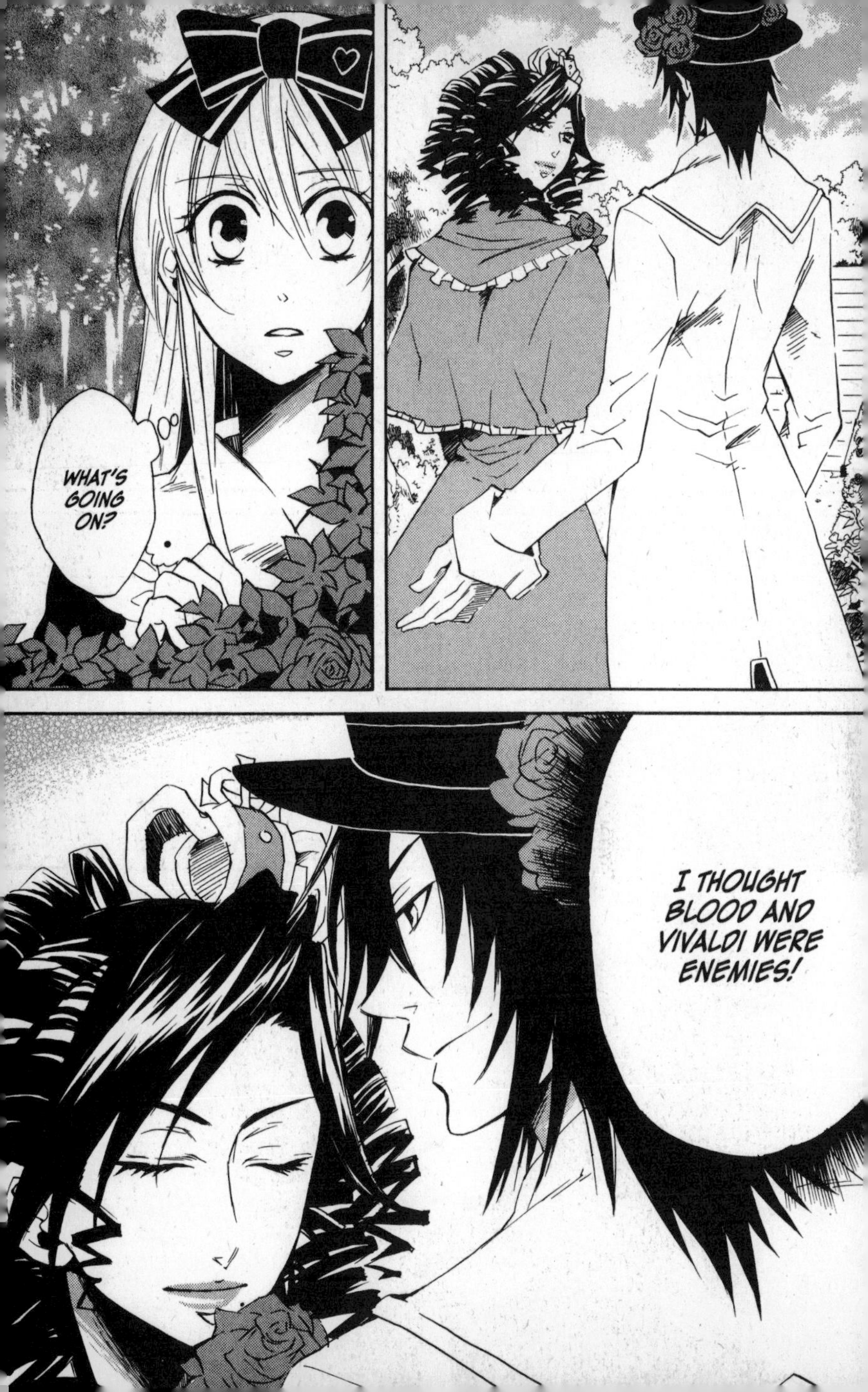
WHAT'S GOING ON?
I THOUGHT BLOOD AND VIVALDI WERE ENEMIES!

# ♥11 Light Weight

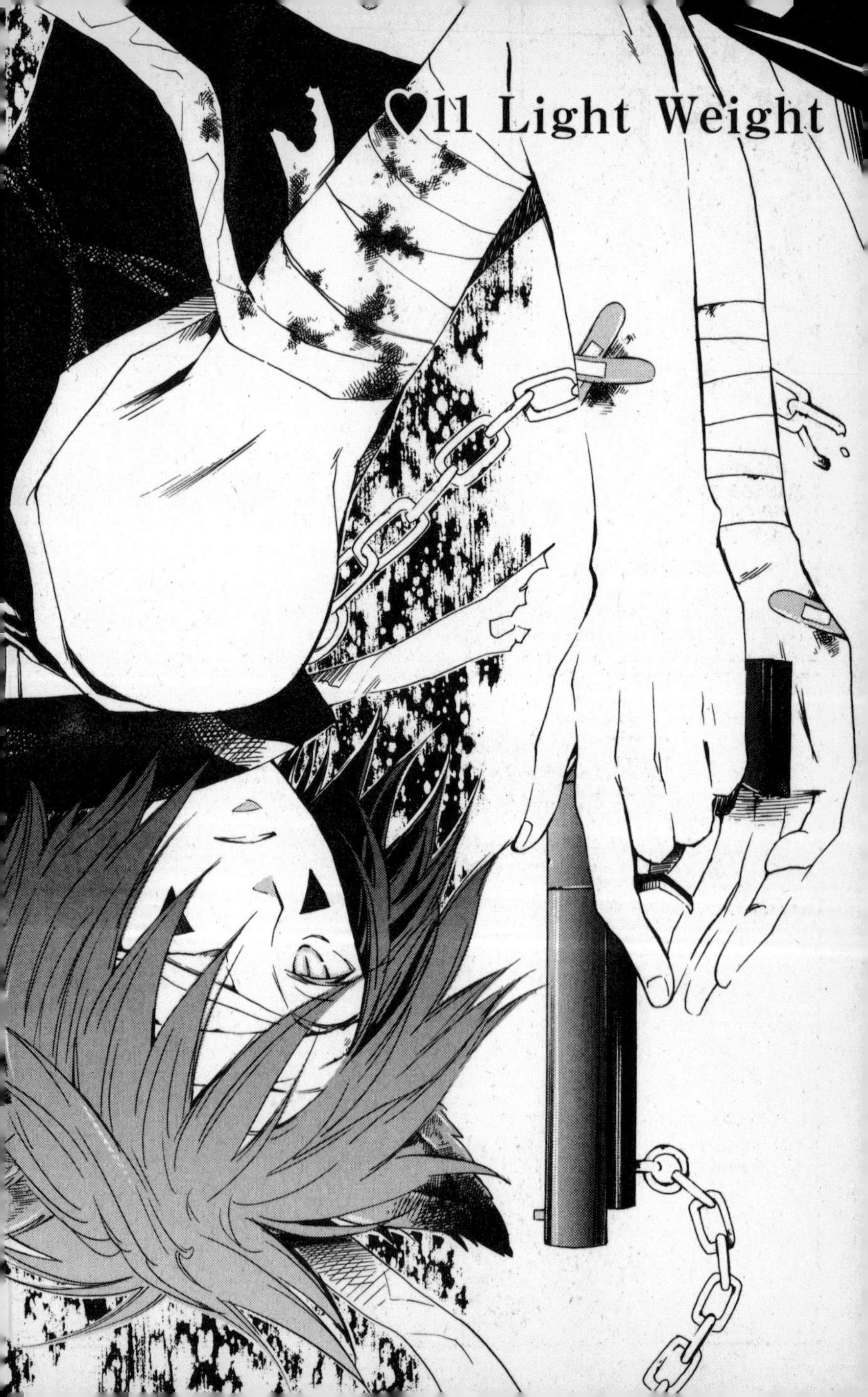

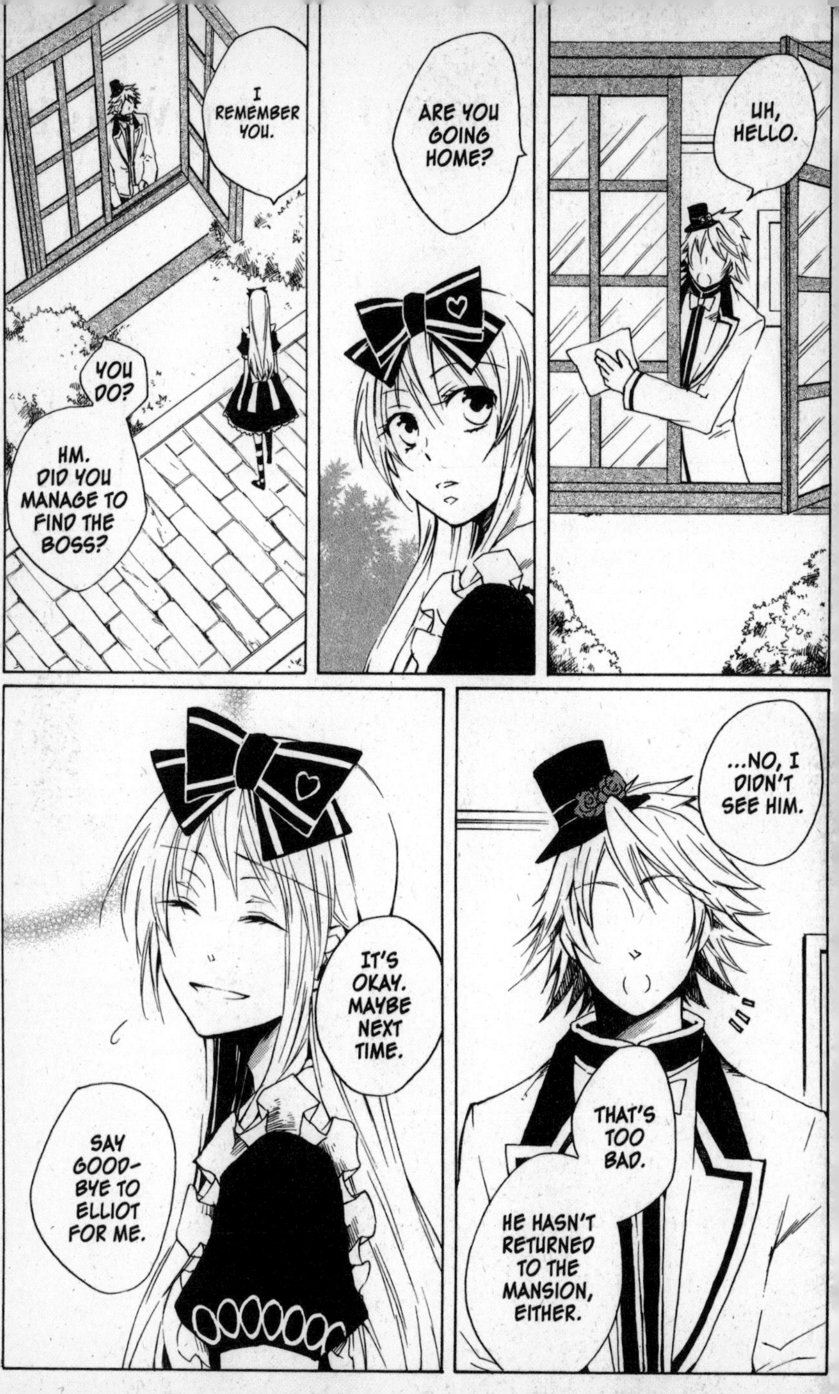
UH, HELLO.
ARE YOU GOING HOME?
I REMEMBER YOU.
YOU DO?
HM. DID YOU MANAGE TO FIND THE BOSS?
...NO, I DIDN'T SEE HIM.
THAT'S TOO BAD.
HE HASN'T RETURNED TO THE MANSION, EITHER.
IT'S OKAY. MAYBE NEXT TIME.
SAY GOOD-BYE TO ELLIOT FOR ME.

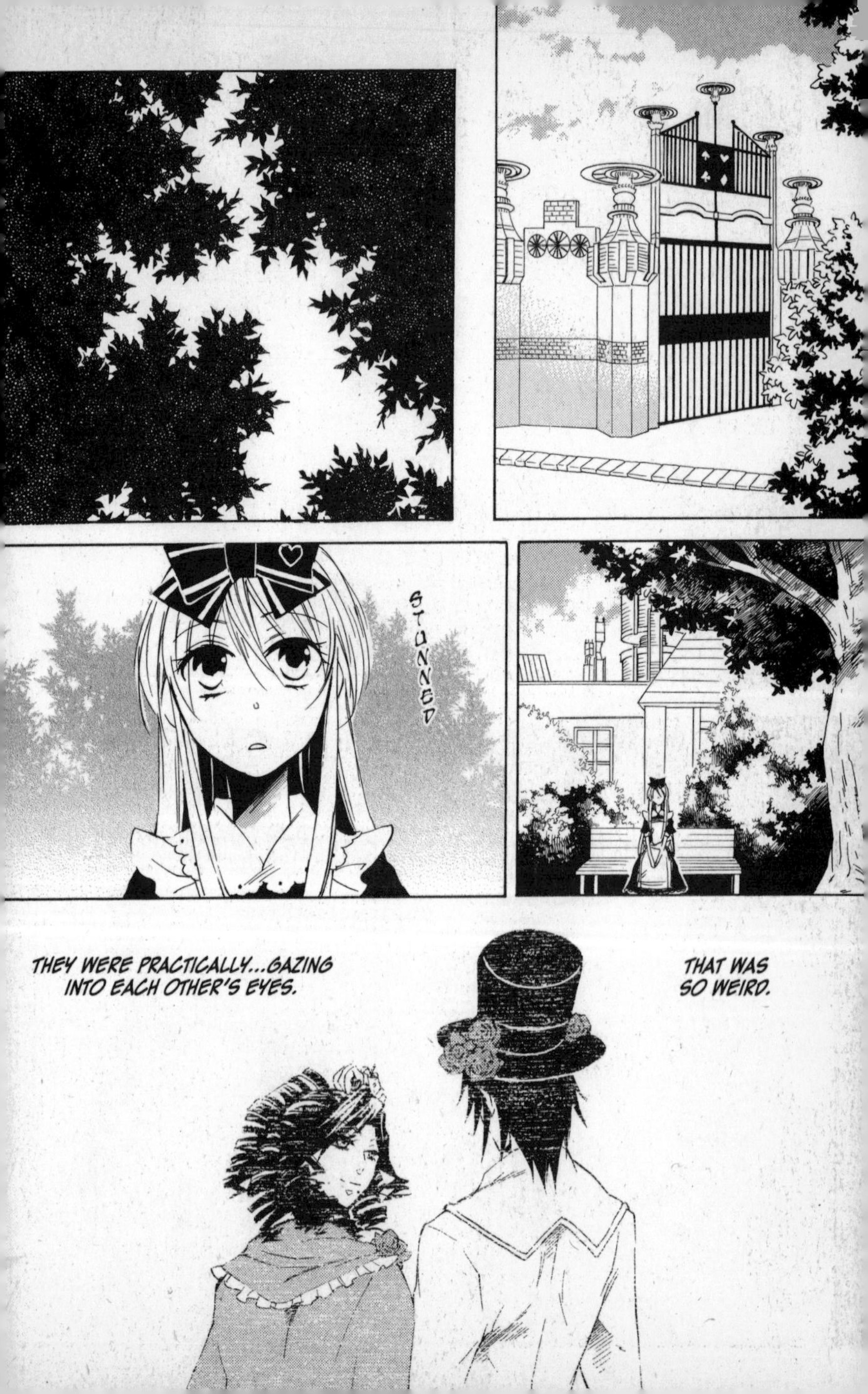
STUNNED
THAT WAS SO WEIRD.
THEY WERE PRACTICALLY...GAZING INTO EACH OTHER'S EYES.

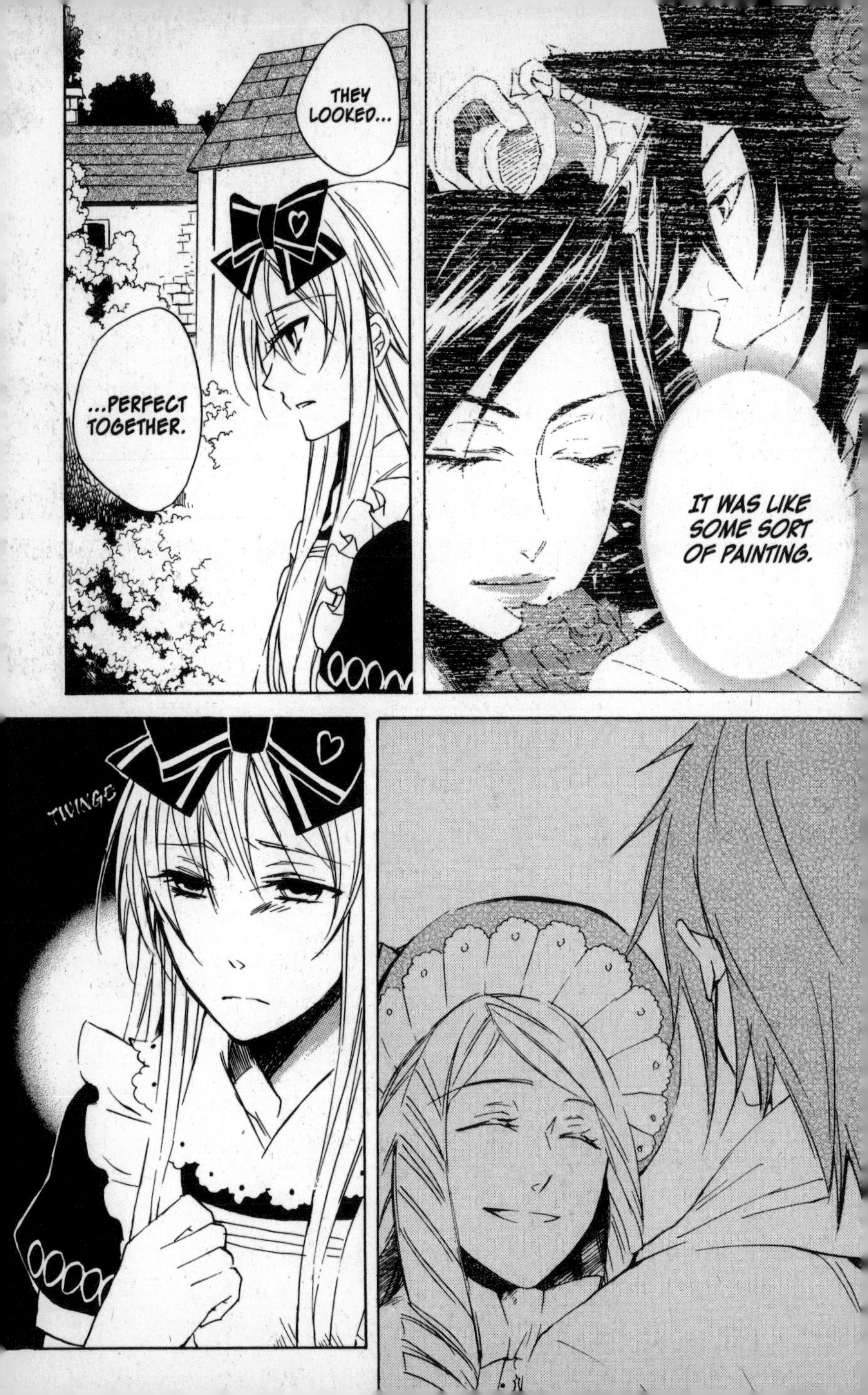
IT WAS LIKE SOME SORT OF PAINTING.
THEY LOOKED...
...PERFECT TOGETHER.
TWINGE

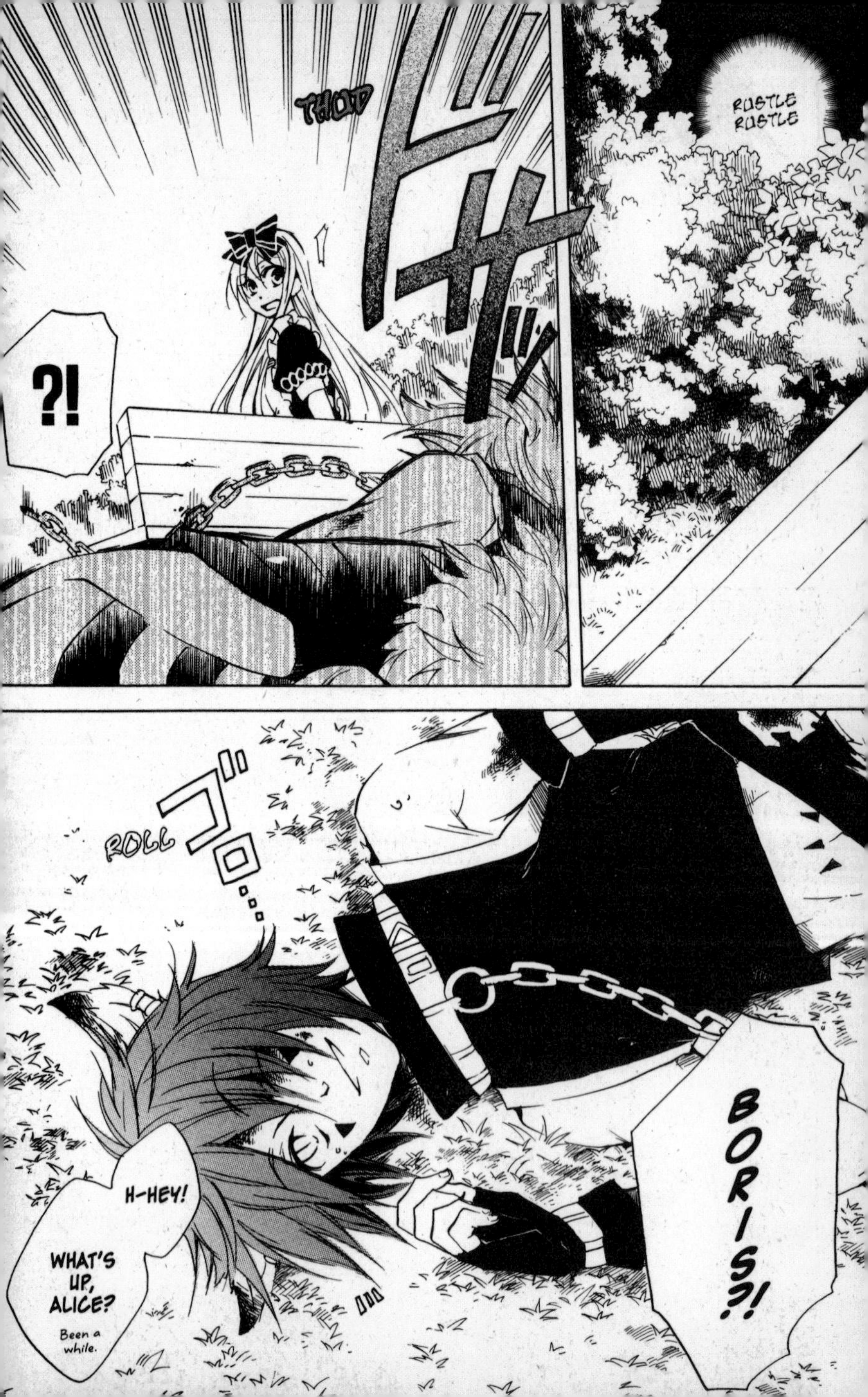

RUSTLE RUSTLE
THUD
ドザッ
?!
BORIS?!
ROLL
ゴロ
H-HEY!
WHAT'S UP, ALICE?
Been a while.

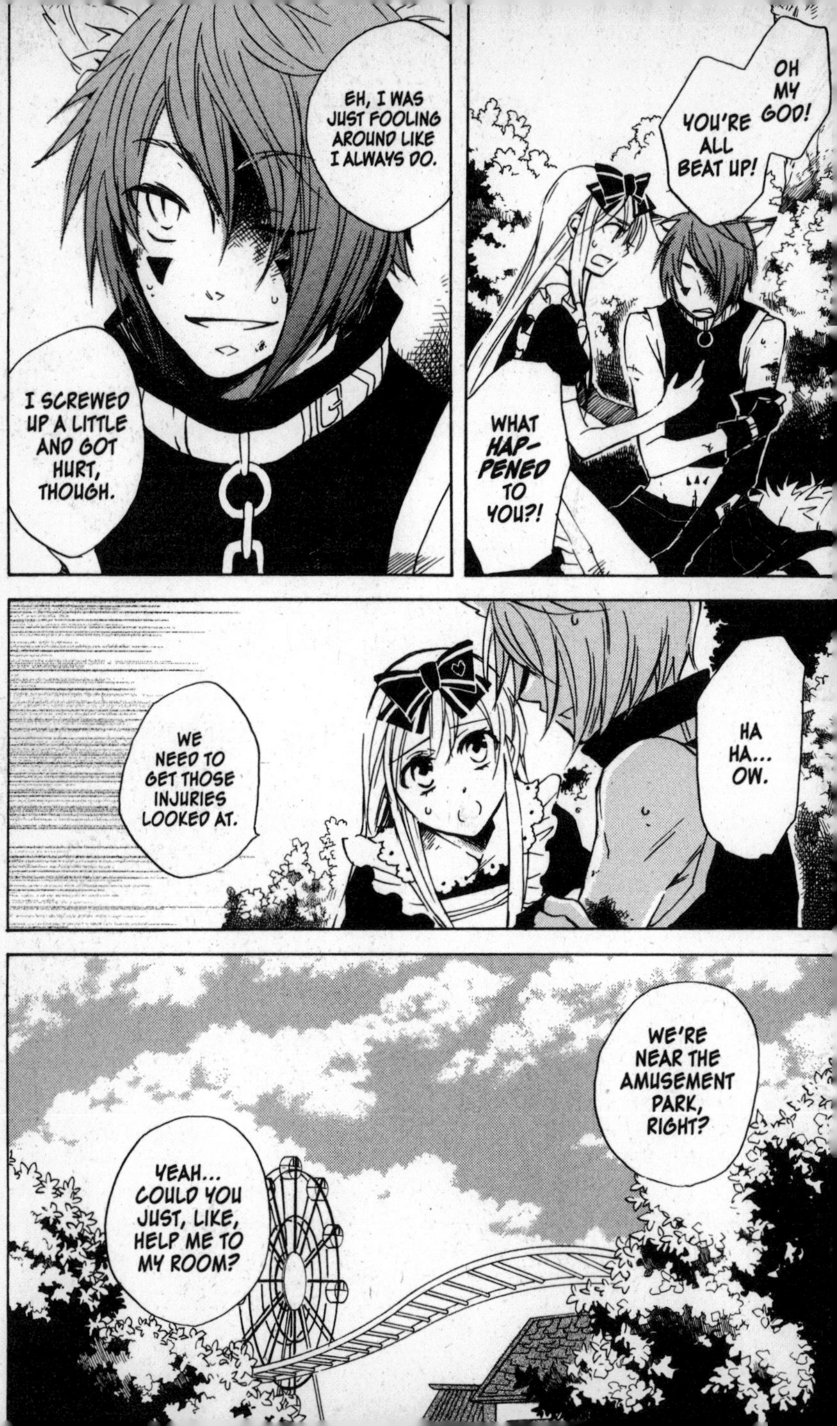
OH MY GOD!
YOU'RE ALL BEAT UP!
WHAT **HAPPENED** TO YOU?!
EH, I WAS JUST FOOLING AROUND LIKE I ALWAYS DO.
I SCREWED UP A LITTLE AND GOT HURT, THOUGH.
HA HA... OW.
WE NEED TO GET THOSE INJURIES LOOKED AT.
WE'RE NEAR THE AMUSEMENT PARK, RIGHT?
YEAH... COULD YOU JUST, LIKE, HELP ME TO MY ROOM?

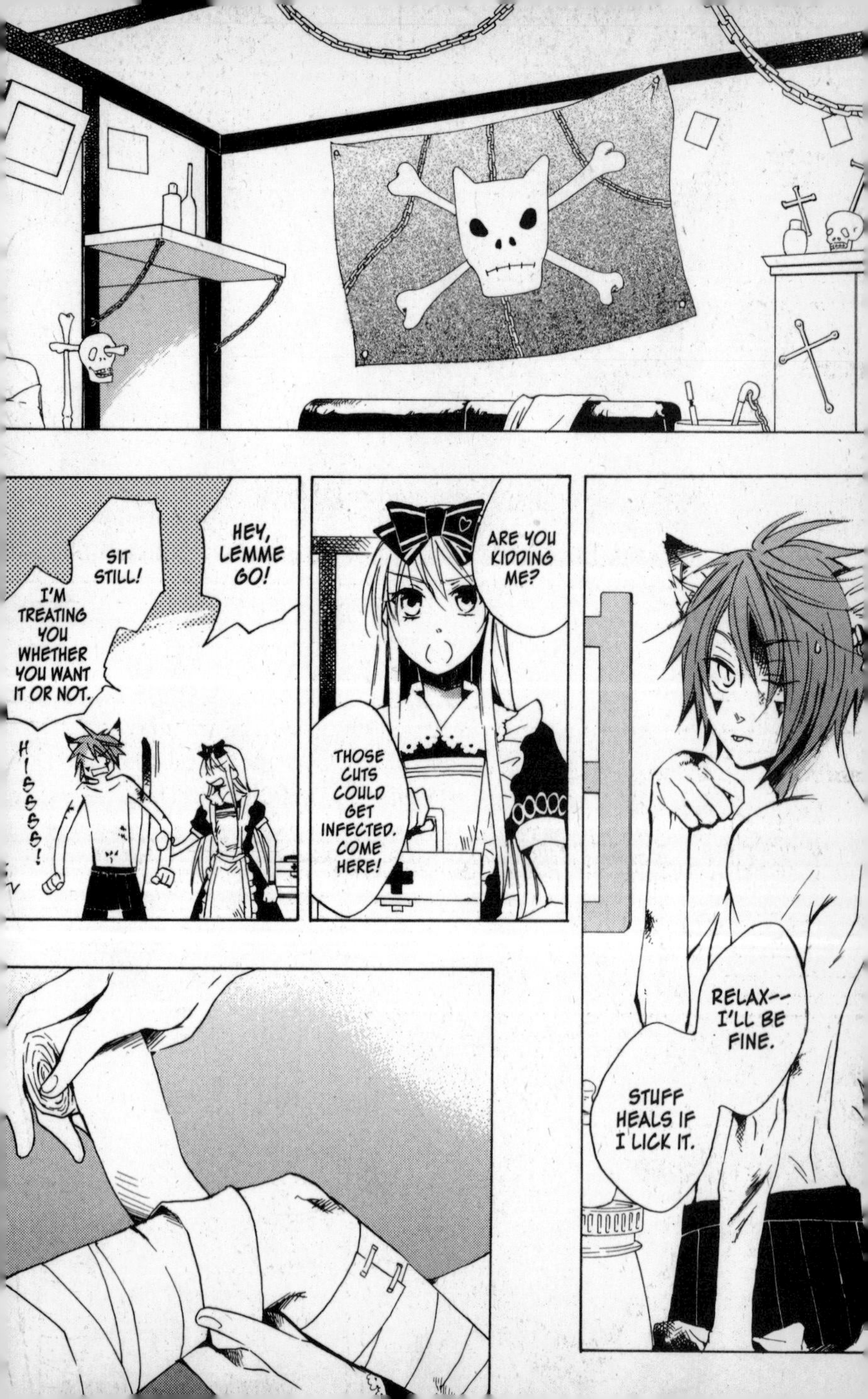
RELAX-- I'LL BE FINE.
STUFF HEALS IF I LICK IT.
ARE YOU KIDDING ME?
THOSE CUTS COULD GET INFECTED. COME HERE!
HEY, LEMME GO!
SIT STILL!
I'M TREATING YOU WHETHER YOU WANT IT OR NOT.
HISSSS!

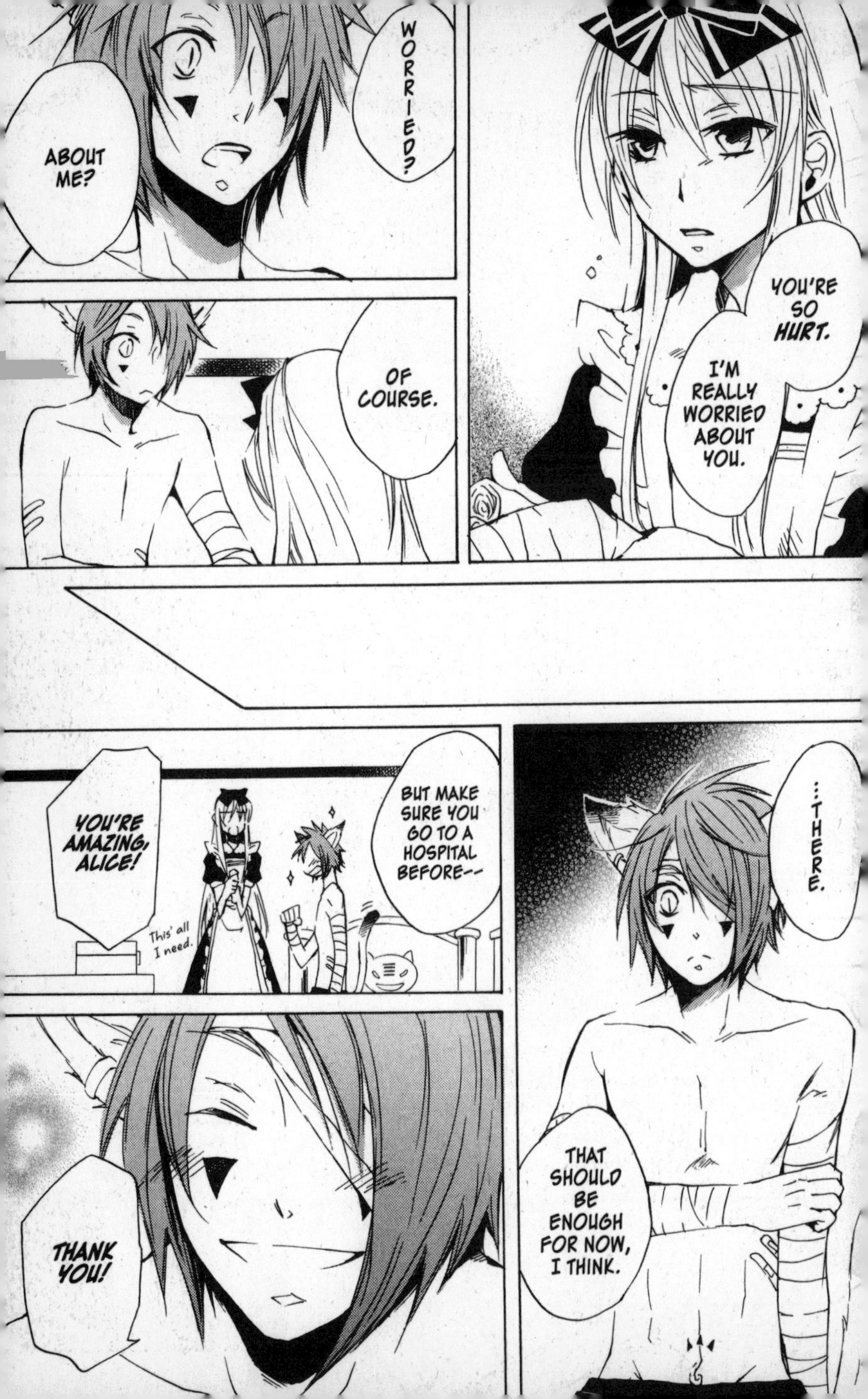

YOU'RE SO HURT.
I'M REALLY WORRIED ABOUT YOU.
WORRIED?
ABOUT ME?
OF COURSE.
...THERE.
THAT SHOULD BE ENOUGH FOR NOW, I THINK.
BUT MAKE SURE YOU GO TO A HOSPITAL BEFORE--
YOU'RE AMAZING, ALICE!
This' all I need.
THANK YOU!

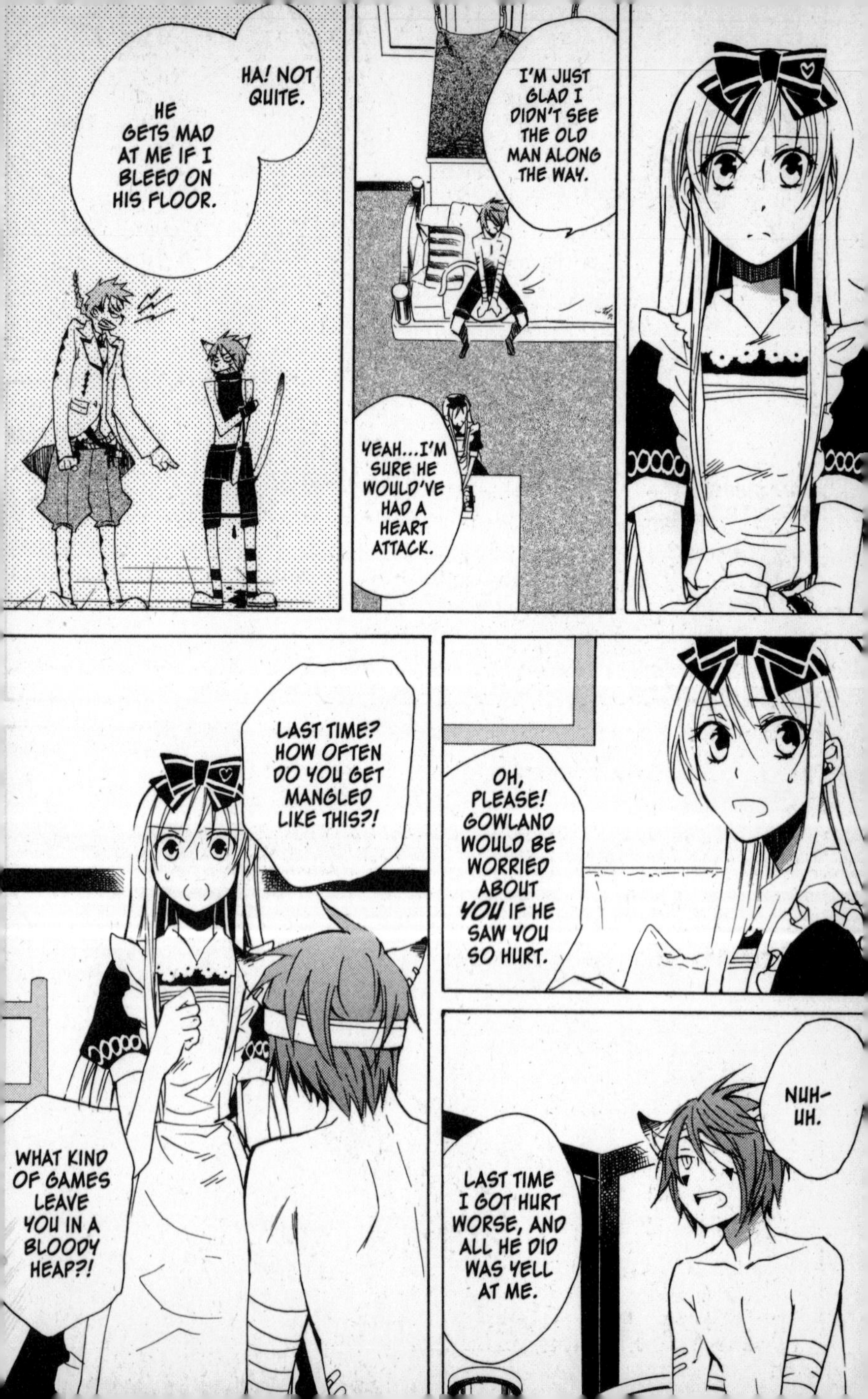
I'M JUST GLAD I DIDN'T SEE THE OLD MAN ALONG THE WAY.
YEAH...I'M SURE HE WOULD'VE HAD A HEART ATTACK.
HA! NOT QUITE.
HE GETS MAD AT ME IF I BLEED ON HIS FLOOR.
OH, PLEASE! GOWLAND WOULD BE WORRIED ABOUT *YOU* IF HE SAW YOU SO HURT.
NUH-UH.
LAST TIME I GOT HURT WORSE, AND ALL HE DID WAS YELL AT ME.
LAST TIME? HOW OFTEN DO YOU GET MANGLED LIKE THIS?!
WHAT KIND OF GAMES LEAVE YOU IN A BLOODY HEAP?!

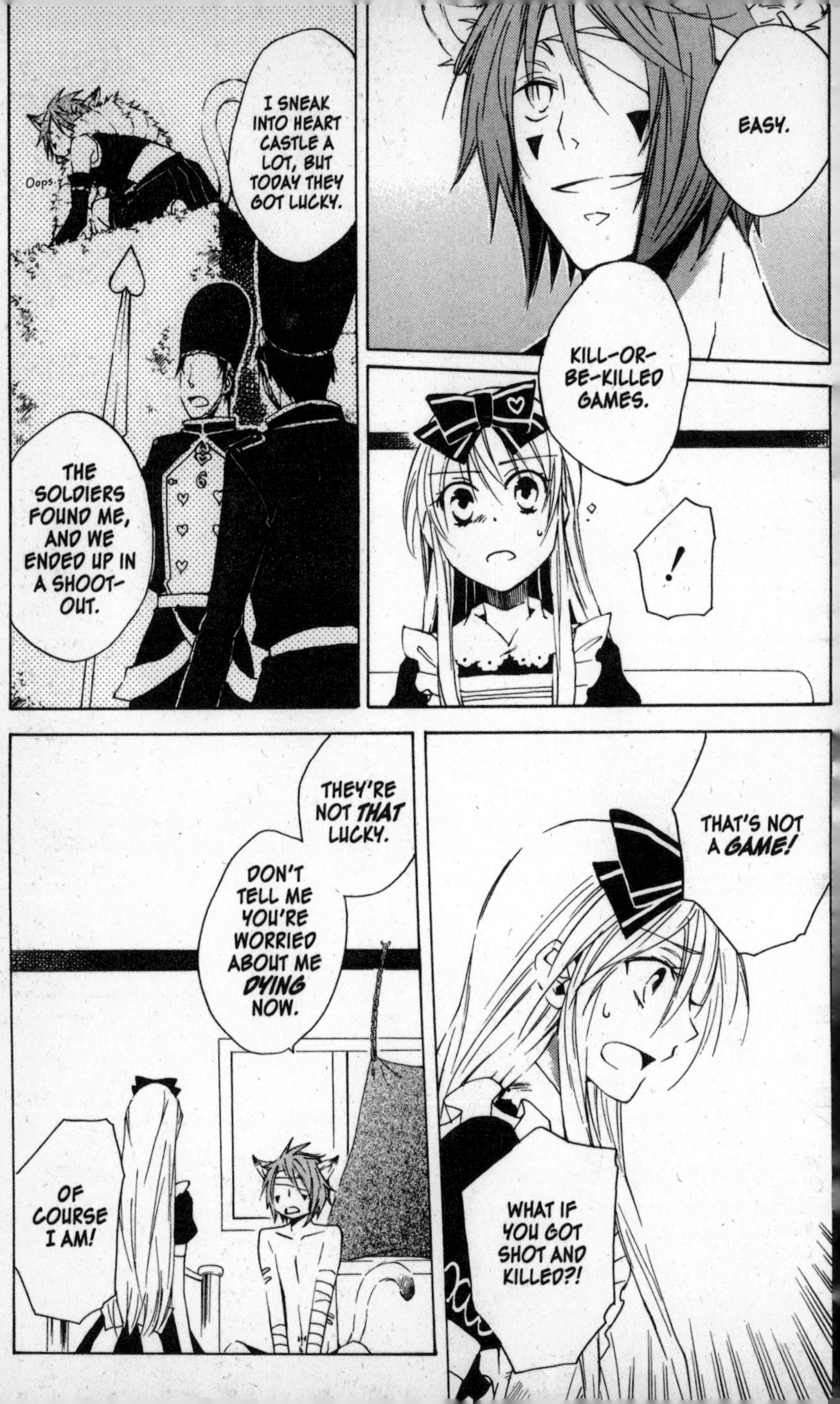
EASY.
KILL-OR-BE-KILLED GAMES.
!
I SNEAK INTO HEART CASTLE A LOT, BUT TODAY THEY GOT LUCKY.
Oops.
THE SOLDIERS FOUND ME, AND WE ENDED UP IN A SHOOT-OUT.
THAT'S NOT A *GAME!*
WHAT IF YOU GOT SHOT AND KILLED?!
THEY'RE NOT *THAT* LUCKY.
DON'T TELL ME YOU'RE WORRIED ABOUT ME *DYING* NOW.
OF COURSE I AM!

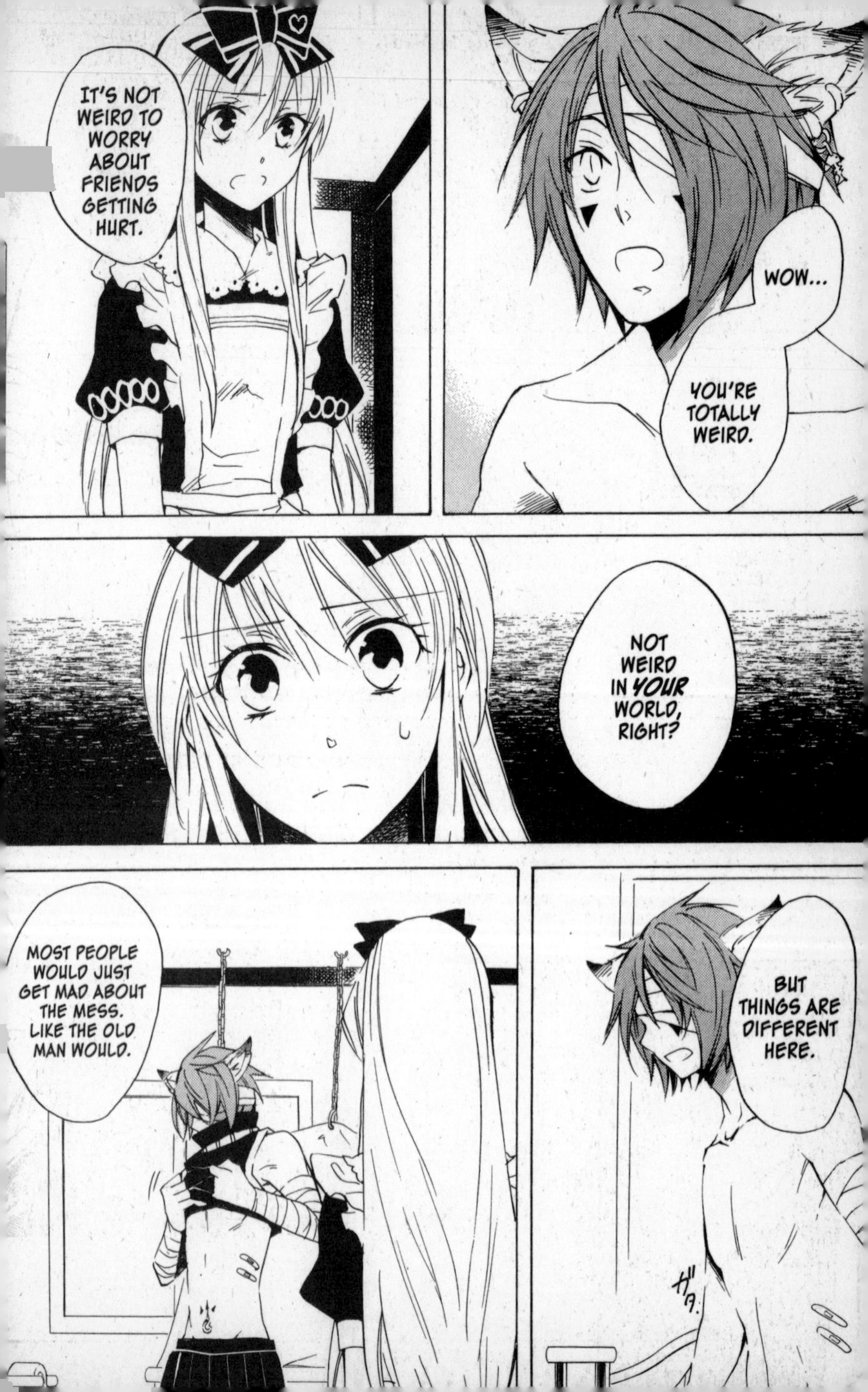
WOW...
YOU'RE TOTALLY WEIRD.
IT'S NOT WEIRD TO WORRY ABOUT FRIENDS GETTING HURT.
NOT WEIRD IN *YOUR* WORLD, RIGHT?
BUT THINGS ARE DIFFERENT HERE.
MOST PEOPLE WOULD JUST GET MAD ABOUT THE MESS. LIKE THE OLD MAN WOULD.

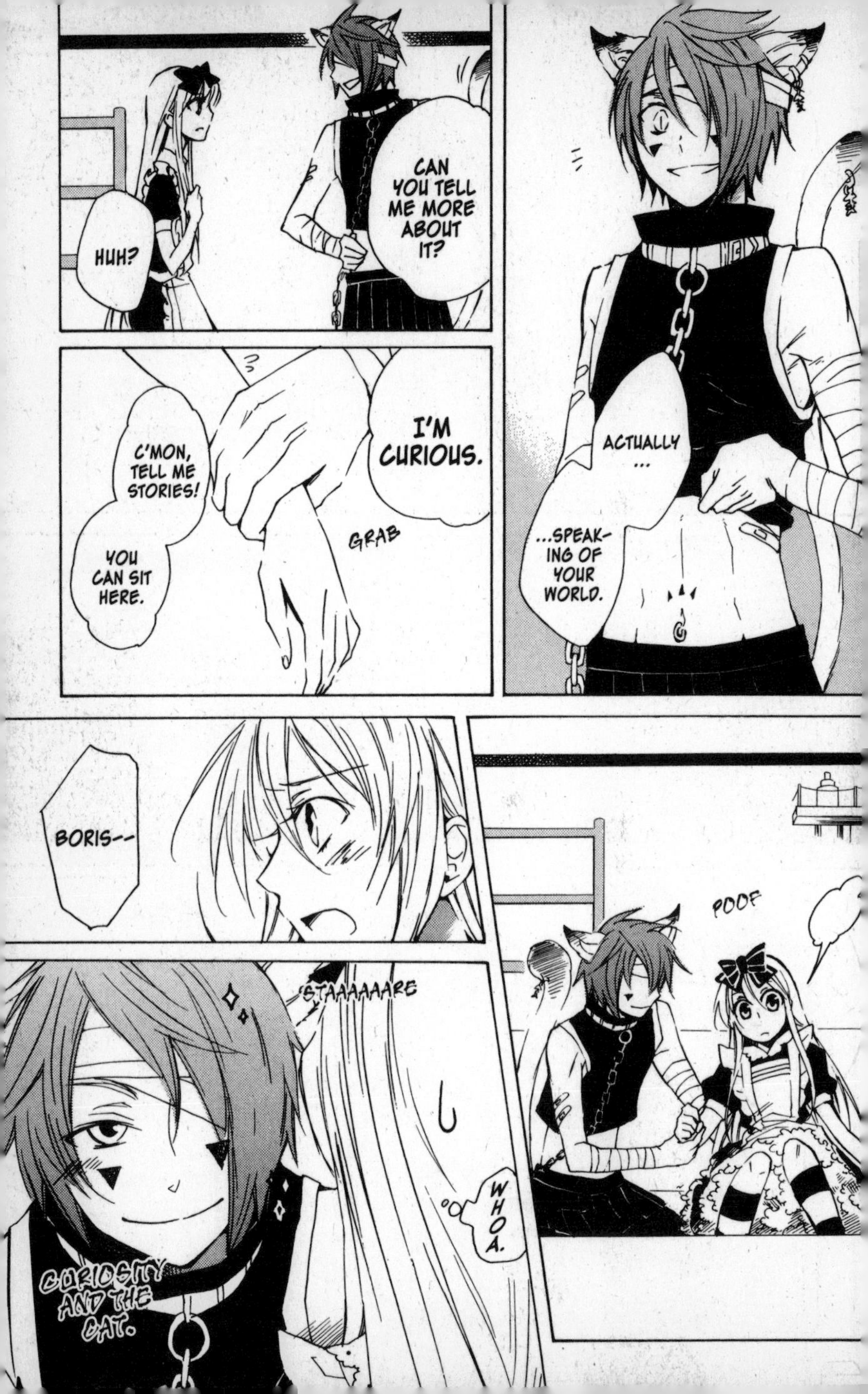
ACTUALLY...
...SPEAKING OF YOUR WORLD.
CAN YOU TELL ME MORE ABOUT IT?
HUH?
I'M CURIOUS.
C'MON, TELL ME STORIES!
GRAB
YOU CAN SIT HERE.
POOF
BORIS--
STAAAAAARE
WHOA.
CURIOSITY AND THE CAT.

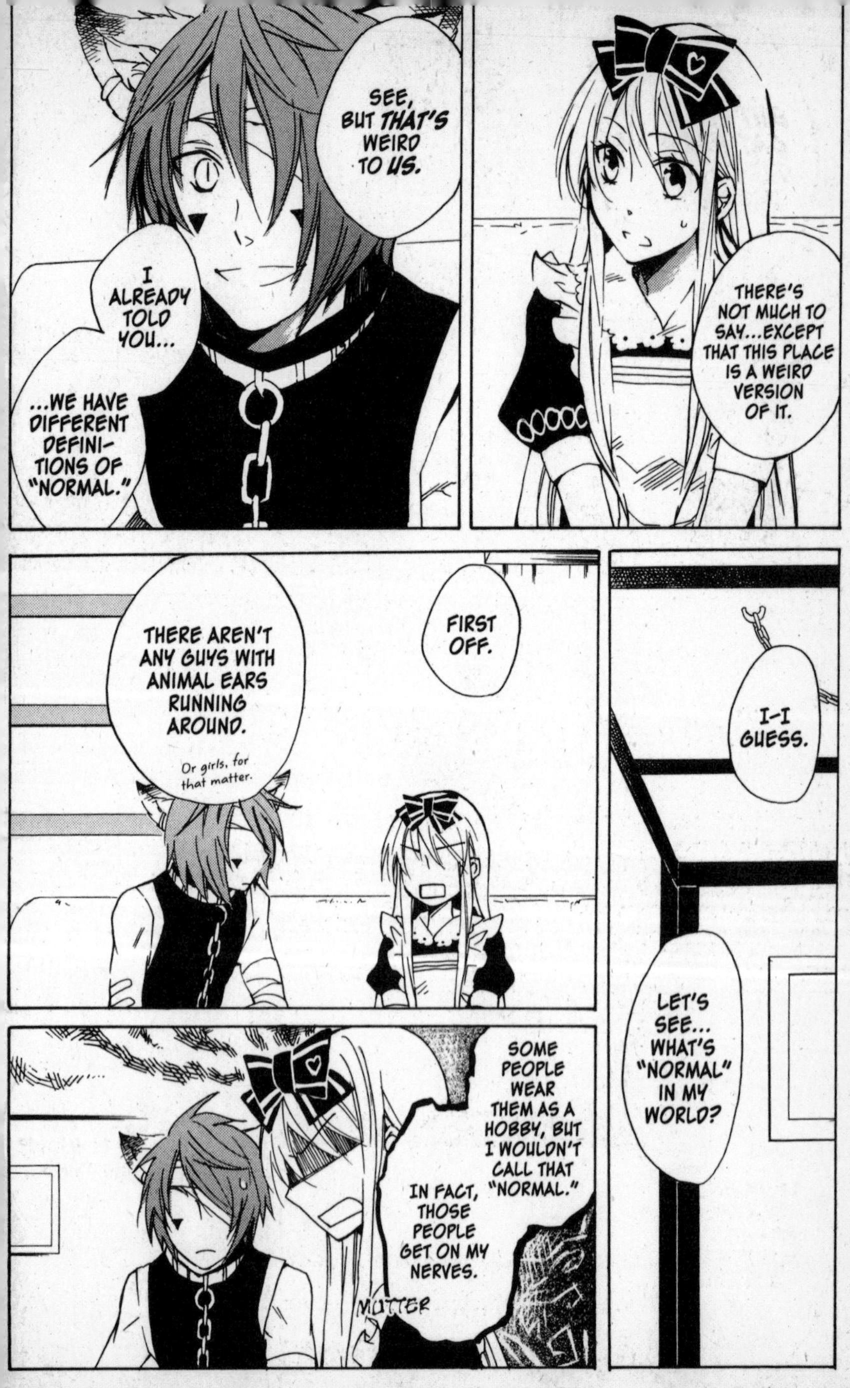
THERE'S NOT MUCH TO SAY...EXCEPT THAT THIS PLACE IS A WEIRD VERSION OF IT.
SEE, BUT THAT'S WEIRD TO US.
I ALREADY TOLD YOU...
...WE HAVE DIFFERENT DEFINITIONS OF "NORMAL."
I-I GUESS.
LET'S SEE... WHAT'S "NORMAL" IN MY WORLD?
FIRST OFF.
THERE AREN'T ANY GUYS WITH ANIMAL EARS RUNNING AROUND.
Or girls, for that matter.
SOME PEOPLE WEAR THEM AS A HOBBY, BUT I WOULDN'T CALL THAT "NORMAL."
IN FACT, THOSE PEOPLE GET ON MY NERVES.
MUTTER

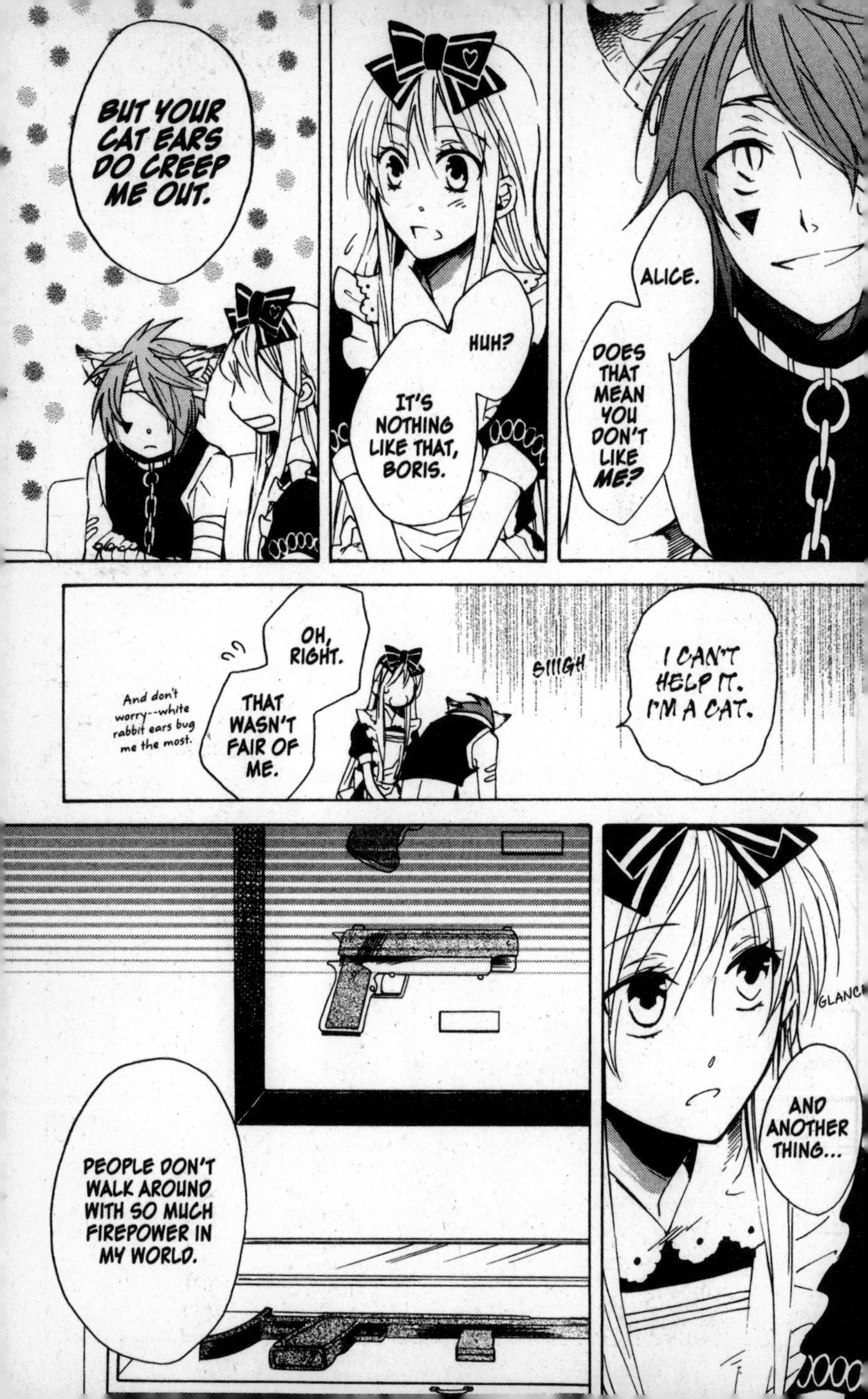
ALICE.
DOES THAT MEAN YOU DON'T LIKE ME?
HUH?
IT'S NOTHING LIKE THAT, BORIS.
BUT YOUR CAT EARS DO CREEP ME OUT.
I CAN'T HELP IT. I'M A CAT.
SIIIGH
OH, RIGHT.
THAT WASN'T FAIR OF ME.
And don't worry--white rabbit ears bug me the most.
AND ANOTHER THING...
PEOPLE DON'T WALK AROUND WITH SO MUCH FIREPOWER IN MY WORLD.

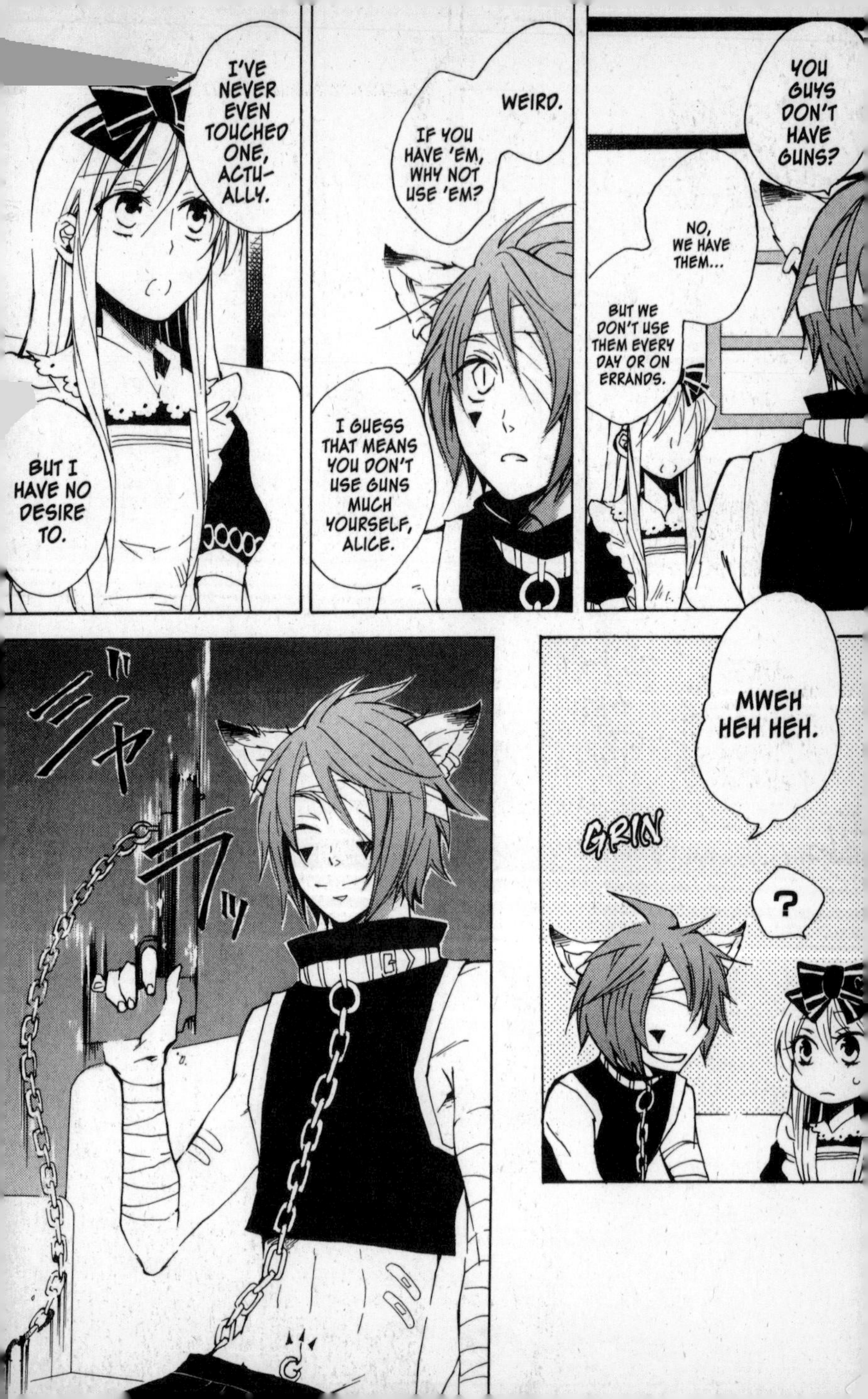

YOU GUYS DON'T HAVE GUNS?
NO, WE HAVE THEM...
BUT WE DON'T USE THEM EVERY DAY OR ON ERRANDS.
WEIRD.
IF YOU HAVE 'EM, WHY NOT USE 'EM?
I GUESS THAT MEANS YOU DON'T USE GUNS MUCH YOURSELF, ALICE.
I'VE NEVER EVEN TOUCHED ONE, ACTUALLY.
BUT I HAVE NO DESIRE TO.
MWEH HEH HEH.
GRIN
?
ジャラッ

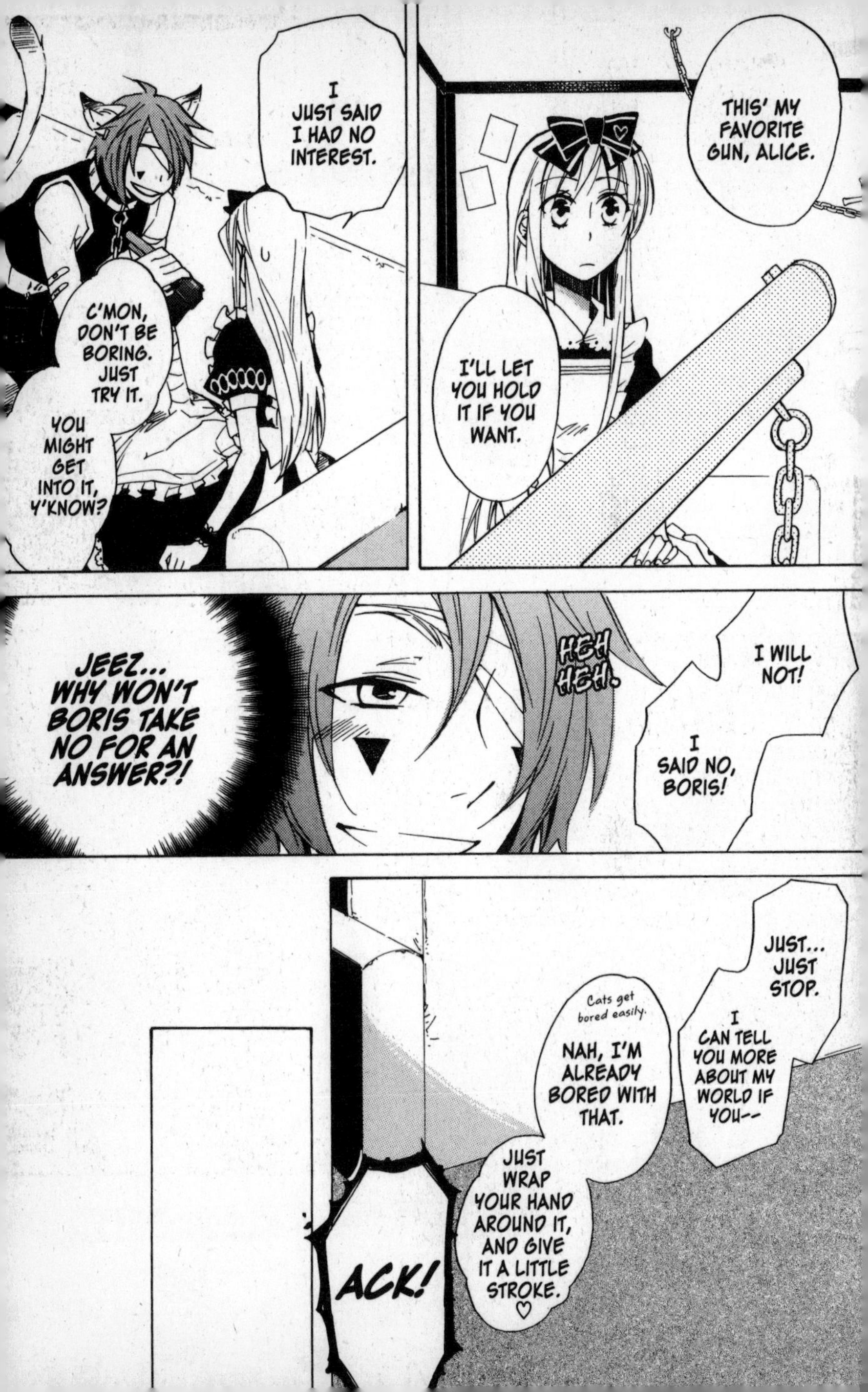
THIS' MY FAVORITE GUN, ALICE.
I'LL LET YOU HOLD IT IF YOU WANT.
I JUST SAID I HAD NO INTEREST.
C'MON, DON'T BE BORING. JUST TRY IT.
YOU MIGHT GET INTO IT, Y'KNOW?
I WILL NOT!
I SAID NO, BORIS!
HEH HEH.
JEEZ... WHY WON'T BORIS TAKE NO FOR AN ANSWER?!
JUST... JUST STOP.
I CAN TELL YOU MORE ABOUT MY WORLD IF YOU--
Cats get bored easily.
NAH, I'M ALREADY BORED WITH THAT.
JUST WRAP YOUR HAND AROUND IT, AND GIVE IT A LITTLE STROKE. ♡
ACK!

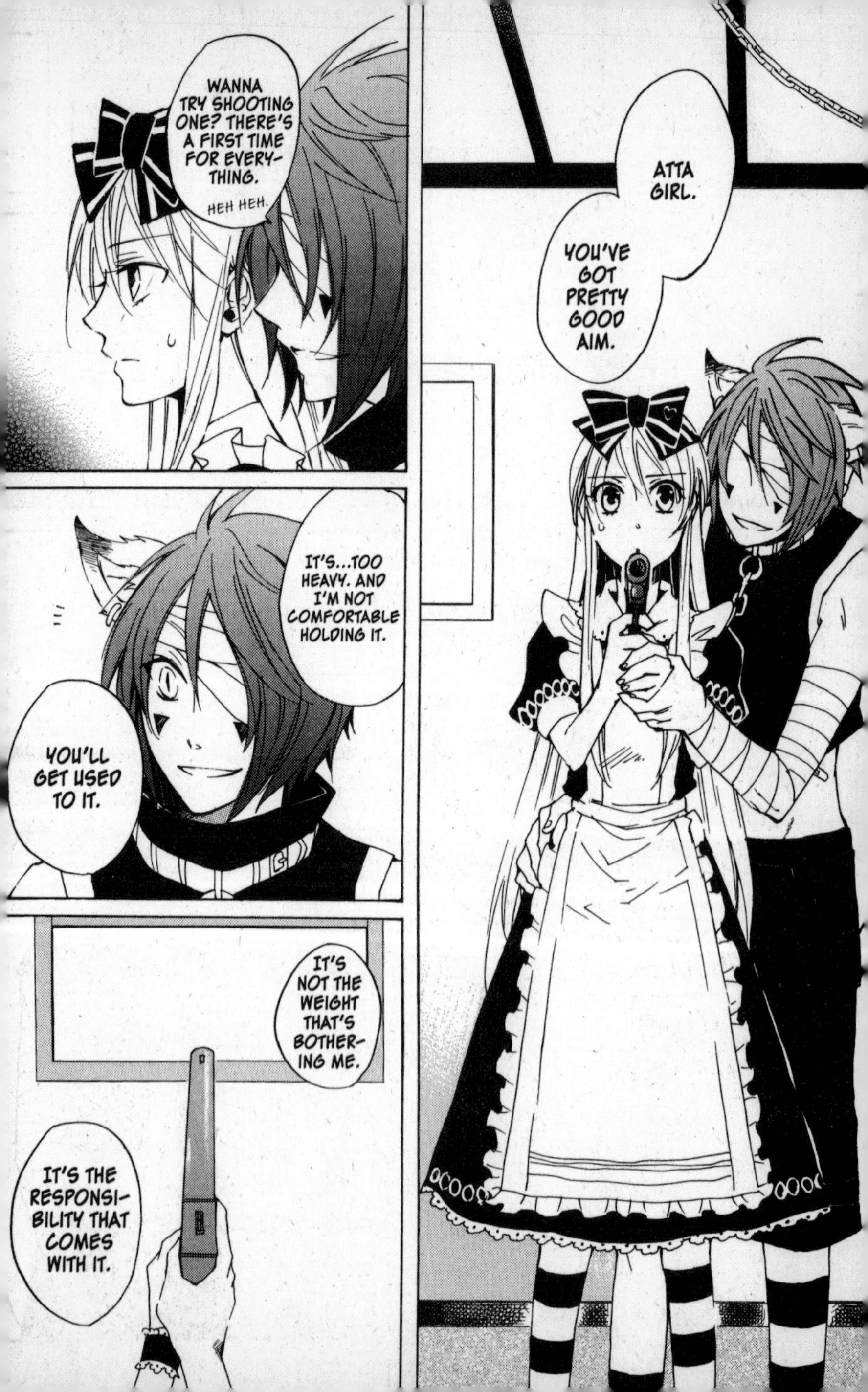
ATTA GIRL.
YOU'VE GOT PRETTY GOOD AIM.
WANNA TRY SHOOTING ONE? THERE'S A FIRST TIME FOR EVERY-THING.
HEH HEH.
IT'S...TOO HEAVY. AND I'M NOT COMFORTABLE HOLDING IT.
YOU'LL GET USED TO IT.
IT'S NOT THE WEIGHT THAT'S BOTHER-ING ME.
IT'S THE RESPONSI-BILITY THAT COMES WITH IT.

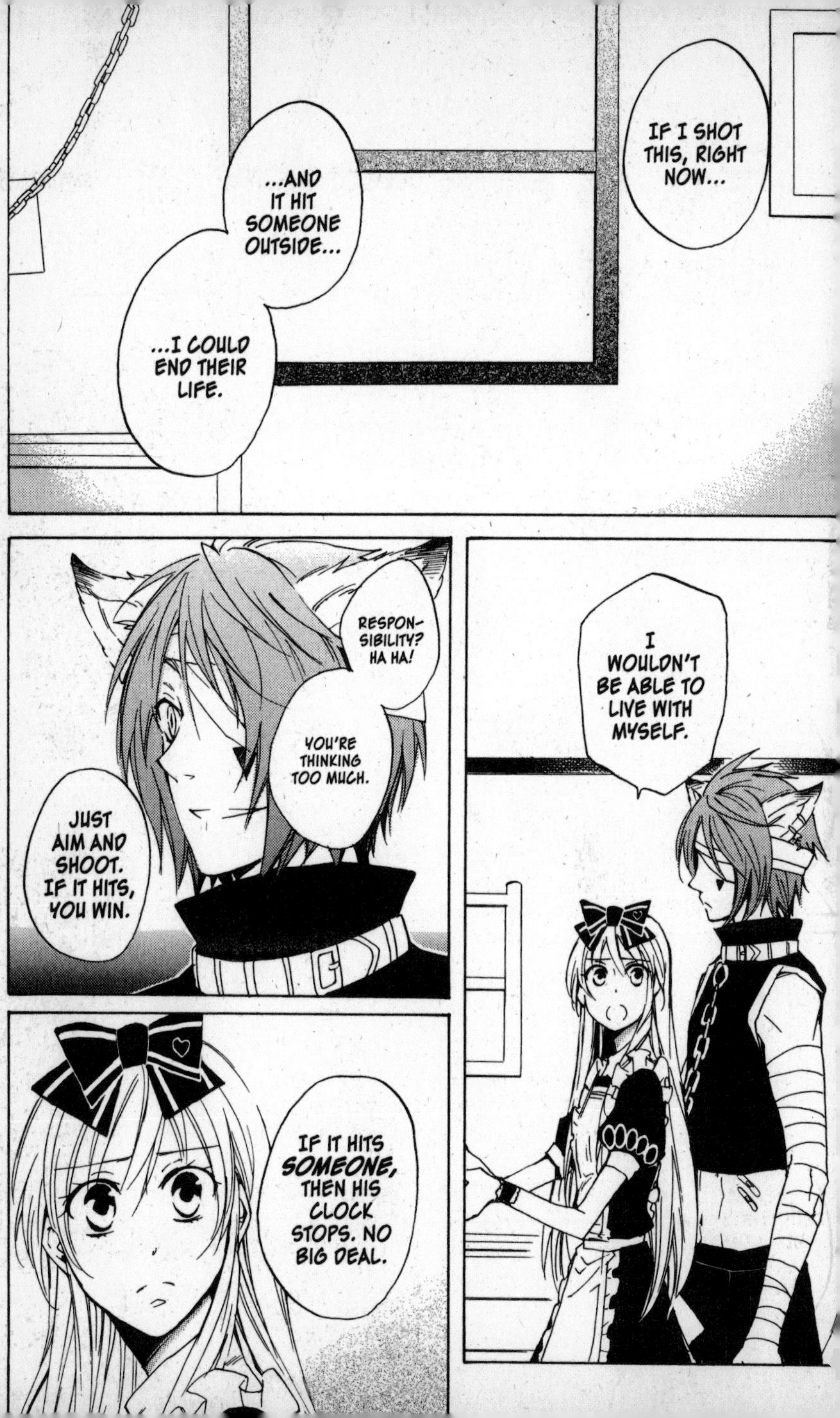
IF I SHOT THIS, RIGHT NOW...
...AND IT HIT SOMEONE OUTSIDE...
...I COULD END THEIR LIFE.
I WOULDN'T BE ABLE TO LIVE WITH MYSELF.
RESPON-SIBILITY? HA HA!
YOU'RE THINKING TOO MUCH.
JUST AIM AND SHOOT. IF IT HITS, YOU WIN.
IF IT HITS *SOMEONE*, THEN HIS CLOCK STOPS. NO BIG DEAL.

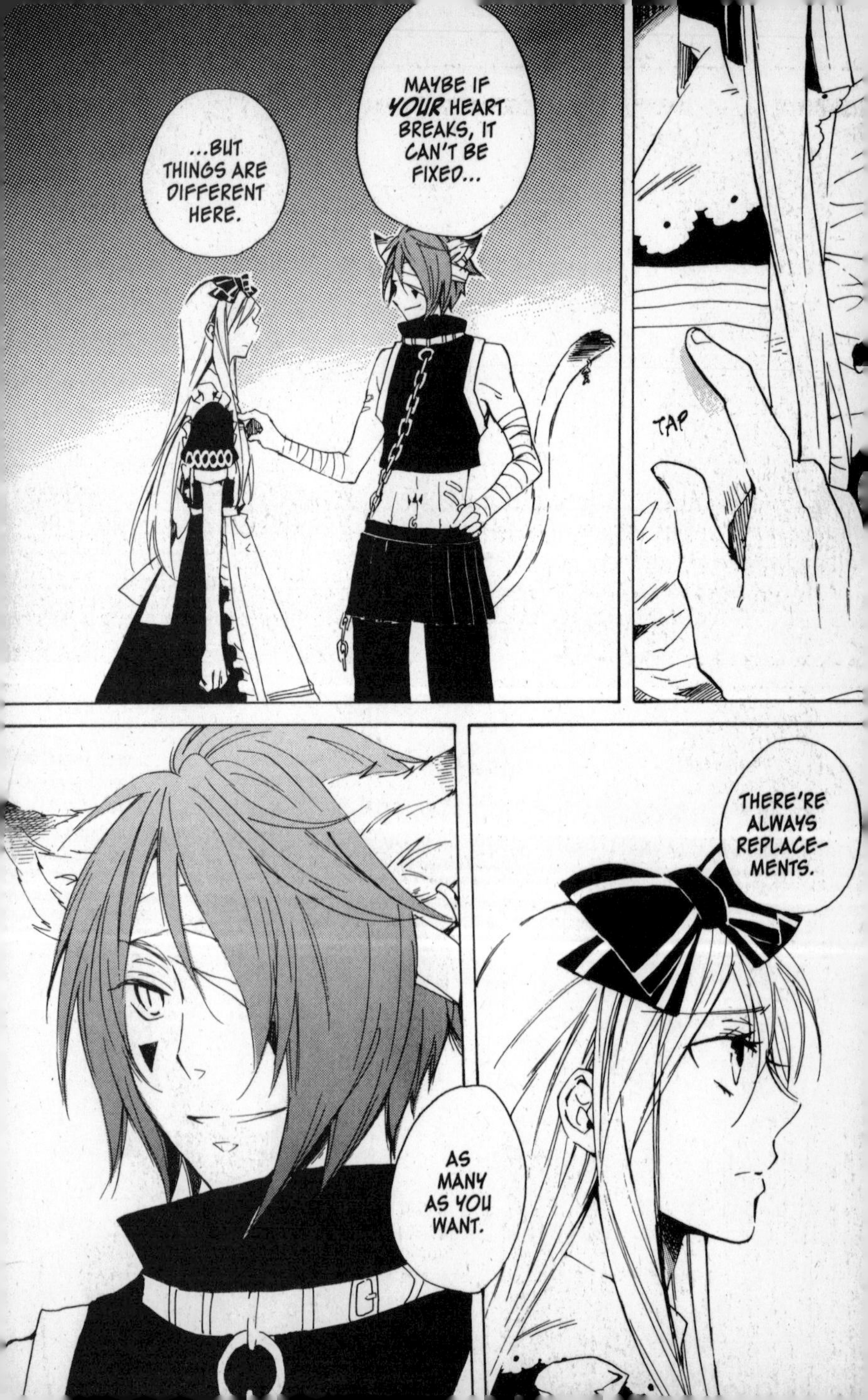
TAP
MAYBE IF *YOUR* HEART BREAKS, IT CAN'T BE FIXED...
...BUT THINGS ARE DIFFERENT HERE.
THERE'RE ALWAYS REPLACE-MENTS.
AS MANY AS YOU WANT.

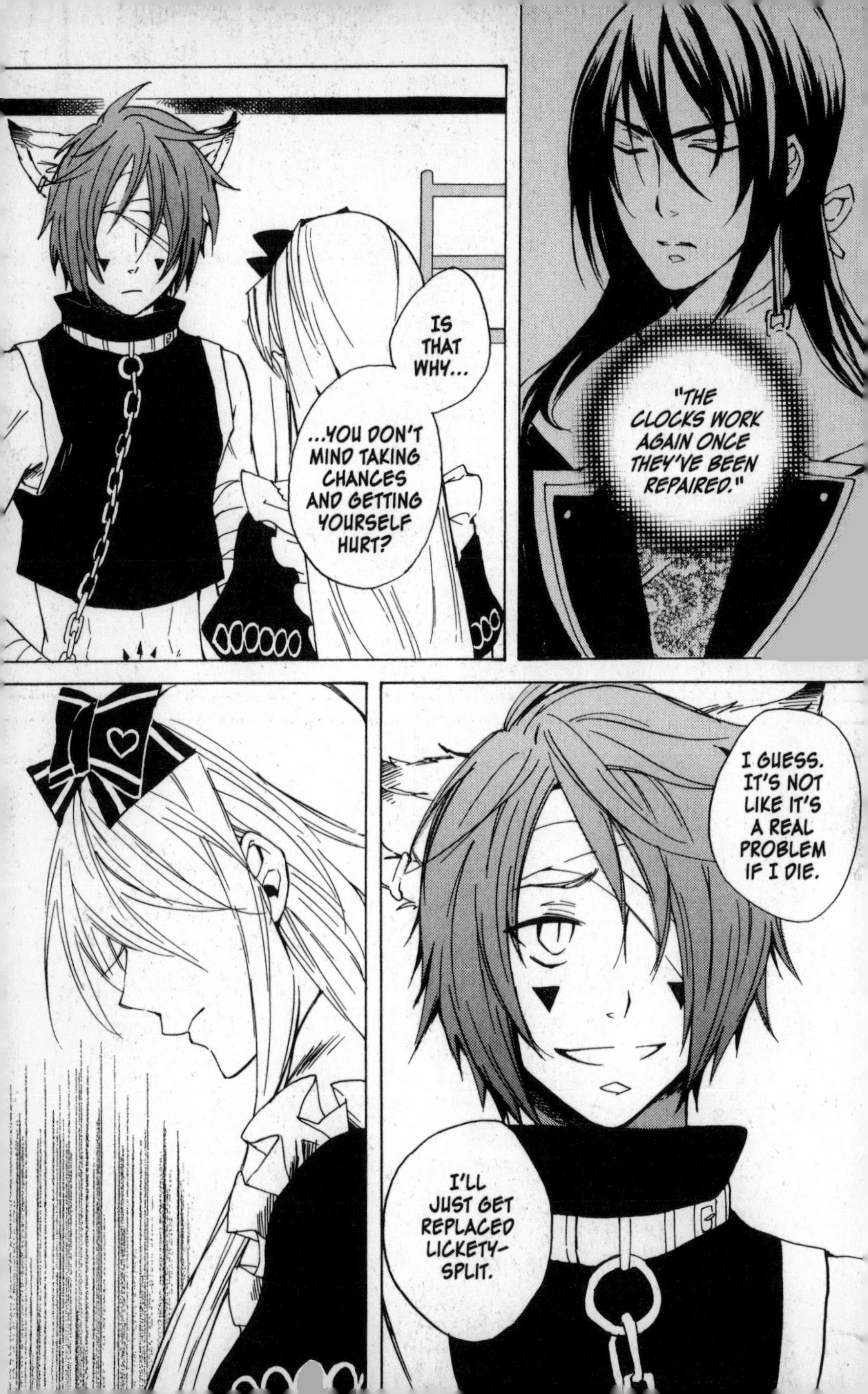
"THE CLOCKS WORK AGAIN ONCE THEY'VE BEEN REPAIRED."
IS THAT WHY...
...YOU DON'T MIND TAKING CHANCES AND GETTING YOURSELF HURT?
I GUESS. IT'S NOT LIKE IT'S A REAL PROBLEM IF I DIE.
I'LL JUST GET REPLACED LICKETY-SPLIT.

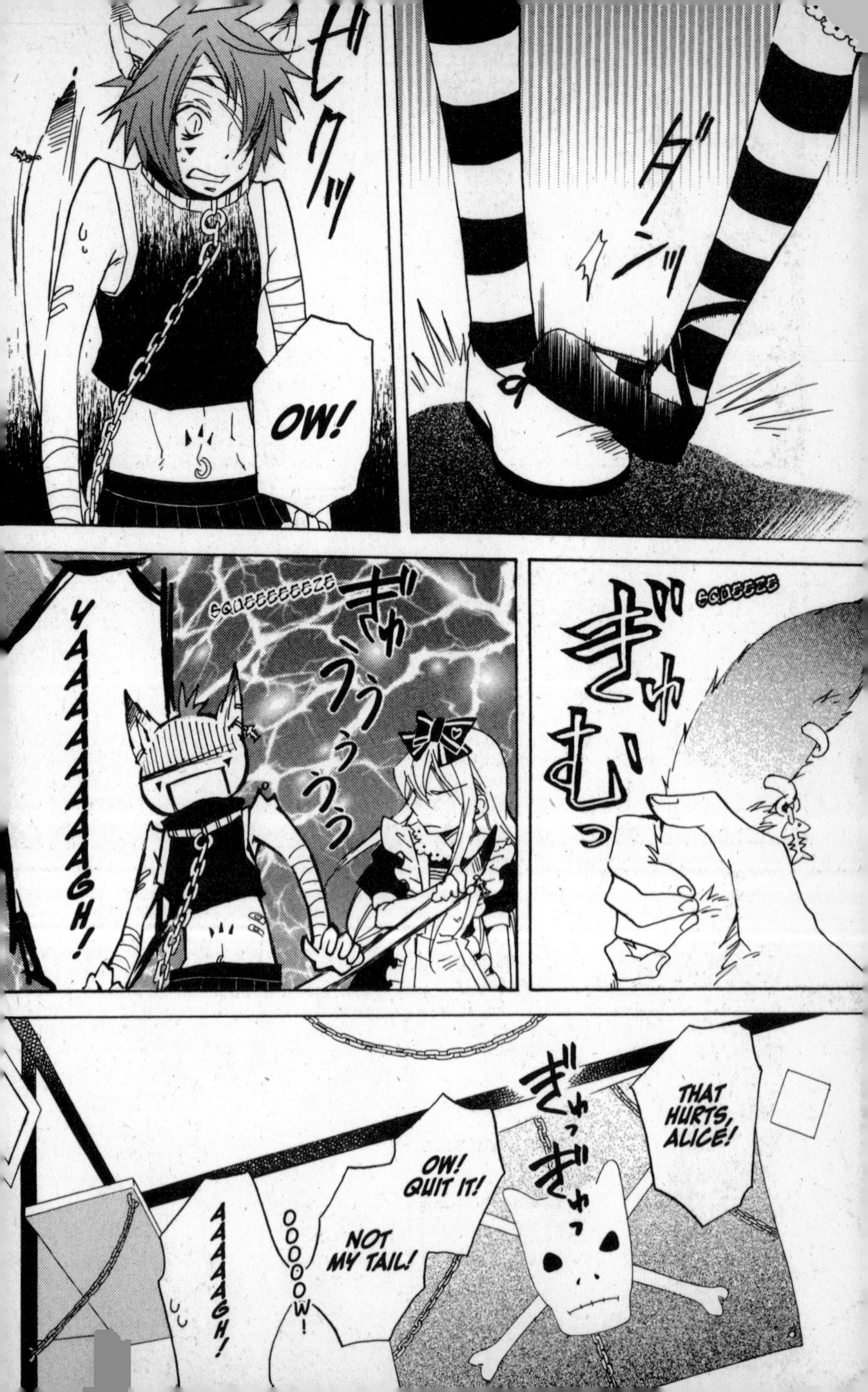
ダンッ
ビクッ
OW!
SQUEEZE
ぎゅむっ
SQUEEEEEEEZE
ぎゅうううう
YAAAAAAAAGH!
THAT HURTS, ALICE!
ぎゅっぎゅっ
OW! QUIT IT!
NOT MY TAIL!
OOOOOW!
AAAAAAGH!

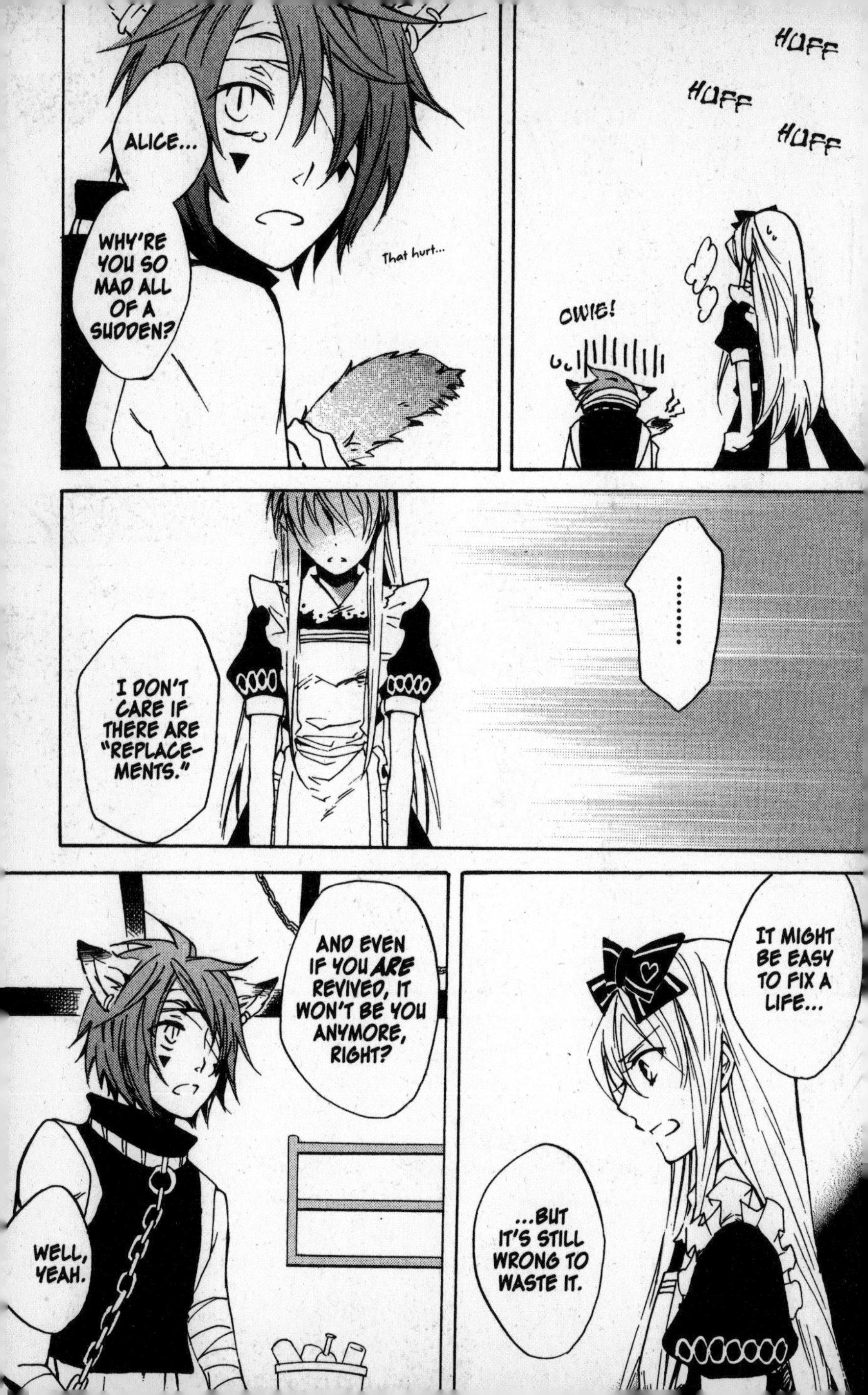
HUFF
HUFF
HUFF
OWIE!
ALICE...
WHY'RE YOU SO MAD ALL OF A SUDDEN?
That hurt...
......
I DON'T CARE IF THERE ARE "REPLACEMENTS."
IT MIGHT BE EASY TO FIX A LIFE...
...BUT IT'S STILL WRONG TO WASTE IT.
AND EVEN IF YOU *ARE* REVIVED, IT WON'T BE YOU ANYMORE, RIGHT?
WELL, YEAH.

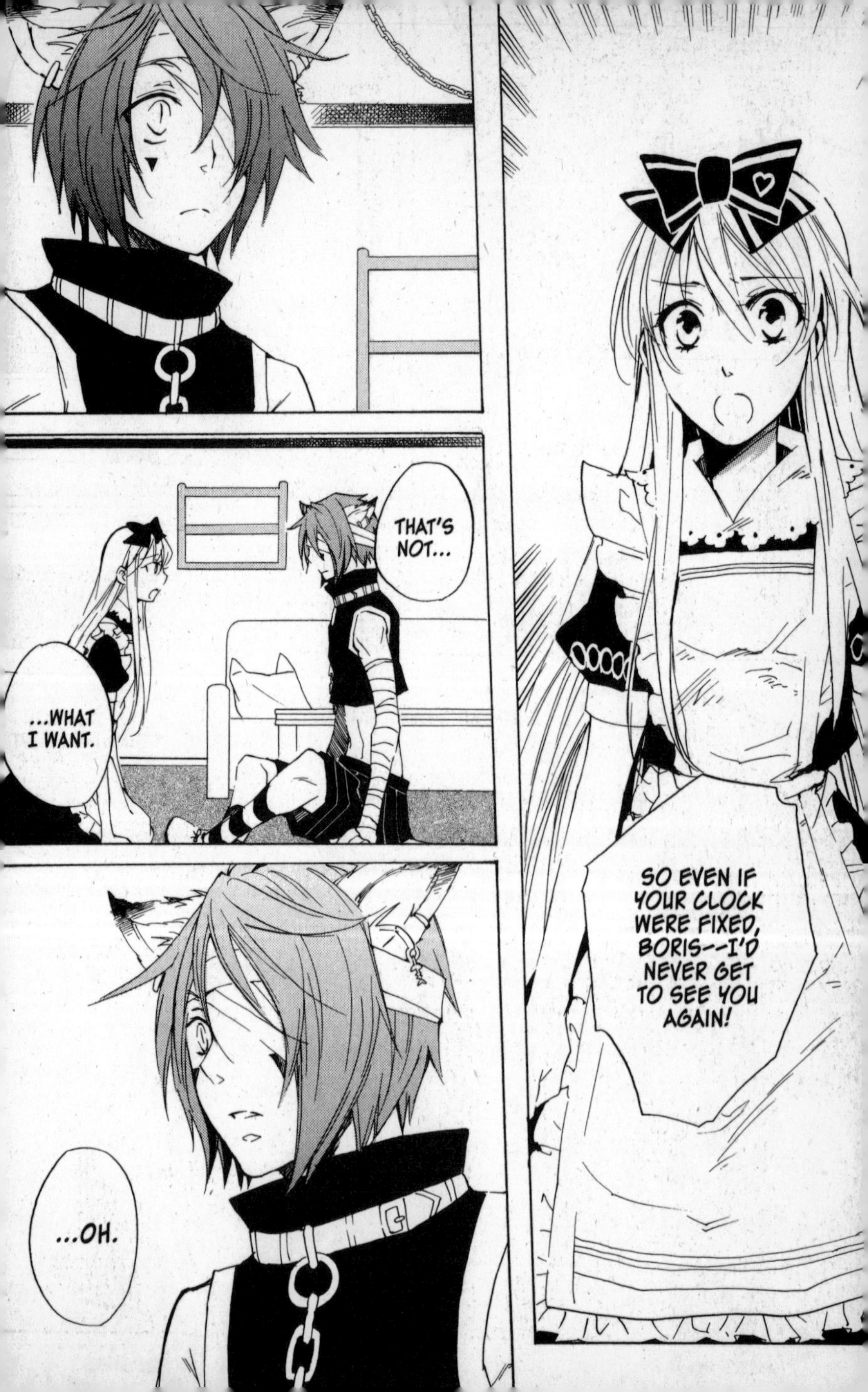
SO EVEN IF YOUR CLOCK WERE FIXED, BORIS--I'D NEVER GET TO SEE YOU AGAIN!
THAT'S NOT...
...WHAT I WANT.
...OH.

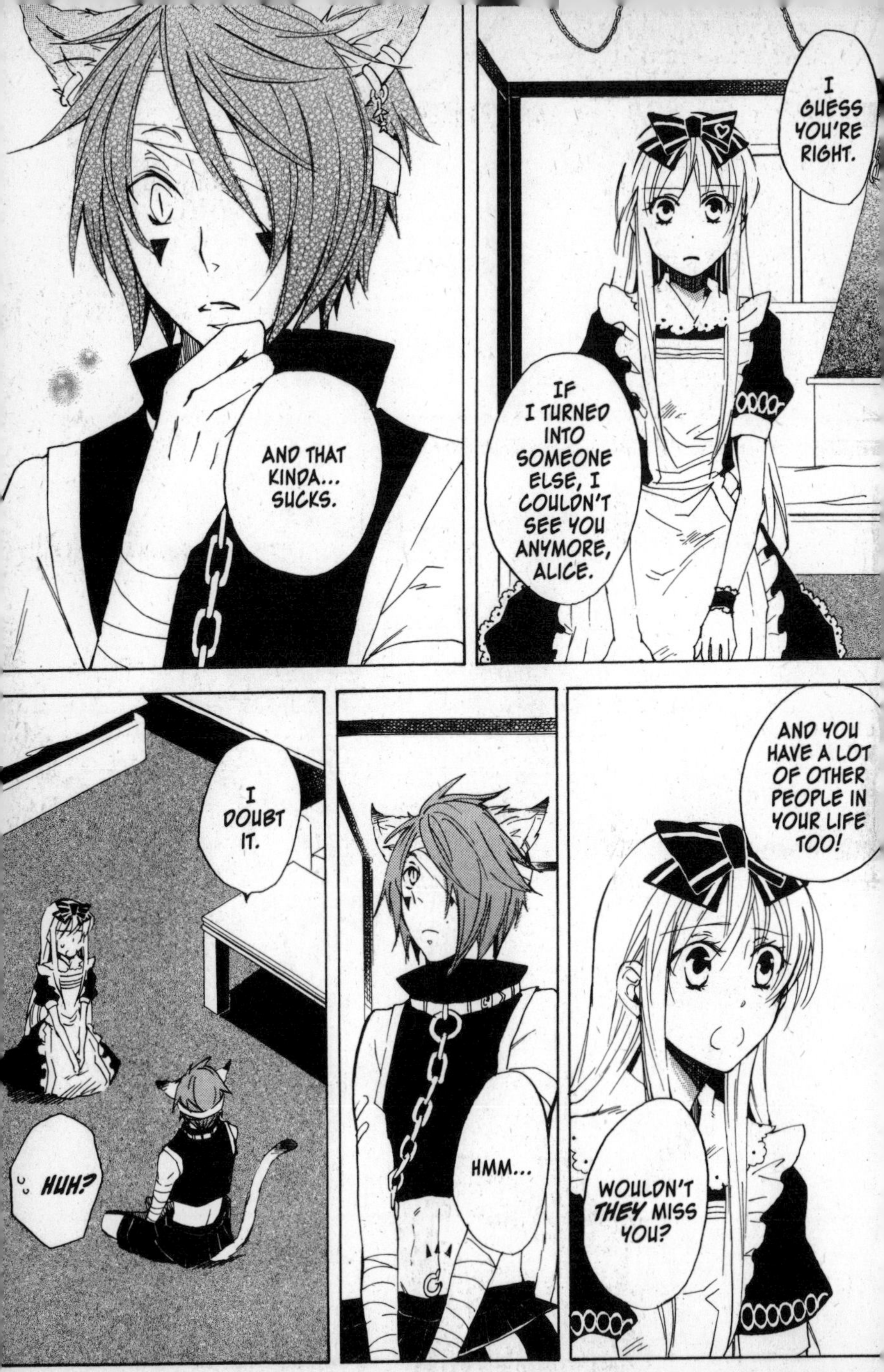
I GUESS YOU'RE RIGHT.
IF I TURNED INTO SOMEONE ELSE, I COULDN'T SEE YOU ANYMORE, ALICE.
AND THAT KINDA... SUCKS.
AND YOU HAVE A LOT OF OTHER PEOPLE IN YOUR LIFE TOO!
WOULDN'T *THEY* MISS YOU?
HMM...
I DOUBT IT.
HUH?

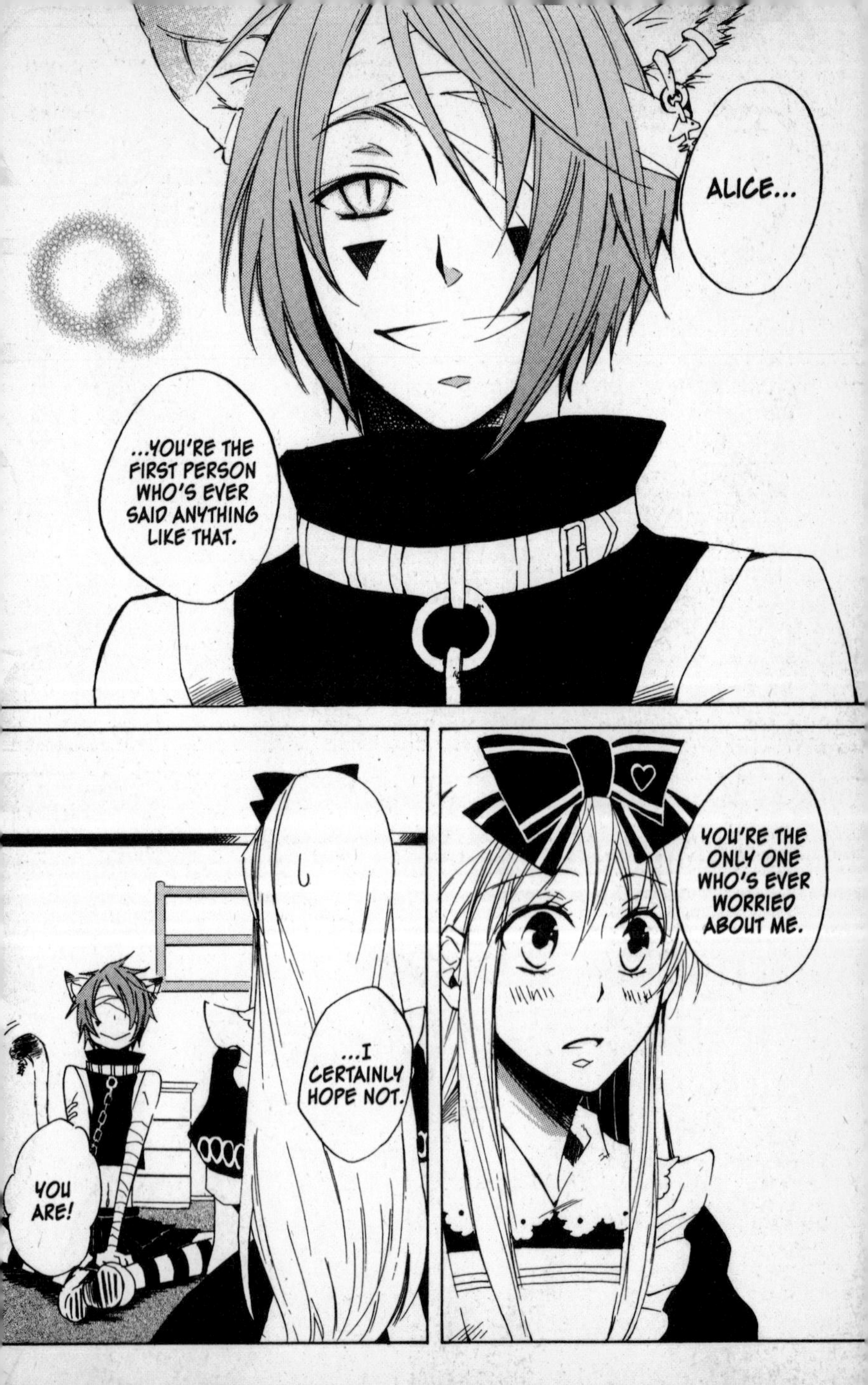
ALICE...
...YOU'RE THE FIRST PERSON WHO'S EVER SAID ANYTHING LIKE THAT.
YOU'RE THE ONLY ONE WHO'S EVER WORRIED ABOUT ME.
...I CERTAINLY HOPE NOT.
YOU ARE!

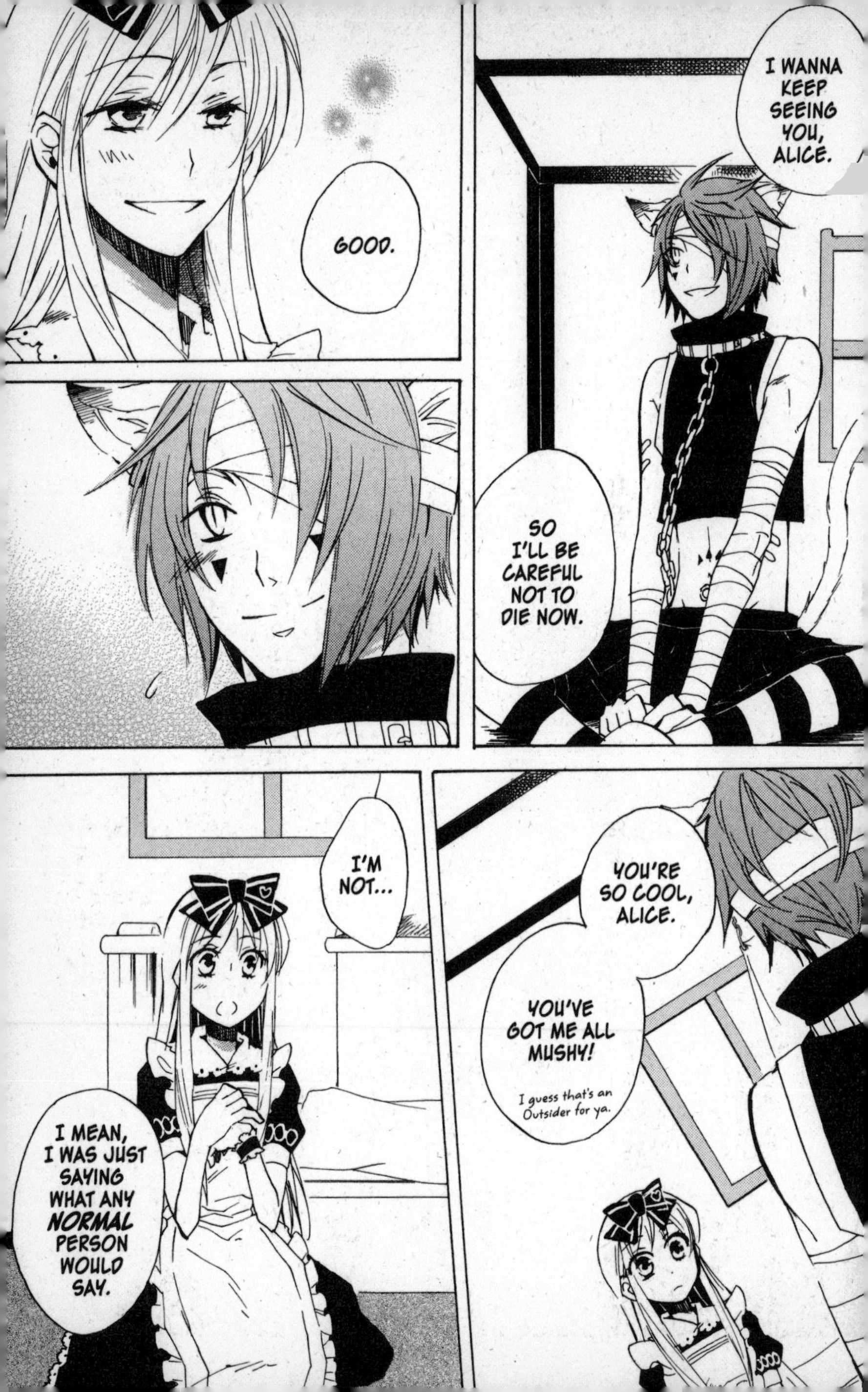
I WANNA KEEP SEEING YOU, ALICE.
SO I'LL BE CAREFUL NOT TO DIE NOW.
GOOD.
YOU'RE SO COOL, ALICE.
YOU'VE GOT ME ALL MUSHY!
I guess that's an Outsider for ya.
I'M NOT...
I MEAN, I WAS JUST SAYING WHAT ANY ***NORMAL*** PERSON WOULD SAY.

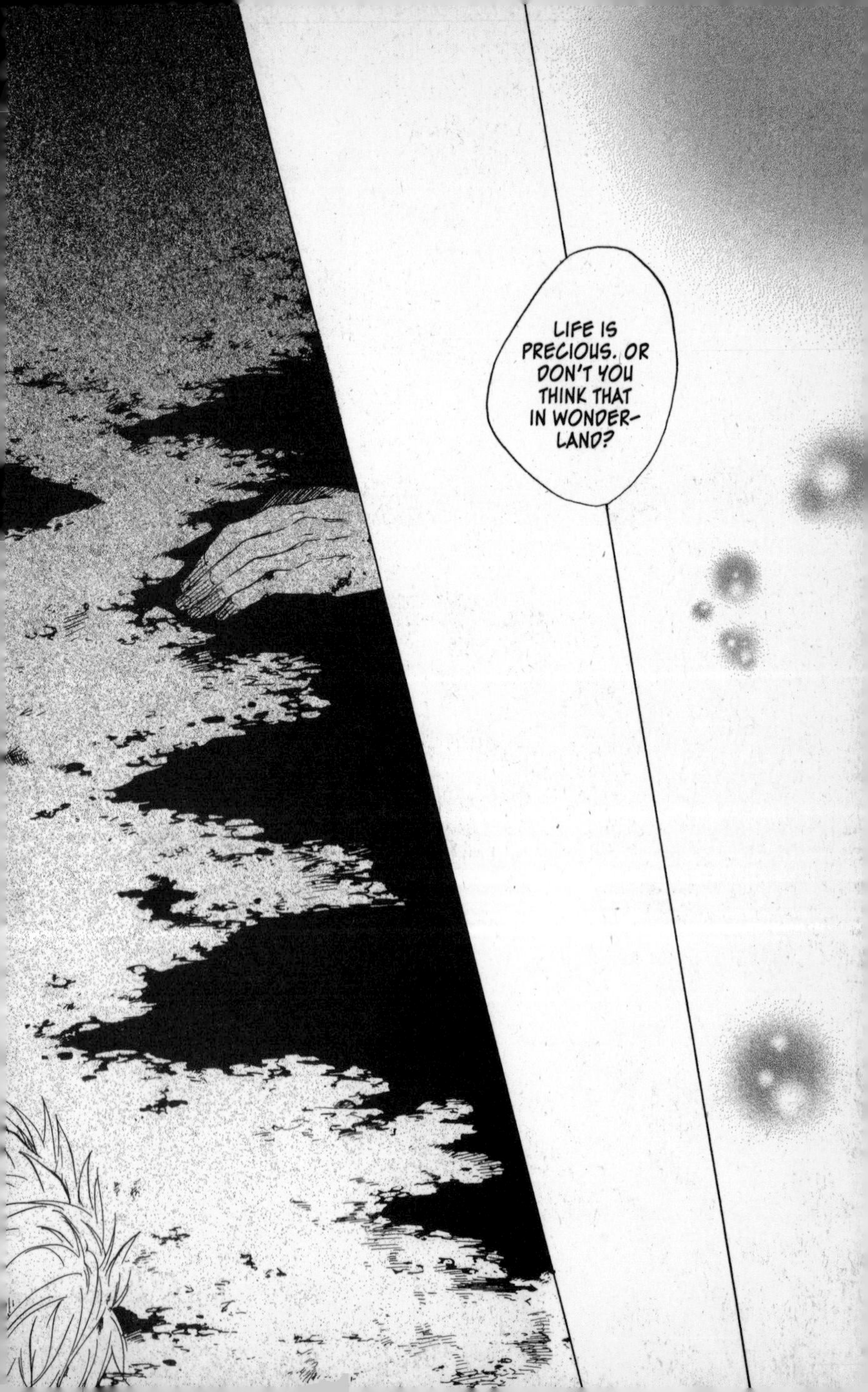
LIFE IS PRECIOUS. OR DON'T YOU THINK THAT IN WONDER-LAND?

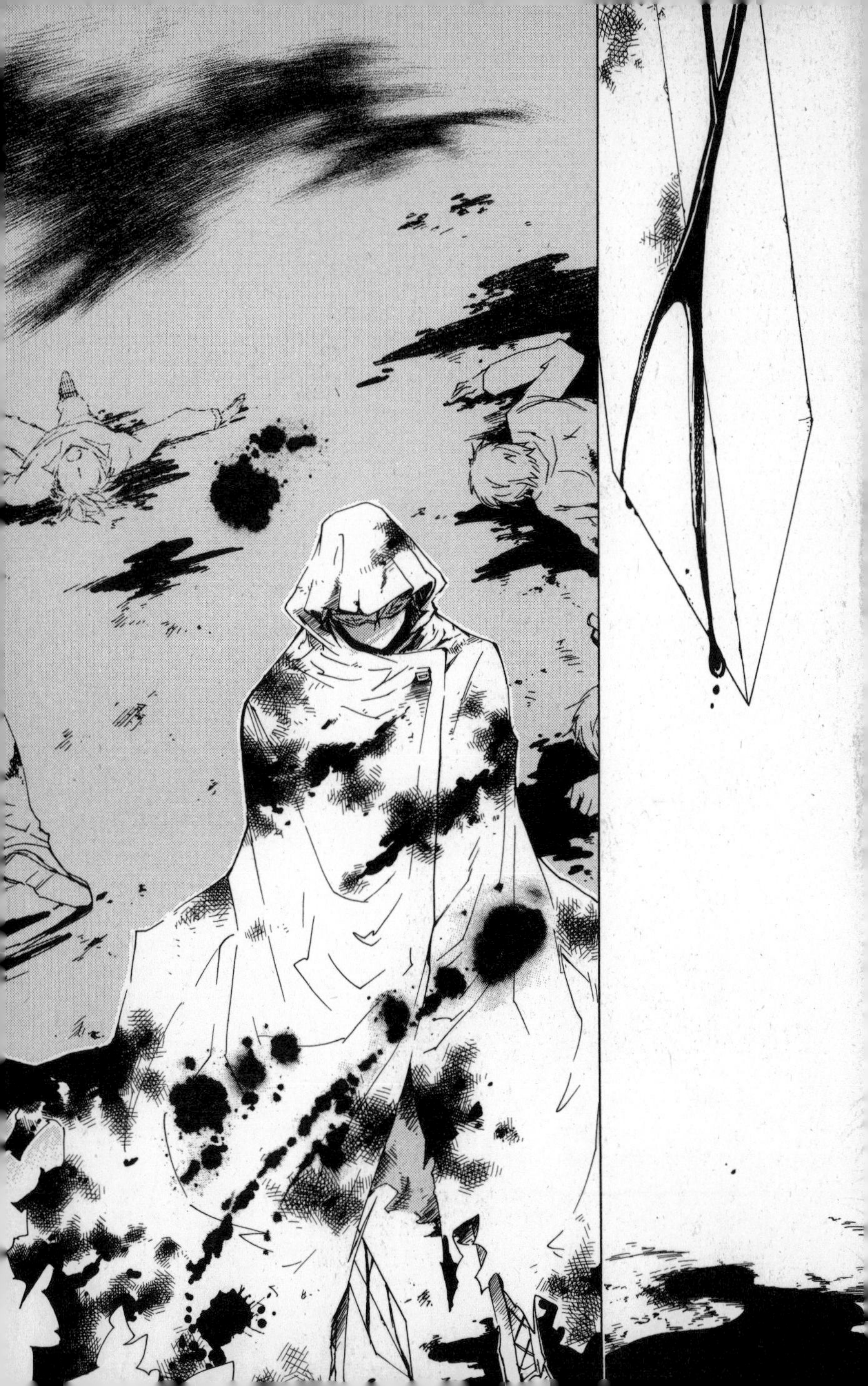

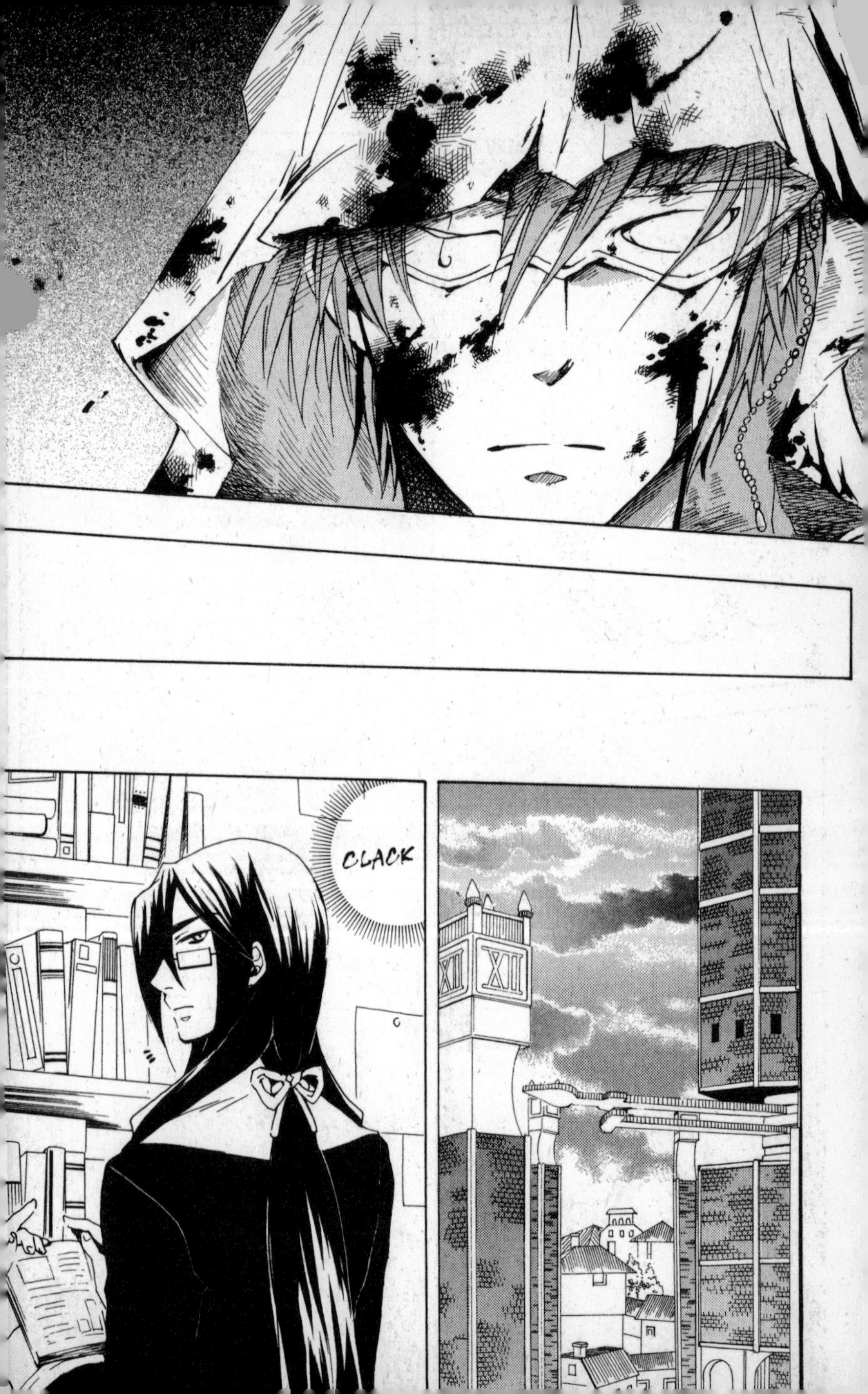
CLACK

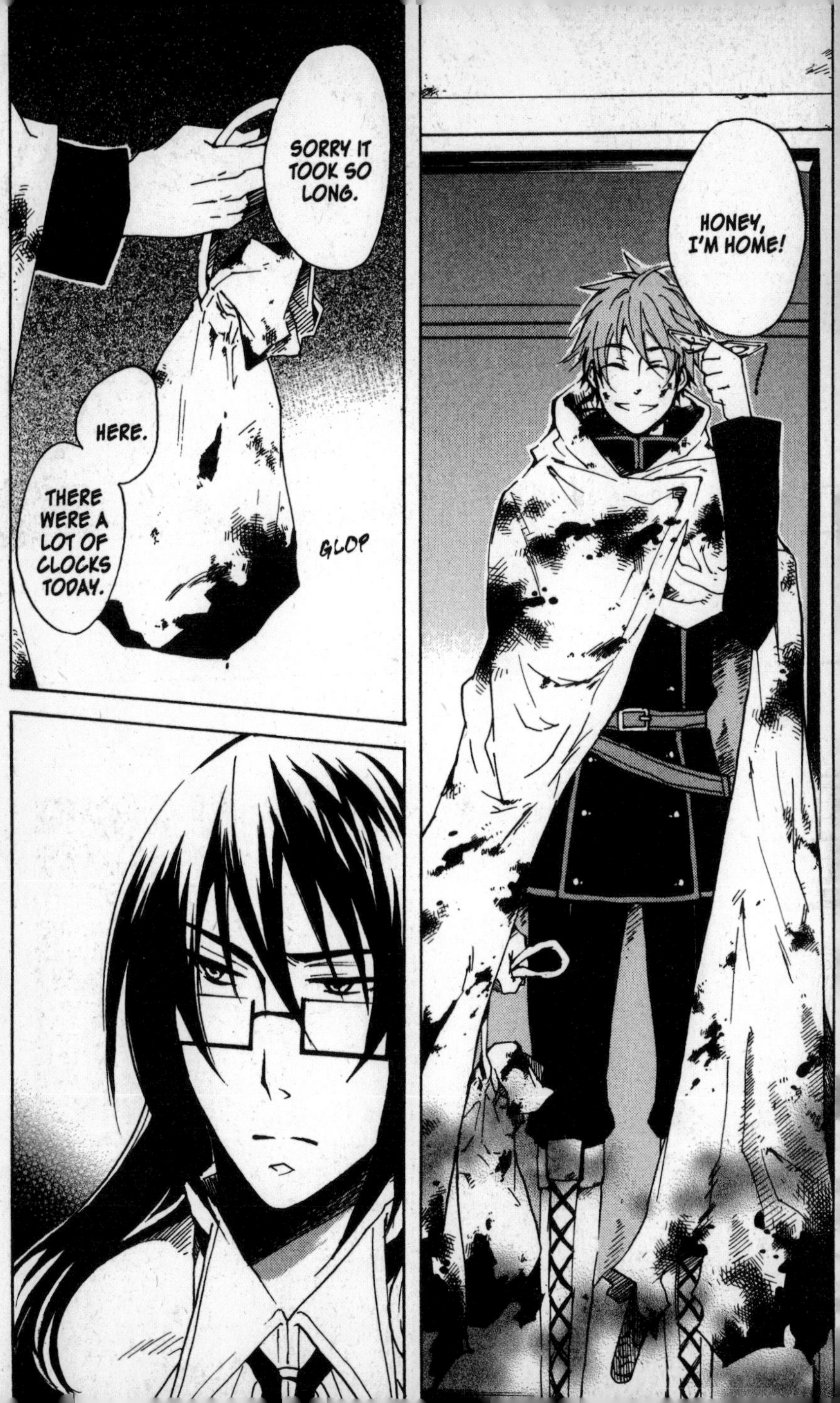
HONEY, I'M HOME!
SORRY IT TOOK SO LONG.
HERE.
THERE WERE A LOT OF CLOCKS TODAY.
GLOP

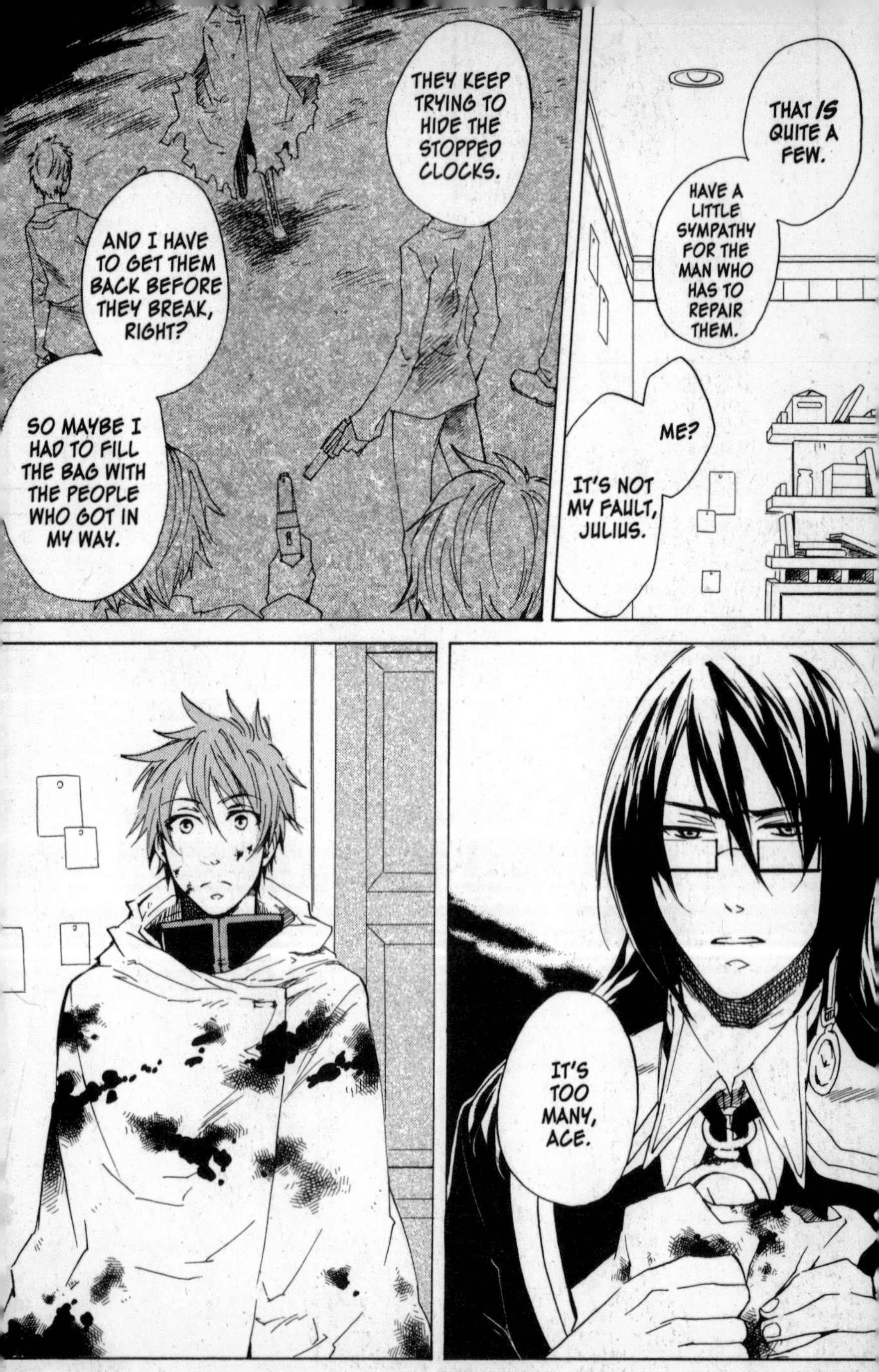
THAT *IS* QUITE A FEW.
HAVE A LITTLE SYMPATHY FOR THE MAN WHO HAS TO REPAIR THEM.
ME?
IT'S NOT MY FAULT, JULIUS.
THEY KEEP TRYING TO HIDE THE STOPPED CLOCKS.
AND I HAVE TO GET THEM BACK BEFORE THEY BREAK, RIGHT?
SO MAYBE I HAD TO FILL THE BAG WITH THE PEOPLE WHO GOT IN MY WAY.
IT'S TOO MANY, ACE.

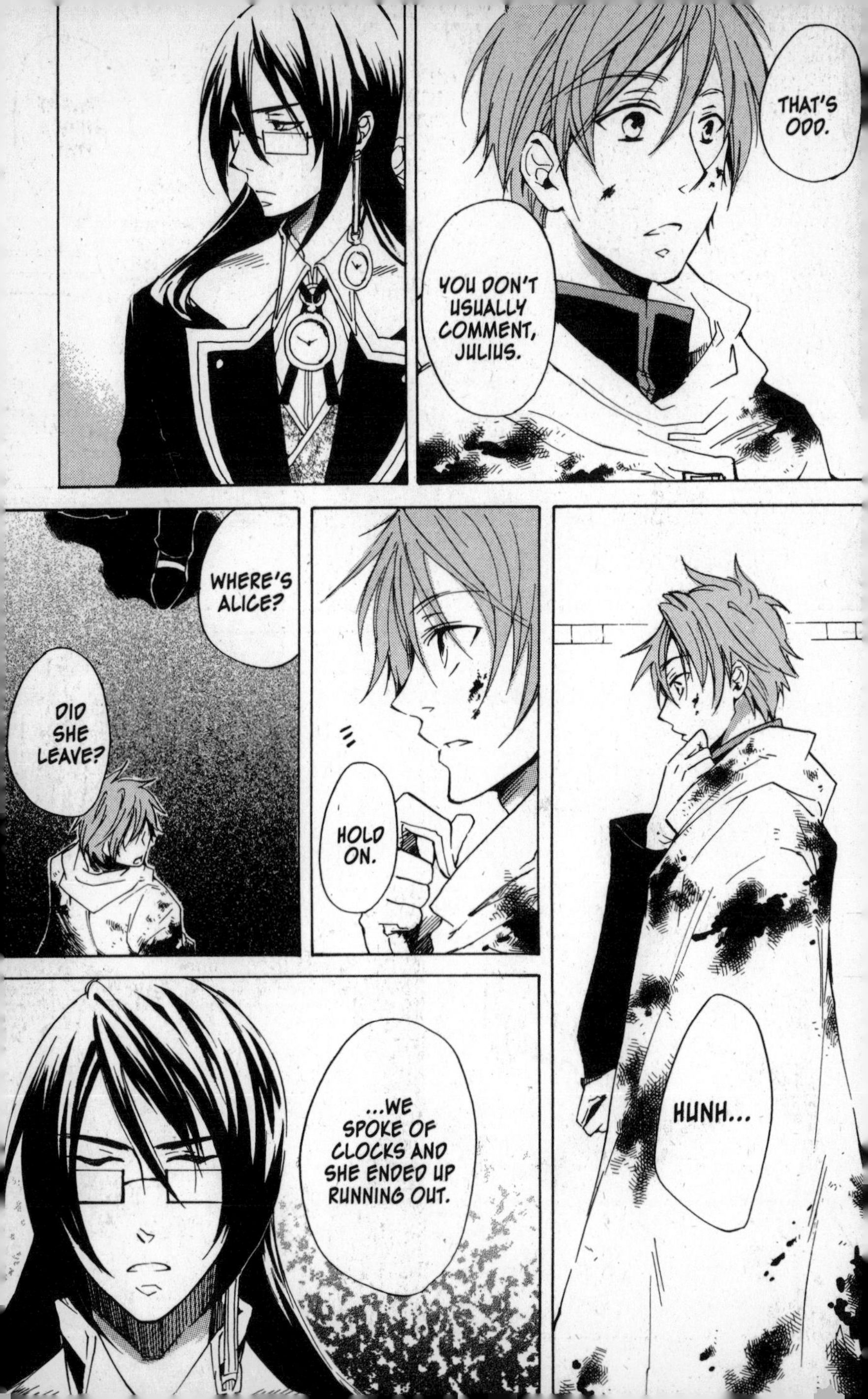
THAT'S ODD.
YOU DON'T USUALLY COMMENT, JULIUS.
HUNH...
HOLD ON.
WHERE'S ALICE?
DID SHE LEAVE?
...WE SPOKE OF CLOCKS AND SHE ENDED UP RUNNING OUT.

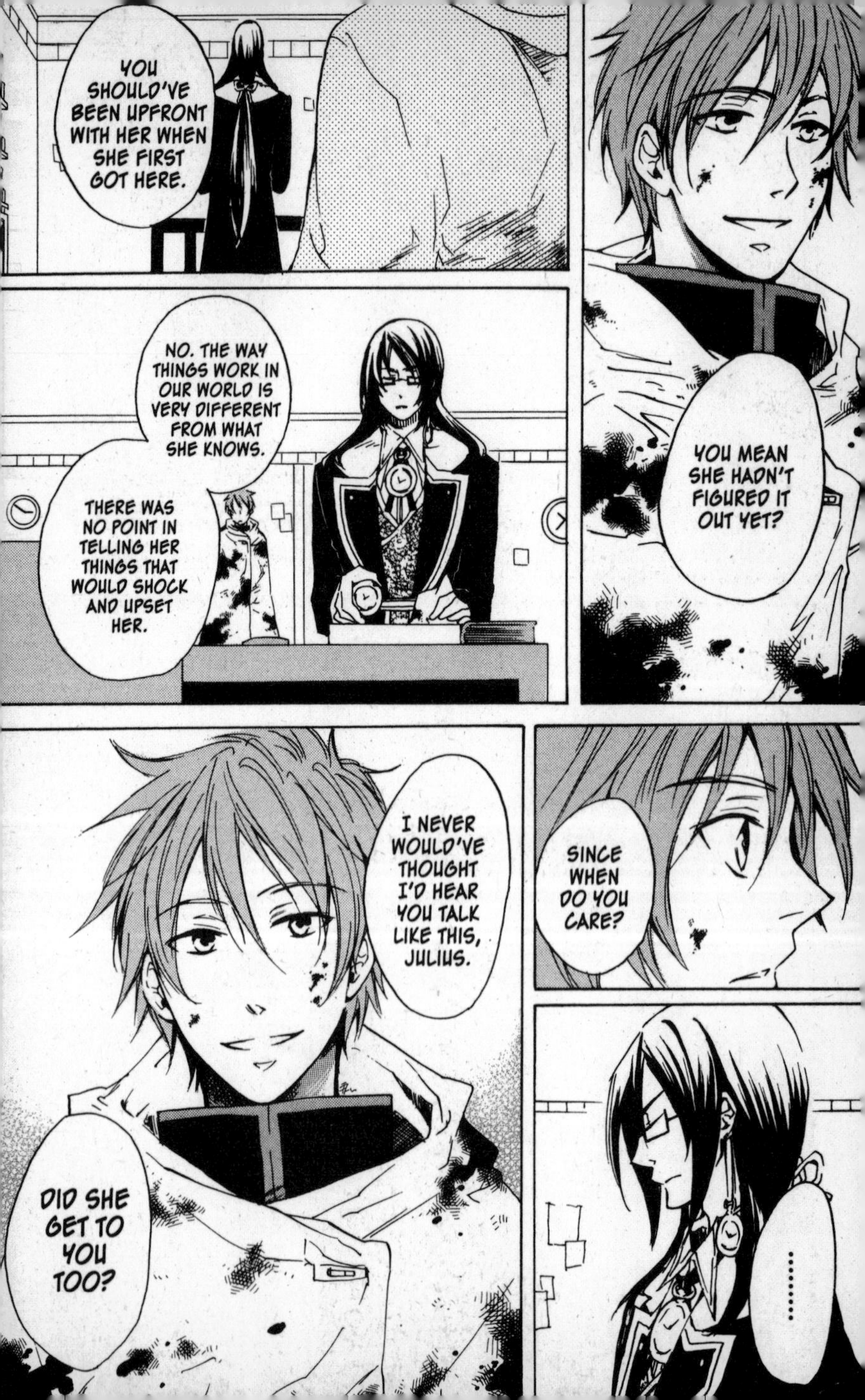
YOU MEAN SHE HADN'T FIGURED IT OUT YET?
YOU SHOULD'VE BEEN UPFRONT WITH HER WHEN SHE FIRST GOT HERE.
NO. THE WAY THINGS WORK IN OUR WORLD IS VERY DIFFERENT FROM WHAT SHE KNOWS.
THERE WAS NO POINT IN TELLING HER THINGS THAT WOULD SHOCK AND UPSET HER.
SINCE WHEN DO YOU CARE?
......
I NEVER WOULD'VE THOUGHT I'D HEAR YOU TALK LIKE THIS, JULIUS.
DID SHE GET TO YOU TOO?

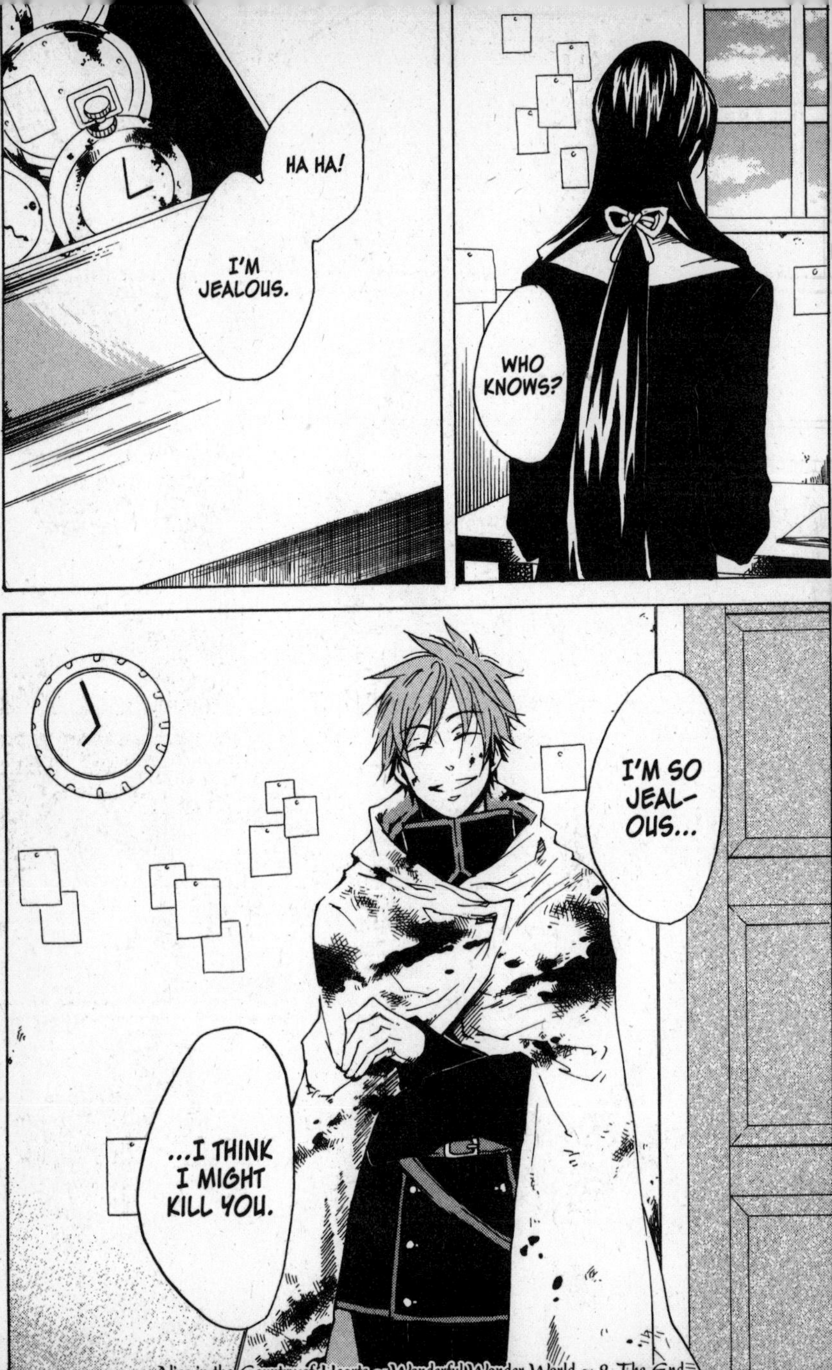
WHO KNOWS?
HA HA!
I'M JEALOUS.
I'M SO JEAL-OUS...
...I THINK I MIGHT KILL YOU.
Alice in the Country of Hearts ~ Wonderful Wonder World ~ 2 The End

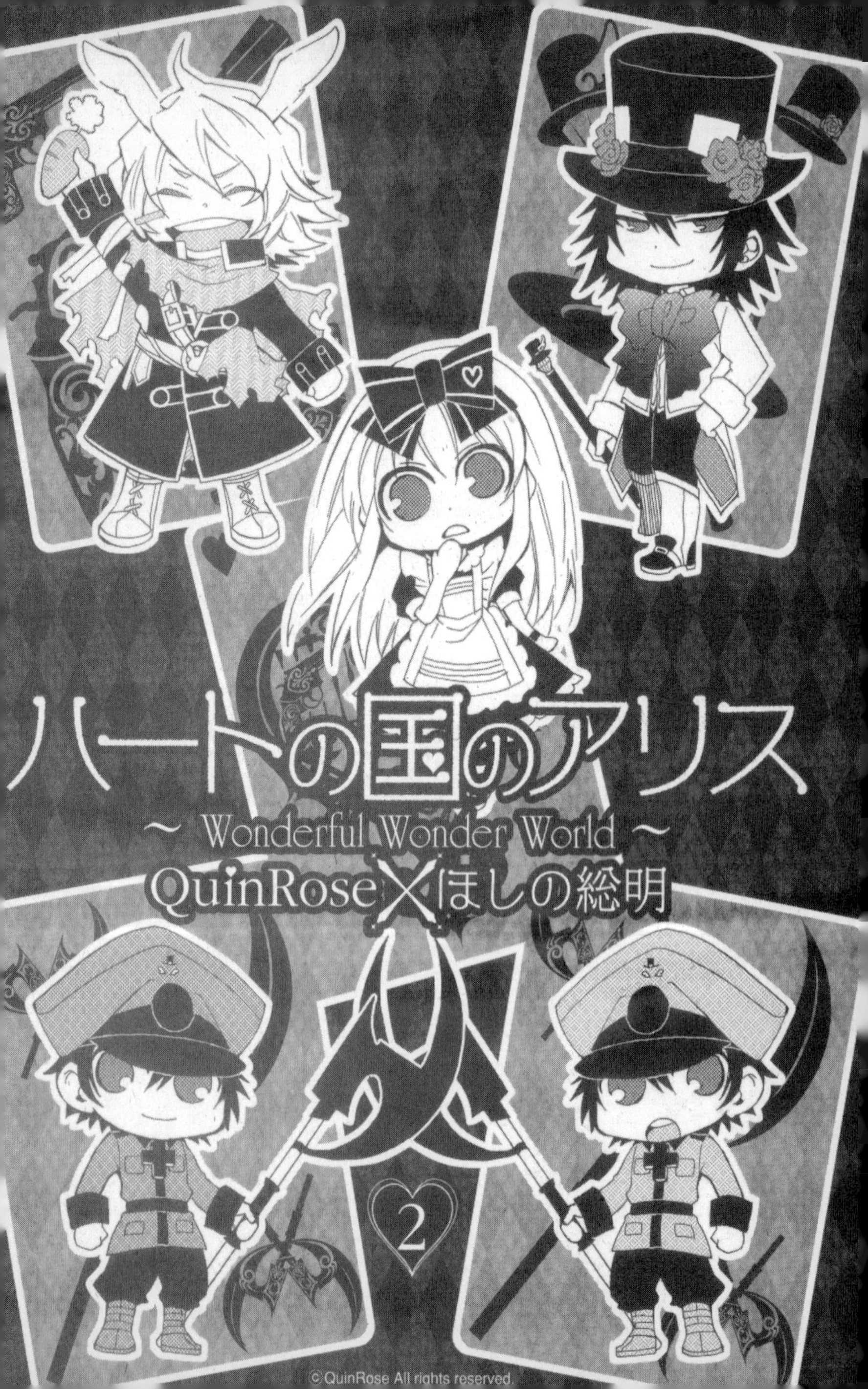
ハートの国のアリス
～Wonderful Wonder World～
QuinRose×ほしの総明
2
© QuinRose All rights reserved.

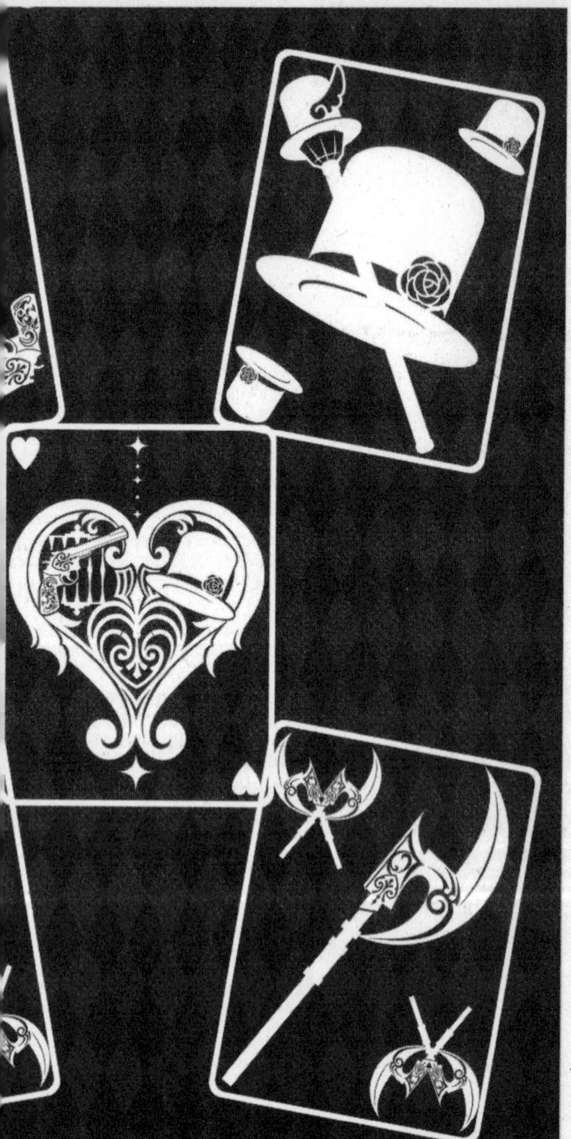

ce in the country of the heart
~ Wonderful Wonder World ~

Presented by
QuinRose & Soumei Hoshino

In the next volume of...

# ♥1 Alice IN THE COUNTRY OF Hearts

Alice's comfort level in Wonderland continues to grow, but something strange is happening. Confusion, memory loss and sudden pain become associated with thoughts of home. In the meantime, Peter cunningly finds a way into Alice's bedroom, and Vivaldi reveals a peculiar secret! And what will Alice do when she is suddenly attacked by Blood Dupre?!

## The class president has a little secret she's keeping from the sexy bad boy in school...

"It's hard to deny this guilty pleasure when it looks like it's having so much fun."
—About.com

The rogue hypnotist strikes again, this time planting the suggestion in Misaki that if she falls asleep, she'll wake up hating Usui! Well, hating him more than usual... So it's up to Usui to preserve their relationship (such as it is) by keeping Misaki awake as long as possible!

# STOP!

## This is the back of the book.
## You wouldn't want to spoil a great ending!

This book is printed "manga-style," in the authentic Japanese right-to-left format. Since none of the artwork has been flipped or altered, readers get to experience the story just as the creator intended. You've been asking for it, so TOKYOPOP® delivered: authentic, hot-off-the-press, and far more fun!

# DIRECTIONS

If this is your first time reading manga-style, here's a quick guide to help you understand how it works.

It's easy... just start in the top right panel and follow the numbers. Have fun, and look for more 100% authentic manga from TOKYOPOP®!